INTERNATIONAL LIBRARY OF AFRO-AMERICAN LIFE AND HISTORY

1. African captives being led to slave markets.
2. An antislavery booklet.
3. A slave auction in the South.
4. Black Americans taking part in the Battle of New Orleans.
5. Crispus Attucks, the first to fall in the Revolutionary cause.
6. The Bethel A.M.E. Church as it appeared early in the nineteenth century.
7. An early abolitionist newspaper.

INTERNATIONAL LIBRARY OF

AFRO-AMERICAN LIFE

AND HISTORY

IN FREEDOM'S FOOTSTEPS

From the African Background to the Civil War

BY

CHARLES H. WESLEY

THE PUBLISHERS AGENCY, INC.

CORNWELLS HEIGHTS, PENNSYLVANIA

under the auspices of

THE ASSOCIATION FOR THE STUDY OF AFRO-AMERICAN LIFE AND HISTORY

In

loving memory

of my daughter

LOUISE J. WESLEY

Preface

THE Association for the Study of Afro-American Life and History joins with Pubco Corporation in presenting this new series of volumes which treat in detail the cultural and historical backgrounds of black Americans. This Association, a pioneer in the area of Afro-American History, was founded on September 9, 1915, by Dr. Carter G. Woodson, who remained its director of research and publications until his death in 1950.

In 1916 Dr. Woodson began publishing the quarterly *Journal of Negro History*. In 1926 Negro History Week was launched, and since that time it has been held annually in February, encompassing the birth dates of Abraham Lincoln and Frederick Douglass. The *Negro History Bulletin* was first published in 1937 to serve both schools and families by making available to them little-known facts about black life and history.

During its sixty-one years of existence, the Association for the Study of Afro-American Life and History has supported many publications dealing with the contributions of Afro-Americans to the growth and development of this country. Its activities have contributed to the increasing interest in the dissemination of factual studies which are placing the Afro-American in true perspective in the mainstream of American history.

We gratefully acknowledge the contributions of previous scholars, which have aided us in the preparation of this *International Library of Afro-American Life and History*.

Our grateful acknowledgment is also expressed to Charles W. Lockyer, president of Pubco Corporation, whose challenging approach has made possible this library.

Though each of the volumes in this set can stand as an autonomous unit, and although each author has brought his own interpretation to the area with which he is dealing, together these books form a comprehensive picture of the Afro-American experience in America. The three history volumes give a factual record of a people who were brought from Africa in chains and who today are struggling to cast off the last vestiges of these bonds. The anthologies covering music, art, the theatre and literature provide a detailed account of the black American's contributions to these fields—including those contributions which are largely forgotten today. Achievement in the sports world is covered in another volume. The volume on the Afro-American in medicine is a history of the black American's struggle for equality as a medical practitioner and as a patient. The selected black leaders in the biography book represent the contributions and achievements of many times their number. The documentary history sums up the above-mentioned material in the words of men and women who were themselves a part of black history.

CHARLES H. WESLEY

Washington, D.C.

Editor's Note

I WISH to thank the following people for the contributions they have made on behalf of this publication: Dan Beagle and Michael Greenberg for their assistance in the research and editing of the manuscript; Allan Kullen for gathering photographs and handling the layout of the volume; and Wendy Schempp for her general assistance. Particular gratitude goes to the following organizations for their invaluable aid in providing materials and photographs to illustrate the book: Mrs. Dorothy Porter at the Moorland Room of Howard University; the staffs of the Library of Congress, the New York Public Library and the New York Public Library-Schomburg Collection; and especially the Historical Society of Pennsylvania, including Mr. John D. Kilbourne, Curator, Mr. Conrad Wilson, Chief of Manuscripts and Mr. Frank W. Bobb, Librarian.

CHARLES H. WESLEY

Washington, D.C.

Table of Contents

Introduction

THE HISTORY of the black man in America before the Civil War has been commonly regarded as a period of slavery, with little or no attention accorded the accomplishments of Afro-Americans themselves. This volume presents the other side of the picture, while at the same time chronicling the central issue of slavery.

The African background is all too often disregarded when discussing the black man in this country out of a misconception that there was no significant history in Africa—except in Egypt—prior to the arrival of the white man. This, however, was not the case. Africa had a long and glorious tradition long before the slave trade and the nineteenth-century explorations of Henry M. Stanley and others.

When the first white traders arrived in equatorial Africa, they found stabilized tribal units occupying villages and outlying areas. They discovered a system of organized government and a stable economy that usually stressed rule by the chief and the elder members of the tribe. The warring elements were made up of the younger males, while the women occupied positions of domestic responsibility. The large supply of Africans, combined with the warring tendencies of many of the tribal units, made it possible for the white traders to begin thinking in terms of the economic exploitation of Africa by the removal of its peoples.

The first large influx of Africans into Europe came as a result of Prince Henry the Navigator's interest in exploration and trade. By the middle of the fifteenth century, Portugal was importing about eight hundred blacks a year. When the explorations reached the Americas later in the century, and as they continued throughout the next century, black Africans were to be found in the company of many of the explorers and taking part in their expeditions. As South America became more profitable economically to the Spanish and Portuguese, the trade in African slaves increased. Of course, as the need for labor grew more pressing and the rape of the African continent continued, the black civilization was gradually drained of its best asset—its future leaders. Africa, therefore, did not develop as it might have but remained somewhat static until the twentieth century.

The first blacks arriving in North America in 1619 came as indentured servants, working out their period of assigned years and gaining their freedom. As the country expanded and developed economically, it became necessary —as it had earlier in Latin and South America—to secure more labor. Since Africans were abundant and cheap to obtain, more attention was given to developing the slave trade. Although laws were passed around the middle of the seventeenth century placing the blacks in perpetual servitude, many Afro-Americans were free and were engaging in business enterprises similar to those pursued by white Americans. Since the economy of the South was more agricultural than industrial, even in the formative years, it was natural for the heavy influx of Africans to be located in the southern colonies, and thus subjugation of the slaves became a primary concern of the whites. They passed laws in every southern colony to restrict and limit the activities of the blacks, both slaves and freemen. The free black man then became a sort of semi-citizen in the South.

Although the North also sanctioned slavery

in the earlier colonial period, the emphasis on industrialization brought many immigrants from Europe to that area. The need for slave labor thus decreased, and as the need diminished the laws in the North were relaxed and slavery died a gradual death. Free blacks became concentrated in the North, especially following the Revolutionary War, and as the Northwest Territory was opened for settlement many free men left the South for the new areas, where they could obtain land and escape the dreaded hand of the bounty-catcher.

The philosophy of the Revolution—equality and the rights of man—seemed to promise the blacks a new type of existence. When the war between Great Britain and the American colonies became a reality, blacks were anxious to enlist and support the doctrine of freedom and equality with their service and their lives. After the controversy was resolved as to whether they should be accepted in the army, many served the Revolutionary cause with valor. But they were to find themselves on the sidelines when freedom came in 1783.

The Constitutional Convention sanctioned slavery and continued the slave trade, although blacks themselves protested and spoke out against these inhumane attitudes of the Founding Fathers. The formation of the Bethel African Methodist Episcopal Church by Richard Allen in 1793 was the beginning of organized activity on the part of Afro-Americans. Soon after Bethel Church was founded, Prince Hall began the organization of blacks into a Masonic Order. These beginnings of institutional life among Afro-Americans gave them an opportunity to organize a platform from which they could verbalize their protests against slavery and the slave trade.

Sympathetic whites, especially among the Quakers, joined with the blacks to work for the abolition of these two evils. The formal rise of abolition as a movement did not occur until the 1830's, when other reform movements took root in American life, even though the slave trade had been legally abolished in 1808. The controversy over whether the Afro-American should remain enslaved, be freed and accorded the rights of citizenship or freed and colonized in some distant land was never far from the minds of the country's leaders from the very beginning of the nation's history until the Civil War.

The black slaves who labored on the southern plantations did not sit idly by and wait for the shackles of bondage to be broken. They revolted, ran away, committed suicide to escape the system, and a few even poisoned their masters. One of the great mysteries of the "peculiar institution" was the network of communication that ran from plantation to plantation, carrying the plans of Afro-Americans for escape or possible insurrection. Gabriel Prosser, Denmark Vesey and Nat Turner are examples of the hundreds of slaves who planned and carried out insurrections on a small scale in their particular areas. The beginnings of the Underground Railroad came as a result of the activity carried on for years by slaves escaping southern bondage.

The history of the black man, as described in this volume, shows the irony of the entire tragic racial pattern in this country. While America grew and developed economically—in large part through slave labor—a steady stream of free black men followed the same pattern of advancement. But always they progressed with the extra burden of their enslaved brothers, whom they sought to free through the democratic processes established by the Constitution.

The liberal use of illustrations in this volume presents graphically those who were active in the slave trade and slavery throughout the centuries so that the people of today may better perceive the history of the black man as he trod in freedom's footsteps.

CHARLES H. WESLEY

Washington, D.C.

CHAPTER ONE

The African Background

AMERICA has become a new homeland for peoples from many parts of the world, and all of her immigrants have had significant cultural traditions and histories. American history, therefore, should be studied within the context of the history of the old world to which America owes its origins. In order to understand our history, we first must consider the cultural contributions of the peoples and nations from which our civilization has been derived.

The contributions of all these peoples—the English, the Germans, the Spanish, the Dutch, the Swedish, the Welsh, the Jews, the Finns, the Poles, the Italians, the Scotch, the Irish and the French—have generally been included in the modern study of our country's history. But American historians have frequently overlooked the contributions of one of the largest of these groups—the Africans. It has been conservatively estimated that fifteen million Negroes came to the western hemisphere during the four centuries in which the slave ships plied the Atlantic.

A BRIEF GEOGRAPHICAL SKETCH

The cultural development of the African people has been profoundly connected to the geography of the African continent. One reason a study of African history is an exhaust-ing task is that the cultural diversity staggers the mind. This variety is matched precisely by the nature of the physical environment. Every extreme is represented—from barren desert to vegetation-choked rain forest. Perhaps, in part, the nature of the land itself is responsible for European ignorance of and misconceptions about African peoples and for the subsequent horrors committed in the name of the "white man's burden." How could an Englishman (or a Portuguese or a Frenchman) understand or even recognize the peculiar nature of an African community's organization? Neither he nor any of his European countrymen had ever been faced with such awesome natural forces. Few features of his own social institutions gave him standards by which to judge those of Africa. Lacking such standards, the majority of early travelers to Africa were blind. Seeing nothing, they concluded that nothing was to be seen. A picture of the land itself is certainly basic to the beginning of understanding.

Africa, a large continent roughly triangular in form, is about twelve million square miles in area. It is three times the size of Europe and nearly four times the size of the United States. A narrow strip of land, now broken by the Suez Canal, connects Africa and Asia. The continent can be divided into five sections. North Africa ranges from the

Explorer Henry M. Stanley with an African guide.

Sahara Desert in the south to the Mediterranean Sea in the north and from Egypt in the east to Morocco in the west. The area is somewhat similar in geography and topography to the countries of southern Europe. While southern Europe, however, is surrounded by humid agricultural lands, the fertile areas of North Africa are encroached upon by desert. The most fertile region is Egypt's Nile Valley. Today this geographical section contains most of Mauritania, the northern parts of Mali, Niger, Chad, Sudan, Spanish Sahara, Morocco, Tunisia, Algeria, Libya and Egypt.

The Sahara Desert has long played an important role in creating both physical and cultural divisions. It is erroneous to assume the Sahara was as forbidding a wasteland in the Stone Age as it is today. After 10,000

B.C. (and probably closer to 5000 B.C.), a climatic change brought rainfall and rivers to the entire region. From thousands of beautiful rock paintings left by the people of the area, scientists have constructed a fairly accurate picture of the civilizations which spanned the Sahara's fertile period. An early and highly developed agriculture gradually formed—based chiefly on the tending of vast herds of cattle. But around 2500 B.C., a slow reversal in climate gradually returned the Sahara to the wasteland it is now and had been before. So the Sahara, which had once attracted North and West African peoples, now expelled them in various directions and ensured their isolation. This great change helps to explain both the puzzling similarities and the differences between North African peoples and those below the Sahara.

West Africa ranges from the southern edge of the Sahara to the Niger Delta. Bounded on the east by a line virtually the same as the current eastern border of Nigeria, it presently encompasses a small southern part of Mauritania and southern portions of Mali and Niger. Senegal, Gambia, Portuguese Guinea, Guinea, Sierra Leone, Liberia, Ivory Coast, Upper Volta, Ghana, Togo and Dahomey are also included. Here, the geography is characterized by coastal swamps leading into thick forests, which in turn give way to savanna grasslands.

Equatorial Africa contains the present countries of Cameroon, southern Chad, the Central African Republic, the Republic of the Congo (Brazzaville), Gabon and the Congo Republic (Kinshasa). The famous explorer Henry M. Stanley described the area:

. . . Imagine the whole of France and the Iberian peninsula closely packed with trees, varying from twenty to a hundred and eighty feet in height, whose crowns of foliage interlace and prevent any view of sky and sun, and each tree from a few inches to four feet in diameter.

The equatorial forests are periodically inundated with rainfall, and since much of the area is flat, swamps and marshes abound.

East Africa, which contains Uganda, Kenya, Ethiopia, the Somali Republic, Rwanda, Burundi and northern Tanzania, is an extraordinarily fertile area. The best lands are on the plateaus, which are the dominant geological features of the region. While deserts abound in East Africa, there are also many savanna grasslands, forests and mountain grasslands. The southern part of the Sudan, sometimes called the Middle Nile Basin, has geographic features similar to those of East Africa.

Southern Africa is characterized by high fertile plateaus, too, but it also contains a substantial area that is best described as desert and steppes. Southern Tanzania, Angola, Zambia, Malawi, Mozambique, Rhodesia, Botswana, South-West Africa, the Republic of South Africa, Lesotho and Swaziland are located in this geographic region. The Malagasy Republic (Madagascar), across from Mozambique and southern Africa, usually receives individual attention in geography books; but, like South and East Africa, it does have highlands and savanna grasslands. On the eastern side of the island is a heavy tropical forest.

The history and civilization of Africa are intimately associated with its geography and physical resources. All approaches to African culture must take into account the internal isolation of its regions. Crossing a desert is no light undertaking; travel through a rain forest has its perils. The rivers also present difficulties. The shallowness of the great African rivers, such as the Senegal, the Niger, the Congo and the Zambesi, sometimes forbids their use as vehicles for intra-continental communication and trade as well as for export activities. Modern ingenuity in communication and transportation is helping to overcome these natural geographical barriers, but progress is being made slowly.

RACIAL DIVISIONS

No adequate definition of "race" has ever been found, and considerable confusion surrounds the concept. Anthropologists have attempted to classify mankind on the bases of skin color, hair texture, shape of head and other physical characteristics. As soon as these classifications have been established, however, the variations that run across the lines supposedly dividing the groups are brought into relief. No attempt should be made to use racial definitions as anything more than a convenient but woefully imperfect system of dividing masses of people into smaller groups. Though scientists will continue to argue whether some of the following categories represent groups or subgroups, these ten divisions (from G. H. T. Kimble, *Tropical Africa*) are most frequently used: Bushman, Pygmy, Hottentot, Negro, Hamite, Half-Hamite, Nilote, Bantu, Semite and Malgache.

Any student of African and Afro-American history should recognize these terms, but only a little study will reveal their limited usefulness. The degree of intermingling of "races" is indeterminable either by extent or by date. Some of the divisions, moreover, rely heavily on linguistic or geographical considerations. Until such time as satisfactory measurements and criteria evolve (and evidence indicates that science will not move in this direction), racial labels should be considered nothing more than arbitrary names to facilitate speaking of people in groups.

EARLY CIVILIZATIONS

European writers have been responsible for most of the written history of Africa. The resulting damage in terms of facts ignored, misinterpreted, overlooked or simply manufactured is only now beginning to be redressed. The attitude common to many who think of, or write about, Africa has been one of easy dismissal: Africa has no history; slavery was a good thing because it took the Africans out of their savage environment and exposed them to the "beneficent influence" of Western civilization. This attitude is, of course, utter nonsense; but it no doubt comforted those who engaged in the slave trade and those who were confronted by the demands of the emancipated Negro. Archeological and sociological studies of the last decade or so have uncovered a wealth of evidence and have disseminated information from little-known older sources to further establish that Africa has a long and distinguished history.

Considerable discussion has developed as to whether our own Western civilization first arose in the valley of the Nile or in the Tigris-Euphrates area. In both areas, evidence of civilization dates from many centuries ago. There could not be more than a thousand years or so of difference in the ages of the two civilizations. The history of the culture of the Nile Valley is particularly significant: it establishes the chronological priority of African civilization and also makes clear the contribution of "colored" peoples to Western civilization.

The great and prosperous civilization of the Nile Valley arose approximately in the fourth millennium B.C. We know very little about the predynastic Egyptians, but there is no doubt that most of them were African farmers from along the Nile, although Egypt certainly must have attracted some immigrants from the Near East. Since most scholars believe that the present land of Egypt could not have existed before 7000 B.C., the culture Egypt had by 3200 B.C. represents a spectacularly rapid development. In the four thousand years or so between the time that the Nile waters receded and left rich soils behind and the date at which all basic elements of the brilliant civilization had been formed, rude farmers had become engineers, artists, high priests and bureaucrats, with an alpha-

bet and a calendar. This remarkably stable society reached fingers of influence into many faraway places.

This is not to say, of course, that relationships between Egypt and her contemporaries were all one-sided. There were the civilizations of Kush and Axum, which definitely possessed independent traits, however much they borrowed from the Egyptians.

Nubian Kush, south of Egypt on the Nile River, lay between the Third and Sixth Cataracts on the Dongola Reach. In early periods (about 2000 B.C.), Kushites were much awed by their Egyptian conquerors; but Kush never became simply a poor carbon of Egypt. At one point in the early eighth century, Kushites ruled Egypt, only to be displaced by Assyrians a hundred years afterward. Even with this extensive intermingling, many features of Kushite religious and secular life emerged unchanged. When the Assyrians fully displaced the Twenty-fifth Egyptian Dynasty in 656 B.C., a glorious heir to Egyptian-Ethiopian civilization remained in Kush.

From their Assyrian conquerors, the Kushites learned techniques of ironworking. Large slag heaps at Meroë, the second Kushite capital, attest the presence of one of the largest ironworking centers in antiquity. The Kushites grew wealthy by exporting ivory, slaves, ostrich feathers, ebony and gold, and through a sophisticated agriculture. Their greatest prosperity occurred in the last three centuries before the birth of Christ. It is still possible to see ruins of their "towns of mortar," where business flourished and art was highly developed. In the middle of the fourth century A.D., Meroë was destroyed by Axumite soldiers under King Ezana.

Axum, near the southern end of the Red Sea, has a history as intriguing as that of Kush. With the conversion of Ezana, Ethiopia began its unique role as the oldest continuously Christian African state. The Ethiopian culture, focused at Axum after the destruction of Kush, was the strongest force

The ruins of the Royal Tombs at Meroë.

This sandstone sculpture found at Meroë is believed to date from the first century A.D.

The large slag heaps at Meroë attest the former existence of one of the largest ironworking centers in antiquity. This model illustrates what the first iron-smelting factories may have looked like.

The ancient city of Timbuktu, an important trade mart for widespread Negro tribes, was also a center of Moslem culture.

in the area until the eighth century. Axum became a major maritime power and a leader in architecture.

Other empires developed in West Africa. In the western Sudan and in the region of the Niger, kingdoms arose characterized by walled and fortified cities and extremely stable political organizations. The kingdom of Ghana, for example, goes back to approximately the fifth or sixth century A.D. By the eleventh century A.D., the kingdom of Ghana had an army of two hundred thousand men, palaces of wood and stone with glass windows, and extreme wealth. Ghana maintained a large export trade with Mediterranean countries. In fact, most of the gold used in western Europe in the Middle Ages was transported from the mines of Ghana. At this time, the borders of Ghana ranged from Timbuktu in the east, to the upper Niger in the southeast, to the upper Senegal River in the south and to the borders of Tekrur in the west. The effective northern border of Ghana lay somewhere in the southern Sahara since Ghanian domination extended over some of the Berber tribes in the southern portion of the great desert.

The grandeur and wealth of Ghana were based on the export of gold and salt. Modern legends and the chronicles of medieval travelers testify to the splendor and power of the Ghanian kings. One traveler recalled that a certain seventh-century king of Ghana possessed one thousand horses and that each one, provided with three attendants, slept on a carpet with a silken rope for a halter. The Ghanian kings were said to have given enormous banquets for their subjects, feeding ten thousand at a time.

As Ghana grew into a large empire, it developed sophisticated bureaucratic and governmental structures, becoming a modern state in every sense of the word, heavily centralized in an attempt to extend the rule of law and order throughout its boundaries. But by the late eleventh century, the Ghanian empire was in ruins. The Berbers of northwestern Africa, displaced and defeated by invading Arabs, began to attack their prosperous neighbors to the south. A Moroccan people, the Almoravides, conquered Ghana after a series of bloody battles. They were never able to consolidate control over the entire empire, but Ghana was in ruins. The Almoravids were assisted in their conquests by the outbreak of revolts from within as Ghanian client states asserted their independence.

The next great Sudanese empire, rising in virtually the same area as the old Ghanian state, was the glorious empire of Mali. It was founded on the basis of the petty state of Kangaba which had revolted from one of the states attempting to take the place of Ghana. Kangaba seized its independence in about 1230 A.D., and it is from this date that we mark the real emergence of Mali.

Over a period of several hundred years, the Malians extended their rule; and by the mid-fourteenth century, the little state of Kangaba had developed into one of the largest empires in the world. Its borders ranged from the Atlantic Ocean on the west to the middle Niger Valley on the east, incorporating the great cities of Timbuktu and Gao. The Malians also controlled a good part of the southern Sahara to the north. To the south, their rule extended to include the gold-producing area just below the borders of ancient Ghana.

Like Ghana, the empire of Mali was highly centralized and stable. Mali was noted especially for the peace and tranquility of life within its borders. According to one Moslem chronicler, the people of Mali

> . . . are seldom unjust, and have a much greater horror of injustice than any other people. Their sultan shows no mercy to anyone who is guilty of the least act of it. There is complete security in their country. Neither traveller nor inhabitant in it has anything to fear from robbers or men of violence. It is a real state whose organization and civilization could be compared with those of the Musselman [Moslem] kingdoms, or indeed the Christian kingdoms of the same period.

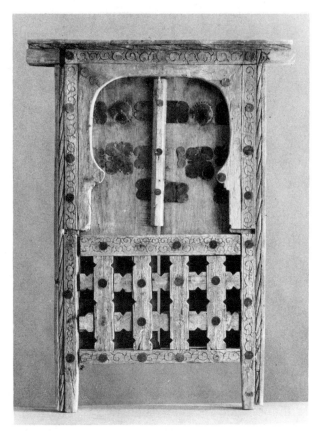

This window from the city of Timbuktu illustrates the intricate craftsmanship of early African artisans.

Mali had become a recognized world power by 1324, when the great Emperor Mansa Musa visited Mecca. The Egyptians and Arabians recognized him as a great king, "lord of the Negroes." They were impressed by the amounts of gold and other precious metals he carried with him, but they found that his spending seriously depressed the value of gold in Cairo and Mecca.

The Emperor of Mali was one of the first Sudanese rulers to accept Islam, and in this respect he was among the first rulers in a long period of increasing Islamic influence. This was the beginning of an increasing cultural unity between the Arabs and Egyptians and the sub-Saharan peoples. Naturally, this cultural contact fostered trade, and Mali was the greatest beneficiary.

Among Mansa Musa's accomplishments in his twenty-five-year reign were the erection of many great palaces and mosques, the rebuild-ing of Timbuktu, the extension of Mali's borders and the very important foundation and patronage of Moslem-oriented universities.

But Mansa Musa's successors were unable to keep the empire together. In 1375, the people of the city of Gao rebelled. The Saharan peoples known as the Tuareg seized portions of the empire, including Timbuktu. These separatist movements continued until, by 1550, Mali was no longer a political unit of any importance. Yet, even in the sixteenth century, the Moroccan traveler Leo Africanus still maintained that Mali's capital, Niane, was a city of six thousand hearths and described the people of Mali as "the most civilized, intelligent, and respected" of all the people of the western Sudan.

One of the vassal states of Mali was the kingdom of Songhay, the last of the great West African empires. After approximately 600 A.D., Songhay developed as a minor commercial civilization around the city of Kulya, near Gao. Close to the beginning of the eleventh century, the ruler of this city-state was converted to Islam, and most of the subsequent rulers retained the faith. While the countryside remained pagan, Islam became the religion of the commercial classes in the cities and of the royal bureaucracy.

Shortly after the conversion, the Songhay capital was transferred to Gao, and that city began its period of great growth. In a favorable position to exploit the expanding trans-Saharan trade, the people of Gao became extremely wealthy. By the first quarter of the fourteenth century, Gao had grown so important that it attracted the conquering armies of Mali.

By 1375, however, Mali had weakened, and the Songhay kingdom won its independence. The next hundred years were of varying fortune for the people of Songhay. Nevertheless, within the century, the Songhay did revive the empire-building efforts of Ghana and Mali. Prominent among the expansionist rulers was Sunni Ali Ber, who ruled from 1464 to 1492. He was especially successful in his military efforts, gaining control of an ever-increasing amount of territory around Gao and conquering the great cities of Jenne and Timbuktu.

The last dynastic rulers of the Songhay Empire, the Askias, reigned from 1493 to 1591. The greatest of the Askias, Askia Mohammed Ture, ruled from 1493 to 1529 and extended the Songhay Empire to the Atlantic Ocean. He was an able administrator who perfected the centralizing techniques and bureaucratic structures that had characterized the empires of Mali and Ghana. Basing his rule on the Moslem urban middle class, he established a university and regulated banking, credit, commerce and taxation. Gao and Jenne became intellectual centers, and at the University of Sankore in Timbuctu, black students studied literature, law, geography and the sciences under black scholars.

ASKIA MOHAMMED TURE

Even after the death of Askia Mohammed Ture, the dynasty flourished. Under Askia Dawud (1549–1582), the empire enjoyed a long period of wealth and prosperity. Again, the Songhay Empire was widely reputed throughout the Middle East, North Africa and among the Europeans. But with Dawud's death, troubles broke out at home. The petty Hausa and Mossi states rebelled against their overlords. And, more important, in 1582 a force of Moroccans seized the Saharan salt works, claimed by Songhay. The soldiers were armed with the arquebus, a primitive rifle, which proved an ominous sign for independent Africa.

In 1591, the sultan of Morocco sent forth an army of mercenaries equipped with modern weaponry. The Moroccans defeated the armies of crumbling Songhay and destroyed the empire. Although the North Africans were unable to hold the Songhay possessions, Songhay never again rose to power.

Ghana, Mali and Songhay were three of the more important political organizations that extended into the late medieval period. But throughout the continent, there were similar developments, all of which reflected a high level of civilization.

The rest of West Africa, for example, saw the rise of several distinct civilizations of great stability and sophistication. In the upper Volta region, five strong states—known as the Mossi states—existed before 1500. Although these states were heavily influenced by the great empires of the north, they remain important examples of African political units that enjoyed long-term stability in the absence of the development of a Moslemized aristocracy.

Far into the interior was the empire of Kanem-Bornu. Extending over an enormous area, it began its existence as a sovereign empire in 800 A.D. and existed well into the nineteenth century. It developed as an important trade center between the kingdoms of the western Sudan, North Africa and the Nile

This cotton robe is typical of the type manufactured in the Hausa confederation during the eighteenth century.

Valley, and was therefore an extremely cosmopolitan area. The upper classes accepted Islam in 1086 A.D.

Between Kanem-Bornu and Songhay were the Hausa states, with a defined political and cultural tradition which dates back to the eleventh century. They maintained their independence until approximately 1800. Hausa cities were centers of trade and exchange, and agriculture prospered in the countryside. The Hausa kingdoms were frequently visited by Arab scholars and developed a written language based on the adaptation of the Hausa spoken language to Arabic script. By the eighteenth century, the Hausa confederation was a center of handicraft industries and had begun to manufacture cotton textiles.

The coastal area between the Niger and the Congo Rivers, the Guinea coast, supplied most of the slaves for the New World. Along this coast, there were many centers of tribal activity that merged purely indigenous ways of life and culture with influences from the kingdoms and city-states of the Sudan. The people of this area were organized in a feudal

manner to such an extent that the Portuguese explorers who landed on the coast in the fifteenth century had little difficulty understanding the political structure.

The South and the East were also seats of great medieval civilizations. As in the Sudan and the Guinea coast areas, these civilizations were mixtures and syncretisms of Moslem, Egyptian and a large measure of other African elements.

In modern Tanzania and Kenya lived a people called by the Arabs the "zanj," who were skilled metal workers and energetic traders. They were heavily involved with Arabs in the Indian Ocean trade. It has been suggested that the famous Persian swords that so amazed the Europeans during the Crusades were forged in India from African iron. As further evidence that this was an advanced culture, anthropologists working in East Africa have found remnants of sophisticated irrigation systems pointing to the existence of a stable and sedentary agricultural community.

Perhaps the greatest monument to this civilization was the fortified city of Great Zimbabwe. This Bantu city of the interior, in the present country of Rhodesia, flourished between about the middle of the thirteenth century and the middle of the eighteenth century, but the culture that produced the city developed over a period of at least one thousand years. According to most modern scholars, Great Zimbabwe was almost exclusively a product of local Africans. The monomotapa, or ruler, of this area was the lord of a state power, which was comprised of a loose tribal-feudal organization.

CULTURAL LIFE

African cultural life was extremely complex, and we can only give the reader a hint of its vast heterogeneity before the arrival of the Europeans. Certain generalizations can be made, nonetheless, concerning African social, political and economic life. And these are useful in understanding the cultural background of the slaves who came to the New World.

The prototypical African political organization was the Sudanic state, or the type of state we can associate with the belt of land extending across Africa south of the Sahara and north of the tropical rain forest. It is with this form of state structure that we associate the ancient West African states and the states of Axum and Kush in the east. While Ghana, Mali and Songhay tended to influence the forms of state organization in the west, it is probable that Kushite patterns directly influenced the forms in the east and south.

Tribal legend and folklore, moreover, suggest that the African state system was inspired primarily by the Kushite monarchs. Historians postulate that the destruction of

the monarchy and the dispersal of the royal family to the south and the west explain many of the similarities in state organization throughout the continent. Many West African legends speak of the ancestors of given tribes coming from the east, whereas many southern and eastern legends point similarly to a Kushite origin.

To varying degrees, African states during the late Middle Ages were tending toward centralization. Throughout the continent, there was a decline of vassalage and increasing development of rationalized monarchy. For example, while Sunni Ali Ber depended upon a temporary army of vassals for his military conquests—men who were loyal to their immediate lord rather than to the person of the emperor—his successor, Askia Mohammed, organized a professional army and

The presence of sophisticated irrigation systems in East African ruins indicates that wells of this type were used by early African farmers.

In early Africa, there were skilled artisans who produced such creations as the delicately tooled ivory and copper armlets (top), decorative brass weights (left) and brass jewelry (right) shown here.

navy that were reliable and owed allegiance to him. Thus, on the one hand, we find an extended family type of government comparable to Tacitus' description of the Germanic tribal government located around the fringes of the Roman Empire. On the other hand, we find an increasing bureaucratization and centralization, which reminds us of the European nation-state in the late medieval and early modern periods of Western history. The general pattern was for large states increasingly to extend their power over smaller ones, either in a feudalistic or absolutist manner.

Some African states had complex electoral systems. Certain men in the community served as advisors to the king, and in fact, the king served at their pleasure. When one king died or was deposed, a new one was selected by the council of electors. This was true, for example, in Bornu, a medieval kingdom in the southern Sudan.

ECONOMIC LIFE

African economic life, by the time of the advent of the slave trade, was a complementary system of agriculture, commerce and manufacturing. Throughout the continent, there was a general tendency toward subsistence agriculture. Along with agriculture, there were the extractive enterprises, such as gold mining in the western coastal region and the trade in ivory tusks along the eastern coast.

In the days before the slave trade, African commerce became increasingly involved in the world market. West African gold, for example, was the medium of exchange in western Europe. Many African kingdoms traded in iron to the Arabs and the Indians. There is considerable evidence of Chinese contacts during the medieval period; for example, much Chinese pottery has been found in many East African ruins. Many of the great

African kingdoms flourished precisely because they were based along trade routes that connected Africa with the Far East and with the Moslem world. When the Europeans came to Africa, they found a people who were experienced in trade and bookkeeping and who had an understanding of the basic laws of commerce. Africa, to a larger extent than most Europeans have been willing to admit, was a continent of cities that carried on a thriving commerce with the rest of the world.

African manufacturing, although pre-industrial, was probably comparable to contemporary European or Asiatic manufacturing. For example, in the eighteenth century the Hausa were beginning to develop a cotton-manufacturing plant. Throughout Africa, the process of iron smelting and manufacturing was well understood. Anthropologist Franz Boas argued:

> . . . It seems likely that at times when the European was still satisfied with rude stone tools, the African had invented or adopted the art of smelting iron. The true advancement of industrial life did not begin until the hard iron was discovered. It seems not unlikely that the people who made the marvelous discovery of reducing iron ores by smelting were African Negroes. Neither ancient Europe, nor ancient western Asia, nor ancient China knew iron, and everything points to its introduction from Africa. At the time of the great African discoveries, blacksmiths were found all over Africa from north to south, and from east to west. With his simple bellows and a charcoal fire, he reduced the ore that is found in many parts of the continent, and forged implements of great usefulness and beauty.

In *Black Mother,* Basil Davidson asserted that nearly all of the peoples of the African continent had experienced some sort of iron age by the time of the first European contacts. Many African peoples also did highly skilled work in gold and other precious metals, and this African craftsmanship in precious metals was increasingly renowned throughout the world.

RELIGION

Many Westerners have adopted an extremely patronizing attitude toward African religion. It has been suggested, for example, that African religion must be inferior to the other great world religions since each tribe had its own gods, implying that there could not be, therefore, any great common theological conceptions. While we criticize the black Africans for their "pagan" religious localism, however, the fragmentations of Christianity, Hinduism and Islam often go unnoticed.

It is impossible to understand African religious life without some knowledge of the influence of Islam. Throughout the medieval period, there was increasing contact between Islamic North Africa and pagan Africa. These contacts were in terms of both trade and warfare. Frequently, the royal families of various African kingdoms would accept the faith of Mohammed. This was often done for economic reasons: it eased trade with the north, which was important for the Sudanic states; and the acceptance of Islam assured the kings of the support of mercantile groups within their own capital cities.

Particularly in the ancient empire of Mali, the kings were faced with the necessity of striking a balance between urbanized Islam and rural paganism. Many feared to offend the pagan country folk, and so, while they embraced Islam, they continued many pagan practices at their courts. This was particularly true of the great king of Mali, Sunni Ali Ber.

The pagan religions of Africa showed remarkable vitality in the face of the Islamic and the later Christian attempts at conversion. Even today, Christianity in Africa is influenced heavily by overlays of paganism. The religious ideology of many nationalist movements in Africa are based on a syncretism of pagan and Christian elements.

African religion is frequently thought of as totally magical in content and devoid, therefore, of any power of abstraction or of any real spiritual content. Recent research has shown that this is untrue. The pagan religions have much in common with the great religions of the world, and there is sound evidence that many African peoples developed remarkably unified sets of sophisticated religious conceptions.

Despite the immensity of the continent and the difficulty of communication, African religions were more homogeneous than many Europeans have been led to believe. Certain religious symbols and concepts, such as the institution of divine kingship, continually reappear throughout the continent. Thus, it is possible for us to make some general remarks about African religions.

Virtually all African religions begin with some concept of a Supreme Being. God is not so much a personality as a primordial force or basic energy that infuses all of life. God is being, the inner essence of life. This Supreme Being is impersonal and all-pervasive.

The African faiths suggest a universe totally infused with spirit. Like the Christians of the Middle Ages, the Africans saw the world as a systematically contrived hierarchy of values and powers in which every person and thing had its place and its role. Thus, African religious folklore is full of legends of men who fell because they challenged God, because they sought to approach God as equals, because they denied the relative insignificance of humanity. In African religions, the spirit of God is primarily a spirit that motivates and drives the universe but also orders it.

Below God in the universal chain of being are vast congeries of nature gods, place gods, family gods, powerful ancestors and tribal hero gods, all of whom stand between man and the Supreme Being. Common throughout Africa, for example, are storm gods, mother-earth figures and sun and moon deities. All of these gods have an established place within the hierarchy. Like many Westerners, Africans concerned themselves with the questions of man's role in the universe and developed notions of purpose, order and spirit that gave them satisfactory answers—answers with which they could live.

Perhaps because of the great sense of order and stability developed by the pagan religions, African moral regulation was always particularly strict. The popular notion of hedonistic Africans living in debauchery is, by all accounts, the product of ignorance and vested interest. Polygamy was practiced not out of a deliberate desire to affront the morals of Christian missionaries but out of a deep reverence for life and love of children. In the debilitating climate of Africa, where infant mortality was high, polygamy was necessary for the mere preservation of the race. The great West African kingdoms were held in high repute by Moslem chroniclers and travelers for the low crime rate and high moral standards that prevailed among their peoples. The anthropologist Leo Frobenius wrote of the Yorubans, who lived within the boundaries of present-day Nigeria, as "the chastest and most ethically disposed of all the national groups in the world which have become known to me."

CONCLUSIONS

It seems to have been proven beyond a doubt that the standard racist picture of Africa as a barbarous land filled with cannibals, head hunters and ignorant, superstitious natives is untrue and unfair. When the Portuguese, and later the English and Dutch, first came to Africa, they found people with whom they could deal on equal terms; they also found political and social structures that they could understand. They found a people who were largely urbanized, who had considerable commercial and industrial experience. They found a people with a sophisticated religious life and a well-developed national and tribal consciousness.

Certainly, African precolonial society was preliterate. But the well-known historian Basil Davidson, whose special field is African culture, suggests that the peoples of Africa were little different from the masses of Europeans, who were similarly ignorant in the sixteenth century. It is true that Africa fell behind industrially and politically. It is true that Africa was conquered and that economically her people were unable to develop on their own. But many of Africa's economic and political problems must be traced to those natural and geographic problems that we have discussed. The barriers to transportation and communication, the intense heat and debilitating atmosphere of much of the continent, these certainly have served to retard African industrial and economic progress.

It is an unfortunate paradox that Africa was also set back by its contact with more "advanced" countries. The impact, for example, of the slave trade on African society has yet to be measured. Virtually fifteen million people were removed from the continent in several hundred years; no area in Africa was entirely unaffected. Along with depopulation, the slave trade corrupted the political life of Africa, especially along the western coast. The trade was so profitable for local kings that they increasingly turned the economies of their countries solely to the slave trade, and after several generations the economic life of the kingdom was dependent on its export of human flesh.

In general, the slave trade seriously weakened the moral, political and social fabric of African life and retarded indigenous development. The coastal states became totally committed to the trade. Native crafts and industries were displaced by cheap European goods. Mild African drinks were displaced by gin and rum. Historian-sociologist W. E. B. Du Bois claimed that "the continued development of African civilization, forecast in the fourteenth and fifteenth centuries by that

Victims of the slave trade, which seriously weakened the moral, political and social fabric of African life.

An African slave-catcher.

in the Sudan, was prevented and turned backward into chaos, flight and death." Henry M. Stanley wrote of the effect of the ivory and slave trade in the eighteenth century on African life:

> Picture, if you can, a territory . . . terrorized and overrun in all directions with hundreds of roving bands of plundering murderers armed with invincible weapons of oppression, a land of blood and might and nights filled with flame and destruction, the days weary with the marching of the coffles and the blood of the despairing, hopeless slaves.

Whole nations of peaceful coastal tribes were turned into raiding slave-catchers penetrating the interior as the mild form of domestic slavery peculiar to West Africa became the savage chattel slavery of the New World.

In conclusion, several points should be emphasized. Most important, perhaps, is that in the field of religion, as well as in economic and political organization, the African people demonstrated a skill and intelligence that disprove the myth of Negro savagery and barbarism. Many of the kingdoms of Africa were certainly on a level with their contemporaries in Europe and Asia. The second important point is that the technological backwardness of the Africans can be traced to the geographical peculiarities of their continent and the demoralizing and destructive influence of the slave trade.

CHAPTER TWO

Exploration and the Advent of the Slave Trade

THE age of discovery began in the fifteenth century. After nearly a century of decline in economic and political well-being, Europe started to emerge and assert her position on the world scene. The explorations that did so much to establish her power were a part and a product of the changes that were taking place in Europe at that time. The Renaissance, and later the Reformation, by rediscovering the world of the individual, freed man from the intellectual confines of the feudal order. Dynastic consolidation established a more centralized political organization than the local rule of feudal barons had provided. The development of commerce, together with the growth of towns, provided the material means as well as the incentives for European expansion.

The first nation to send explorers out beyond the confines of the European coast was Portugal. An important factor in the Portuguese explorations was the support given them by the Royal Court of Lisbon. Henry the Navigator, the son of John I (1385–1433), was an important patron of these early voyages. His father had established the Aviz dynasty in Portugal. Prince Henry was to benefit greatly from this consolidated political base; it provided him with the resources necessary to finance these early voyages.

Prince Henry had various motives in extending his patronage to these early explorations. Materially, he was concerned with reversing the drain on Portugal's gold reserves by finding additional sources of gold on the African continent or through the discovery of a new route to India. The latter would enable Portugal to break the Egyptian-Venetian monopoly of the Asiatic spice trade, which had created an unfavorable balance of trade between Portugal and the East and was one of the prime factors responsible for the shortage of gold.

Christianity as well as economics had its place in these adventures. As a defender of the faith and a vassal of the Lord, Henry naturally desired to win converts to the church. The crusading spirit was particularly strong on the Iberian Peninsula, which was just emerging from Moorish control. Henry sought not only to win converts to the church, but to make contact with Prester John, an apparently mythical Christian prince, who was believed at that time to have established a kingdom somewhere in the Middle East.

In 1415, Henry and his brothers captured the Moroccan seaport of Ceuta. The Cape of Bojador, which is just south of the Canary Islands, had long stood as a barrier to further

Ships on the high seas transporting their cargoes of gold and slaves to Europe.

exploration. Untold dangers were believed to lie beyond the Cape, but when it was rounded in 1434, the sailors found nothing more than calm seas. Two years later, the Portuguese sailors had ventured as far south as Rio d'Oro. Spurred by the hopes of finding gold and winning converts, they moved farther south along the African coast. At the time of Prince Henry's death, in 1460, they had reached as far south as Sierra Leone, stopping just short of Liberia.

A profitable trade was developing between Africa and the newly arrived Europeans. The Island of Arguin was established as the center of this business. Portuguese ships laden with various luxury goods, such as tapestry and linen, arrived regularly. They exchanged their cargo for gold and slaves, which they carried back to Europe. Diego Gomez, a participant in the traffic, asserted that from seven to eight hundred slaves entered Portugal annually.

After Henry's death, direct participation of the Portuguese monarchy in the trade and discoveries was briefly halted. Fernao Gomes secured the monopoly of the trade from 1469 to 1474. He agreed as part of the stipulations of the grant to send out exploring expeditions. His ships traveled along the Gold, Ivory and Slave Coasts, halting just short of the mouth of the Congo River. Though he had dutifully carried out his part of the bargain, his grant was not renewed. The monarchy, under King John II (1481–95), was again taking direct control over the operation.

John was primarily interested in gaining direct access to the trade with the Far East. He therefore stressed the need to find a route around Africa that would lead to India. A base for further Portuguese operations was established at Elmina in 1481. This combination fort and trading post was located on the Gold Coast. Diogo Cão, under the sponsorship of the new monarch, discovered the

Congo River in 1482; he then moved southward along the coast of Angola down to the tip of Cape Cross. In a few short years, Africa would be rounded and the route to India would be opened.

THE START OF THE SLAVE TRADE

Thus Africa almost accidentally entered again into the European consciousness. At first, it had been viewed primarily as an obstacle to be traversed. Then, as news of the potential wealth to be gleaned from the continent reached Europe, it became more and more sought after for its own sake. Though Portugal at this time was still primarily interested in the more profitable trade with India, activities on the African coast foreshadowed things to come.

It was during one of the early explorations that the slave trade quietly entered the European economy. Antam Gonçalvez, in 1441,

sailed from Portugal along the coast of Africa. His travels were recorded by the Portuguese chronicler Zurara, who quotes Gonçalvez as declaring: "O how fair a thing it would be, if we, who have come to this land for a cargo of such pretty merchandise, were to meet with the good luck to bring the first captives before the face of our prince."

He then proceeded the next night to capture a Moor, probably a Berber of the Sanhaja Tuareg, and a woman who may have been the Berber's slave. Besides the happiness of his prince, Gonçalvez sought information about Africa. There would also be social status and commercial profit in the capturing of people who could be sold as slaves.

Gonçalvez's ship was joined by that of another trader, Nuño Tristão. Thus reinforced, he went ashore with Tristão and raided a small party of Africans, capturing ten more slaves. They returned to Portugal, bringing their captives before the Prince. Henry

In the execution of the slave traffic, Africans were treated as merchandise to be traded on the open market for desired commodities.

immediately turned to Pope Eugenius IV for spiritual guidance. When the Pope learned what had occurred, he quickly gave his approval, giving "to all those who shall be engaged in the said war, complete forgiveness for all their sins."

The prospect of profitable trade enabled Gil Eannes and Lançarote to raise the capital necessary for the first significant entrance into the African slave trade. Their six ships returned to Portugal laden with 235 slaves, which marked the true beginning of the trade. Initially, the Portuguese had secured the slaves through raids on the coastal areas, but they quickly discovered that it was more profitable to obtain their human cargoes through trade rather than through haphazard raids. With Arguin as the center of this trade, Portuguese traders and those of the Sanhaja Berbers and other tribes met and exchanged their goods.

The court at Lisbon constantly pushed the trade farther south, so that within the first fifty years the number of Africans entering Portugal tripled. Slaves were not yet the primary export of Africa; in the mid-fifteenth century, they were just one of the many goods being sought. Gold and ivory were deemed equally desirable by the European traders. The demand for slaves was limited primarily to the domestic needs of Spain and Portugal, which meant that the trade was not yet an important economic factor.

SPAIN AND THE DISCOVERY OF AMERICA

Portugal soon found herself pressed by other European powers. Christopher Columbus, returning from his discovery of America, was forced by bad weather to enter the harbor at Lisbon. There he described his adventures to King John II. John doubted that Columbus had discovered a westward route to the Indies, but he was aware of the potential threat of a rival Spanish empire. He proceeded to claim all the lands discovered

for Portugal, but Spain appealed to the Papacy for ratification of its claims. The Spanish Pope Alexander VI was quite sympathetic to the claims of the Spanish monarchy, and in June 1494, a compromise was effected when all parties signed the Treaty of Tordosillas. The new lands were divided between the two powers in such a way that it was assumed that Spain would control the Western Hemisphere and Portugal the Eastern. In 1500, Pedro Alvares Cabral stumbled onto Brazil, which was soon found to be in Portugal's half of the divided world.

The discovery of America was to change drastically the relationship of Europe to the African continent. Before the discovery of the New World, the slave trade had seemed destined to play but a small role in Europe's economic and social life. It was the coincidence of finding a virtually unlimited reservoir of manpower, followed shortly by the discovery of a vast and sparsely settled land area, that was to gain for slavery its crucial position in the development of the modern world. The Americas, Europe and the African continent were to be drawn together in an intimate, if unequal, bond.

The Spanish took the lead in establishing the first colonies in the New World. Alexander VI, in securing this area for the Spanish Crown, assumed that the monarchy would, as its first obligation, tend to the religious needs of the "heathens." Spain was at that time governed by King Ferdinand and Queen Isabella, who had united Spain through their marriage, combining the Aragon and Castilian territories into one dynasty. Ferdinand and Isabella had defeated the Moors and forced them from Granada, their last stronghold on the Iberian Peninsula. They had also expelled the Jews from Spain in 1492.

Their previous maneuvers had demonstrated an ability to balance material needs with religious obligations. It was thought, therefore, that they would not be unmindful of the Pope's desires but would try to

TOP: *Christopher Columbus explains his exploration plans
          to King Ferdinand and Queen Isabella.*
MIDDLE: *Spanish explorer Pedro Alvares Cabral.*
BOTTOM: *The bustling harbor of Lisbon, Portugal, as it ap-
          peared in the early sixteenth century.*

VASCO NUÑEZ DE BALBOA

balance them against the material needs of the colonies. The issue would be complicated by the colonies' need to secure a dependable labor supply. Lesley Simpson (*The Encomienda in New Spain*) explained that while "on the one hand the government undertook to see that the natives were well protected and made Christians; on the other it was bound to favor the multitude of Spaniards who had gone to the Indies in the hope of some material reward, while the needs of the poverty-stricken Crown could not be lost sight of."

Columbus returned to Hispaniola, as the Spanish colony in the West Indies was called, in 1494. Upon his return, he discovered that the natives had risen in rebellion against their Spanish visitors. Columbus crushed the uprising and in the process took many Indian prisoners, whom he sent back to Spain. Columbus had always favored a policy of imitating the Portuguese and engaging in the slave trade. He argued that it would eliminate

troublemakers among the Indians and provide a source of revenue for the Crown. The Indians would profit from the situation also, he claimed, as they would be taken to Spain, where they could be Christianized.

NEGROES IN EXPLORATION

Following the initial discovery of the New World, men began exploring the unknown territory within its borders. Accompanying these adventurers were Negroes, some of whom played a prominent role in the discoveries on the continent.

When Balboa reached the Pacific Ocean in 1513, crossing the Isthmus of Panama, he reportedly had thirty Negroes with him. In 1520, Spanish conquistador Cortez explored the area now known as Mexico. He had about three hundred Negroes in his company, one of whom planted the first wheat in the New World.

The Spaniard Lucas Vasquez de Ayllón was among the first to bring blacks to the coast of what is now the state of Virginia. According to Woodbury Lowery (*Spanish Settlements within the Present Limits of the United States*), de Ayllón established a colony in the proximity of the Jamestown colony later established by the English. In founding the colony, de Ayllón brought Negro and Spanish settlers from Haiti. The Negroes were treated so harshly that they revolted and burned several of the dwellings they had erected. The discontent of the blacks contributed to the eventual abandonment of the colony, whose settlers returned to Haiti.

Blacks were brought to the Mississippi River under De Soto's orders after his initial discovery of the lower river region. They also were part of the expeditions led by Spanish explorers in the South American areas of Chile, Peru and Venezuela, and took part in the expeditions of Panfilo de Narváez and Cabeza de Vaca, Spanish explorers credited with the discovery of New Mexico.

In 1527, Panfilo de Narváez left Spain for the New World, with a commission to serve as governor of three Spanish territories. The number of Negroes in his company is not known. At least one was present, however, and he became the most prominent of the black conquistadors. Estevanico, or Little Stephen, is credited with locating Cibola, one of the Seven Cities of the Zuni Indians.

The de Narváez expedition suffered repeated misfortune. Starting with more than five hundred men, it ended a little over a year later with only four—one of them the Negro Estevanico. The men wandered from place to place over an eight-year period, serving for a time as slave laborers and medicine men to the Indians. Three of the men eventually returned to Spain, but Estevanico remained. During the years they were lost, the men became familiar with the legends of the Indians, one of which included the story of the famous Seven Cities.

FERDINAND DE SOTO

Estevanico traveling with the Spanish explorer Panfilo de Narváez in search of the Seven Cities of the Zuni Indians.

Under the leadership of Fray Marcos, an expedition was undertaken to find these cities, with Estevanico as guide. The black man was to search ahead of his party and report back to de Vaca, who had become leader of the Spanish explorers after the death of de Narváez. Estevanico was to send back wooden crosses to the other members of the party, thereby notifying them that he was still alive and scouting. Should Estevanico discover that he was near the Seven Cities, he was under instructions to send back a large wooden cross and then wait for the remainder of the party. Upon making his discovery, however, Estevanico disobeyed the orders, rushed into the city, and thus became the actual discoverer. Unfortunately, he was murdered by the Indians shortly after his arrival. Upon learning of Estevanico's murder, Fray Marcos turned back without ever seeing the Seven Cities.

The following year, 1540, Coronado led an expedition, which included Negroes, into New Mexico in search of the Seven Cities. Negroes were also with the French explorers in their quest for new territories in parts of Canada and later in Louisiana.

The traditional historical approach to the period of exploration and discovery has not included mention of the presence of these black men, who are thought to have been neither slaves nor savages but probably servants who had been converted to either the Muslim or the Catholic faiths before their departures from Europe.

THE *ENCOMIENDA*

The early colonists in the West Indies needed food to survive and gold to prosper. The settlers were for the most part members of the Spanish nobility or Catholic clergy and were thought to have a higher calling than that of manual labor. There were, however, large numbers of Indians, who, it was reasoned, could provide whatever manpower was needed. In 1498, Columbus wrote to Isabella and Ferdinand, asking permission to use Indian labor until the economy was stabilized. The colonists had availed themselves of this indigenous source of labor from almost the beginning, and without it, they probably could not have survived the first year. Thus, Columbus was merely asking for legal sanction for an already established practice.

The West Indian colony continued to have its troubles, and in 1501 Isabella appointed Nicolas de Ovando royal governor. It would be his task to restore order to the colony and to stabilize the Spanish presence in the New World. His instructions reflect the conflicts to which the monarchy was subject. On the one hand, he was told to teach the Catholic faith to the Indians, to allow them to maintain their freedom of movement and to pay them wages for their labors in extracting gold. On the other hand, the Indians were forced to work in the gold mines, were subject to Spanish taxation and were forbidden to bear arms.

Ovando arrived in Hispaniola at the head of a Spanish army of 2,500 troops. The Indians now realized that the Spanish were here to stay. They knew that they were unable to defeat the superior Spanish firepower, so they began a campaign to starve the Spaniards out. They refused to plant any food at all, hoping they would outlast the Spaniards, who would be forced to leave. Ovando reacted quickly, asking the Crown for explicit recognition of the legality of forced Indian labor.

In 1503, the Spanish monarchy issued a *cedula*. This royal proclamation, which became known as the *Encomienda,* provided the framework for the system of forced Indian labor. The attempt to solve the colonists' need for a dependable and disciplined labor force through the system of the *Encomienda,* however, was short-lived. The Indians rapidly succumbed to the extremely hard labor and poor working conditions to which they were

Captive American Indians being sold into slavery.

subjected. The diet provided for them was insufficient, and many Indians were killed by the diseases that the white man was introducing into the New World. Fernando Ortiz wrote of the situation that confronted the Indians as they performed their tasks as a "free people": "To subject the Indian to the mines, to their monotonous, insane and severe labor, without tribal sense, without religious ritual, . . . was like taking away from him the meaning of his life. . . . It was to enslave not only his muscles but also his collective spirit."

There were some attempts to bring indentured servants to replace the Indians, but the cost of labor proved to be too dear. The high ratio of land to population made it relatively easy for an indentured servant, once his time of service had been completed, to obtain his own land. There was, however, one source of labor that could resolve this dilemma. Africa, it seemed, possessed an unlimited supply of manpower, which combined with the system of slavery could ensure both adequate numbers of workers and a system of control over the labor force. It would thus solve the problems that the early settlers in the New World then faced.

The Spanish quickly recognized the possibilities of Negro slavery. They soon estimated that it took four Indians to do the work of one African slave. A Spanish official wanted "permission . . . to bring Negroes, a race robust for labor, instead of the natives, so weak that they can be employed in tasks requiring little endurance, such as taking care of the maize fields or farms."

THE FIRST NEGRO SLAVES
IN THE NEW WORLD

Apparently, Negroes were not brought to the New World before 1501, although it has been stated by some historians that a Negro, Niño, accompanied Columbus on his maiden voyage. In that year, a royal decree excluded Jews and Moors and authorized the transportation of Negroes born in Christian lands (i.e., Europe). Some accompanied Ovando when he arrived in Hispaniola in 1502; but the following year, he asked for an end to the shipment of Negroes to the New World. Ovando complained that they tended to be insubordinate and were stirring up trouble among the Indians. Isabella consented to allow only the import of white slaves, hoping, as Davidson put it, "that Christian slaves would help in the work of converting the heathen, not knowing, of course, that most of the heathen would soon be dead."

Ovando soon realized the necessity of having Negro slaves, and in the following year Ferdinand rescinded the prohibition. In 1505, the bureau in charge of colonial trade was instructed to promote the sending of Negroes to the New World for the next ten years. The Negroes were to come from Spain, as the transporting of slaves directly from Africa was still prohibited in accordance with the general policy of allowing only Catholics to settle in the new lands. The use of Indians and Negroes imported from Europe failed to solve the acute labor shortage, and soon Ovando was asking for more slaves.

It was still necessary to satisfy the sincere desire of the Crown to ensure that the religious motives of the colonizing process would not be ignored. The Crown found itself caught, as before, between its desire to meet its Christian obligations and the economic realities of the New World. The problem, however, was quickly resolved. The Africans had been more and more looked upon as having no religion at all, and it was reasoned that

Charles V granting the license allowing the direct importation of African slaves to the New World.

taking these heathens to the New World, rather than threatening the Catholic goals of the venture, would complement them. The journey to the Americas would take the Africans that much closer to their own salvation.

The profits of this new trade quickly grew, and in 1513 the Crown levied a royal tax on each license (the permit for shipping a single slave). In 1515, the first shipment of slave-grown West Indian sugar arrived in Spain. The growing economic incentives for a full-scale involvement in the slave trade received a boost from Bartholomé de las Casas. This Dominican priest became the most influential advocate of the Indian's cause. He suggested that one way of alleviating the suffering of the Indians was to replace them with robust Africans. On August 18, 1518, Charles V, the new monarch, granted a license for the importation of slaves directly from Africa. The same year, a cargo of slaves shipped to the West Indies directly from Africa arrived in the New World.

A new, exclusive grant for the shipment of 4,000 slaves over a period of four years was issued in 1528. This differed from the previous grants in its attempt to placate the islanders by restricting the price of slaves. The grant, however, was still distinct from the later *asientos,* which granted a particular company a monopoly of the trade. Its prime function was to enrich courtiers rather than to meet the needs of the colonists. When this grant expired, the slave trade fell under the control of the regular administrative boards, which attempted to maintain a competitive trade and rejected bids for an *asiento*.

THE SLAVE TRADE IN THE LATE SIXTEENTH CENTURY

In 1580, Spain annexed Portugal and began granting *asientos,* which reflected the Spanish monarchy's growing concern with the labor needs of her colonies. The Crown was still preoccupied, of course, with its own need for revenue, but more and more it was balancing its own immediate interest with the necessity of securing an adequate labor supply for the colonies. Spain, despite her immense power and prestige, suffered from serious internal weakness. Since the Spanish had failed to develop a middle class, they were constantly forced to use the bankers of Italy, Belgium and Holland to conduct their business. Goods shipped to Spain were quickly dispatched to Antwerp, which had become the center for redistributing goods throughout Europe. Portugal suffered from similar problems, for neither Spain nor Portugal was capable of meeting the demands of the colonies for an adequate labor supply. Despite the efforts of the Crown, the prices of slaves remained high throughout this period, and the growth and development of the colonies were restricted.

As the Spanish attempted to meet the demands of their colonists for slaves, Africans in increasingly larger numbers were being transported to the West Indies. By the 1540's, thousands of slaves per year were shipped directly from Africa. The demand continued to grow, and in 1592 a license was granted to Gomes Reynal to deliver 38,250 slaves at the rate of 4,250 a year. The latter figure is apparently the number of slaves leaving Africa,

for the grant also stipulated that 3,500 of these slaves must be landed alive. The license cost Reynal close to a million ducats.

During this period, the English made their first significant attempts to break the Portuguese-Spanish monopoly of the slave trade. In 1562, with the backing of several English merchants, John Hawkins attempted to enter the slave trade. He sailed from England to Africa with three ships. Once in Africa, he acquired some three hundred slaves through piracy and other means. He then proceeded to the West Indies, where he exchanged his cargo for sugar and hides and other such goods. His third voyage, however, ended in disaster. He was captured, and the Spanish confiscated his cargoes. This misadventure discouraged English interest in the slave trade. Not until nearly a century later would England enter the trade in any serious way.

The French failed in their attempt to gain a significant hold on the slave trade, although they were able to upset Portugal's monopoly

JOHN HAWKINS

on the African coast and to enter into the trade for gold and ivory. Spain's prevailing position in the New World made it extremely difficult for other nations to break into the Atlantic slave trade. Throughout much of the sixteenth century, therefore, the Iberian interest dominated the trade.

THE DUTCH AND THE ENGLISH

In the seventeenth century the European powers continued to intensify their struggle over the lucrative lands in the New World and the profitable enterprise of transporting the black cargo to America. The *asiento* in this century ceased to be an instrument of Spanish policy and became an international prize, symbolizing for the recipient the achievement of naval supremacy. In the latter half of the century, it would be held by the Dutch, the French and, finally, in 1713, it would become the property of the British. The Spanish monopoly over the West Indies began to falter as various European powers started to avail themselves of these newly discovered sources of wealth.

The Dutch began their activity on the African coast late in the sixteenth century and were responsible for the final collapse of the Portuguese monopoly. At this time, the natives of Fetu, in part because they wanted free trade with the Dutch, drove the Portuguese almost completely away from the Gold Coast. The Dutch quickly moved in and established themselves. In 1611 or 1612, they gave visible evidence of their presence by constructing Fort Nassau at Mowree. In 1617, the Dutch purchased the island of Goree, which, together with Fort Nassau, afforded them an excellent position for trade on the Gambia River and the Gold Coast.

The Dutch West India Company was formed in 1621 by combining the Guinean trade and the West Indian settlement under one interest. It was given a monopoly on all the African trade, as well as the right to establish settlements in the New World. In 1637, Portugal's strongest African fort, Elmina, was taken by the Dutch. With the loss of Fort St. Anthony at Axum in 1642, the Portuguese were finally driven completely from the Gold Coast.

An important reason for the success of the Dutch was their ability to gain the support of the Africans. The Portuguese monopoly had always been opposed by much of the tribal leadership, who naturally preferred to be free to trade with all. The French and the English were both unable to take advantage of this situation. They did not at this time establish permanent outposts but would merely trade and leave. This left the natives open to Portuguese retaliation. The Dutch, by establishing permanent forts, put themselves in a better position to replace the Portuguese.

Certain Dutch merchants opposed the monopoly of the Dutch West India Company and attempted to operate under the cover of Swedish nationality. Under the leadership of Louis de Gear of Liège, the Swedish African Company was formed in 1647. A Danish citizen, Henry Carloff, in the employ of the company, established Cabo Corso, an outpost on the Gold Coast. The Dutch West India Company vigorously protested what they considered to be an intrusion on their monopoly. They did not, however, take any action at that time to remove the interlopers. Denmark seized the colony and held it for a brief period, ultimately losing it to the Dutch. The Dutch victory, however, was short-lived, because by then a more powerful rival was ready to establish its position.

England's first venture into the African trade had ended with the third voyage of John Hawkins. In the seventeenth century, though continually wracked by internal disorder and revolution, England began systematically to apply herself to the search for wealth and power in Africa and the New World. During much of the seventeenth century, she found herself in a desperate struggle with the

KING JAMES I OF ENGLAND

major powers of Europe. Finally, in 1713, the Treaty of Utrecht ratified the dominant position that England had come to hold in the slave trade.

In 1618, James I chartered the Company of Royal Adventurers in London. The company was given the right to trade along the African coast south of Barbary. Richard Jobson was one of the traders who operated on the company's behalf near the coast and along the Gambia River. He was accompanied on one trip into the interior by a native merchant named Buckor Sano. During the course of their journey, Jobson was offered some slaves. His indignant reply is recorded in his memoirs, *The Golden Trade:*

> I made answer, we were a people who did not deal in any such commodities; neither did we buy or sell one another, or any that had our shapes; at which he seemed to marvel much, and told us it was the only merchandise they carried down, and that they were sold to white men who earnestly desired them. We answered, they were another kind of people, different from us; but for our part, if they had no other commodities, we would return again.

U. B. Phillips (*American Negro Slavery*) added a footnote to these noble sentiments: "the company speedily ended its life [and] was quickly followed by another."

There is some evidence to indicate, however, that by 1623 England was renewing her interest in the slave trade. Elizabeth Donnan's *Documents Illustrative of the History of the Slave Trade to America* notes that a "list of names of 1623 is endorsed 'Adventurors [*sic*] in the slave trade taken out of the map,' with no further explanation." When the *James Bonaventure* and the *Benediction* were seized by the French, their owners, in their petition for restitution, claimed that the *Benediction* had been carrying 180 slaves at the time of its capture.

The Puritan Revolution enabled a new group to acquire the grant for the African trade. Formed as the Guinea Company, it obtained a monopoly for fifteen years, although the area of the African coast set aside for free trade was increased. The central problem facing any company operating in the African trade still remained: the merchants were in a state of constant warfare with foreign competitors. Whatever the gains acquired in the trade, at times they barely matched the losses incurred by the various European powers as a result of these hostilities.

The Guinea Company continued to increase its activity in the slave trade. In 1651, Bartholomew Howard sailed under its auspices for the African coast. He was instructed to locate the company's factor, Mr. J. Pope, with whom he was to exchange his cargo for "so many Negers as your ship can carry." But the company failed to prosper, and in 1657 the trade was entrusted to the East India Company.

The monarchy was restored to England in 1660, and with it came a renewed interest in the African trade. The development of the sugar plantations in the West Indies was exerting enormous pressure to provide an adequate labor supply. From 1640 to the

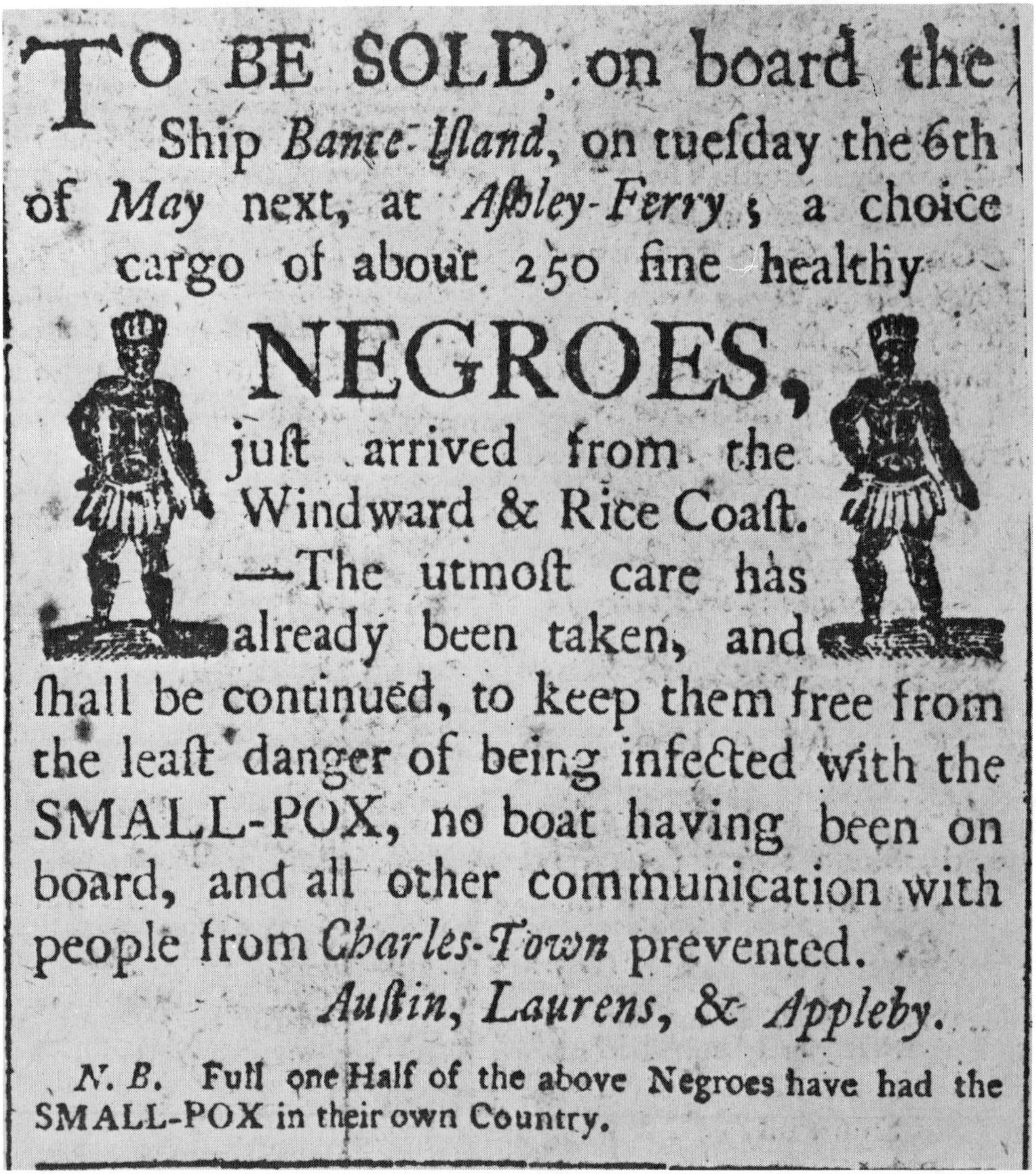

TO BE SOLD, on board the Ship *Bance-Island*, on tuesday the 6th of *May* next, at *Ashley-Ferry*; a choice cargo of about 250 fine healthy

NEGROES,

just arrived from the Windward & Rice Coast. — The utmost care has already been taken, and shall be continued, to keep them free from the least danger of being infected with the SMALL-POX, no boat having been on board, and all other communication with people from *Charles-Town* prevented.

Austin, Laurens, & Appleby.

N. B. Full one Half of the above Negroes have had the SMALL-POX in their own Country.

One of the greatest dangers facing slave traders was bringing back a shipload of diseased slaves. This broadside was posted to reassure the public that the cargo of slaves advertised for sale had been carefully selected and transported to prevent their becoming infected with smallpox.

Restoration, the trade had been dominated by the Dutch, who still posed a formidable barrier to successful English involvement.

The slave trade, though it provided great profits, also involved enormous risks. On March 20, 1664, Sir Thomas Modyford and Peter Colleton, factors for the now reorganized African Company, recorded the arrival of some ships from Africa. This account reflects the uncertainties and dangers inherent to the trade: "The *Speedwell* arrived with 282 negroes, who have greatly lost in value owing to the small-pox breaking out among them. The *Success* brought 193 blacks, and these with Capt. Nowbrook's have produced the best of any."

The Dutch were still able to maintain their position on the coast. A letter received in 1663 from one of the company's agents in Africa gives insight into the reasons for the continued success of the Netherlands. The Dutch were adept at gaining the crucial confidence of the Africans. For the European powers did not have at that time the strength actually to conquer the Africans. They were dependent, therefore, on treaties and friendly relations. The English agents recorded that "The Dutch give daily presents to the King of Futton and his 'capeshiers' to exclude their honors [the Royal African Company] from this trade." The tenacity of the Dutch merchants is also reflected in the Treaty of Breda, July 21, 1667, which maintained their position on the African coast.

The Royal African Company's attempt to establish a monopoly position was opposed by many Englishmen as well as by the Dutch. Those English merchants who would be kept from operating on the African coast if the grant were successfully enforced constantly lobbied for free trade. Their position received important support from English settlers in the New World. The governing bodies of Barbados petitioned the King, asking that free trade be permitted on the African coast. This unrest was caused by high slave prices as well as by the company's inability to meet the growing colonial demand.

In 1667, Francis Lord Willoughby wrote to the Crown, explaining the difficulties of the planters. He urged that the island "be granted free trade to Guinea for Negroes by which they may be as plentifully furnished as formerly, so excessive scarce and dear are they now that the poor planters will be forced to go to foreign plantations for a livelihood." By 1669, the company was giving licenses to others to engage in the trade. Finally, in 1672, the company's operations were drastically reorganized.

In 1672, the Royal African Company was chartered. It maintained a monopoly on the African slave trade for approximately fifteen years. During this time, the continually increasing demands of the islands, together with the growing demand of the North American mainland, conspired to give the African Company the most prosperous years of its existence. The clamor of the colonies against the monopolistic restrictions continued unabated, and the steady flow of profit increased the interest in free trade of those excluded from a share in the booty. These two arguments finally were successful; for, as a by-product of the Glorious Revolution of 1689, the Royal African Company's monopoly was broken permanently. In 1697, the slave trade was thrown open to all Englishmen.

THE PORTUGUESE AND THE FRENCH IN THE SEVENTEENTH CENTURY

Compared to the English, the French played a minor role in Africa during the seventeenth century, establishing themselves only at Senegal. The French Minister of Finance, Jean Baptiste Colbert, quickly sought

JEAN BAPTISTE COLBERT

to emulate the Dutch and the English by giving one company the exclusive rights to the slave trade. The French company, however, experienced the same difficulties as its English counterparts. The demand of the French islands for slaves proved to be beyond the capabilities of a single company, while domestic and foreign interests opposed the exclusive privileges that the French Crown had granted. The attempt to operate the slave trade through one company was abandoned in 1685, when a second company was established by the French government and given official permission to participate in the African slave trade.

During the seventeenth century, Portugal attempted with less and less success to maintain its position on the African coast. Its chief advantage over its European counterparts was its position as supplier of slaves to the Spanish colonies. Either because they felt bound by the Treaty of Tordosillas or because they lacked a middle class capable of handling the trade, the Spanish had maintained a policy of permitting outsiders to supply her colonies. Portugal, which itself was under the rule of the Spanish monarchy between 1580 and 1640, usually received the *asiento*. In 1620, Richard Jobson wrote concerning the Portuguese activities on the African coast:

> They do generally imploy themselves in buying such commodities the country affords, where in especially they covet the country people . . . but the black people are brought away by their own nation, and by them either carried or sold unto the Spaniard, for him to carry into the West Indies, to remain as slaves, either in their mines or in any other servile uses.

In 1640, Portugal broke free of Spanish domination, and Spain retaliated by refusing to grant the Portuguese the *asiento*. The Dutch had broken with the Spanish Crown at the beginning of the century and were thus in a position similar to the Portuguese. For the next fifteen years the Spanish did not grant *asientos*. As a result, an illegal trade flourished. These developments threatened Spain's commercial position and cut off an important source of revenue to the Crown. In 1662, the *asiento* was issued to two wealthy Genoese, Domingo Grillo and Ambrosio Lomelin. The Anglo-Dutch War, however, so upset trade that these two gentlemen were unable to meet the requirements of the grant. Instead of transporting slaves directly from Africa to the Spanish colonies, they were forced to use the English and the Dutch as intermediaries. They would pick up their slaves from the Dutch colony at Curaçao or from the English islands and then ship them to the Spanish colonies. The Spanish monarchy, of course, opposed this practice, but was left with no alternative.

In the latter half of the seventeenth century, the Dutch acquired the legal right to supply the Spanish colonies. The power of the Netherlands, however, was on the wane. The Dutch suffered repeated defeats at the hands of the English. In 1702, the French Guinea Company gained the *asiento*. Its contract required the delivery to the Spanish colonies of 38,000 Negro slaves (or 48,000 if the war between France and England should end) over a ten-year period.

In 1713, as part of the terms of the Treaty of Utrecht, the *asiento* passed to England. The English contracted to deliver to the Spanish colonies 144,000 slaves over a thirty-year period, or an average of 4,800 slaves per year.

At the close of the seventeenth century, the European powers had established positions on the African coast. The English were in Gambia and shared the Gold Coast with the Dutch. The French dominated the trade in Senegal. In lower Guinea, Portugal held the advantage, dominating the trade southward from the Congo River. The Slave Coast was now open to all the major European powers.

CHAPTER THREE

The Rise of the Slave Trade

THE forced migration of Africans to the New World lasted for nearly four centuries. Slavery and the slave trade became important elements in the development of the modern world: the profits that resulted from the enterprise helped to build the machines and factories of the Industrial Revolution. The slave system created an expanding market that facilitated the transformation to large-scale manufacturing. The millions of Africans transported to America provided the labor force for the colonies' most profitable endeavors. Men were broken; fortunes were made.

The Treaty of Utrecht, signed in 1713, left England in a position to dominate the slave trade. W. E. B. Du Bois estimated that in the years following the treaty from forty to a hundred thousand slaves were exported from Africa annually. In *An Introduction to the History of West Africa,* J. D. Fage states that approximately seventy thousand new slaves arrived at the Caribbean Islands annually. The number being shipped directly to the American mainland during this period was also increasing. Conservatively estimated, between four and seven million Africans were sent into slavery in the New World during the eighteenth century.

ENGLAND

London was the headquarters for the Royal African Company. This company's monopoly of the slave trade was broken in 1698, and Bristol soon replaced London as the focal point for the enterprise. Liverpool entered the trade late, but in a few short years slaving was so important to the city's economic life that it had become synonymous with its name.

Liverpool's principal export in 1700 was coarse linen. The goods produced at Manchester met the need of American planters for cheap clothing for their slaves, and by 1730, these goods dominated the West Indian market. In 1719, the port at Liverpool had more

A colonial slave market in the seventeenth century.

than eighteen thousand tons of registered shipping.

Liverpool's position in the slave trade soon surpassed that of Bristol. In 1730, Liverpool had fifteen ships engaged in the African enterprise, while Bristol had more than one hundred. In 1764, the number of ships sailing for Africa from Liverpool was more than twice the number leaving Bristol. In 1786, the profits accruing to Liverpool in slaving alone were almost 300,000 pounds sterling. When the famous English actor George Frederick Cooke was booed while on stage in that flourishing city, he responded to his critics by stating that he had not come there "to be insulted by a set of wretches, every brick in whose infernal town is cemented with an African's blood."

The profits were not just limited to the supplying of slaves to the West Indies. The trade was three-cornered, with lucrative gains at each point. Goods manufactured in Manchester would be sent to Africa and exchanged there for slaves. Ships laden with this human cargo would then cross the Atlantic. In the West Indies, the Africans would be exchanged for sugar, cocoa, coffee, indigo and ginger. These goods would then be sold in England.

The profits resulting from the trip could be reinvested immediately in another such journey. The capital that was accumulated in this business was also invested in textile mills, foundries, coal mines and, of course, shipping. Historian Frank Tannenbaum of Columbia University estimated that in a typical year, 1774, about half of England's shipping was engaged in this African trade.

This intercontinental trade expanded the market for English manufactures, providing additional incentives for the technological advances that played an important role in the Industrial Revolution. As the output of the factories increased, they created a continual strain on England's coal mines. The need for deeper penetration of the mines was finally met with Thomas Savery's invention of the steam pump in the early eighteenth century and by Thomas Newcomen's subsequent improvements. Merchants who obtained their incomes from the slave trade financed James Watt's steam engine.

AFRICA

Slave ships loaded with cargo sailed from Europe to African ports. The prime concern of the captain was to spend as little time close to the African coast as possible, because of the risks involved in mooring off the African continent. It was essential, therefore, that the slaves that were going to be purchased be previously assembled. To ensure this, the companies sent down representatives, known as factors, who kept a supply of Negroes on hand in stockades, known as factories.

These factors were a generally disreputable lot. They were poorly paid and tended to be drunk most of the time. William Bosman, a Dutch factor, who was an exceptionally capable official, described the general situation: "'Tis incredible how many are consumed by this damnable Liquor (pardon the expression) which is not only confined to the soldiers but some of the principal People are so [addicted] to it."

The usual method of obtaining slaves was through trade with native African suppliers. Jean Barbot, a Frenchman, was a fairly competent official who worked for the English Royal African Company. He made two trips to the continent, one in 1678 and the other in 1682. He greatly admired the religion of the Africans with whom he came in contact and found their governmental systems to be very advanced. His most reliable suppliers were the Whydah, or Ouidah, whom he referred to as the Fida. "The Blacks of Fida," he claimed, "are so expeditious at the trade of slaves that they can deliver a thousand every month." Another French representative was André Brue, who arrived in Africa in 1697.

Because of the great risks involved in mooring off the African coast, slave traders held their captives in stockades until it was possible to load them on a slave ship.

He obtained his slaves by dealing with the Damel, the King of Cayor, a strong and tyrannical monarch, shrewd in politics and successful at playing off each European power against the others.

An African could become a slave in one of several different ways. A king might sell a criminal as part of his punishment. Individuals sold themselves or members of their families into slavery during famine. People were kidnapped by European slavers or native gangs; those who were already enslaved often were sold to the Europeans. Many slaves were obtained as captives in war. As the slave trade with the Europeans developed, these processes all accelerated.

In the eighteenth century, native kings were to number among the largest of the merchants operating in the trade. These kings did not replace the European factors, but rather complemented their work. It still took approximately two or three months to acquire the requisite number of slaves to fill one ship. Thus, while the factors who had the necessary capital to maintain supplies of slaves were still important, most of them could not operate without the consent of the local king.

The King of Barsally was one such slave merchant. Francis Moore, a British factor sent to Africa by the Royal African Company, was appalled by the operation of the trade as he observed it at James Fort at the mouth of the Gambia River in 1730. In order to obtain the brandy, rum, gunpowder and weapons he desired from the governor at James Fort, the king would barter bodies. When he was not at war with a neighboring king, he would even plunder his own towns, selling his subjects into slavery. Moore gave a vivid description of the king's system:

> . . . He often goes out with some of his Troops by a Town in the Day-time and returns in the Night and sets fire to three parts of it, placing Guards at the Fourth to seize the People that run out of the Fire, then ties their Arms behind them and . . . sells them.

Moore also discussed the effects of the slave trade on African life and custom. He found a tendency to subordinate everything else to the interests of the slave trade. The criminal code was modified so that it operated to facilitate the accumulation of people for sale. "Since this Slave-Trade has been us'd," wrote Moore, "all Punishments are chang'd into Slavery."

While there is much evidence to document the cruel conditions to which Africans were subjected, there are few records by the individuals who were victimized by the process. Most of the Negroes who were taken into slavery could not write and lacked any opportunity to express their reactions to slavery. One exception was Job ben Solomon, an extremely well-educated Moslem.

Job ben Solomon was sold into slavery in 1730. He sailed to the New World on the slave ship *Arabella* and was sold to a tobacco farmer in Maryland, who used him as a field hand. Solomon refused to adjust to life as a slave and escaped, but was recaptured and sent to jail. While there, he impressed many officials with his literacy and scholarship. James Oglethorpe, who was at that time an official of the Royal African Company, was so impressed by Solomon's brilliance that he purchased him from his master and brought him to England. Later, at his own request, Solomon was returned to his home in Africa. Job ben Solomon was a rare exception who survived the ordeal relatively unharmed. Generally, however, those Africans who became slaves found their loss of freedom to be permanent, and rarely did any return—a fact probably responsible for the belief widely held among the Gold Coast Negroes that white men were cannibals.

In the middle of the eighteenth century, slave trading changed for the worse. The Royal African Company had tried always to remain on good terms with the natives. Since its ships returned continuously, the company reasoned that it had more to gain in the long run from good relationships with the African powers. Therefore, the company was willing to forego any advantages it might have gained through fraud or the use of force.

The individual private merchants had neither the capital nor the inclination for such an approach. Their vessels tended to be overcrowded and undermanned, with crews that were overworked, underfed and constantly flogged. These slavers were more prone to take the quick profit rather than worry about long-term considerations. An African town that asked too high a price for its merchandise often found itself being shelled by a British merchant vessel. Such abuses lasted for approximately fifteen years before consolidation eliminated much of the competition that had fostered these ills.

Much of the information about the nature of the slave trade has come from people who served on board the ships. There are also records of the ships and the testimony taken by the Privy Council during its investigation of the slave trade. The testimony before the council was condensed into readable form by Thomas Clarkson, in his *Abstract of the Evidence*. In 1788, two books were published by former participants in the trade—Alexander Falconbridge, a surgeon on a slave ship, and John Newton, a captain of one of the vessels.

Even before the investigation by the Privy Council, Parliament attempted to regulate the conditions aboard the slaving vessels. Most of these early regulations dealt with minimal space requirements. The net effect of the laws was to strengthen the growing monopoly position of the large houses since they were in the best position to afford the required changes.

By the middle of the eighteenth century, two approaches had come to dominate the method of obtaining slaves. More and more Africans were losing their freedom through kidnapping or local wars, which were fast becoming slave-raiding expeditions. The whole process had become well organized and was

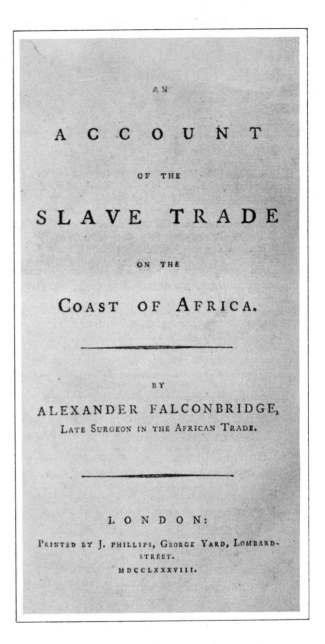

AN

ACCOUNT

OF THE

SLAVE TRADE

ON THE

COAST OF AFRICA.

BY

ALEXANDER FALCONBRIDGE,

LATE SURGEON IN THE AFRICAN TRADE.

LONDON:

PRINTED BY J. PHILLIPS, GEORGE YARD, LOMBARD-STREET.

MDCCLXXXVIII.

operating on an increasingly larger scale. Falconbridge stated in his book, *An Account of the Slave Trade on the Coast of Africa,* that he had "good reason to believe that of the one hundred and twenty Negroes purchased for the ship to which [he] belonged . . . by far the greater part, if not the whole, were kidnaped." Many of the kidnappers were white men, the most famous of whom was a man named Griffiths, who operated between Cape Le Hout and Apollonia.

The main source of slaves was the tribal wars. Falconbridge described the process:

"The slaves are not prisoners of war as we understand the word war. In Africa, a piratical expedition for making slaves is termed a war." The Europeans also took part in this activity. A lieutenant of the 75th Regiment stationed in Goree in 1779 stated that a grand pillage would be "executed by the King's soldiers, from three hundred to three thousand at a time, who can attack and set fire to a village and seize the inhabitants as they can."

As the demand for slaves increased, the supply in the coastal area greatly decreased, and more and more slaves were taken from Africa's interior. They were marched to the coast in groups called slave coffles. Though many of the slaves were taken from the interior, most of the Africans who made the journey to the New World had lived on the western coast of the continent.

Daniel P. Mannix (*Black Cargoes*) and Melville Herskovits (*The Myth of the Negro Past*) have supplied valuable information on the geographical and tribal distributions of peoples contributing slaves to the New World. The vast majority of American and West Indian Negroes are descended from coastal peoples removed from the area between the mouth of the Gambia River and the Bight of Biafra. By far the most popular with the English traders during most of the eighteenth century were the Gold Coast slaves (or Coromantees), the majority of whom were supplied by the Fanti and Ashanti tribes. Although they were renowned for their industry, many planters were wary of their reputation for being rebellious and unresponsive to punishment.

Next prized were those from the Slave Coast, those lands facing the Bight of Benin. Here Ewe-speaking and Yoruba-speaking slaves were marched to the coast and ferried through the surf to the waiting ships. Most of these slaves came from tribes highly skilled and disciplined in agriculture, and were therefore greatly valued for field work.

Many slaves also came from lands located on the Bight of Biafra, although many purchasers avoided the Ibo because they were known to sulk, to become despondent to the point of debility and to commit suicide. Other buyers valued them for their gentleness.

Liberia and the Ivory Coast areas sometimes provided slaves, although these were not particularly favored. Somewhat more sought after were slaves from what is now Portuguese Guinea and Guinea. While many tribes contributed slaves, the Baga and the Susu seem to have been the most popular. The Mandingos, inhabiting the interior lands between the Senegal and Gambia Rivers, were industrious farmers and merchants. They were not regarded as energetic enough for field work but were often bought to work as house servants and craftsmen. Other peoples of the area (Fula, Wolof, Serer and Felup) usually served in the same capacity.

Lower Guinea, as it was referred to by the eighteenth-century geographers, extended down the coast from Cameroon through Angola. Its peoples were not popular as slaves: their civilizations were less "advanced" (that is, their customs did not permit them to adapt easily to a foreign way of life), and they seemed constitutionally unable to withstand the rigors of the long ocean journey. However, they were cheap. During the late eighteenth century, after slave prices farther up the coast had risen, they became quite popular with the British. Since the legal slave trade had nearly ended by then, however, lower Guineans do not form a large fraction of modern Afro-American ancestry.

THE EXTENT OF THE TRADE

There is no reliable information available on the exact number of blacks from Africa as a whole who made the journey to the New World as slaves. Père Dieudonné Rinchon (*La Traité et l'esclavage des Congolais par les Européens*) estimated that from the Congo

An Account of the Number of Negroes delivered in to the Islands of Barbadoes, Jamaica, and Antego, from the Year 1698 to 1708, since the Trade was Opened, taken from the Accounts sent from the respective Governours of those Islands to the Lords Commissioners of Trade, whereby it appears the African Trade is encreas'd to four times more since its being laid Open, than it was under an Exclusive Company.

Between what Years deliver'd.	No. of Negroes delivered into Barbados.	Number delivered into Jamaica.	Number delivered into Antego.
Between the 8 April, 1698 To April 1699	} 3436		
To April 1700	3080		
To 5 ditto 1701	4311		
To 10 ditto 1702	9213		
To 31 Mar. 1703	4561		
To 5 April 1704	1876		
To 2d. ditto 1705	3319		
To 5 ditto 1706	1875		
To 12 May 1707	2720		
To 29 April 1708	1018		
Between 29 Sept. 1698 and 29 Decemb. 1698		1273	
Between 7 April 1699 and 28 March 1700		5766	
From 28 Mar. to 3 Apr. 1701		6068	
3 Apr. 1701 to 20 dit. 1702		8505	
20 dit. 1702 to 12 dit. 1703		2238	
12 dit. 1703 to 18 dit. 1704		2711	
18 dit. 1704 to 24 dit. 1705		3421	
24 dit. 1705 to 27 dit. 1706		5462	
27 dit. 1706 to 22 dit. 1707		2122	
22 dit. 1707 to 26 dit. 1708		6623	
To June 1708		187	
1698			18
June 1699			212
Between June 1700 and 24 April 1701			364
Between 24 April 1701 and 30 March 1702			2395
To April 1703			1670
To Nov. 1704			1551
To 1705			269
To 1706			530
To 1707			114
	35409	44376	7123

Besides which there are 7 Separate Ships named in the foregoing List for *Antego*, but not the Number of Negroes, so we may well compute them at 1200 more, which arriv'd between 1699 and 1700.

An Account of the Number of Negroes delivered by the Royal African Company, *between* 1698. *and* 1707. *given in to the* Lords Commissioners *of Trade by the said Company.*

Years.	Number of Negroes imported by the Company.
1698	941
1699	1500
1700	2045
1701	1511
1702	2014
1703	1138
1704	2745
1705	2921
1706	1144
1707	1801
	17760

From the foregoing Account, given in by the Company, 'tis plain how many Negroes they imported Annually. So it must naturally follow, that what more than these were delivered into the Plantations, in that time, must be on Account of the Separate Traders.

Also from the Account of Negroes delivered into *Barbadoes, Jamaica,* and *Antego,* it appears, that the Numbers imported into those three Islands, (allowing 1200 for the said 7 Ships, whose Numbers are not included by the Governour of *Antego* in his Account) amount to 88108. And even allowing the whole Number which the *African* Company sent out, being 17760, were all deliver'd at those three Islands only, yet then it appears, the Separate Traders have delivered 70 odd Thousand to the Company's 17760, in about the same time, besides what were delivered into *Virginia, Maryland,* and all the other Colonies, which must amount to at least thirty or forty Thousand more.

It appears also from the said Account, that there were imported into those 3 Colonies only 42000 and odd Negroes in the Years 1700, 1701, and 1702, whereof not above 4000 by the *African* Company, which being compared with the Company's Imports of Negroes into all the Plantations, when Exclusive, between 1680 and 1688, amounting but to 46396, or 5150 Negroes per An. as is to be seen by their own Account, given in to the Lords Commissioners of Trade. It is very plain, there were near as many Negroes deliver'd into those 3 Plantations in 3 Years, since the Trade was open'd, as were deliver'd in 9 Years by the Company into all the Plantations, when Exclusive to all others.

It farther appears from the said Account, that there were more Negroes deliver'd into those 3 Plantations in one Year by Separate Traders, between *April* 1701, and *April* 1702. being 18602, than the Company deliver'd in the nine Years and half since the Act, being 17760, because the Total of Negroes, imported both by the Company and Separate Traders in that Year, amounted to 20113, out of which, deducting even the full Number deliver'd by them into all the Plantations that same Year, being 1511, the Remainder is above 18602.

Again, it must be observed, that the Import of Negroes in that Year for those 3 Colonies only, are within 2000 and odd of as many as the Company deliver'd in 4 Years, when Exclusive (even in time of Peace) into all the Plantations.

No reliable information exists on the exact number of blacks imported from Africa, but estimates can be made by examining the reports that were made by slave-trading organizations to various regulatory bodies. This list was submitted by the Royal African Company to the Lord Commissioners of Trade for the years 1698 through 1707.

alone seven thousand slaves were exported, primarily to South America, each year during the sixteenth century. During the next century, approximately fifteen thousand slaves were shipped from the Congo each year. In the eighteenth century, about thirty thousand Congolese slaves made the journey each year; and between one and two hundred thousand were exported during the first part of the nineteenth century. The trafficking finally decreased to two thousand a year before it came to an end in 1885. This would mean that about thirteen million slaves were exported from the Congo alone. Joaquim Pedro Oliveira Martins (*O Brazil e as Colonias Portuguezas*) estimated that approximately twenty million Africans were involved in the trade.

Other estimates of the trade are somewhat lower. Edward Ely Dunbar (*History of the Rise and Decline of Commercial Slavery in America*) stated that between 1500 and 1850 close to fourteen million slaves were imported throughout the Americas. Thus, even conservative estimates of the total population that Africa lost as a result of the slave trade run to scarcely imaginable numbers of human beings.

The Privy Council estimated that 4.5 per cent of the slaves died waiting in the harbor to be sold, 13 per cent died during the trip to America, and 33 per cent died while being seasoned in the West Indies. According to these figures, only 50 per cent of the Africans survived to work as slaves throughout the New World.

Frank Tannenbaum estimated that approximately one-third of the slaves died on their way to the harbor or at the embarkation points and that only about one-third of the slaves actually survived the entire process. If allowance is made for the cost of the wars, Basil Davidson's estimate of the African loss of fifty million people as a result of the slave trade does not seem too high.

EFFECTS ON AFRICA

Slavery had existed in Africa long before the coming of the Europeans. In the eleventh century, when Africa came under the influence of the Moslem religion, slavery had increased. But the indigenous slavery had been more a social institution lending prestige than an economic institution creating wealth. The slave in Africa could marry, own property and enjoy normal legal rights. Slavery in the New World differed in kind, for it was always primarily a method of producing wealth.

The effects of the trade on Africa went beyond depopulation: it caused an increase in internal warfare and contributed to the disintegration of the culture. On the west coast of Africa, the slave trade subverted all social and political institutions. Davidson wrote that "Wherever the trade found strong chiefs or kings it prospered almost from the first; wherever it failed to find them it caused them to come into being."

When the Europeans arrived, the continent was divided into a series of stable feudal states. The long-term effects on Africa were a disruption of social, economic and political conditions, which led to a breakdown of the social structure and a loss of security and self-respect.

THE MIDDLE PASSAGE

The ocean voyage from Africa to the Americas became known as the middle passage. This phase of the slave trade was the source of many of the horror stories that later

The infamous middle passage was the source of many of the horror stories that resulted from the slave trade. It is well known that slaves were beaten, branded and in other ways treated with extreme cruelty on the slave ships.

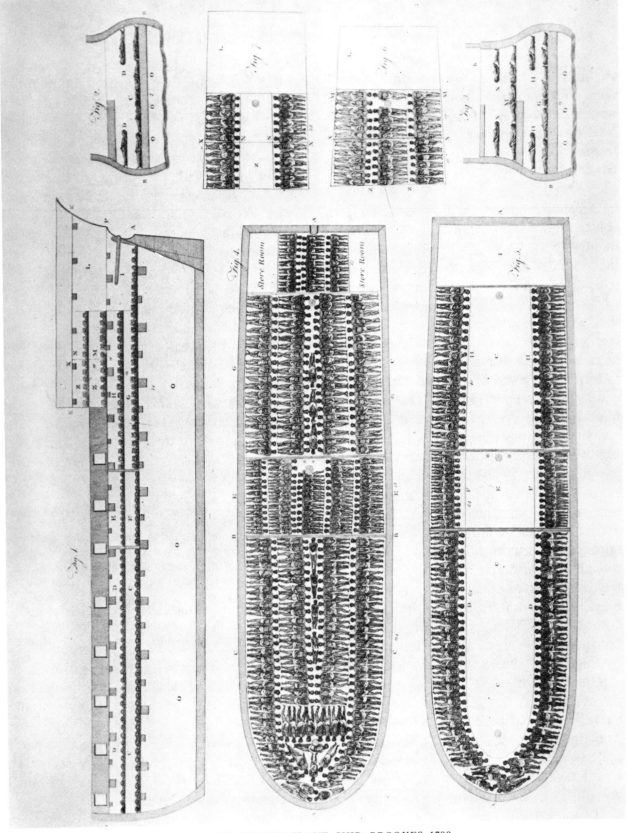

PLAN OF THE SLAVE SHIP *BROOKES* 1790.

		Feet	Inches
AA	Overall length of Lower Deck	100	0
BB	Breadth of beam inside Lower Deck	25	4
OOO	Depth of Hold	10	0
	Height between each deck	5	8
CC	Length of Men's Room on Lower Deck ..	46	0
	Breadth of Men's Room on Lower Deck .	25	4
DD	Length of Platforms in Men's Room	46	0
	Breadth of Platforms in Men's Room ...	6	0
EE	Length of Boys' Room	13	9
	Breadth of Boys' Room	25	0
FF	Breadth of Platforms in Boys' Room	6	0
GG	Length of Women's Room	28	6
	Breadth of Women's Room	23	6

		Feet	Inches
HH	Length of Platforms in Women's Room .	28	6
	Breadth of Platforms in Women's Room .	6	0
II	Length of Gun Room on Lower Deck ..	10	6
	Breadth of Gun Room on Lower Deck .	12	0
KK	Length of Quarter Deck	33	6
	Breadth of Quarter Deck	19	6
LL	Length of Cabin	14	0
	Height of Cabin	6	2
MM	Length of Half Deck	16	6
	Height of Half Deck	6	2
NN	Length of Platforms on Half Deck	16	6
	Breadth of Platforms on Half Deck	6	0
PP	Upper Deck		

served to discredit the whole venture. Conditions aboard the slave ships were pictured as wretched. Stanley M. Elkins (*Slavery: A Problem in American Institutional and Intellectual Life*) compared the detached barbarism of the voyages to the Nazi incarceration of the Jews.

Depending on the situation on the African coast, it took approximately two to twelve months to load a slave ship. The period during which a ship was moored off the coast was extremely dangerous. The crew would be weakened by the African diseases to which they easily succumbed, and the proximity to freedom made control of the slaves already on board extremely difficult.

European powers, whatever their differences, usually cooperated in crushing slave mutinies. The fear of insurrection was so great that nations whose navies had been firing at each other a few years before would join together to defeat the mutineers. A British sailor, William Richardson, described the time his shipmates helped to crush a revolt aboard a French ship: "I could not but admire the courage of a fine young black who, though his partner in irons lay dead at his feet, would not surrender, but fought with his billet of wood until a ball finished his existence. The others fought as well as they could but what could they do against fire-arms?"

Conditions aboard the slave ships were extremely cramped. There had been some discussion as to whether it paid to crowd as many Africans as possible in the ships. Those who argued against this practice thought that the loss of life and health that would result would tend to keep the profits below those brought in by more loosely packed ships. By 1750, however, the advocates of tight packing had demonstrated the superiority of their method and dominated the trade.

The hold of a slave ship was generally about five feet high. Shelves would be built in the middle and they extended about six feet out on both sides. When the bottom was full, the slaves would be packed on the platform. "The poor creatures," according to John Newton, "thus cramped, are likewise in irons for the most part which makes it difficult for them to turn or move or attempt to rise or to lie down without hurting themselves or each other. Every morning, perhaps, more instances than one are found of the living and the dead fastened together." Falconbridge describes how it was necessary for him to take off his shoes to avoid crushing the slaves as he crawled over them.

The men and women were crowded underneath the ship's deck for ten or fifteen hours a day when the weather was good. They lived there in darkness, with no running water or sanitation facilities. They were naked and each slave was chained to another. They sat in a space five or six feet long, sixteen inches broad, and two or three feet high. The Reverend Robert Walsh graphically described the situation in his *Notices of Brazil:*

> . . . The height, sometimes, between decks was only eighteen inches; so that the unfortunate human beings could not turn round, or even on their sides, the elevation being less than the breadth of their shoulders; and here they are usually chained to the decks by the necks and legs. In such a place the sense of misery and suffocation is so great, that the Negroes like the English in the black-hole at Calcutta, are driven to frenzy.

While they had some exercise and fresh air when the weather was clear, during the rains they would be kept under all day. A sailor aboard one of these ships, Henry Ellison, stated: "In rains, slaves [are] confined below for sometime. I have frequently seen them faint through heat, the steam coming through the gratings like a furnace."

Many slaves went mad on board ship. Walsh described voyages in which the crews heard "horrid dins and tumults" coming from the hold below, where the slaves were stowed. The noise would signify that the slaves were struggling frantically to extricate themselves before dying of suffocation. Any slaves who

Despondent slaves often were chained to the ship's hatches to prevent them from killing themselves.

went mad were clubbed and thrown overboard. Those suspected of faking were flogged to death.

Slaves had to be watched very carefully, as many attempted to take their own lives. Captain Thomas Phillips, in his journal, recounted an incident that took place aboard the *Hannibal:* "We had about 12 Negroes did wilfully drown themselves, and others starv'd themselves to death; for 'tis their belief that when they die they return home to their own country and friends again."

Many slaves responded less actively to their situation but with the same results. Many died of what was then called "fixed melancholy," which meant they had no wish to remain alive. The ship's captain did all he could to prevent this unnecessary loss of life and to protect his company's investment.

Falconbridge described the usual treatment of slaves refusing to take food: "I have seen coals of fire, glowing hot, put on a shovel and placed so near their lips as to scorch and burn them. And this has been accompanied with threats of forcing them to swallow the coals if they persisted in refusing to eat." If this and continual flogging didn't work, the slaves would be force-fed through a device known as a "speculum oris." This "mouth opener" would force the slave to open his mouth so that food could be poured in through a funnel.

The slaves on board ship were subject to a wide variety of diseases. Europeans brought smallpox, measles, gonorrhea and syphilis. Africa contributed yellow fever, dengue, blackwater fever and malaria. Before limes were available, many sailors died of scurvy.

Slaves were confined to the hold of the ship during the major part of their trip to the port of sale. The ship's crew then gathered them together and brought them out for examination and sale.

There were many rebellions aboard the slave ships. For any attempt at revolt, execution was the mandatory penalty. From 1699 to 1845, detailed accounts were recorded of fifty-five slave mutinies, and there were references to over a hundred additional revolts.

THE WEST INDIES

When a ship arrived in the West Indies, bodies of the slaves were polished with oil so they would look as healthy as possible. A gun was fired to announce the arrival of a slave ship. The usual practice was for a factor on the island to sell the slaves for a commission. Sometimes, a single planter bought an entire shipload of slaves.

Occasionally, the captain of a slave vessel attempted to sell the slaves himself. It was not uncommon to see a group of slaves being paraded through a town to the tune of bagpipes. The sale was then held in the public square. Officer J. G. Stedman, of the Scots Brigade, which was used by the Dutch to quell the slave revolts on Surinam, described one such scene: "The whole party was . . . a resurrection of skin and bones . . . risen from the grave or escaped from Surgeons Hall." They were "walking skeletons covered over with a piece of tanned leather."

The most common methods of sale used were the "scramble" and auction. The ship's captain, along with the factor, would inspect the slaves, segregating the diseased and the maimed to be sent to town and sold at auction. The remaining slaves were separated into groups of men, women and children. After a set price had been agreed upon for each category, the purchasers scrambled on board to obtain their slaves.

Falconbridge described a typical scene:

> The purchasers on shore were informed a gun would be fired when they were ready to open sale. A great number of people came on board with tallies or cards in their hands, with their own names upon them, and rushed through the barricade door with the ferocity of brutes. Some had three or four handkerchiefs tied together to encircle as many as they thought fit for their purpose.

In this manner, the frightened and physically debilitated slaves were introduced to their new owners.

BREAKING IN

Before the closing of the British slave trade, few slaves were taken directly from Africa to the northern colonies of the United States. U. B. Phillips summarized the situation cogently in *American Negro Slavery:*

> Small parcels, better suited to the retail demand, might be brought more profitably from the sugar islands whither New England, New York and Pennsylvania ships were frequently plying than from Guinea whence special voyages must be made. Familiarity with the English language and the rudiments of civilization at the outset were more essential to petty masters than to the owners of plantation gangs, who had means of breaking in fresh Africans by deputy. But most important of all, a sojourn in the West Indies would lessen the shock of acclimatization, severe enough under the best circumstances.

In contrast, the southern colonies imported the vast majority of their slaves straight from Africa.

A discussion of the role of the West Indies must be included in any serious consideration of American Negro history. As a result of the slave trade, at least before the Revolutionary War, the United States and the West Indies were economically interdependent. Events such as slave revolts or the passage in the West Indies of ameliorative measures di-rected toward the treatment of slaves had their effect in the United States.

The "breaking in" period for the newly arrived sick, bewildered and despondent slave was likely to be harsh in either the South or in the West Indies—and usually worse in the latter area owing to the practice of absentee ownership of estates, which left overseers in full command. A period of introduction to what lay before them was necessary in order to transform them into financial assets. Since slaves in the West Indies greatly outnumbered the whites, this transitional period relied heavily on cruelty to impress upon the slave his responsibilities. Fear by reason of numerical inferiority was not the only element accounting for the savagery of the overseers. Although the slave was an economic asset, he was never more than that. There were plenty more to be had from the ships arriving regularly: better to beat to death immediately the recalcitrant or weak Negro rather than support him for a longer period only to be repaid later by a rebellion or a death.

Historian Elsa Goveia (*Slave Society in the British Leeward Islands*) cited the peculiar reluctance of West Indian planters to see breeding as a profitable alternative to importation. She quoted contemporary economists who insisted that breeding was less expensive, but she concluded that "the planters do not seem to have shared this view." Involved with the production of sugar for quick financial return, they seem obstinately to have refused to allow the slightly more humane conditions which would have produced a slave "crop." Of course, it is a moot question as to which approach—the southern border states' breeding farms or the West Indian import system—was the more degrading to the slaves. Each had its own ingenious methods of perpetrating indignities and barbarities.

It is certainly true, however, that the West Indian system tended to use worse cruelties than did the system in the southern United

As valuable economic assets, slaves often were branded to make it easy for their owners to identify them.

States. The slaves in the breaking-in period, whether turned over to reliable, trained slaves in small groups or trained by an overseer as one large class, were not handled with patience and understanding. One long, often-quoted passage from Sir Hans Sloane, who visited the islands in 1688, will suffice to show the penalty for lessons ill-learned: slaves were punished for major crimes by being nailed

> . . . down on the ground with crooked sticks on every Limb and then applying the Fire by degrees from the Feet and Hands, burning them gradually up to the Head, whereby their pains are extravagant; for Crimes of a lesser nature Gelding or chopping off half of the Foot with an Ax. . . . They are whip'd till they are Raw; some put on their Skins Pepper and Salt to make them smart, at other times their Masters will drop melted Wax on their Skins and use several very exquisite Torments.

As might be expected, this breaking-in period exacted a large toll of those Negroes who had survived the middle passage. Disease ran rampant: the slaves had been starved aboard ship, and their resistance was low to the new diseases they encountered, which surely would have taken the lives of a large number had they been healthy. Malnutrition continued on the islands, for the planters were so greedy for land to grow sugar that land appropriations for raising slave rations were scanty. Elsa Goveia wrote: "In 1788 the legislature of St. Kitts reported that the slaves there were generally allowed from 4 to 9 pints of flour, corn, peas, or beans, and between 4 to 8 herrings or other salted fish per slave per week. . . . This allowance appears to have been about average for the Leeward Islands as a whole." During the Revolutionary War, when shipments from the United States were curtailed, famine conditions existed in some islands.

Beatings and other punishments caused many deaths. Suicide and infanticide also exacted their toll—amounting to a surprisingly large number, although recorded figures tend to be unreliable. Herskovits quotes an interesting passage from *Alien Americans* by Bertram Schrieke that tells of the birth of Nat Turner, famous Negro insurrectionist. His mother was reported to have been "so wild that at Nat's birth she had to be tied to prevent her from murdering him." She was, significantly, African born. This event occurred in the United States, but there is ample evidence to prove that the problem was an annoying one for West Indian planters.

The period of the slave's orientation into his new way of life was a crucial one for him, whether he was brought first to the West Indies or to the United States. Charles Leslie, in *A New and Exact Account of Jamaica*, published in 1740, estimated that "almost half of the new imported Negroes die in the seasoning." U. B. Phillips, in a more modern estimate, placed the rate at 20 to 30 per cent.

THE PLANTATION SYSTEM

It was in the Sugar Islands that the plantation system had its beginnings, and from there it spread to the North American mainland. Many of the features of the system in the United States, therefore, had their origins in the West Indies. In the final analysis, the ultimate reason for Negro slavery was its economic superiority over other forms of labor tried in the New World.

In the West Indies, the large plantation soon replaced the small subsistence farm as the sugar industry developed. Sugar culture was favorable to slavery. Operations such as clearing the land, holing, planting, weeding and cane cutting could be done in gangs, which made it simple to provide maximum supervision with the fewest number of overseers. Slavery usually was less successful in diversified agriculture and more profitable where routine tasks were required.

John Stuart Mill believed that slavery was favorable to the quick development of the

Slaves cultivating sugar cane on a large plantation in the West Indies.

islands. "It is likely," he wrote, "that productive operations which require much combination of labour, the production of sugar, for example, would not have taken place so soon in the American Colonies, if slavery had not existed to keep masses of labour together."

Slavery also served a useful political function. Until late in the eighteenth century, it was regarded as a way of keeping the colonies tied to the mother country. Thus, in 1766, Governor Charles Pinfeld of Barbados, where economic welfare depended on slavery, reported on the island's compliance with the Stamp Act. He was relieved that the act had remained in effect for four months in his area without adverse incident, "especially as the North American Correspondents have spared neither Threats, or entreaties to persuade us to imitate their outrageous and Rebellious Conduct." In 1640, Barbados had a few Negro slaves but was populated mostly by whites owning small farms. In 1643, there were about eight thousand Negro slaves and eighteen thousand white males capable of bearing arms. There were at that time approximately ten thousand separate holdings. As the sugar economy developed, the marginal farmers were forced out, so that in 1666 there were about nine thousand white males and forty thousand slaves. Until the eighteenth century, Barbados was the leading producer of British sugar and the most valued English colony. As its soil lost fertility, it was replaced in importance by Jamaica.

Jamaica, in 1673, had about nine thousand slaves and seven thousand whites. Despite the initial efforts of the government there to limit the imports of slaves, from 1698 to 1707 there were over forty thousand slaves shipped to Jamaica. In 1734, there were over eighty-five thousand slaves, and ten years later the number had increased to well over a hundred thousand. By 1787, there were more than two hundred thousand slaves on the island of Jamaica.

Most of the plantations in the West Indies were owned by absentee landlords who were concerned primarily with maintaining the highest possible return on their investments. The Lords of Trade generally did not interfere but allowed the planters to develop their own policies toward the slaves. The overseers who ran the plantations in the owners' absence maintained their positions by making enough money to keep the owners happy. Henry Coor visited Jamaica in 1774 and was told by an overseer, "I have made my employers 20, 30 and 40 more hogsheads per year than my predecessors and tho I have killed 30 or 40 Negroes per year more, yet the produce has been more than adequate to the loss."

Once the slaves were broken in, they lived in family huts in the slave quarters. They were allotted small farms on the outskirts of the plantation to raise their own crops, which were supplemented by food allowances. Still, the food was never adequate, and the birth rate was far below the death rate. During one year on the island of St. Vincent, 2,656 births and 4,205 deaths were recorded.

The slave began work at daybreak and worked until sundown. He was allowed thirty minutes for breakfast and the semi-relaxation of doing lighter work for two hours during the hottest part of the afternoon. During the harvest period, slaves were worked for eighteen hours a day. Half the group worked in the boiling house for twelve hours; they were then replaced by another group of slaves, who worked the second twelve-hour shift. After twelve hours in the boiling house, the slaves worked an additional five or six hours cutting and bringing in the cane.

There were a number of slave revolts, the first taking place in Hispaniola in 1522. When the English seized the island of Jamaica, many of the slaves escaped to the hills. These bands of slaves, known as maroons, encouraged other slaves to escape. In 1730, England sent troops to the island to crush the maroons. The war lasted for a number of years and was finally concluded with a treaty of peace.

THE ECONOMICS OF THE SLAVE TRADE

Economist Adam Smith did not exaggerate when he wrote in *The Wealth of Nations* that "The profits of a sugar plantation in any of our West Indian Colonies are generally much greater than those of any other cultivation either in Europe or America." In economic importance, the Caribbean area, with its numerous slaves, dwarfed the colonies of North America during the eighteenth century. In 1697, British imports from Barbados, an island with an area of a mere 166 square miles, were five times the total of the imports from the bread colonies and New England combined. British exports to Barbados at that time were slightly higher than its total exports to its colonies north of Baltimore. In 1773, British imports from Jamaica were five times greater than the combined total imported from the bread colonies. Its exports to the island were one-third larger than those to New England and slightly less than those to New York and Pennsylvania combined.

During the eighteenth century, Barbados, which is pictured here, and the other islands of the Caribbean were of far greater economic importance to the European powers than the colonies on the North American mainland.

A clear picture of the relative economic importance of the few small islands of the West Indies to England's wealth can be gleaned from the overall statistics of the period from 1714 to 1773. The exports of the island of Montserrat to Britain were three times the exports of Pennsylvania to Britain. The island of Nevis exported twice as much as New York. The tiny island of Antigua had three times the exports of all New England. During these years, Barbados experienced a period of economic decline yet managed to export twice as much as the bread colonies. Jamaica's exports were six times as great as those of the mid-Atlantic states. The exports of Britain to Jamaica equaled its exports to New England. British exports to the islands of Barbados and Antigua equaled the total of British goods sent to New York. The British goods entering Montserrat and Nevis were greater than those exported to the colony of Pennsylvania.

It is clear that the major source of colonial wealth that accrued to England was from the small islands of the West Indies. The source of this wealth was the day-to-day arduous labor of the Negro slaves. When one adds to this the profits of the slave trade, the importance of slavery to the development of modern capitalism can be more fully appreciated.

CHAPTER FOUR

Slavery in the English Colonies

IN the seventeenth century, the colonies of the North American mainland were of less interest to the empire builders of England than were their more tropical possessions. The growing season was short compared with that of the West Indies (Jamaica had been taken from the Spanish in 1655), winters were cold and the prospects for the discovery of gold or of a northwest passageway to the Far East had gradually diminished. The founding companies' profits were minimal. In 1608, Captain John Smith wrote to his English backers, "As yet you must not looke for any profitable returnes"; indeed, by 1623, the Virginia Company was bankrupt. Throughout the colonial period, therefore, both the colonies and the system of slavery developed slowly and unevenly.

THE NEW ENGLAND COLONIES

Slavery is associated traditionally with the southern colonies—Virginia, Maryland, the Carolinas and Georgia. But it should not be forgotten that the heart of the slave trade lay in New England at one time and that the Puritan and mid-Atlantic colonies continued the institution of slavery until the turn of the nineteenth century. In New Jersey, for example, slavery was not abolished officially until the passage of the Thirteenth Amendment in 1866.

Any discussion of slavery in New England must begin with the role of the slave trade. During the seventeenth century, enterprising

CAPTAIN JOHN SMITH

Yankee seamen who had been driven from the Guinea coast by the monopolistic Royal African Company went as far as Madagascar in their search for human cargoes. In 1696, the company's slave-trading monopoly was broken, and West Africa was opened to the New Englanders. After the English acquired the *asiento* in 1713, they found that they were incapable of providing unilaterally the requisite 4,800 slaves per year to the Spanish. Thus, New England merchants were permitted to enter the slave trade in full force to assist England in her program of Atlantic domination.

The slave trade was most lucrative for New Englanders during the first half of the eighteenth century. Ships from Boston, Salem, Providence, Newport and New London were extremely active. Even New Hampshire and Connecticut seamen became involved. New England merchants exported rum, fish, dairy products and many other goods and shipped great numbers of slaves to the southern colonies. By the middle of the eighteenth century, roughly one-half of the tonnage of the New England shipping community was involved in some manner in the slave trade.

Newport, Rhode Island, increasingly became the center of the trade. A small, wealthy aristocracy gradually emerged from the ranks of the early slave merchants. By mid-century, Newport had from twenty to thirty stills working to supply rum for use in the slave trade.

Not all of the slaves in the charge of the New England merchants went to the south, however; during the early years of the colony's existence, many Massachusetts leaders seem to have been enthusiastic over the prospects of the widespread use of slaves. During the 1640's, John Winthrop's brother-in-law, Emmanuel Downing, hoped for a war with the Narragansett Indians for two reasons: first, to stop their "worship of the devill"; and second, to gain slaves.

. . . If upon a just warre the Lord should deliver them into our hands, wee might easily have men, women and children enough to exchange for Moores, which will be more gaynful pilladge for us than wee conceive, for I doe not see how wee can thrive untile wee get into a stock of slaves sufficient to doe all our buisines, for our children's children will hardly see this great continent filled with people, soe that our servants will still desire freedome to plant for themselves and not stay but for verie great wages. And I suppose you know verie well how wee shall mayntayne 20 Moores cheaper than one Englishe servant.

By 1700, out of a total population of about 90,000, New England contained only about 1,000 blacks. By Revolutionary days, however, the number had risen to almost 20,000. During the early eighteenth century, Massachusetts had more Negroes than the other New England colonies. In 1715, Massachusetts had about 2,000 Negroes, most of whom lived in or around Boston. By 1735, when the white population was 141,000, there were approximately 2,600 Negroes. By 1776, there were about 5,200 Negroes in the colony and 343,000 whites.

As the century wore on, Rhode Island developed the greatest concentration of blacks relative to population. In 1710, there were about 375 Negroes and 7,500 whites. By 1750, there were about 3,350 Negroes and 33,200 whites. In 1770, there were about 3,700 blacks and 58,000 whites.

There probably were never more than fifteen thousand Negroes in all of colonial New England. Only Rhode Island was as much as 5 per cent black. Although Negroes scarcely played an important economic role in colonial New England, their very presence was significant. Their Puritan masters were perhaps the most devout of the settlers; they thought of themselves as creating the Kingdom of God on earth. Yet these same men dominated the colonial slave trade in the Western Hemisphere and owned slaves of their own.

The Puritans were perhaps the first Americans to create an ideological justification for

COTTON MATHER

slavery. They suggested that the slaves were the children of the Biblical Ham, who had been condemned to eternal servitude. Although some leaders, such as Cotton Mather, expressed uncertainty, Roger Williams and other eminent theologians viewed blacks and Indians as the "unregenerate seed" who could in no way be considered as part of the Elect, or the body of persons whom God, in his mercy, had chosen for salvation. In general, the Puritans disregarded the violent aspects of slavery and saw the slave as occupying a place in the order of the world that was sanctioned by God. Most Puritan theologians granted that the slave had a soul and acknowledged that his supreme master was God; yet they felt that it would be wrong for him to resist his lot in life. He should act in a Christian fashion and trust God to deliver the necessary justice. Naturally, the Puritans depended heavily on the Bible as defense and support for their arguments.

The Puritans considered slavery not so much as an industrial system but more in the manner of the Old Testament, in which slaves became part of the family rather than chattel. They were, therefore, very interested in contractual matters. "Innocent" slaves, those who had been kidnapped and were guilty of no crime for which slavery was a fit punishment, were in at least several cases ordered returned to Africa and set free. Legal purchase was later expanded to include those Negroes taken in war, a broadening that produced a greater supply of "legitimate" slaves. In 1641, the famous Body of Liberties provided:

> There shall never be any bond slaverie, villinage or captivitie amongst us unless it be lawfull captives taken in just warres, and such strangers as willingly selle themselves or are sold to us. And these shall have all the liberties and Christian usages which the law of God established in Israell concerning such persons doeth morally require.

With this one stroke, the Puritan fathers legitimized slavery and gave to it the cast that was to be peculiar to New England. Slavery in New England resembled Old Testament bondage in its mildness: many slaves were taken into the master's family and most New England slaves retained the fundamental rights of personality.

Having so early given legal status to slavery, subsequent generations slowly elaborated the means by which this new institution operated in American life and law. In 1670, Massachusetts moved toward fixing slave status as a hereditary position by making it possible to sell the children of slaves into bondage. Ten years later, a new law was enacted to forbid slaves in Massachusetts to board any ship without a permit. In 1693, whites were forbidden to trade with Negroes. In 1660, Connecticut passed a law that barred Negroes from military service. Most New England colonies forbade Negroes to be on the streets at night without a pass. It was

An Act concerning Indian, Molatto, and Negro Servants, and Slaves.

BE it Enacted by the Governour, Council, and Representatives, in General Court Assembled, and by the Authority of the same, That whatsoever *Negro, Molatto,* or *Indian* Servant, or Servants shall be found Wandring out of the Bounds of the Town, or Place to which they belong without a Ticket, or Pass in Writing under the Hand of some Assistant, or Justice of the Peace, or under the Hand of the Master, or Owner of such *Negro, Molatto,* or *Indian* Servants, shall be Deemed, and Accounted to be Run-aways, and may be Treated as such: And every Person Inhabiting in this Colony, Finding, or Meeting with any such *Negro, Molatto,* or *Indian* Servant, or Servants not having a Ticket, as aforesaid, is hereby Impowred to Seise, and Secure him, or them, and Bring him, or them before the next Authority to be Examined, and Returned to his, or their Master, or Owner, who shall satisfy the Charge Accruing thereby.

This Connecticut law is typical of the restrictive legislation passed in New England during the colonial period.

illegal to sell liquor to blacks. And in many places, laws were passed that forbade Negroes from striking or attacking whites.

The actual slave regimen, however, was relatively mild. As previously mentioned, slaves were frequently treated as members of the family in the Old Testament tradition. Few slave crimes were punishable by death. The codes were neither as exhaustive nor as rigidly enforced as those in the southern colonies, and masters did not have the power of life or death over their slaves. Slaves had recourse to the courts and, throughout the colonial period, could testify against whites. They were permitted to own property. Marital ties among the blacks were ordinarily respected, and their marriages were solemnly consecrated by the Puritan churches.

Thus, in law and in fact, slaves in New England never became as systematically de-graded as in the tobacco and rice colonies. As the New Englanders evolved a legal and moral setting for the institution, they found themselves allowing the bondsman some element of personality: the slave was not totally a commodity or a chattel.

This can be explained partially, of course, by the fact that gang labor had no real roots in New England. Most Negroes, therefore, became personal servants or artisans rather than field hands. Throughout New England, many of the skilled and semi-skilled trades were, indeed, permeated with men who had learned their crafts in Africa. In the eyes of their masters, therefore, the New England blacks had a certain degree of spiritual and moral personality. While slavery was still slavery, and all the benevolence in the world could not make it a humane institution, the Negro of colonial Boston was allowed greater personal freedom than his brother on a rice plantation in South Carolina.

There were other mitigating factors. The intellectual climate of New England, with its stern emphasis on education, certainly tempered New England restrictions on slaves and provided an atmosphere which did benefit the slaves somewhat. Many Puritan leaders, John Eliot and Cotton Mather among them, were apparently sincerely concerned with educating and Christianizing the slaves of colonial New England. The Anglican Society for the Propagation of the Gospel in Foreign Parts was active in all the colonies, and became increasingly active in New England as the Puritan theocracy lost its monopoly on political power in the late seventeenth century. These efforts account for the fact that the Negroes of New England were much better educated than were Negroes elsewhere.

Only in one area did the condition of the New England blacks approach that of their southern brethren. The land surrounding the Narragansett Bay in Rhode Island was the most fertile area in all of New England, and the proportion of blacks to whites there was the highest. Many farms were of plantation size, ranging from six hundred to one thousand acres. Historian U. B. Phillips *(American Negro Slavery)* said: "prosperity from tillage, and especially from dairying and horse breeding, caused the rise in that neighborhood of landholdings and slave-holdings on a scale more commensurate with those in Virginia than with those elsewhere in New England." Some planters owned as many as forty-five slaves. In 1730, in South Kingston, one of the areas in this region, there were about a thousand whites, over three hundred Negroes and over two hundred Indians. For a number of years afterward, slaves constituted a group from one-third to one-half as large as the community of freemen.

It is important to realize, however, that the slaves in the Narragansett Bay area were not working with a labor-intensive cash crop like tobacco, rice or indigo, which would require depersonalizing gang labor. Instead, this area specialized in stock-raising and dairy-farming. Phillips has even suggested that the high

JOHN ELIOT

concentration of blacks in this area occurred not because of the demands of fertile soil for a large group of unskilled laborers, but rather because of its proximity to a great center of the slave trade, Newport. Many slave ships returned from the Indies with extra slaves and disposed of them cheaply in Newport and the Narragansett Bay area. Even here, however, there was no break with the fundamental New England tendency towards domestic, as opposed to chattel, slavery.

The relatively high proportion of blacks in Rhode Island made the issue of slavery more urgent there than elsewhere in New England, and it forced the colony's leaders and citizens to grapple with the problem earlier. Their initial reaction was ambiguous. On the one hand, the Rhode Island slave code was perhaps the harshest in New England. Rhode Island officials were particularly concerned with penalizing any meetings or exchanges between free Negroes and slaves. Not even cider could be sold to a Rhode Island slave. Punishment seems to have been harsher and more rigorous than in other New England areas. On the other hand, Rhode Island was historically a center of progressive political and religious thinking. In 1652, for example, the joint government of Providence and Warwick ruled that all slaves must be freed within ten years, and a heavy penalty for noncompliance was established. This measure was not repealed for many years—although, of course, it was never enforced. It was in Rhode Island, therefore, where the issue of social control was potentially most serious, that tension first developed between the forces of abolition and repression.

Although slavery in New England was undeniably mild, this did not ensure the docility of the Negroes, who demonstrated their antipathy to the system in various ways. Many ran away or showed their antagonism through continued criminal behavior. Organized insurrections also took place. In Hartford, as early as 1658, Negroes and Indians

The first settlement of New York, founded by the slave-trading Dutch West India Company.

destroyed some of the houses of their masters and attempted to escape into the wilderness. An insurrectionary plot was uncovered in 1690 in Newbury, Massachusetts, in which Negroes and Indians had combined forces. In 1723, Boston was terrified by black arsonists: ten or twelve fires were set during a single week in April. Laws were passed immediately to clear the streets of slaves and to prohibit them from "idling or lurking together."

THE MID-ATLANTIC COLONIES

The story of the mid-Atlantic colonies is more complex than that of New England. From the beginning, there was little ideological uniformity. We cannot meaningfully speak of the mid-Atlantic colonies as a religious or political unit in the same way we can discuss early New England in these terms.

Of all the northern states, New York probably had the most difficulty with the whole question of slavery. Perhaps this was because the colony had been founded by a great slave-trading corporation, the Dutch West India Company. The company owned and stocked several large plantations in the colony and generally favored importations. As early as 1628, there were complaints of Negro recalcitrance.

Under the English, slavery grew. In her message to the colonial governor of 1702, Queen Anne ordered officials to "take especial care that the . . . Province may have a constant and sufficient supply of merchantable Negroes at moderate prices." Increasing numbers of people developed an interest in the institution and bought only one or two slaves. New York City traders became active in the traffic.

The number of Negroes in New York, therefore, had increased considerably by the end of the eighteenth century. In 1640, there had been more slaves in New York than in any other colony; by 1650, there had been an estimated 500 Negroes in a population of slightly more than 4,000. The proportion had changed by 1700 to about 1,900 blacks to 20,000 whites. In 1750, there were 11,000 Negroes and more than 75,000 whites. By 1771, slaves comprised almost one-ninth of the total population of New York.

The slave codes enacted in New York were relatively harsh. White citizens were not allowed to trade with slaves, and penalties for harboring fugitive slaves were severe. Slaves were not permitted to hold meetings with more than three in attendance. No slave could testify in court against a white citizen. The problem of runaway slaves became so serious that, after 1705, any slave caught traveling forty miles north of Albany could be executed.

As in most of the colonies, a certain amount of benevolent paternalism was operative in New York. In 1702, Queen Anne had requested that "a law be passed for restraining any inhuman severity." The Anglican Society for the Propagation of the Gospel in Foreign Parts also urged humanity. Elias Neau was one of the first active agents of the society, working in New York during the first quarter of the eighteenth century. The slave owners resented and mistrusted Neau. They feared that, if baptism were to be conferred upon slaves, it would become as impossible and illegal to hold them in bondage as it was in England. Neau, however, attempted to explain to masters and slaves that the church could provide only spiritual freedom through

baptism: freedom from sin. Religion, he countered, had nothing to say on the matter of abolition. Indeed, Neau was instrumental in 1706 in persuading the colonial governor to sponsor legislation to the effect that conversion and baptism did not alter the civil status of slaves. After this legislation was passed, it is hardly surprising that slaveholders grew more willing to permit their chattels to attend Neau's classes. In this way, benevolence and paternalism served to fasten the bonds of slavery ever tighter.

New York was plagued with more slave unrest than any other northern colony. There were continual complaints of criminal behavior, insubordination and rowdiness on the part of the slaves. Many Negroes ran away and found a ready welcome with the Indians. In 1696, the mayor of New York was assaulted by a group of slaves. In 1708, a Negro woman and an Indian man were executed for murdering their master and his family. Organized insurrectionists were barely thwarted in New York in 1712. Twenty-one slaves were executed: some were hanged, some were burned at the stake and others were broken on the rack.

The slave codes were stiffened as a result of the 1712 rebellion; but in 1741, popular hysteria rose again upon the rumor of more uprisings. After a series of trials, eighteen Negroes were hanged, thirteen were burned alive, and seventy were expelled from the colony. Several whites were also prosecuted for assisting the blacks. There is still considerable dispute as to whether any slaves actually attempted to rebel or whether the threatened insurrection of 1741 was only the product of the overheated imaginations of the white New Yorkers. In any case, it is clear that by the middle of the eighteenth century free New Yorkers had found it necessary to come to grips with the agony of keeping a subject population in their midst.

Colonial New Jersey, stretching between New York City and Philadelphia, without a major port of its own, reflected the influences of the two metropolises. While western New Jersey used Pennsylvania currency throughout the colonial period, the eastern section used New York currency. This sectional division also manifested itself in the various ways in which slavery was institutionalized in the state.

Among the mid-Atlantic colonies, New Jersey was second only to New York in size of slave population during the colonial period. When the British took over control from the Dutch in 1664, they offered every settler seventy-five acres for each slave or servant brought into the colony. Between 1670 and 1680, the number of Negro slaves increased from sixty to about two hundred; and by 1690, nearly every family in eastern New Jersey owned at least one slave. In 1726, there were about 2,600 Negroes in the colony out of a total population of 32,500. In 1740, there were 4,300 Negroes and slightly over 51,000 whites. By 1750, there were about 5,300 Negroes and 71,400 whites. The greatest period of growth took place after 1750, for by 1790 there were about 11,500 slaves in the colony and 2,800 free Negroes.

The distribution of slaveholdings reflected religious and political differences in the state. The Negro population was more or less stabilized after 1726 at 8 per cent of the total population; however, there was an increasingly greater concentration in the eastern part of the state, while the west moved toward total manumission and emancipation because of the Quaker influence.

As in virtually every northern colony, the blacks of New Jersey worked at many diversified occupations. As early as 1680, Lewis Morris of Shrewsbury had over sixty blacks working at his iron mill. Many worked on farms, in mines and on the docks at Perth Amboy or Camden. Since most enterprise was on a small scale, there was considerable personal interaction between black and white.

The New Jersey slave code had been similar to the New York laws but became harsher after western and eastern Jersey were united in 1702. The penalty for petty theft was whipping; grand larceny was punishable by branding; castration was inflicted for rape; and death was the punishment for murder.

Despite its harsh legal code, New Jersey's slave system does not appear to have incited a great deal of insurrectionary activity on the part of the Negroes. In 1741, there was an arson scare in Hackensack, but there was no hysteria among the white community comparable to that in New York in the same year.

The situation in New Jersey was ameliorated somewhat by the work of the Quakers. The New Jersey Quakers were part of the Philadelphia Yearly Meeting of Friends and were therefore in contact with the most articulate supporters of black freedom in the country. The leader of the opposition to slavery in New Jersey, John Woolman of Mount Holly,

JOHN WOOLMAN

began his long career in 1743. He was apparently a gifted orator and organizer and did much to create antislavery sentiment in the state, particularly in the western area. By 1758, the Quakers were not only opposed to the importation of new slaves but also advocated complete emancipation of those slaves already in the state.

The Society for the Propagation of the Gospel in Foreign Parts was also active in New Jersey. As in New York, the society's main aim was to provide a religious education for the slaves, and it never attempted to oppose the institution of slavery.

In Pennsylvania, there was a sharp confrontation between a beneficent social ideology, Quakerism, and the proponents of slavery. Perhaps only in colonial Georgia was the ideological contest as severe. On the one hand, a large majority of the Friends, a group of German farmers and many of the small artisans in Philadelphia despised the institution; on the other hand, commercial interests and the Royal African Company were determined to plant bondage in the fertile hinterland of Penn's woods.

The number of Negro slaves in Pennsylvania grew slowly. In 1680, there were 25, out of an estimated 7,000 Negro slaves in the American colonies. In 1721, the slave population was about 2,500. In 1750, it was estimated at 2,800. In 1790, there were about 3,800 slaves in the colony and about 6,500 free Negroes. Thus, although Pennsylvania's black population was considerable, it never equaled that of either New York or New Jersey. Given the labor needs of Philadelphia and the fertile farming districts immediately to the west, one can only assume that the importation of blacks was at least partially minimized by the joint activities of the antislavery elements in Pennsylvania.

The story of the struggle over the slave issue in colonial Pennsylvania becomes more clear when we examine the attempts of the legislature to place prohibitive duties on slave

An Act for Laying a Duty on Negroes Imported into This Province

We, the representatives of the freemen of the province of Pennsylvania, desire that it may be enacted:

[Section I.] And be it enacted by Charles Gookin, Esquire, by the royal approbation Lieutenant-Governor, under William Penn, Esquire, Proprietary and Governor-in-Chief of the Province of Pennsylvania, by and with the advice and consent of the freemen of the said Province in General Assembly met, and by the authority of the same, That for every negro which shall be imported, landed, or brought into this province at any time after the first day of June, in the year of our Lord one thousand seven hundred and fifteen, and before the first day of June in the year one thousand seven hundred and eighteen (other than such negroes as are actually shipped for sailors and shall continue in the service of the vessel they are brought in, and not be exposed to sale in this province, and other than such negroes as shall be brought or sent to this province upon their master's immediate business, and not for sale) there shall be paid for the uses hereafter mentioned the sum of five pounds lawful money of America.

And that all masters of vessels, and others, who shall within the time aforesaid bring into this province, by land or water, any negroes, shall forthwith make entry and give or cause to be given upon oath or affirmation, to the person hereinafter appointed to collect the said duty, a true and just account of all the negroes so imported, or brought in, and to whom they respectively belong, which the said collector shall duly enter in a book for that purpose, and thereupon shall grant a permit, gratis, for landing the same.

In 1715, the legislature of colonial Pennsylvania tried to decrease the number of slaves being imported into the province by levying a five-pound duty on each new slave.

imports. In 1700, a duty of twenty shillings was placed on every Negro entering the colony. In 1705, the duty was raised to forty shillings. In 1712, the influence of the slave-trading firms in London sufficed to nullify a

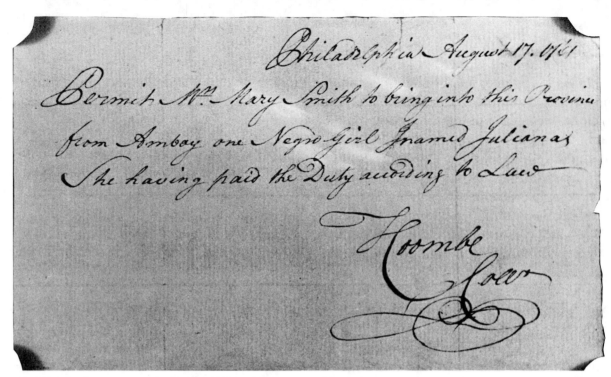

Despite the duty imposed by the legislature, slaves were still brought into Pennsylvania, as this receipt indicates.

law that the legislature had passed prohibiting all future slave imports; nonetheless, the number of slaves entering the colony fell. In 1715, the duty was raised to five pounds. It was vetoed but re-imposed in 1722. Between 1729 and 1761, the duty was reduced to two pounds; but by mid-century, the slave trade to Pennsylvania had all but ceased. Between 1761 and 1780, the duty was ten pounds; and after 1780, the slave trade was forbidden altogether.

Only after 1700 was the status of the Pennsylvania slave legally defined. Prior to this, slaves and indentured servants had enjoyed roughly similar positions. After 1700, the special status of the slave was recognized. A special slave court was established, where murder, rape and burglary were punishable by execution. Attempted rape incurred castration. After 1726, intermarriage between the races was forbidden. Curfews were established, and limitations on travel for blacks were imposed.

Slavery in Pennsylvania, as one may suspect, was relatively mild. Labor was diversified, as it was throughout most of the North. According to several witnesses, the laws restricting mobility were often softened or ignored in practice, and the Negroes of Pennsylvania, especially in Philadelphia, enjoyed considerable personal freedom. At no time during the colonial period did Pennsylvania suffer a slave insurrection, although large numbers of slaves, of course, attempted to run away.

Delaware was part of Pennsylvania until 1703, and the colony did not develop its own legal system for slavery until 1721. The first act set up a special slave court, forbade meetings among the slaves, prohibited slaves from carrying arms and forbade fornication and adultery. Legislation was enacted in the 1760's to minimize manumissions as Delawarians became increasingly fearful of the presence of a large group of free Negroes within the colony. In 1700, there were only 135 Negroes to 2,335 whites. By 1750, Delaware contained nearly 1,500 Negroes out of a total population of about 29,000. However, Delaware did not develop a plantation-style economy during the colonial period. U. B. Phillips has suggested that "the retention of slavery seems to have been mainly due to public inertia and to the pressure of political sympathy with the more distinctly southern states."

Before the Revolution, therefore, slavery's hold on the colonies north of Maryland was tenuous. And even in the three colonies where it had any chance of achieving some sort of permanence—New York, Rhode Island and New Jersey—strong social and political factors operated against it. New England, despite the slave trade, could not hope to support slavery on its thin soil. And Northerners were increasingly influenced by an articulate and militant antislavery element.

THE SOUTHERN COLONIES

In 1619, Virginia planter John Rolfe wrote that "about the last of August a Dutch man of war, of Flushing, brought in twenty negars." These "twenty negars" were the first blacks in the English colonies, but their arrival did not suddenly transform the South into a society based on black labor. In fact, the slave population of Virginia grew slowly until the last quarter of the seventeenth century. In 1625, there were only 25 blacks in the colony, and they had been brought in as indentured servants rather than as slaves. Twenty-five years later, there were still only 400 Negroes in the colony, along with about 19,000 whites.

By the closing years of the seventeenth century, however, Virginia was moving in the direction of becoming a slaveholding society. At that time, more than 1,000 slaves were entering the colony each year. By 1700, Virginia had more than 16,000 Negroes out of a total population of 58,000. By 1710, there were more than 22,000 blacks out of a total of close to 80,000 inhabitants. Finally, in 1770, there were an estimated 187,000 Negroes in Virginia living among nearly 260,000 whites. In many counties, whites were increasingly fearful that they would soon be outnumbered by their bondsmen.

During the two generations in which there had been very few Negroes in the colony, Virginia had the leisure, unlike some of the other colonies formed later in the century, to work out the status of slaves. It was during this period that a line was gradually drawn between the status of the black slave and the status of the white worker.

It should not be forgotten that the English colonists had little experience, prior to colonization, with chattel slavery or, for that matter, with Negroes. While the Spanish and Portuguese, through their maintenance of the ancient Justinian codes and through their contacts with the Moslem world, had a legal structure that could assimilate slavery, the English colonists had to work out a new system, with no legal precedent. Slavery had long since died out in most of western Europe, while remaining at least a marginal institution on the Iberian peninsula.

Although the English, like other western Europeans, lacked direct experience with

A formal agreement of indenture for the Negro Shadrach.

slavery, they were well acquainted with other forms of dependent labor. As the historians Oscar and Mary Handlin have suggested, the crucial difference in the seventeenth century was not between slavery and freedom but rather between freedom and various forms of "unfreedom." Thus, the seventeenth-century Englishman was more or less familiar with outright villeinage—which still existed in some areas of Scotland—and with the sale of debtors, sometimes even for life, the sale of members of a family by an indebted head of household and formal indenture for a period of years. In all cases, the laborer was "unfree" and was subject to his master's control.

The first Negroes in Virginia—and very likely in all of the English colonies—were servants rather than slaves. They entered as unfree persons into a society in which large numbers of people were similarly unfree. Their status was similar to that of many Indians, Englishmen, Scots and Irishmen. In 1661, Virginia passed the first law making Negroes formally and legally slaves for the duration of life. Until this time, Negroes had rights similar to those of white servants. In English law, for example, any servant became "enfranchised" after baptism. In 1624, a Virginia Negro named John Phillip was permitted to testify at the trial of a white man because he could prove that he had been baptized in England in 1612 and was therefore considered a free man.

It is striking that Negroes hired other servants. By 1650, a free Negro named Anthony Johnson was hiring other blacks as servants. Significantly, Johnson had probably been one of the "twenty negars" who had been brought into Virginia in 1619. Other cases showed that Negro servitude during these years was quite different from Negro slavery. In September 1625, one court ordered that "the Negro that cam in with Capt. Jones shall remaine with the [Lady] Yeardley till further order be taken for him, and that he shall be allowed by the Lady Yeardley monthly for

> Whereas complaint was this daye made to ye court by ye humble peticion of Anth. Johnson Negro ag[ains]t Mr. Robert Parker that hee detayneth one John Casor a Negro the plaintiffs Serv[an]t under pretense yt the sd Jno. Casor is a freeman the court seriously considering & maturely weighing ye premises doe fynd that ye sd Mr. Robert Parker most unrightly keepeth ye sd Negro John Casor from his r[igh]t mayster Anth. Johnson as it appeareth by ye Deposition of Capt. Samll Gold smith & many probable circumstances. be it therefore ye Judgement of ye court & ordered that ye sd Jno. Casor negro, shall forthwith bee turned into ye service of his sd master Anthony Johnson and that the sd Mr. Robert Parker make payment of all charges in the suite and execution.

In sustaining the claim of Anthony Johnson, a free black, to the perpetual service of John Casor, the court gave judicial sanction to the right of Negroes to own slaves of their own race.

his labors forty pownd waight of good merchantable tobacco . . . so long as he remayneth with her."

Throughout this period, both Negroes and white servants were referred to as "servants" rather than as "slaves." Whereas the word "slave" was used occasionally, in colloquial usage it was usually synonymous with servant or "low born." Thus Hamlet declaims "O, what a rogue and peasant slave am I!" A sixteenth-century report says that of two hundred soldiers, eight were gentlemen and the rest were "slaves." As late as 1660, the Carolina constitution, while recognizing the legal status of black slavery, assumed that most of the work on the plantations would be done by white villeins.

The distinction between white and black servants gradually grew sharper. At first, laws to enforce discipline upon Negroes "who are servants" were of the same sort as the Bermuda legislation that commanded that the Irish workers should "straggle nor night nor dai, as is too frequent with them." But in order to encourage the immigration of white laborers, certain guarantees had to be given: they needed to understand that their status in the New World would not be one of perpetual bondage. In the 1640's, a series of laws was passed in Virginia to limit the term of indenture, but the courts construed the laws as not applying to blacks. It was decided that the law only applied to those whose migration had been voluntary.

Finally, by 1660, Virginia formally recognized the existence of slavery. An act passed to encourage trade with the Dutch and other foreigners specifically mentioned the importation of "Negro slaves." In 1661, the assembly legislated that if any white servants ran away in company with "any Negroes who are incapable of making satisfaction by addition of time," the white fugitive must serve the Negro's master for as long as the black had been away, in addition to suffering the usual penalties for his own misdeeds. As Phillips pointed out, "a Negro whose time of service could not be extended must needs have been a servant for life—in other words, a slave." In 1662, the ruling finally came that slavery was a hereditary condition among blacks and that the status of the child was determined by the status of the mother.

Lifetime chattel slavery was clearly contemplated in the legislation of 1667 that declared that baptism did not necessarily imply civil freedom. The act assured owners that they might allow their slaves to receive a Christian education without any threat of altering the slaves' legal status. Sincere interest in the Christian salvation of the slaves was present, no doubt, but the legislators' first concern was obviously with the needs of the slave owners. In 1670, it was determined that all non-Christian servants were to be reduced to two classes. Those who came into the colony by sea (Negroes) would remain slaves all their lives; those coming by land (Indians) would serve a period of indenture, after which they would be freed.

Through this series of judicial decisions and legislative enactments, therefore, the oldest of the plantation colonies fixed the status of the slave. This judicial and legislative process ran parallel to several other occurrences: the increase of the black population and the rise of the plantation. It was the tobacco plantation, after all, that created the vast labor shortage which called for importation of the black African into America in such large numbers. By the end of the century, the classic pattern of large tobacco plantations was beginning to emerge in the most fertile areas in the colony. This implied, for the first time, the development on a large scale of the gang-labor system. By the end of the century, one Virginia planter could write that his plantations were being worked by "fine crews of Negroes"; planter John Carter owned as many as 106 slaves, and many others owned extremely large numbers of blacks.

Because of its economic advantages, black slave labor increasingly came to displace white labor. In his *History of Agriculture in the Southern States to 1860,* Lewis C. Gray discussed the two main economic advantages of the slave system. According to Gray, an adult slave could be obtained at the beginning of the eighteenth century for less than twice the cost of an adult servant whose term expired in four years. The slave belonged to the planter for life and so did all his descendants. A further economic advantage to the planter lay in the fact that he was obligated only to provide his slaves their subsistence. With intelligent, efficient farming, however, the land of the New World could be made to produce a volume of goods that went far beyond the minimum required for the subsistence of those working the land. Under the slave system, the planter could legally appropriate whatever "surplus value" accrued from the efforts of his laborers. Obviously, this was advantageous. For, under a more normal system, the planter would have found it necessary to share some of those excess profits with his employees in the form of higher wages.

The triumph of the plantation system and the displacement of white labor by slave labor was directly related to the increased size of the tobacco crop. The sot-weed export from Virginia in 1619 was 20,000 pounds. In 1664, Virginia and Maryland together exported about 25 million pounds. In 1760, England imported from these two colonies plus Carolina over 52 million pounds.

The Virginia slave code also had been elaborated by the turn of the eighteenth century. Slave travel was restricted. Slaves found guilty of murder or rape were to be hanged. For other offenses, the penalties ranged from whipping to being pilloried with one's ears nailed to the posts for half an hour. The harshness of the Virginia slave code was based, apparently, on a realistic fear of Negro recalcitrance. Settlements of runaway slaves were reported in 1672, 1691 and 1711. The runaways were so destructive that special laws were passed to encourage the hunting down and killing of them. In 1691, a slave named Mingoe headed a band of blacks in Rappahannock County who took cattle and sheep and "two guns and a Carbyne and other things."

In 1687, the slaves of the Northern Neck area plotted to kill all the whites in the vicinity. By 1694, lawlessness had become endemic among the Negroes, and Governor Edmund Andros complained that the codes were being inefficiently administered.

The institutionalization of slavery in Maryland followed a pattern roughly similar to the developments in Virginia. The statistics of the Negro population are fragmentary, but by 1663, it was apparently so large that the colony began to pass laws giving statutory recognition to slavery. By the turn of the eighteenth century, several hundred Negroes were coming into the colony annually. For example, about 700 blacks arrived during one ten-month period in 1708. By 1750, there were 43,000 Negroes in the colony and 100,000 whites. In 1780, there were 80,500 blacks and 169,000 whites.

Maryland's agriculture was based largely on the tobacco economy, and large units of production were common throughout the colonial period. By 1790, for example, in the slaveholding counties in Maryland, the average holding ranged from between 8 to 13 slaves. Thus the slaves in Maryland became increasingly subject to depersonalizing gang-labor conditions.

Records are available of some attempts on the part of Maryland's Negroes to strike out against the slave system. There are several cases of poisoning and arson but no instances of attempted mass insurrection. By the late seventeenth century, Maryland had evolved a slave code somewhat similar to Virginia's. In 1659, laws were passed covering the return and treatment of fugitive slaves. A few years later, statutes were enacted that forbade slaves to deal in stolen goods and liquor. In the elaboration of her slave code, Maryland profited from the experience of her neighbors—and especially from Virginia's experience in establishing a firm legal basis for slavery early in her existence.

The founders of the Carolinas provided in the Fundamental Constitutions that "every freeman of Carolina shall have absolute power and authority over his Negro slaves, of what opinion or religion soever." Thus, with one blow, they established the legal basis for slave status that was developed so painfully in Virginia over a period of three generations. Four of the original eight lords proprietors of the colony were members of the Royal African Company. In 1663, they offered each settler twenty acres for every Negro man brought into the colony and five acres for every black woman.

Rice was introduced into the colony in 1694, and from this date on slaves were imported rapidly to work the enormous plantations in the South Carolina tidewater region.

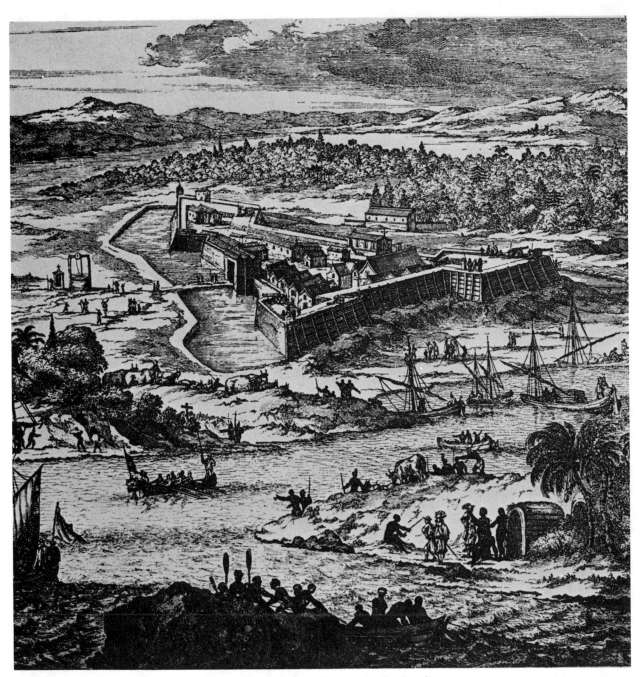

One of the earliest settlements in the Carolinas.

As early as 1710, there were over 6,000 whites in the colony and 4,000 black slaves. And the Negro population continued to grow with the size of the rice crop. In 1724, for example, when 4,000 tons of rice were exported from South Carolina, there were 14,000 whites and 32,000 slaves in the colony. In 1749, the exports had risen to 14,000 tons, and the colony contained 25,000 whites and 39,000 slaves. In 1765, a rice crop of 33,000 tons was worked by 65,000 slaves, while there were 40,000 whites in the colony.

More than any other colony, South Carolina suffered from fear of its slaves. The overwhelming numbers of blacks required rigidly enforced slave codes if any sort of social order and peace were to be maintained. Thus, the South Carolinians borrowed their slave codes largely from Barbados, where a similar situation prevailed. Laws to ensure discipline were passed as early as 1686. Negroes were forbidden to engage in any sort of trade. Negroes could not leave their master's place between sunset and sunrise without a note of explanation. Murder, burglary and arson were punishable by death. For the first time, patrols of slaves were established and given disciplinary authority over less trusted blacks. Even a chronic light offender was subject to execution.

South Carolina, like New York, suffered terribly from black violence and insurrections. As early as 1711, the inhabitants of Charleston were held "in great fear and terror" by menacing runaway slaves, or maroons. Following a revolt near Charleston in 1720, several slaves were burned alive and others were banished. There was another outbreak near Charleston in 1730. The famous Cato conspiracy began in 1739 on a plantation about twenty miles west of Charleston. A large group of slaves seized guns from a warehouse and prepared to fight their way to freedom in Florida. They were stopped at the expense of thirty white and forty-four black lives.

In 1733, the governor of South Carolina offered a reward of "twenty pounds alive" and "ten pounds dead" for maroons in South Carolina. The number of maroons in 1765 was apparently so large that many leading colonists actually feared open rebellion, and, indeed, several pitched battles were fought between white troops and black runaways. In June of 1740, 200 Negroes in the Charleston area once again attempted insurrection. This particular plot was uncovered, but during this same year Negroes were suspected of causing a fire that did considerable damage to the city.

During the colonial period, the development of slavery in Georgia also was related to the development of the rice crop, for rice was as important in that colony as it was in South Carolina. Georgia, however, was unique in its inception. James Oglethorpe, a wealthy and public-spirited man, is largely credited with the founding of the colony in 1732. The colonization of Georgia was seen by Oglethorpe to have many advantages; it could provide a refuge for debtors and for persecuted Protestants; could act as a defensive force against French and Spanish expansion; and could eventually provide raw materials, such as skins, silk, hemp, flax and lumber to the mother country.

With these mixed goals, Georgia was opened to "charity" settlers and adventurers. Rules at first were strict. Ownership of land was not permitted; holdings were in the form of grants and could not be sold, although a son could inherit them. Furthermore, slaves were not allowed, chiefly for two reasons. First, the area was extremely vulnerable to Indian attacks, and it was thought that the presence of slaves would increase the danger of revolts. Second, the products England

JAMES OGLETHORPE

hoped to obtain from Georgia needed skilled labor. Georgia, however, did not develop according to plans and expectations.

The political history of Georgia for the first few decades of its existence is largely the history of the attempts of the colonists to avoid the restrictions placed upon them by Oglethorpe and other underwriters. The Georgia colonists, seeing the success of their South Carolina neighbors with large rice plantations, fought bitterly against the restrictions on slave purchasing and the consolidation of estates. After several petitions were rejected by their London overlords, in 1741 many settlers began to hire slaves on one-hundred-year terms from sympathetic Carolinians. Gradually, it became clear to the proprietors that Georgia faced economic disaster if the settlers were not given some free rein. There were about five thousand whites in Georgia in 1737; by 1741, all but five hundred were gone.

The prohibition against the purchase of Negroes was repealed in 1750. Certain restrictions were introduced: the sanctity of Negro marriages was held inviolate; Negroes were to be inspected upon entrance by health officers; and Negroes were to be tried according to English common law. These laws were weakly enforced, if at all, and within the decade, Georgia was on its way to becoming a slave colony. By 1760, there were about 3,500 Negroes in the colony and 6,000 whites. By 1770, there were about 10,500 blacks and 13,000 whites. In 1780, there were about 21,000 blacks and almost 36,000 whites.

The Georgia slave code was a nearly complete adaptation of the South Carolina code. It was equally as severe—the result of South Carolina's experience of insurrection, arson and insubordination. It is surprising, then, that there appear to have been few if any insurrections in Georgia during the colonial period. It may be that Florida, then a Spanish colony, drew the more rebellious slaves to it

And be it further Enacted by the Authority aforesaid that if any Slave shall presume to Strike any White person such Slave upon Trial and Conviction before the Justice or Justices and Freeholders aforesaid according to the direction of this Act shall for the first and Second Offence suffer such punishment as the said Justice and Freeholders or such of them as are impowered to try such Offences shall in their discretion think fitt not extending to Life or Limb and for the Third Offence shall suffer Death but in Case any such Slave shall greviously Wound Maim or Bruise any White person tho' it shall be only the first Offence such Slave shall suffer Death . . ..

In Georgia, the slave codes were quite severe—a major reason, perhaps, for the low number of insurrections experienced there during the colonial period.

as runaways. During the seventies, however, many colonies of fugitive slaves gradually developed.

In certain respects, North Carolina was the polar opposite of South Carolina and Georgia. Slavery never took root there, which probably accounts for the fact that North Carolina was one of the strongest southern antislavery states. The colony had been settled by poorer Virginia farmers, Scotch-Irish, Germans and Quakers, who had little interest, moral or economic, in slavery. There was no good port for the entrance of the black cargoes or for the export of great quantities of tobacco. The soil was poorer, except in a few counties in the east, than in most of the southern colonies, and there was therefore no incentive to plantation-style agriculture, which would have required a larger labor force.

When North Carolina separated from South Carolina in 1729, there were only about 6,000 Negroes among 24,000 whites. In 1750, there were 19,800 Negroes and 53,000 whites. Economic conditions, plus the presence of an active Quaker group, tended to limit the black population. There were no slave insurrections in North Carolina during this period, a fact probably best explained by the lack of impersonal treatment on large plantations.

THE COLONIAL EXPERIENCE AND THE ORIGINS OF RACIAL PREJUDICE

In order to understand modern American racial problems, it makes sense to search for their sources in the colonial era. In the first confrontation between black and white, attitudes and values were formed that ultimately influenced the present situation.

Nineteenth-century historians more or less assumed that Virginia's first blacks were enslaved immediately upon debarkation. A later historian explained their attitude in the following statement: "So close was their acquaintance with the problem of slavery that it could not occur to them that Negroes could ever have been anything but slaves." Implicit in this assumption was the concept that Negroes were naturally inferior and the notion that the white settlers, in recognizing this, were inherently prejudiced.

During the course of the first half of the twentieth century, these attitudes underwent some important modifications. Increasingly, it was shown that the slave system had evolved gradually. It was argued that there had been a period, in many of the northern and southern colonies, during which Negro servants had lived and worked alongside white servants. Oscar and Mary Handlin, in their discussion of the evolution of the slave system, asked, "If whites and Negroes could share the same status of half-freedom for forty years in the seventeenth century, why could they not share full freedom in the twentieth?" Prejudice was not "natural" and therefore could be eradicated.

In 1959, Carl Degler (*Out of Our Past*) returned to the nineteenth-century assumptions. He attempted to disprove the assertion that slavery had preceded race prejudice and argued that race prejudice, in fact, had actually caused slavery. It has been suggested that Degler's theory was at least indirectly proven by the rigid attitude of the southern states on desegregation and the general pessimism that prevailed concerning the future of American race relations during this period.

In 1962, however, a new formulation was suggested by a southern historian, Winthrop Jordan, writing in the *Journal of Southern History*. In attempting to put an end to a fruitless controversy that, given the paucity of documentation, could not be solved, Jordan found evidence to suggest slavery and racial prejudice had begun at the same time. Slavery and racial prejudice were twin aspects of the general debasement of the African in the New World. Jordan suggested that the ideology of racial prejudice and the economic system of slavery had interacted throughout the years, and that historians, therefore, should not look for mechanistic answers to the question of causation.

It is clear that there is a fundamental connection between our knowledge of the past and our ability to understand the present. It is inevitable, therefore, that the literature on this question will grow as American historians attempt to understand the roots of present problems.

CHAPTER FIVE

The Free Negro in the Colonial Era

THE record of the increase in the number of free Negroes during the colonial period is unreliable. Even the records for the slave population are largely matters of estimation because there were no tabulations prior to the United States Census of 1790. However, we do know that even after the Revolution, during which so many people came to question the morality of Negro enslavement, there were still relatively few free Negroes in the United States.

According to the first census, there were 59,557 free Negroes in the country. They were distributed as follows:

FREE NEGROES IN THE UNITED STATES IN 1790

NEW ENGLAND SECTION		MIDDLE SECTION		SOUTHERN SECTION	
Massachusetts	5,369	Pennsylvania	6,531	Virginia	12,866
Rhode Island	3,484	New York	4,682	Maryland	8,043
Connecticut	2,771	New Jersey	2,762	North Carolina	5,041
New Hampshire	630			Delaware	3,899
Maine	536			South Carolina	1,801
Vermont	269			Georgia	398
				Tennessee	361
				Kentucky	114
TOTALS:	13,059		13,975		32,523

We must assume, of course, that the percentage of free Negroes in the population was even smaller during the colonial period proper, for many were manumitted as a direct result of the Revolutionary War.

If the free Negroes formed such a small percentage of the colonial population, it may be reasonable to ask why modern historians seek to understand them and their behavior. The answer is that, in studying the lives of the free Negroes in the colonial era, we can perhaps begin to understand one aspect of our own modern race problem. Beginning in the colonial period, a predominantly white Protestant society was confronted with a group of cultural "outsiders" who were free men and yet were not treated as equals, whose legal and social status was somewhere between freedom and slavery. An understanding of this first confrontation from the point of view of white men and from the point of view of the free Negroes can cast some light upon the general course of the history of American race relations.

SOURCES OF THE FREE NEGRO POPULATION

The free Negro population came into being and grew in three main ways. Many Negroes came to this country as regular indentured servants and obtained their freedom when their stipulated term of service had expired. Freedom also accrued to the offspring of several types of interracial unions; and many

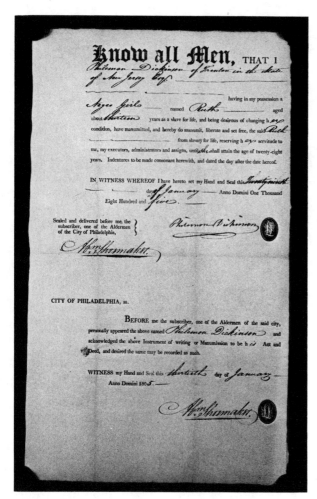

In this manumission document, an owner declares that his slave Ruth is to be set free, but he reserves the right to her services until she reaches the age of twenty-eight.

slaveholders freed their slaves by the process of manumission.

An important source of free Negroes was the indentured servant class. Many of the first blacks brought into Virginia won their freedom after serving for a specific number of years. The following contract, which was agreed upon in 1648, illustrates the changing status of many blacks during the seventeenth century:

> Be it thought fitt and asserted unto by Mr. Steph. Charlton in Court, that Jno. G. Hamander Negro, his servant, shall from ye date hereof serve ye sd Mr. Charlton . . . until ye last days of November who shall be in ye year of our Lord . . . one thousand six hundred Fifty eight and then said Negro is to be a free man.

There is reliable evidence that as late as 1665 a Negro who came into the colony was indentured for only five years.

In 1661, in Virginia, the status of the black slave became hereditary and increasingly irrevocable. E. Franklin Frazier (*The Negro in the United States*) suggested that slavery had triumphed generally over servitude for Negroes in the 1680's. There can be no doubt that a large segment of the colonial free Negro population was created before the distinction between servitude and slavery was drawn clearly.

As late as the eighteenth century, in some of the older colonies, some free Negroes could trace their ancestry to Negroes who had never been enslaved. In New Jersey, for example, Negro servitude continued to exist side by side with slavery well into the eighteenth century.

Many Negroes were born into freedom during the colonial era as the offspring of interracial unions. Such children stood a much better chance than average of avoiding slave status. It is recorded, for example, that in Maryland in 1755, 0.87 per cent, or 357, of the state's 41,143 Negroes were free. In sharp contrast, however, 1,760, or 35.1 per cent, of all mulattoes in the state were free.

Many of these mulattoes, of course, were offspring of free masters and slave women. Frequently, these children were doted upon by their wealthy fathers and freed when they reached maturity. Many were products of unions between slaves and Indians. We know of many Negro families of the colonial period, both in the North and in the South, who intermarried with Indians. In Virginia, one tribe, the Pamunkeys, became virtually Negro over a period of generations because of the steady admixture of African elements. Another Virginia tribe, the Gingaskin, by the end of the century had at least half black blood in them. According to the local whites, the reservation afforded "a Harbour and convenient asylum to an idle set of free

13. And for prevention of that abominable mixture and spurious issue, which hereafter may increase in this government, by white men and women intermarrying with indians, negroes, mustees, or mulattoes, *be it enacted by the authority aforesaid,* That if any white man or woman, being free, shall intermarry with an indian, negro, mustee or mulatto man or woman, or any person of mixt blood, to the third generation, bond or free, he shall, by judgment of the county court forfeit and pay the sum of fifty pounds, proclamation money to the use of the parish.

14. *And be it further enacted by the authority aforesaid,* That no minister of the church of England, or other minister or justice of the peace, or other person whatsoever within this government, shall hereafter presume to marry a white man with an indian, negro, mustee or mulatto woman, or any person of mixt blood, as aforesaid, knowing them to be so, upon pain of forfeiting and paying, for every such offence, the sum of fifty pounds, proclamation money; to be applied as aforesaid.

This North Carolina law imposed a fifty-pound penalty on any white man or woman who married an "indian, negro, mustee, or mullato." It also imposed a fifty-pound penalty on the minister who performed the ceremony.

Negroes." In Massachusetts and in New England in general, there were similar examples of intermarriages, especially with members of the Pequote tribes. The children of unions between slave men and Indian women were, of course, free, as were the children of free Negro men and Indian women, or free Negro women and Indian men.

The children of black men, slave or free, and white women also were considered free, for the child inherited the status of the mother. That Negro-white unions occurred frequently enough to arouse the ire of the white citizenry is indicated by the fact that, in 1715, North Carolina imposed a fifty-pound penalty on each party in such a marriage. In 1691, a Virginia law fated to perpetual banishment "any white woman marrying a negro or mullatoe, slave or free." Shortly after the law was enacted, Ann Wall, an Englishwoman, and two of her mulatto children were bound out for indenture to a man in Norfolk County and ordered never to return to their home in Elizabeth City under threat of banishment to the Barbados. In Maryland, the children of Negro-white unions also comprised a sizable portion of the free Negro population.

Other increases in the free Negro population in the seventeenth century came about because of the ambiguous legal status of the blacks. The fact that slavery was ill defined as an institution for at least the first half of the century in Virginia resulted in a larger number of free Negroes. Perhaps this explains why the free Negro population of Virginia, in 1790, was over 12,000, so much larger than that of South Carolina, which was about 1,800. The status of slavery in South Carolina, as has already been illustrated, was more or less precisely defined from the outset.

Many seventeenth-century documents attest the existence of a class of free Negroes who gained their freedom much as did white indentured servants. Scarcely a decade after slavery was legally recognized in Virginia, a law was passed stating that "No Negro or Indian, though baptized and enjoyned their own freedome shall be capable of any purchase of Christians, but yet not debarred from buying any of their owne nation." Thus, limits were placed on the ability of free Negroes to enslave whites, but their legal existence and their lawful prerogative to purchase other blacks as slaves were formally recognized.

The third source of the free Negro population was manumission, that is, the setting free of slaves by their masters. Many masters throughout the colonies appear to have contributed to the free Negro population by manumitting their old slaves so they would not be in the position of having to support them in their unproductive years. New Jersey passed a law, in 1713, claiming "that free negroes are an idle and slothful people, and prove very often a charge to the place where they are." It was decreed that anyone planning to manumit a slave had to give some assurance that the freed man would be able to support himself. Similar laws were passed in Pennsylvania (1726), Delaware (1739), Massachusetts (1703), Connecticut (1702), Rhode Island (1728 and 1755), Maryland (1728), North Carolina (1752) and New York (1712 and 1717).

Manumission frequently was based on the personal relationship between master and slave. That is, indulgent masters sometimes freed slaves after long and meritorious services, because of a particular act of heroism, or because they had promised them freedom. These private manumissions were increasing in frequency in Virginia when they were limited in 1691 to cases wherein the master paid the charges for transporting the Negro out of the colony. In New York, there were for many years no restrictions on private manumission. There were simply regulations assuring that the freed slaves would be able to provide for themselves. One historian has suggested, interestingly, that "most manumissions were motivated not by philanthropy, but by pressures brought by the slaves themselves. Most masters recognized that freedom made the blacks more productive. Many blacks brought pressure for manumission by malingering, stalling, and in general, making it clear that they would perform better as wage workers rather than as slaves." In Maryland, although there were few manumissions during the colonial period, the majority were based upon either a blood relationship to the master or long service.

During the late colonial period, a new phenomenon developed. An increasingly large number of slaveholders began to free their slaves for ideological instead of merely for sentimental or practical reasons. Slavery was

And be it further enacted by the authority aforesaid, That when the owner or owners of any slave, under fifty years of age, and of sufficient ability to provide for himself, or herself, shall be disposed to manumit such slave, he, she or they, shall previous thereto, procure a certificate, signed by the overseers of the poor, or the major part of them, of the city, town or place, and of two justices of the peace of the county, where such person or persons shall dwell or reside; and if in the cities of New York or Albany, then from the mayor or recorder, and any two of the aldermen, certifying that such slave appears to be under fifty years of age, and of sufficient ability to provide for himself, or herself, and shall cause such certificate of manumission, to be registered in the office of the clerk of the city, town or place, in which the owner or owners of such slave, may reside; that then it shall be lawful for such person or persons, to manumit such slave, without giving or providing any security, to indemnify such city, town or place. And every slave so manumitted, shall be deemed, adjudged and taken, to be free; and the clerk for registering such certificate, shall be entitled to two shillings, and no more.

The New York legislature's requirements for manumission of slaves under fifty years of age.

an evolving institution during this period, and therefore was subject to considerable criticism from a moral and even from an economic standpoint. Thus, before we can deal with ideologically motivated manumissions, we must understand something of their ideological background.

THE ROOTS OF ANTISLAVERY SENTIMENT

Abolitionists were seen on the one hand as wild-eyed fanatics who were believers in a "higher law" than the Constitution, who sought to impose their own particular moral vision on a perhaps less uplifted, but more practical, citizenry. On the other hand, the said "practical" citizens usually viewed the abolitionists as soft-headed visionaries with no understanding of economic or social realities.

Early abolitionism—or perhaps emancipationism—began, in certain of its aspects, as a highly pragmatic movement. Many seventeenth- and early eighteenth-century mercantilists, for example, disliked slavery because it discouraged and limited white migration. Thus, in Georgia, perhaps the purest incarnation of mercantilist ideas of what a colony should be, slavery was barred until 1750. The earlier mercantilist thinkers also opposed slave labor for fear of difficulty in assimilating the Negro into colonial culture and his potential as an internal enemy. They opposed slavery because it created a large class of nonconsumers and because the importation of slaves only put the colonies further into debt. In 1738, for example, one Carolina writer expressed the fear that slavery would, in the long run, hold back the economic future of the colony:

> I cannot avoid observing that altho' a few Negroes annually imported into the province might be of Advantage to most people, yet such large importation of 2,600 or 2,800 every year is not only a loss to many, but in the end may prove the Ruin of the Province, as it most certainly does that of many industrious Planters who unwarily engage in buying more than they have occasion or are able to pay for.

The mercantilists began to change their attitude toward the end of the colonial period, for it had become accepted that slave labor was virtually the only source of economic manpower available to the colonies.

Antislavery sentiment was encouraged by members of the religious sect known as the Society of Friends, or Quakers. The Quakers had originally settled in Pennsylvania and western New Jersey and were responsible for the fact that slavery never really took hold in either of these areas. Quakers on Long Island, New York, and in western North Carolina also made their voices heard increasingly

on the moral as well as the practical problems of slavery. The Quaker opposition to slavery was based primarily on a simple appeal to the Golden Rule: one did not uphold slavery because one would not want others to enslave him. Quaker pacifism also opposed slavery because most slaves had been taken by violent and immoral means from their homelands, and to possess slaves was to encourage this practice. Finally, the Quakers opposed slavery on the grounds that it maintained a population in subjugation and thus placed the whole society in danger of continued bloody slave insurrections.

In 1688, the Quakers of Germantown, Pennsylvania, wrote to the Friends' Yearly Meeting in an attempt to get the Meeting to pronounce forcibly against slavery. At that time, the Quaker position had not fully developed, and there were still many slaveholders active in the sect. Even at the Yearly Meeting of 1696, the Quakers were not fully prepared to confront the issue directly. Rather, it was suggested that: "Friends do, as much as may be, avoid buying such Negroes as shall hereafter be brought in, rather than offend any Friends who are against it; yet this is only a caution and not a censure."

It was not until 1758 that the Friends' Yearly Meeting in Philadelphia adopted the rule that all Quakers who imported slaves should themselves be excluded from church. In the same year, the Quakers appointed a committee to visit and "treat with" those who kept slaves, to see what the possibilities were for emancipating all Quaker-owned slaves. By 1776, most northern Quaker Meetings had formally banned all slave-owners from membership; Maryland and Virginia Quakers followed their example in 1788.

Although the formal Yearly Meeting took three-quarters of a century to ban slavery among its members after the issue was first raised, the Quakers produced many antislavery leaders during this period who did obtain *de facto* emancipation of slaves in many

THIS IS TO Yᵉ MONTHLY MEETING HELD AT RICHARD WORRELL'S.

These are the reasons why we are against the traffick of men-body, as followeth. Is there any that would be done or handled at this manner? viz. to be sold or made a slave for all the time of his life? How fearful and faint-hearted are many on sea, when they see a strange vessel,—being afraid it should be a Turk, and they should be taken, and sold for slaves into Turkey. Now what is this better done, as Turks doe? Yea, rather is it worse for them, which say they are Christians; for we hear that yᵉ most part of such negers are brought hither against their will and consent, and that many of them are stolen. Now, tho they are black, we can not conceive there is more liberty to have them slaves, as it is to have other white ones. There is a saying, that we shall doe to all men like as we will be done ourselves; making no difference of what generation, descent or colour they are. And those who steal or robb men, and those who buy or purchase them, are they not all alike? Here is liberty of conscience, wᶜʰ is right and reasonable; here ought to be likewise liberty of yᵉ body, except of evil-doers, wᶜʰ is an other case. But to bring men hither, or to rob and sell them against their will, we stand against. In Europe there are many oppressed for conscience sake; and here there are those oppressed wʰ are of a black colour. And we who know that men must not comitt adultery, —some do committ adultery, in others, separating wives from their husbands and giving them to others; and some sell the children of these poor creatures to other men. Ah! doe consider well this thing, you who doe it, if you would be done at this manner? and if it is done according to Christianity? You surpass Holland and Germany in this thing. This makes an ill report in all those countries of Europe, where they hear off, that yᵉ Quakers doe here handel men as they handel there yᵉ cattle. And for that reason some have no mind or inclination to come hither. And who shall maintain this your cause, or pleid for it? Truly we can not do so, except you shall inform us better hereof, viz., that Christians have liberty to practise these things. Pray, what thing in the world can be done worse towards us, than if men should rob or steal us away, and sell us for slaves to strange countries; separating housbands from their wives and children. Being now this is not done in the manner we would be done at therefore we contradict and are against this traffic of men-body. And we who profess that it is not lawful to steal, must, likewise, avoid to purchase such things as are stolen, but rather help to stop this robbing and stealing if possible. And such men ought to be delivered out of yᵉ hands of yᵉ robbers, and set free as well as in Europe. Then is Pennsylvania to have a good report, instead it hath now a bad one for this sake in other countries. Especially whereas yᵉ Europeans are desirous to know in what manner yᵉ Quakers doe rule in their province;—and most of them doe look upon us with an envious eye. But if this is done well, what shall we say is done evil?

If once these slaves (wᶜʰ they say are so wicked and stubborn men) should joint themselves,—fight for their freedom,—and handel their masters and mastrisses as they did handel them before; will these masters and mastrisses take the sword at hand and warr against these poor slaves, licke, we are able to believe, some will not refuse to doe; or have these negers not as much right to fight for their freedom, as you have to keep them slaves?

Now consider well this thing, if it is good or bad? And in case you find it to be good to handel these blacks at that manner, we desire and require you hereby lovingly, that you may inform us herein, which at this time never was done, viz., that Christians have such a liberty to do so. To the end we shall be satisfied in this point, and satisfie likewise our good friends and acquaintances in our natif country, to whose it is a terror, or fairful thing, that men should be handeld so in Pennsylvania.

This is from our meeting at Germantown, held yᵉ 18 of the 2 month, 1688, to be delivered to the Monthly Meeting at Richard Worrel's.

　　　　　　　　　　　　　　　Garret henderichs
　　　　　　　　　　　　　　　derick up de graeff
　　　　　　　　　　　　　　　Francis daniell Pastorius
　　　　　　　　　　　　　　　Abraham up Den graef.

At our Monthly Meeting at Dublin, yᵉ 30—2 mo., 1688. we having inspected yᵉ matter, above mentioned, and considered of it, we find it so weighty that we think it not expedient for us to meddle with it here, but do rather commit it to yᵉ consideration of yᵉ Quarterly Meeting; yᵉ tenor of it being nearly related to yᵉ Truth.

　　　　　　　　　　　　　On behalf of yᵉ Monthly Meeting,
　　　　　　Signed,　　　　　　P.　　　　　　Jo. HART.

This, above mentioned, was read in our Quarterly Meeting at Philadelphia, the 4 of yᵉ 4th mo. '88, and was from thence recommended to the Yearly Meeting, and the above said Derick, and the other two mentioned therein. to present the same to yᵉ above said meeting, it being a thing of too great a weight for this meeting to determine.

　　　　　　　　Signed by order of yᵉ meeting,
　　　　　　　　　　　　　　　　ANTHONY MORRIS.

YEARLY MEETING MINUTE ON THE ABOVE PROTEST.

At a Yearly Meeting held at Burlington the 5th day of the 7th mouth, 1688.

A Paper being here presented by some German Friends Concerning the Lawfulness and Unlawfulness of Buying and keeping Negroes, It was adjudged not to be so proper for this Meeting to give a Positive Judgment in the Case, It having so General a Relation to many other Parts, and therefore at present they forbear It.

The Germantown Friends' protest against slavery, 1688, and the ruling of the Yearly Meeting on their protest.

In 1754, Woolman wrote a pamphlet entitled *Some Considerations on the Keeping of Negroes, Part I*; and shortly afterward he followed this with his essay *Considerations on Keeping Negroes, Part II*. So convincing were his arguments, both written and spoken, that he had a considerable influence on the acceptance of antislavery thought. According to his biographer, Janet Payne Whitney, "Deeply was the Society of Friends affected by Woolman's labor, especially throughout the Philadelphia Yearly Meeting. Quakers became uneasy about owning a slave. . . ."

Anthony Benezet wrote a caustic article, *A Caution and Warning to Great Britain and Her Colonies*, lashing out at the slave trade. He stated:

> . . . much might be justly said of the temporal evils which attend this practice [the trade] as it is destructive of the welfare of human society, and of the peace and prosperity of every country in proportion as it prevails. It might also be shown, that it destroys the bonds of natural affection and interest, whereby mankind in general are united . . . it is inconsistent with the plainest precepts of the Gospel, the dictates of reason, and every common sentiment of humanity.

areas of New Jersey and North Carolina. Perhaps the leading antislavery agitators among the Quakers of this period were Anthony Benezet of Philadelphia and John Woolman of New Jersey. Both of these men put forth a steady stream of propaganda against slavery, urging their fellow Quakers and fellow Americans to manumit their slaves. A flood of leaflets, articles, books, speeches and petitions flowed from the pens of these agitators. The peak of their activity was roughly 1740–60, and in many ways they laid the basis for the revulsion against human bondage that was to come with the Revolution.

Long before the Yearly Meeting had declared that slavery was forbidden, therefore, many individual Quakers had begun to put their principles into action by manumitting their slaves. So active were the North Carolina Quakers in manumitting their slaves that, as early as 1741, the provincial legislature, to counteract their "promiscuous manumission," declared that manumission was to be regulated by the courts and was to be awarded only for meritorious services. The Quaker sentiment for manumission even influenced non-Quakers, and as the Revolution grew closer, manumissions grew in number. In New York, for example, one master freed all his slaves "believing it to be consistent with the will of kind Providence who hath created all nations with one blood." There are many records of New Yorkers manumitting their slaves "in order to serve the community." It is not known that their masters were Quakers, but it is certain that they were influenced by this benevolent group. It is known also that, when manumissions were actually forbidden in North Carolina, many Quaker groups actually bought slaves and formally owned them but in practice permitted them to operate as though they were free.

Antislavery sentiment in New England, in the words of Negro historian Lorenzo Greene, "down to the revolutionary period manifested itself only in spasmodic utterances by a few high-souled and humanely sympathetic men." During these pre-Revolutionary years, moral outcry against slavery does not appear to have been a significant factor in New England's cultural life, perhaps because the New England ideology found a place for the idea of slavery in its Old Testament heritage.

Several New England men, nonetheless, did begin early to lay the groundwork for the creation of a popular antislavery movement. Perhaps the foremost of these was Chief Justice Samuel Sewall of Massachusetts, who published *The Selling of Joseph* in 1700. Here he combined moral arguments against slavery with mercantilist notions to the effect that slavery was damaging to the colonial economy. Negroes, he said, were unassimilable into the body politic and therefore contributed nothing to it. Their ineligibility for military service, for example, added nothing to colonial security. White labor, he said, was more productive—and a white working class would consume as well as produce. He claimed that the presence of slave women, pliant to their masters' wishes, destroyed the moral fabric of society. Finally, he concluded that "Liberty is valued next to life, none should part with it themselves or deprive others of it, save upon most mature consideration."

SAMUEL SEWALL

Sewall published, in 1706, *An Essay or Computation That the Importation of Negroes Is Not So Profitable As That of White Servants*. Sewall argued again that Negroes were lazy and thievish and that a white working class would be far more reliable and productive. He argued that a white working class would add to the body politic, while the children of slaves would not. Sewall himself had a Negro slave, whom he employed for wages.

The Quaker agitators also were active in colonial New England. Elihu Coleman of Nantucket, a Quaker minister, wrote, in 1737, *A Testimony against That Anti-Christian Practice of Making Slaves of Men*. Along with the Quakers of Philadelphia and New Jersey, he simply argued that the primary rule of life was the Golden Rule, and that slavery, therefore, was inexcusable.

We can see that the antislavery agitation had at least some effect in New England, or at any rate was not totally isolated from the

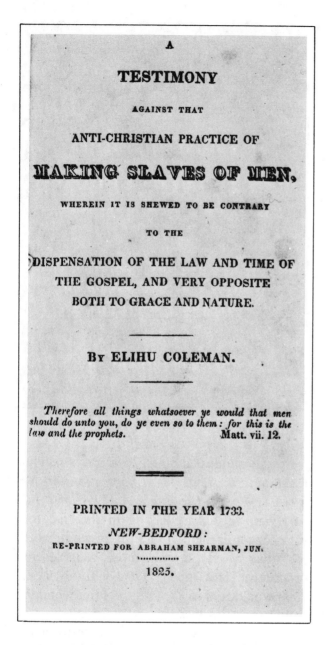

A

TESTIMONY

AGAINST THAT

ANTI-CHRISTIAN PRACTICE OF

MAKING SLAVES OF MEN,

WHEREIN IT IS SHEWED TO BE CONTRARY

TO THE

DISPENSATION OF THE LAW AND TIME OF
THE GOSPEL, AND VERY OPPOSITE
BOTH TO GRACE AND NATURE.

———

By ELIHU COLEMAN.

———

*Therefore all things whatsoever ye would that men
should do unto you, do ye even so to them: for this is the
law and the prophets.*   Matt. vii. 12.

———

PRINTED IN THE YEAR 1733.

NEW-BEDFORD:
RE-PRINTED FOR ABRAHAM SHEARMAN, JUN.
....
1825.

mainstream of New England thought. As early as 1652, the independent government of Providence and Warwick in Rhode Island had decreed that slavery was to be abolished within ten years. And in 1701, the selectmen of Boston read into their minutes a resolution to the effect that white labor was to be preferred over black.

The final source of the free Negro population in the colonial period of our country was, therefore, ideologically motivated manumission. We have no way of knowing how large a percentage of the colonial slaves were manumitted because their masters opposed slavery as a system. We do know, however, that in many areas the agitation of these principled men led to some manumissions. During 1726, for example, the Quakers of North Carolina secured the freedom of a number of slaves in two counties of the colony. These Negroes were seized and later resold into slavery, for it was claimed that they had never been legally emancipated. The Quakers brought suit in the Superior Court of the Edenton District, and the Court held that the slaves had been deprived unlawfully of their liberty and accordingly must be set free.

Although we cannot make any quantitative judgments about the extent of manumissions, and particularly about those that were ideologically motivated, there are two major conclusions that many historians have drawn from the fragmentary evidence that does exist. First, manumissions in general were an extremely important source of the free Negro population during the early part of the century; and, second, they declined in importance as the ideology of the approaching American Revolution gave new impetus to antislavery sentiment and many slaveholders became fearful of total abolition.

Early in the eighteenth century, most states passed laws limiting private manumissions, apparently hoping to end the manumission of superannuated or otherwise incompetent slaves, so as to avoid the burden of caring for unproductive chattels. Virginia, with perhaps the most severe free Negro problem, attempted to deal even more decisively with the situation. In 1723, manumission was prohibited, except in the case of some meritorious services. These meritorious services—which ordinarily consisted of informing on other slaves—were to be judged and allowed by government council. South Carolina passed a similar law in 1735, adding to this that manumission was voided if the freed slave was found in the colony twelve months after manumission. In the North, New Jersey began restricting manumissions in 1704, and New York followed suit in 1712. New York required the manumitter to legally ensure the good behavior of the freeman by posting a bond. The point of the law of 1712 was to make manumission financially prohibitive. It was repealed, however, in 1717.

By the middle of the eighteenth century, the free Negro population had grown large enough to cause considerable trepidation among the master class and among the white community in general. The colonial Americans thought of the free Negroes as an alien element within the body politic, an element not subject to the same sort of social discipline as slaves.

We have seen that each colony attempted to make manumission into a public function, or to otherwise limit it. The first such public manumission occurred in Charleston, South Carolina, in 1712, when a slave was freed for informing on an insurrectionary plot. During most of the eighteenth century, therefore, flight remained the primary course of action open to those Negroes who wanted freedom. Numerous colonies of runaway Negro slaves existed, especially in the southern states; although the members of these communities were not legally free, they were certainly no longer subject to the will of the white community. Colonies of this sort were found largely in South Carolina, but also in North Carolina, Virginia and Georgia. Hundreds of slaves, as evidenced by advertisements of rewards offered for recapture, ran away during the colonial period and a certain percentage of them actually gained their freedom. They took refuge in Canada and among the Spaniards in Florida.

In 1715, there were reported to be 58,850 free Negroes in the colonies out of a total Negro population of approximately 434,600. By

During the eighteenth century, when flight was the primary course open to Negroes who wanted freedom, the tracking down of runaway slaves by both bounty-hunters and slave-owners was common.

1790, there were only about 59,557. The greatest increase in the free Negro population appears to have occurred in the seventeenth and early eighteenth centuries, while the remainder of the eighteenth century saw an increasing reaction against the spirit of manumission and liberalism.

By the late eighteenth century, the greatest concentrations of free Negroes appear to have been in and around the cities. It was in the cities that the ideas of the Enlightenment had their first impact and led to manumissions; it was there also that slavery seemed most useless. It was in the cities that slaves were able to develop, in those early years, close personal relations with their masters. Class and caste lines were less rigid than on the plantations, and the cities, therefore, seem to have provided the best haven for a class that was not enslaved yet not fully free.

THE LEGAL STATUS OF THE FREE NEGRO

The free Negro's legal status was never certain. Obviously, he was not a slave, and there were even attempts to minimize his association with the slaves. Yet it was continually made clear to him that neither was he the equal of a white man.

The laws of the 1660's and later, recognizing the existence of slavery, also recognized the existence of the free Negro class. The free Negroes were guaranteed the right to employ servants and slaves as long as they were Negro. This did not mean, however, that the free Negro in Virginia was to be treated as a citizen. By the act of 1723, for example, free Negroes in Virginia were forbidden to hold meetings or to visit with slaves. They were also deprived of any voting rights they might previously have held. By laws of 1751, 1755 and 1757, Negroes in the militia of Virginia were prohibited from bearing arms. As far back as 1680, it had already been determined that no free Negro would be permitted to possess weapons.

In North Carolina, discrimination against the free Negro in a legal sense was inaugurated in 1746, when all free Negroes to the third generation were disqualified from appearing as witnesses in courts, except against each other. Discrimination against free Negroes in New Jersey is evident from the state supreme court ruling of 1701 that all Negroes in the colony were prima facie slaves and that the burden of proof of freedom was upon the Negro. By law in 1714, all Negroes in New Jersey traveling outside of their home counties had to carry proof that they were free. In the same year, it was also ruled that no free Negro could own property in his own name.

Throughout the colonies, there were legal restrictions on the free Negro. During the seventeenth century, the free Negroes of Virginia were enfranchised, but this was revoked in 1723. In North Carolina, some free Negroes were able to vote throughout the colonial period, but the high property qualifications made the majority ineligible. In Pennsylvania, they were tried by special courts, and there were special laws forbidding them to bear arms or to mix with the slaves, and laws prohibiting vagrancy. In most colonies, free Negroes had to give bond for good behavior upon entering the colony. Of the Connecticut free blacks, an anonymous writer said it was "no more expected that Negroes should have the right of suffrage in freemen's meetings and in town meetings than the Indians or women or children should have the right." Free Negroes lost the franchise in Georgia in 1754. A South Carolina statute of 1716 denied voting privileges to free Negroes and to Jews. Massachusetts similarly denied the ballot to free Negroes prior to the Revolution.

Free Negroes were restricted in their personal movement as they were not allowed to travel without passes. They were subject to special jurisdiction in the courts, and in most colonies they did not have the right to trial by jury.

Colonial authorities were frequently fearful that the free Negro population would attempt to influence or to demoralize the slaves. In Massachusetts, free Negroes were not permitted to entertain slave friends in their homes without the master's permission. The Maryland legislature passed an act, in 1723, to "prevent the tumultuous meetings and other irregularities of Negroes and other slaves." An act of Rhode Island, in 1703, prohibited free Negroes from walking the streets after nine o'clock in the evening. In Boston, Negroes were restrained under pain of imprisonment from carrying walking sticks or canes, both during the day and at night.

THE ECONOMIC POSITION OF THE FREE NEGRO

Free Negroes occupied an increasingly marginal position in the economic life of colonial society. Free white and free Negro laborers were gradually replaced by slave labor in the South; and in the North, free white labor tended to be predominant. Thus, the free Negro found his economic role more and more circumscribed.

A large proportion of the free Negro population was without secure employment since many white businessmen refused to hire blacks. Without the opportunity to work, many free Negroes became vagabonds, like similar types in the white community. Facing legal obstructions to their economic opportunity, it is not surprising that many free Negroes were without adequate employment. But as time passed, and as the country became industrialized, the number of free Negro wage earners increased.

Free Negro labor tended to be diversified wherever slave labor was also diversified—in the cities and the small farming districts. In plantation areas, free Negroes tended to operate in the interstices of economic life. Although most of the agricultural work on the plantations was performed by the slave population, the planters did employ some free Negroes for this type of labor. Some of these employers were persons who were opposed to the use of slave labor, usually on the grounds that slavery was morally wrong. Many planters in the western parts of Virginia and North Carolina preferred the free labor of Negroes to slave labor. And in the northern and middle colonies, it was not uncommon to see free Negroes at work in the fields. A small proportion of them were landowners and farmers who had come into the possession of their lands either by bequest or purchase.

A study of the county records of Virginia in the seventeenth century shows that there were many Negro mechanics in this colony. In the towns and cities, they were at work as barbers, coopers, carpenters, cabinet-makers, wheelwrights, bricklayers, tanners and as skilled craftsmen of many other types. Some of the best mechanics were free Negroes, and some Negroes were master workmen in both northern and southern colonies. They were employed in the iron factories and foundries as forgemen, firemen and helpers. White workmen frequently declined to compete with them and chose rather to become proprietors of land than to enter the trades that were followed by Negroes.

Some free Negroes were property owners and substantial citizens. The journal of a Hessian officer in 1778 stated that he observed in the English colonies that "many families of free Negroes, who live in good houses, have property and live just like the rest of the inhabitants." Their skilled labor was invaluable to the southern colonies.

Catering and the preparation of food provided employment opportunities for many. At Newport, Rhode Island, a free Negro woman with the surname Quamino, who was known as the "Duchess," conducted a very successful catering business. In the 1730's, in Providence, Rhode Island, Emmanuel Manna Bernoon opened and maintained a catering establishment. He was so successful that he and his wife later opened an oyster house. Other catering houses were opened by free Negro proprietors in New York and Philadelphia.

Competition between the races for work was keen in the middle and northern colonies. In Pennsylvania, in 1722, white workers presented a petition to the assembly urging the passage of a law to prevent the employment of Negroes. The petition stated that "the practice of the blacks being employed was a great disadvantage to them who had emigrated from Europe for the purpose of obtaining a livelihood." The assembly refused to pass a law to this effect and expressed the opinion that such opinions were dangerous.

Nonslaveholders frequently found it necessary to employ Negro laborers since no others were available. This was especially true in Maryland, Virginia and North Carolina. In many areas, the labor supply was insufficient to meet the demand, and this made it profitable for some free blacks to gain proficiency at several trades. One free Negro in Talbot County, Maryland, worked as a shoemaker, wheelwright and woodworker.

THE EDUCATION OF THE FREE NEGRO

The appeals made by religious and philanthropic organizations and individuals encouraged more humane treatment of slaves. Benevolent, paternalistic masters frequently sought to educate their slaves. Wills and bequests freeing slaves often carried provisions for their education. The Society for the Propagation of the Gospel in Foreign Parts did effective work toward the establishment of schools for free blacks. The society also attempted some work in the South. In 1741, the organization purchased two free Negroes, Harry and Andrew, and educated them to

serve as schoolmasters. Eventually, the two opened a school for free Negroes in Charleston, South Carolina. Unfortunately, legislation passed by the colonial assembly soon brought this work to a halt.

The first efforts to enlighten Negroes grew out of a desire to convert them. Puritans, Quakers and Anglicans were particularly interested in this work. The religious sects believed that the slaves should be instructed as a preparation for emancipation. Some were persecuted because of this program, which was particularly unacceptable in the southern areas. Efforts were somewhat successful in New Jersey, Pennsylvania and New York. Anthony Benezet became a teacher in Philadelphia, in 1742, and established a school for the daughters of the most prominent families. In 1750, he opened an evening school for free Negroes, and noteworthy results were obtained.

This movement for education of the free Negro spread in the years immediately before the Revolution. In Newport, Rhode Island, there was a school for free Negroes by 1773; one existed in Boston by 1798; and seven, in Philadelphia, the Quaker City, by 1797.

As a general rule, however, the colonists were indifferent about education for Negroes. Both free Negroes and slaves were relatively unenlightened, and the opportunities for one were scarcely more favorable than for the other. The records of the incorporation of Negro schools and churches in the eighteenth century have demonstrated that many of the Negro founders of these organizations were incapable of writing their names. While the education of the free Negro began with his freedom in the colonial era, it did not really become widespread until the American Revolution.

CHAPTER SIX

The Negro and the American War for Independence

AN account of the struggle of the American colonies for independence from Great Britain, of its causes and results, is beyond the scope of this book. Yet the ferment of ideas which created the intellectual climate in which the Revolution could take place, the influence of such thinkers as Locke and Rousseau, reflected in such documents as the Declaration of Independence and the Constitution, could not fail to have an effect on the "Peculiar Institution."

Almost inadvertently, the American Revolution began the destruction of American slavery. For treatises on the nature of freedom, on natural rights and natural law, on inalienable rights and guarantees of freedom could not but produce an atmosphere in which chattel slavery seemed a vicious atavism. Among Negroes and whites, opposition to slavery grew.

EARLY STEPS TOWARD ABOLITION

The intellectual atmosphere at the end of the eighteenth century, the "Age of Reason," was a catalyst for a certain type of Negro activity. As early as November 1766, Massachusetts Negroes attempted to destroy the entire legal structure of slavery by bringing an action of trespass against their masters. John Adams reported that he had "heard there have been many" such actions. There are also records of many slave petitions for freedom. In May 1774, a "Petition of a Grate Number of Blackes" was sent to the governor and general court of Massachusetts denouncing slavery as evil and destructive of natural rights.

JOHN ADAMS

There were cases in New England of Negro and white cooperation in the antislavery struggle. In western Massachusetts, a group of slaves in 1775 petitioned a local Committee of Correspondence for assistance in obtaining their freedom. The white inhabitants convened shortly after receiving the petition and resolved, "That we abhor the enslaving of any of the human race, and particularly of the Negroes in this country, and whenever there shall be a door opened, or opportunity presented for anything to be done for the emancipation of the Negroes, we will use our influence and endeavour that such a thing may be brought about."

NOTES on the ſtate of VIRGINIA;

written in the year 1781, ſomewhat corrected and enlarged in the winter of 1782, for the uſe of a Foreigner of diſtinction, in anſwer to certain queries propoſed by him reſpecting

MDCCLXXXII.

In January 1777, many Massachusetts slaves, in a petition to the legislature for freedom, remarked on the contradiction between the ideology of the Revolution and the practice of slaveholding. They expressed "their Astonishment that It has Never Bin Considered that Every Principle from which America has Acted in the Cours of their Unhappy Dificulties with Grat Britain Pleads Stronger than A thousand arguments in favours of your petitioners."

The beginnings of an abolition movement among whites during the colonial period has been discussed. But during the Revolutionary period, many important men joined the cause, and the movement for abolition developed a new scope and depth. Statesmen began to see how dangerous was the continuance of the unlimited slave traffic. Jefferson, in *Notes on the State of Virginia,* wrote: "Indeed, I tremble for my country when I reflect that God is just, that his justice cannot sleep forever." Patrick Henry wrote of slavery, "I will not—I cannot justify it! I believe a time will come when an opportunity will be offered to abolish this lamentable evil." In 1761, James Otis stated boldly that the colonists, black and white, were freeborn British subjects and that they were entitled to all the rights of Englishmen.

There were other colonial whites who, influenced by the spread of Revolutionary ideas, spoke out against slavery. One of these was the Rev. Isaac Skillman of New England who published his *Oration On the Beauties of Liberty* in 1772. In it he argued that slaves had even a natural right to rebel against their masters. Thomas Paine devoted his first published article, in 1775, to "African Slavery in America." Paine argued that Negroes not only should be liberated but also should be given land as payment for their many years of free labor.

Antislavery sentiment also was growing on a public and governmental level. During the early 1770's, the New Jersey and Connecti-

JAMES OTIS

cut legislatures received several petitions for the abolition of slavery. In 1774, Rhode Island ruled that any Negro slave brought within its borders was thenceforward free. Many towns adopted resolutions promising to participate no longer in the slave trade. In 1777, Vermont's new constitution forbade slavery; and in 1780, the Connecticut legislature discussed the possibilities of abolition, finally enacting a law in 1784. The Pennsylvania abolition law was passed in March 1780. During this period even Virginia eased the requirements for manumission of slaves.

Growing antislavery sentiment was also expressed on a national level. One of the agreements passed by the First Continental Congress in 1774 mentioned the nonimportation of slaves. It was agreed that the colonies would not import or purchase slaves after December 1, 1775, and that they would not hire their vessels or sell their goods to those who were involved in the slave trade. All the colonies except Georgia were represented at this convention. This move, however, was

more an attempt to rectify an unfavorable balance of payments than to correct a moral evil.

The original draft of the Declaration of Independence prepared by Thomas Jefferson contained an indictment of the King of England because of his interest in the slave trade. It declared that he had:

> . . . waged cruel war against human nature itself, violating its most sacred rights of life and liberty in the persons of a distant people who never offended him, captivating and carrying them into slavery in another hemisphere, or to incur miserable death in their transportation thither. This piratical warfare, the opprobrium of INFIDEL powers, is the warfare of the CHRISTIAN King of Great Britain.

According to Jefferson, these sentences were omitted to comply with the desires of South Carolina and Georgia. But he added that "our Northern brethren also, I believe, feel a little tender in these censures, for though their people have very few slaves themselves, yet they have been pretty considerable carriers of them to others."

THOMAS PAINE

During all of this period, the Pennsylvania Quakers continued their work, and by 1785 virtually no Quakers owned slaves. In April 1775, the first abolition society in America, the Pennsylvania Abolition Society, was organized.

The antislavery sentiment was obviously not universal. Most of it appears to have been limited to the northern colonies. North Carolina hardened its laws in 1777 against manumissions, suggesting that "the evil and pernicious Practice of freeing slaves in this State ought at this alarming and critical Time to be guarded against by every friend and Wellwisher to his Country." In 1780, South Carolina reinforced the slave system by granting a slave as bounty to every Revolutionary soldier. In the southern colonies the slaveholders attempted to ensure the maintenance of their labor force despite the dislocations they knew a war would cause. The slaveowners were aware that the Revolutionary ideas had found their way into the slave quarters, and they made certain that they would not be acted upon.

During the war the slaveholders customarily attempted to remove their slaves from zones of British influence. Laws were passed to provide harsh punishment for those slaves who attempted to flee. Early in 1776, four captured runaways in Virginia were hanged, and twenty-five were shipped to the West Indies. The money from the sale was to be given to the masters of these delinquent blacks, "provided they are not unfriendly to American liberty."

The British were well aware of the contradiction between the American rhetoric and the American reality and frequently sought to capitalize on it. In November 1775, Virginia's royal Governor, Lord Dunmore, issued a proclamation that recited the causes of the Revolution from the British point of view. He then declared: "All indentured servants, Negroes or others appertaining to the rebels, free, who are willing to bear arms, they

joining His Majesty's troops as soon as may be, for more speedily reducing this colony to a proper sense of their duty to His Majesty's crown and dignity."

The British, therefore, cooperated in loosening the bonds of slavery. Once the British had established freedom as a reward for military service, they had set a precedent that could only weaken the institution. Throughout the war, slaves from the South flocked to the British lines. Many more than three thousand Negroes sailed for Europe with the British troops from New York City after the signature of the Treaty of Paris in 1783. Five thousand escaped slaves left from Savannah, Georgia, with the evacuating British in the summer of 1782, and more than six thousand debarked from Charleston, South Carolina. Given the fact that many slaves died in the

LORD DUNMORE

British armies and died in British camps before they could be debarked, and given the fact that many escaped to Canada or to French and Spanish colonies, one historian has estimated that at least one hundred thousand slaves actually escaped from slavery during the course of the Revolution.

There was one other way in which the Revolution aided the Negro struggle for freedom. Despite the precautions of slave-owners, the Revolutionary War lessened social stratification in the colonies and weakened plantation discipline. Many slave insurrections occurred during the war years, though none was ultimately successful. The insurrectionary experience was important for slaves insofar as it taught them of their own power and instilled in them an ever intensifying desire for freedom. During the course of the war years, colonies of runaway slaves gathered in Georgia, North Carolina, New York, New Jersey and Virginia. Even as late as 1787, some of the colonies established during the Revolution remained. One unusual group at Accomack County, Virginia, caused the following report to be written: "We have had the most alarming times this Summer, all along the shore from a sett of Barges manned mostly by our own Negroes who have run off—These fellows are really dangerous to an individual singled out for their vengeance whose property lay exposed —They burnt several houses."

In addition to these slave colonies, there were attempts at insurrections throughout the war years in virtually every colony. They were caused by the spread of the spirit of liberty and the general loosening of social discipline that wars frequently cause. Perhaps the largest of these conspiracies and rebellions developed in Pitt, Craven and Beaufort Counties, North Carolina, in the summer of 1775. After considerable investigation, "a deep laid Horrid Tragic Plan" was uncovered. Scores of slaves were arrested and jailed. Prosecutions and punishments contin-

GENERAL GEORGE WASHINGTON

ued throughout the summer. Another center of disaffection in the late seventies was around Albany, New York. Apparently, there were several attempts at wholesale flight; and early in 1779, a slave named Tom was reported at large, "endeavouring to Stir up the minds of the Negroes against their Masters and raising Insurrections among them."

PROPOSALS TO ENLIST NEGROES IN THE CONTINENTAL ARMY

Historian Benjamin Quarles (*The Negro in the American Revolution*) told of the attitude toward Negro participation in military service: "Although general policy in early America was to exclude Negroes from military service, manpower shortages often outweighed the reluctance to give the Negro the gun; hence official attitude did not always mirror actual practice." Prior to the Revolution, blacks had served on board navy vessels and had participated in the colonial militia during the French and Indian Wars.

Even though many Negroes had served in the colonial militia, there were objections raised to their service in the Continental Army. When Washington took command of the militia, he retained those blacks who were already in it. Opposition to further enlistments developed rapidly, however. In the South, it was decided that every objection should be brought to bear against "a measure of so threatening an aspect and so offensive to that republican pride which disdains to commit the defense of the country to servile hands or those with a color, to which the idea of inferiority is inseparably connected, the profession of arms."

In July 1775, both the congress of Massachusetts and General Gates, an aide to Washington, barred enlistment of Negroes. Conferences with army officers were held in which it was agreed that slaves were to be excluded; and according to the reports from at least one of these conferences, all Negroes were to be excluded from the army, even though Negroes had been serving as Minutemen. John Rutledge of South Carolina, in the Continental Congress, on September 26, 1775, proposed that General Washington should be called upon to discharge all Negroes, slave and free, from the army. This was approved by the Continental Congress in October.

A council held at Washington's headquarters on October 8, 1775, had already agreed to reject all Negroes, slave and free. On November 12, 1775, Washington issued an order that "neither Negroes, boys unable to bear arms, nor old men unfit to endure the fatigue of the campaign are to be enlisted." General Gates' instructions to officers on recruiting service stated that they were "not to enlist any deserter from ministerial army, nor any stroller, Negro or vagabond, or person suspected of being an enemy to the liberty of America nor any under 18 years of age."

Events later in the war helped to change the attitudes of Americans who had previously opposed the military service of Negroes. Lord Dunmore's proclamation, previously cited, impressed upon the minds of the American leaders that if they did not use the slaves, the British would. George Washington

GENERAL HORATIO GATES

declared that Lord Dunmore's Tory operations must be crushed "for if he gets formidable, numbers of them will be tempted to join who would be afraid to do it without." In December 1775, Washington wrote of Dunmore:

> If . . . that man is not crushed before spring, he will become the most formidable enemy America has; his strength will increase as a snowball, by rolling; and faster, if some expedient cannot be hit upon to convince the slave and servant of the impotency of his design.

Many Revolutionary War leaders had begun to suggest the enlistment of Negroes: James Madison, Alexander Hamilton, Samuel Hopkins and John Laurens were among them. John Hancock, perhaps typical, suggested that the Revolution should "give them their freedom with their swords," for, "if we do not take them, the enemy probably will."

On December 30, 1775, General Washington made an entry in his Orderly Book that "as the General is informed that numbers of free Negroes are desirous of enlisting, he gives leave to the recruiting officers to entertain them and promises to lay the matter before the Congress, who, he doubts not will approve it." Washington wrote the President of the Congress stating that he had departed from the resolution of Congress concerning Negro soldiers, since the free Negroes were "much dissatisfied at being discarded," and that he had given license for their enlistment. He added that "if this is disapproved of by Congress, I will put a stop to it."

When the proposal reached Congress, a committee composed of George Wythe, John Adams and James Wilson reported on the matter, and Congress agreed on January 16, 1776, that "the free Negroes who have served faithfully in the army at Cambridge may be re-enlisted therein but no others." This restriction was not adhered to, and in spite of legislative hesitation and compromise, numbers of Negroes were enlisted into the Continental Army.

In February 1778, the Rhode Island Assembly enacted:

> . . . that every able bodied Negro, mullatoe or Indian man slave in this state may enlist into either of the . . . two battalions to serve during the continuance of the present war with Great Britain; that every slave so enlisting shall be entitled to and receive all the bounties, wages and encouragements allowed by the Continental Congress to any soldiers enlisting in this service.

The Rhode Islanders also declared that liberty was to be given to "every effective slave to enter into the service during the war; and upon his passing muster he is absolutely free." Similar laws were passed in Massachusetts in April 1778. In March 1781, New York authorized the formation of two regiments of slaves, who were to be freed after the completion of their tour of duty. Slaves were also enlisted in the other New England and mid-Atlantic states.

Even in the South, there appears to have been some enlistment of Negroes. A North Carolina law of 1778, passed to penalize runaway slaves, proves this. In its discussion of the punishment of escaped slaves, the law states that "nothing herein contained shall deprive of Liberty any Slave who having been liberated and not sold by order of any Court has enlisted in the service of this or the United States." In 1780, Maryland legislated to the effect that both slaves and free Negroes could be enlisted in the Revolutionary armies.

In most of the South, enlistments were forbidden. However, by May 1777, even in Virginia free Negroes—although not slaves —were permitted into the army. Taking

ALEXANDER HAMILTON

advantage of this duality, many whites attempted to enlist their slaves as substitutes for themselves and then re-enslave them after the war. By May 1777, it had become necessary for the legislature to declare it unlawful for any recruiting officer to enlist in the service of state or nation any Negro or mulatto who could not produce a statement from the justice of the peace in his county of residence certifying that he was, in fact, a free man.

In spite of the restrictions, however, some slaves did manage to get into the Revolutionary armies. A Virginia law of 1783 stated that all slaves who had served in the army, the majority of whom had been enlisted by their masters as substitutes, could not be re-enslaved. For they had "contributed toward the establishment of American liberty and independence, and should enjoy the blessings of freedom as a reward for their toils and labors."

In 1779, Congress recommended to South Carolina and Georgia that they enlist 3,000 slaves. These slaves were to be both fed and clothed at the expense of the United States government and were to be manumitted at the close of the war with a fifty-dollar bonus. A bill for this purpose was introduced in the South Carolina legislature, but it was defeated. The same thing happened in Georgia. On hearing of these results, Washington wrote that the spirit of freedom that was once so evident had now subsided. He was of the opinion that it was private and not public interest that influenced the majority of the people.

In 1778 and 1779, when the people of South Carolina and Georgia were threatened by the British army, the Continental Army could not afford the extra troops to assist them. Colonel Henry Laurens recommended, therefore, that a regiment of Negroes be raised in South Carolina and Georgia. His letter of March 16, 1779, emphasized the growing need for reinforcements. Laurens wrote: "Had we arms for three thousand

COLONEL HENRY LAURENS

such black men as I could select in Carolina, I should have no doubt of success in driving the British out of Georgia, and subduing East Florida." Congress approved the proposal, but no action was taken on it at the time.

Congress recommended to these states on March 29, 1779, that they enlist Negroes if they so desired and suggested that "the said Negroes be formed into separate corps and battalions—to be commanded by white officers." Congress had approved the measure

ORGANIZED COMPANIES AND REGIMENTS   89

because it was of the opinion that the Negro troops would be formidable "to the enemy from their numbers, and the discipline of which they would very readily admit and would also lessen the dangers from revolts and desertions by detaching the most vigorous and enterprising from among the Negroes." General Robert Armstrong, in a letter to Horatio Gates on April 3, 1779, described this action and stated that the proprietors were to receive from Congress one thousand dollars for each Negro and that the measure was fostered by the delegates from these states.

NUMBERS IN THE ARMY

In 1775, there were over five hundred thousand Negroes in the colonies. Opinions vary on the number of Negroes who served in the American Revolution. One estimate is that there were at least thirty-five Negroes in every regiment; others state that there was one Negro for every fifty or sixty whites, and that there was an average of fifty-four in each brigade. The estimates of the total number vary from three thousand to six thousand. In October 1778 a Hessian officer wrote that "The Negro can take the field instead of the master; and therefore no regiment is to be seen in which there are not Negroes in abundance; and among them are able-bodied strong fellows." In this connection George L. Clark (*A History of Connecticut*) stated:

> In the stress of conflict it came to pass that neither the selectmen nor the commanding officers questioned the color; white and black, bond and free, if able bodied, went into the rolls together, accepted as the representatives or substitutes of their employers. Many slaves were promised their freedom on the condition that they serve for three years in the army, and many displayed superior bravery when death was near.

Weighing these sources and drawing upon other facts, most historians have concluded that there were from four to six thousand Negroes scattered through the Continental Army. The majority of them, predictably, were from the North.

ORGANIZED COMPANIES AND REGIMENTS

Companies of Negro soldiers were not unusual after 1779. In Connecticut, in addition to the Negroes dispersed throughout its regular regiments, there was a company composed entirely of Negroes in Meig's Regiment, afterwards known as Butler's Regiment. On March 20, 1781, New York provided for the raising of two Negro regiments. There is no record of how many slaves were brought into these regiments, but it is known that there were many enlisted. Maryland resolved in 1781 to make provisions to enlist 750 Negroes to be incorporated into a separate unit. New Hampshire offered Negroes the same bounty it offered whites for three years of army service.

Similar movements were undertaken in Rhode Island, South Carolina and Georgia. It was proposed by General James Mitchell Varnum to General Washington in 1778 that the two Rhode Island regiments at Valley Forge be united and that the officers of one be sent to Rhode Island to enlist a battalion of Negroes. Governor Nicholas Cooke of Rhode Island approved the proposal and submitted it to the General Assembly. The assembly adopted the plan on February 23, 1778, and the officers began the organization. It was provided that up to 120 pounds would be paid to the owner of each slave enlisted who would be "immediately discharged from the service of his master or mistress, and be absolutely free, as though he had never been encumbered with any kind of servitude or slavery." Opposition arose to the plan. It was said that there were not enough Negroes in the state who would be inclined to enlist; that it would lead to the opinion that the state had purchased slaves for its defense, which would be wholly inconsistent with the

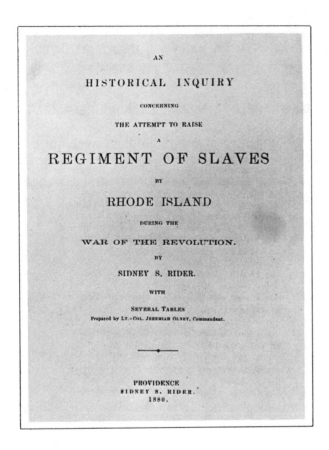

AN

HISTORICAL INQUIRY

CONCERNING

THE ATTEMPT TO RAISE

A

REGIMENT OF SLAVES

BY

RHODE ISLAND

DURING THE

WAR OF THE REVOLUTION.

BY

SIDNEY S. RIDER.

WITH

SEVERAL TABLES

Prepared by LT.-COL. JEREMIAH OLNEY, Commandant.

PROVIDENCE

SIDNEY S. RIDER.

1880.

principles of liberty for which they were fighting; and that the expense involved in purchasing and equipping such a regiment would exceed the expenses of raising a regiment of white men.

Governor Cooke had estimated that at least three hundred Negroes would enlist, but there is some disagreement on the number actually enlisted. Sidney S. Rider (*An Historical Inquiry concerning the Attempt to Raise a Regiment of Slaves by Rhode Island during the War of the Revolution*) claimed "their number did not exceed one hundred and thirty or one hundred and forty men." A separate unit, the Black Regiment, was organized, although it does not seem to have reached the proportions of a battalion.

Later in the year, the legislature of South Carolina refused to adopt Colonel Henry Laurens' plan for Negro enlistment. Its author was discouraged, but he made another attempt to obtain an approval of his plan. Of this second effort he said: "I was outvoted,

having only reason on my side and being oppressed by a triple-headed monster, avarice, prejudice, and pusillanimity." Washington expressed the opinion to him later that it would have been surprising if he had succeeded in this effort. The emancipation of the slaves as a reward for fighting was a strong deterrent to acceptance of his plan.

Another instance of the presence and activity of Negro soldiers appeared near the close of the war. John Hancock, then governor of Massachusetts, presented a banner with his initials to a regiment of Negro soldiers as a tribute to their devotion to the cause of American freedom.

NEGROES IN THE NAVY

Negroes served in the navy, and on the privateers that preceded the organization of the navy, as well as in the army during the American Revolution. As early as 1775, a sign was posted at Newport recruiting "ye ablebodied sailors, men white or black, to volunteer for naval service in ye interest of freedom." A free Negro gunner, Benoni Brown, of Providence, Rhode Island, served on a vessel commanded by Commodore Esek Hopkins. Johnny Braenmer was a gunner on the *Bonhomme Richard,* commanded by Commodore John Paul Jones. The battle in which this vessel fought with the *Serapis* was one of the famous episodes of the Revolution. There were twenty Negro seamen on board the *Royal Louis,* a ship with twenty-two guns, commanded by Captain Decatur (senior). At least two Negro sailors were crew members on the *Alliance,* commanded by Commodore Christopher R. Perry: Joshua Tiffany and David Mitchell. A Negro named Caesar was a crewman on the brig *Hazard,* Cato Blackney was on the *Deane.* Negroes served on the *Trumbull,* commanded by Captain Nicholson, and on the *South Carolina,* the *Confederacy,* the *Randolph* and many other ships.

JOHN PAUL JONES

The great naval battle between the Bonhomme Richard *and the* Serapis.

Commodore John Paul Jones leading the crew of the Bonhomme Richard *to victory over the* Serapis.

STEPHEN DECATUR

Negro sailors were on the *Patriot,* the *Liberty,* the *Tempest,* the *Gloucester,* the *Diligence* and the *Hero,* vessels of war operated by the state of Virginia during the Revolution. It has been estimated that Negroes fought on at least one-third of the fifty vessels maintained by Virginia. Many Negroes also manned Georgia's defensive coastal galleys. Negro sailors served on the first merchantmen bought by the Continental Congress in 1775. Several of these Negroes had records for distinguished service. The sailors received money payments during the war, and at its close some received land grants as well. The evidence is scanty for the presence of large numbers of Negroes in the naval forces, since quite often they were not listed on the ships' rolls. There are, however, individual records that show blacks were in the navy rendering service to their country.

Two American Negro seamen of note were Joseph Ranger and Caesar Tarrant. Ranger served on four vessels during the war, the *Hero,* the *Dragon,* the *Jefferson* and the *Patriot.* He was taken prisoner by the British in 1781, later gained his freedom, and after the war was given a grant of one hundred acres by the Commonwealth of Virginia. Seaman Tarrant was a pilot in the Navy for four years, serving on the *Patriot* on the eve of the Battle of Yorktown. He received his freedom for participation in the Revolution from the Virginia legislature in 1786, and his heirs were allotted one hundred acres in the Ohio military reserve land in the 1830's.

Perhaps the most prominent of the Negroes in the Revolutionary Navy was James Forten of Philadelphia, who began his service on the *Royal Louis* with Stephen Decatur as commander. Later, this vessel was captured by the British frigate *Amphyon,* and a friendship began between Forten and the son of the captain. As a result, Forten was offered passage to England. He refused to renounce his American citizenship, however, and spent the rest of the war as a naval prisoner in the floating dungeon, the *Jersey.* Forten later became wealthy and famous as the inventor of an improved mechanism for sail-handling and as a leading abolitionist.

NEGRO LOYALISTS

Americans were not unanimous in desiring independence from England. John Adams even suggested that as many as one third of the colonists were loyal to the mother country. This division among the American colonists was reflected in the Negro population and emphasized by Lord Dunmore's appeal to the Negroes. When Rutledge came to Philadelphia in 1780, he reported that the Negroes there were praying for a British victory because they believed that the English were more likely to give them freedom than were the Americans.

Many Negroes left with the British at the end of the war. It is reported that from three-fourths to seven-eighths of the Negroes in Georgia were carried off or left voluntarily with them. There are some historians who believe that 100,000 Americans eventually reached Canada, which was in sympathy with the British. There were Negroes in this number. The state of Virginia reported 30,000 missing in 1780; and South Carolina, 25,000. They were valued at 12 million dollars, and diplomatic negotiations for their return were continued into the nineteenth century. Some of these slaves were taken by the British vessels to the West Indies, and some were resold into slavery. They were also used by the British as spies, informers and guides.

Many blacks were employed as soldiers by the British. There were at least 230 Negroes and Tories who were the last to be routed at the battle of Great Bridge on December 9, 1775. Several were captured by the Americans. Those who had served by compulsion with Lord Dunmore, former Governor of Virginia, were treated kindly; but those who had volunteered were manacled and imprisoned. Lord Dunmore had sought the aid of several hundred Negroes in his effort to regain his place as ruling authority in Virginia. The British Army in Georgia, at Fort Cornwallis in Augusta, was garrisoned by 400 British and 200 Negro soldiers in 1781. After the war, a band of Negroes about the Savannah River, calling themselves "the King of England's Soldiers," kept the inhabitants of this area alarmed by their marauding activities.

It should be pointed out that many of the slaves who went behind British lines were deceived in their expectations of treatment. Many were sold into slavery in the British West Indies. The letters of Dunmore himself show that many found only sickness and death on board the crowded and unsanitary British ships. In June 1776, Dunmore reported to London that a large number of slaves had joined him but that sickness "has carried off an incredible number of our people, especially the blacks." That same summer, in Maryland, it was reported that "the shores are full of dead bodies, chiefly Negroes, washed ashore from the British boats."

NEGRO SOLDIERS

Many Negroes, individually in white regiments and in the ranks of all-black regiments, distinguished themselves fighting for the Revolution. There are countless stories of bravery and sacrifice. One of the first men to die for the ideals of the Revolution, for example, was Crispus Attucks, an escaped slave who had run away to sea at an early age.

On March 5, 1770, there occurred a popular outbreak in Boston that resulted in the Boston Massacre. Here the first blood of the Revolution was spilled. On this day, Crispus Attucks, with a cordwood stick in his hand, joined with twenty or thirty other sailors similarly armed and moved to the head of a crowd on King Street facing Captain Preston's company of redcoats. Attucks in front, urging the other citizens to fight, was the first to fall in the Revolutionary cause. From this time on, the Revolution gathered momentum until war broke out in earnest five years later.

Peter Salem distinguished himself in the opening days of the Revolution with the American forces under Colonel William Prescott. Salem had served for seven years in the Framingham Militia in Massachusetts and had taken part in the early battles around Lexington and Concord. At the Battle of Bunker Hill, he dashed forward and is said to have fired the shot that mortally wounded Major John Pitcairn, the leader of the British forces. The gun used by Salem is displayed at the Bunker Hill monument, with a sign reading: "Gun belonged to Peter Salem, a colored man, who carried it at Lexington, Concord and Bunker Hill, and with it shot Major Pitcairn."

Crispus Attucks, the first to fall in the American revolutionary cause.

The shooting of Crispus Attucks during the Boston Massacre.

The Crispus Attucks Monument on the Boston Common,
dedicated in 1888 in honor of the victims of the Boston Massacre.

PETER SALEM

Peter Salem charging the British forces during the Battle of Bunker Hill.

The Battle of Long Island.

The Battle of Monmouth, where Samuel Charlton served with distinction.

The bravery of Salem Poor at the Battle of Bunker Hill attracted such attention that a statement was sent to the Massachusetts legislature by fourteen white officers describing his conduct. This statement was dated December 5, 1775, and reported that "a Negro man called Salem Poor of Col. Frye's regiment, Capt. Ames' company in the late battle at Charlestown, behaved like an experienced officer as well as an excellent soldier . . . in the person of this said Negro centers a brave and gallant soldier."

Austin Dabney of Georgia was the hero of several conflicts with the British. The legislature of Georgia granted him a tract of land as a reward for his services, and the United States government awarded him a pension. With this start, he soon acquired other property and became a wealthy man.

A Negro soldier named Prince assisted in the capture of General Richard Prescott at Newport. An account of his daring has been preserved:

> Lieutenant-Colonel Barton of the Rhode Island militia planned a bold exploit for the purpose of surprising and taking Major-General Prescott, the commanding officer of the royal army at Newport. Taking with him in the night about forty men, in two boats, . . . and having arrived undiscovered at the quarters of General Prescott, . . . the general was not alarmed till the captors were at the door of his lodging chambers which was fast closed. A Negro man named Prince, instantly thrust his beedle head through the paned door and seized his victim while in bed. This event . . . is considered an ample retaliation for the capture of General Lee by Colonel Harcourt. . . . it puts General Lee in a position by which means an exchange of prisoners may be obtained.

James Armistead, former Virginia slave, became a spy for General Lafayette in 1781 and provided information on the strength and position of the British. As a reward for his outstanding service to the country, Armistead was granted his freedom in 1786 by the Virginia legislature.

LEMUEL HAYNES

Seymour Burr, who desired freedom from slavery, was captured fleeing to the British lines while serving with the 7th Massachusetts Regiment. He later was freed by his master after he bravely served his country at the siege of Fort Catskill.

Samuel Charlton fought in the Battles of Brandywine, Germantown and Monmouth. After the war, he was liberated and given a pension at the time of his master's death. Oliver Cromwell served in the Continental Army for six years and nine months. During this time, he fought in the Battles of Trenton and Princeton, Brandywine, Monmouth and Yorktown. He also crossed the Delaware River with George Washington on Christmas Day in 1776. Another black soldier during the Revolution was William Flora, a free Negro who served in the defense of Great Bridge near Norfolk, Virginia, in 1775.

Lemuel Haynes was both soldier and minister, beginning his military activities in 1774 as a Minuteman. He served in the Battle of Lexington during the war and went on to become the first Negro minister to a white congregation in Torrington, Connecticut. Edward Hector was a private in the 3rd Pennsylvania Artillery and saw action in the Battle of Brandywine Creek in 1777. Barzillai Lew, Negro patriot of the 27th Massachusetts Regiment, engaged in anti-British activities in New England.

GENERAL WILLIAM WHIPPLE

GENERAL LAFAYETTE

CHARLES PINCKNEY

Still another black participant in the American pursuit for independence was Saul Matthews. He was sent by Colonel Josiah Parker of Virginia to infiltrate the British lines, where he was to gather information pertaining to troops, positions of armaments, and movements on the James River. Because of his activities in the war, the Virginia legislature granted Matthews his freedom in 1792.

James Robinson was awarded a Gold Medal by General Lafayette for valor at Yorktown. Because of the service he had rendered, Robinson had been promised his freedom. However, on his master's death, the heirs denied the black veteran the freedom he had fought to win for his country. Tack Sisson took part in commando raids on British forces and helped capture a British commander. A free-born native African, Prince Whipple, served as bodyguard to General William Whipple and also is mentioned as having crossed the Delaware River with George Washington.

Several individual deeds of bravery were noted in the Battles of Long Island and Monmouth. Said Frederic Bancroft, in telling of the Battle of Monmouth: ". . . nor any history omit to record that of the Revolutionary patriots who on that day offered their lives for their country more than 700 black men fought side by side with the white." And of course it should be noted that there were Negro soldiers who endured the rigorous winter at Valley Forge.

At the siege of Savannah in 1778, the famous Black Legion, composed of free Negroes from Haiti serving with the French under Admiral D'Estaing, covered the retreat of the Americans and by their fierce counterattacks upon the British saved the American Army from a crushing defeat and probable capture.

The Rhode Island regiment of Negro soldiers fought with valor at the defense of Red Bank, where 400 Negroes successfully defended their position against 1,500 Hessians.

In describing the work of Negro soldiers in the American Revolution, Charles Pinckney of South Carolina said in 1820:

> They were then, as they still are, as valuable a part of our population to the union as any other equal number of inhabitants. They were in numerous instances the pioneers and, in all, the laborers of your armies. To their hands were owing the erection of the greatest part of the fortifications raised for the protection of our country, some of which, particularly Fort Moultrie, gave at that early period of the inexperienced and untried valor of our citizens, immortality to American arms, and in the Northern States numerous bodies of them were enrolled into and fought by the sides of the whites, the battles of the Revolution.

And yet these individual instances of heroism represent only a fraction of the sacrifices that the Negro population made during the War for Independence.

CHAPTER SEVEN

From Revolution to Constitution

THE American colonies were part of a greater community of nations bordering on the Atlantic Ocean, and the cultural and economic contacts Americans had had with Europeans were only temporarily interrupted by the War for Independence. In order to fully understand the development of thought on slavery in the United States in the eighteenth century, it is necessary to have some knowledge of parallel developments on the European continent and in Great Britain.

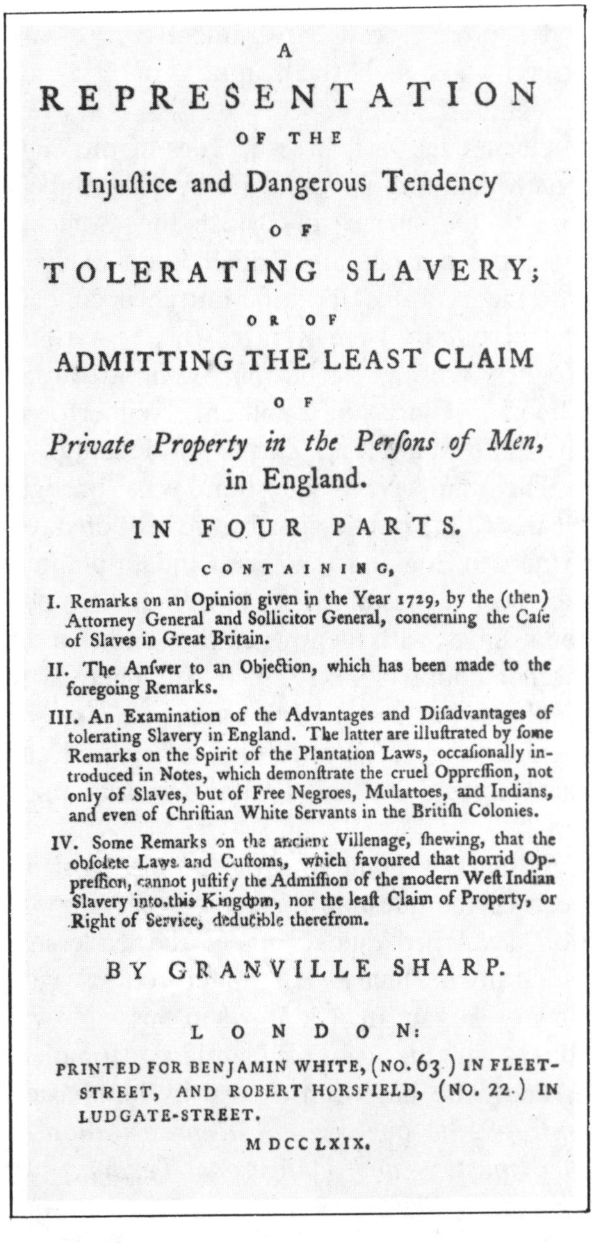

DEVELOPMENTS IN EUROPE

While the English Colonies in America were contending for their legal rights, liberal thinkers in other nations were spreading new ideas concerning the rights of man. It was in France that the more abstract of these ideas were forming. One outgrowth of this trend was the founding in 1788 of La Société des Amis des Noirs (the Society of the Friends of the Blacks). Honoré Gabriel Riqueti, comte de Mirabeau, General Lafayette, the Marquis de Condorcet and Jacques Pierre Brissot de Warville were associated with this movement, which had as its objectives the abolition of slavery, and equal rights for all men.

In England, a new humanitarianism developed during the "Age of Enlightenment." A new religious impulse was felt, and steadily increasing agitation for parliamentary reform

A

REPRESENTATION

OF THE

Injuſtice and Dangerous Tendency

OF

TOLERATING SLAVERY;

OR OF

ADMITTING THE LEAST CLAIM

OF

Private Property in the Perſons of Men,
in England.

IN FOUR PARTS.

CONTAINING,

I. Remarks on an Opinion given in the Year 1729, by the (then) Attorney General and Sollicitor General, concerning the Caſe of Slaves in Great Britain.

II. The Anſwer to an Objeƈtion, which has been made to the foregoing Remarks.

III. An Examination of the Advantages and Diſadvantages of tolerating Slavery in England. The latter are illuſtrated by ſome Remarks on the Spirit of the Plantation Laws, occaſionally introduced in Notes, which demonſtrate the cruel Oppreſſion, not only of Slaves, but of Free Negroes, Mulattoes, and Indians, and even of Chriſtian White Servants in the Britiſh Colonies.

IV. Some Remarks on the ancient Villenage, ſhewing, that the obſolete Laws and Cuſtoms, which favoured that horrid Oppreſſion, cannot juſtify the Admiſſion of the modern Weſt Indian Slavery into this Kingdom, nor the leaſt Claim of Property, or Right of Service, deducible therefrom.

BY GRANVILLE SHARP.

LONDON:

PRINTED FOR BENJAMIN WHITE, (NO. 63.) IN FLEET-STREET, AND ROBERT HORSFIELD, (NO. 22.) IN LUDGATE-STREET.

MDCCLXIX.

THOMAS CLARKSON

WILLIAM WILBERFORCE

RICHARD BAXTER

EDMUND BURKE

and a press free of government control disturbed the established modes of life and thought.

During the last three decades of the eighteenth century, the controversy over slavery rose to the surface of British life. Some of the most outstanding British humanitarians who incorporated abolition into their concept of Christianity were Richard Baxter, Griffith Hughes, Wesley Warburton, Edmund Burke, Thomas Clarkson, William Wilberforce, Granville Sharp and Zachary Macaulay.

The antislavery question was brought clearly to the public view by the visit of slave-owners to England. The West Indian planters had been accustomed to bringing their personal slaves with them when they came to the mother country. In 1729, it was decreed in England that a slave did not become free by coming from the West Indies to England and that baptism did not bestow freedom upon him.

While this opinion governed the legal aspects of the question for many years, opposition developed quickly under the leadership of Granville Sharp. His direct contact with slavery began in 1765, when his aid was sought in the case of a slave, Jonathan Strong, who had been abused by his master. In 1769, he published *A Representation of the Injustice and Dangerous Tendency of Tolerating Slavery.*

THE SOMERSET CASE AND BRITISH OPPOSITION TO SLAVERY

The most famous among several eighteenth-century slave cases was that of James Somerset. He was brought to England by his master, Charles Stewart of Boston, in 1769. Somerset became ill and was abandoned by his master. On his recovery, he refused to return to Jamaica and was seized and carried on board a vessel to be returned to slavery. Granville Sharp was instrumental in bringing the question before the English courts to decide whether a slave, by coming to England, became free. On June 22, 1772, Lord Chief Justice Mansfield handed down the decision that slavery could not be maintained under English law, that the only kind of servitude in English law was villeinage and that slavery could be sustained only by the legal system of the country in which the condition existed.

The precedent set by this decision was never reversed. Although slavery began in Canada as in other English colonies, an act of 1793 stated it was "unjust that a people who enjoy freedom by law should encourage the introduction of slaves" and that it was highly expedient to abolish slavery in the Province: "No Negro or other person who shall come or be brought into this Province—shall be subject to the condition of a slave." Slaves in

Canada were to be free at the age of twenty-five and no indenture was to be longer than five years. Almost immediately there began a movement of runaway slaves from the United States to Canada.

John Wesley, the founder of Methodism, denounced slavery in *Thoughts Upon Slavery,* published in 1774. Adam Smith, both in his *Theory of Moral Sentiments* and in *The Wealth of Nations,* both published in 1776, described the economic disadvantages of slavery. In the same year, David Hartley introduced a motion in Parliament that "the slave trade is contrary to the laws of God and the rights of man." The English Quakers formed a committee for the publication and distribution of these writings. Thomas Clarkson's untiring efforts to produce irrefutable facts about the cruelties of the slave trade, gained distinction for him and placed him among the leaders of the antislavery sympathizers. A committee made up mainly of Quakers was formed in 1783 to oppose the slave trade and to press for liberation of the Negro slaves in the West Indies. This marked the first organized effort to abolish the slave trade in Great Britain.

EFFECTS OF THE REVOLUTION ON AMERICAN SLAVERY

The founders of the American Republic generally were not happy with the institution of slavery. Even some southerners, for example, George Washington, Samuel Hopkins, Thomas Jefferson, George Wythe and Henry Laurens, expressed opposition to slavery. The American Revolution's emphasis on liberty brought the status of the Negro directly to the attention of the founding fathers. A Negro writer known only as Othello declared in 1788 that it was "inconsistent with the declared principles of the American Revolution" to hold slaves; that our institutions were "painted sepulchres" characterized by

JOHN WESLEY

THOUGHTS

UPON

SLAVERY.

By *JOHN WESLEY,* A. M.

GENESIS, Chap. iv.
*And the Lord said—What haft thou done? the voice of
thy brother's blood crieth unto me from the ground.*

LONDON, PRINTED;
Re-printed in PHILADELPHIA, with notes,
and fold by JOSEPH CRUCKSHANK.
MD,CC,LXXIV.

ABIGAIL ADAMS

"naught but rottenness and corruption." Othello suggested that the slaves should either be free or colonized in the west "so that it may become a known and fixed point, that ultimately universal liberty in these United States, shall triumph." Abigail Adams wrote to her husband, John, "it always appeared a most iniquitous scheme to me to fight ourselves for what we are daily robbing and plundering from those who have as good a right to freedom as we have."

In 1791, the famous Negro scientist Benjamin Banneker wrote to Jefferson:

> Suffer me to recall to your mind the time, in which the arms of the British crown were extended, with every powerful effort, in order to reduce you to a state of servitude; look back, I entreat you . . . you were then impressed with proper ideas of the great violation of liberty and the free possession of those blessings to which you were entitled by nature; but sir, how pitiable is it to reflect, that although you were so fully convinced of the benevolence of the Father of Mankind, and of his equal and impartial distribution of these rights and privileges which he hath conferred

> upon them, that you should at the same time counteract his mercies, in detaining by force and violence, so numerous a part of my brethren under groaning captivity and cruel oppression, that you should at the same time be found guilty of that most criminal act, which you professedly detested in others.

The Revolution, therefore, engendered considerable antislavery sentiment and thereby weakened the institution. Feeling against slavery was probably hastened by the failure of the tobacco, rice and indigo markets immediately after the war, but the pervasive influence of Revolutionary ideology is undeniable. In the four years immediately following the end of the Revolution, the movement to abolish slavery grew steadily, and a new black consciousness and self-awareness began to develop.

The first abolition society was founded in Philadelphia in 1775 and reconstituted in 1784. John Jay led New York's first abolition society in the 1780's; and by the end of the decade, New Jersey, Delaware, Connecticut, Maryland and Rhode Island had organized

JOHN JAY

abolition groups. Besides the organizations, many local abolition groups also formed in these states. And at the first national convention of antislavery groups, held in 1794, even Virginia was represented.

These early abolition groups, although the forerunners of the later groups of the 1840's and 1850's, were vastly different in temper. The founders were men of wealth and stature who disdained "rabble-rousing" techniques. While the standard picture of the nineteenth-century abolitionist is one of a wild-maned fanatic, the men of the eighteenth century preferred to work quietly—and, as it developed, unsuccessfully. They sent petitions to state and national legislatures urging the abolition of the domestic and foreign slave trade and the gradual abolition of slavery itself. Frequently, they bought slaves in order to free them. They tried to mount campaigns to persuade their fellow citizens to boycott the products of slave labor. They assisted free Negroes in finding employment and attempted to educate the blacks. In 1787, the African Free School was formed and sponsored by the New York Manumission Society.

The propaganda of these societies frequently persuaded individuals to manumit their own slaves. In 1787, Philip Graham of Maryland freed all his slaves, declaring that the holding of "fellow men in bondage and slavery is repugnant to the golden law of God and the unalienable right of mankind as well as to every principle of the late glorious revolution which has taken place in America." Richard Randolph of Virginia, likewise, upon his coming of age wrote to his guardian: "With regard to the division of the estate, I have only to say that I want not a single Negro for any other purpose than his immediate liberation. I consider every individual thus unshackled as the source of future generations, not to say nations, of free men; and I shudder when I think that so insignificant an animal as I am is invested with this monstrous, this horrid power."

After the Revolution, churches became increasingly active in antislavery work. The Quakers remained dedicated, and it was largely because of their influence that Pennsylvania barred slavery in 1780. The Baptists licensed many black preachers, slave and free. A Methodist Convention held in Baltimore in 1780 expressed disapproval of members who held slaves and required all traveling Methodist preachers to rid themselves of the slaves they owned. This regulation remained in force until 1785. Many early Methodist congregations were racially mixed. Of fifty-one churches reported in 1789, thirty-six had Negro communicants.

Some antislavery sentiment was based less on Revolutionary morality than on economic interests. We have already noted that some southern colonial leaders feared that the purchase of slaves would misdirect economic resources. Thus, for example, the Revolutionaries attemped to boycott the slave trade, and South Carolina actually barred the importation of slaves for a brief period after the Revolutionary War. George Mason of Virginia said at the Constitutional Convention:

> Slavery discourages the arts and manufactures. The poor despise labor when performed by slaves. . . . Slaves produce the pernicious effect on masters. Every master of slaves is born a petty tyrant. They bring the judgement of heaven on a country. As nations cannot be rewarded or punished in the next world, they must be in this. By an inevitable chain of causes and effects, Providence punishes national sins by national calamities.

ANTISLAVERY LEGISLATION BY STATES

The American Revolution made it possible for the colonies to assume an authority which they had not exercised before. This authority was exercised first in matters of government, and constitutions were formed to take the place of colonial charters. Vermont was the first of the new states to assert the inherent right of all men to freedom. In the Declaration of Rights, which preceded its constitution of 1777, it was stated that every man was entitled to life, liberty and happiness and that no person should serve another after he reaches maturity. Later, the state expressly abolished slavery. The Virginia Bill of Rights adopted in 1776 included a liberty clause. Since it did not expressly forbid slavery, however, the institution continued there undisturbed. In 1783, the Massachusetts courts outlawed slavery. The case of *Walker* v. *Jemison* in 1783 was based on the first article of the Massachusetts Declaration of Rights. Jemison was indicted for an assault upon Walker, his slave. Chief Justice Cushing, speaking for the Massachusetts Supreme Court, ruled that "the idea of slavery is inconsistent with our own conduct and Constitution; and there can be no such thing as perpetual servitude of a rational creature, unless his liberty is forfeited by some criminal act or given up by personal consent or contract."

In 1784, Connecticut and Rhode Island passed gradual abolition laws. New York and New Jersey passed manumission acts in 1785 and 1786, respectively, although further legislation in 1799 and 1804 was necessary to make this legislation operative. Thus, in 1799, New York declared that a female born in slavery would be free on her twenty-fifth birthday, and a male on his twenty-eighth birthday. This applied only to slaves born after passage of the legislation. In New Hampshire, as in Massachusetts, slavery was abolished by the courts.

The move toward abolition even affected some southern states, however temporarily or marginally. Virginia made private manumissions possible once again in 1782. In 1785, a law was passed to manumit a slave who had been brought into the state and kept there for one year. In that same year, the antislavery forces in Maryland were able to muster twenty-two votes against slavery in the legislature, as opposed to thirty-two votes for it. Manumission was also facilitated in North Carolina. There was no question as to the proslavery sentiment of the lower South.

THE ARTICLES OF CONFEDERATION

The debates over the adoption of the Articles of Confederation and the laws which were passed under the document's aegis saw the infant nation reach a "high-water" mark of liberalism in relation to slavery. During the debates that took place in the Continental Congress over the Articles, there were incidental references to Negroes. On October 30, 1777, it was proposed by amendment that "colored" men be excluded from taking part in the vote. The only voices in favor of this amendment were from Virginia. On November 13, the acceptance of the fourth article was under consideration: "The better to secure and perpetuate mutual friendship and intercourse among the people of the different states, in the Union, the free inhabitants of each of these states, paupers, vagabonds and fugitives from justice excepted, shall be entitled to all the privileges and immunities of

CHIEF JUSTICE CALEB CUSHING

free citizens in the several states." The delegates from South Carolina proposed and supported an amendment to this article that would insert the word "white" before "inhabitants." This amendment lost by a vote of eight to two, and the article was adopted as presented.

The slaveholding states gained a victory, however, in the discussion of the requisitioning of state men and money for federal purposes. In assessing the attitudes of the Founding Fathers, Benjamin Quarles suggested: "The main Negro problem considered by the Continental Congress and that of the Confederation was whether slaves should be considered part of the state's population in laying obligation—manpower and money—upon it and in giving it increased powers." The basic problem was whether or not states were to be assessed on the basis of population or land. The New England states preferred to have assessments based on population, for land values were high and people fewer. In the heavily populated South, where land was cheap, it was hoped that assessments would be based on land. The South, therefore, was unwilling to consider its slaves as persons for the sake of taxation. A delegate from South Carolina declared that slaves should be conceived of as property. He asked: "Being our property, why should they be taxed more than sheep?" The matter was finally decided in favor of the South, so that requisitions were to be levied according to land values in each state.

FREEDOM IN THE TERRITORIES

At the beginning of the Revolutionary War, Massachusetts, Connecticut, New York, Virginia, North Carolina and Georgia all claimed territory west of the Atlantic Ocean on the basis of their respective charters. Their claims were opposed by the states whose charters restricted their own claims to a definite territory. The smaller states, particularly

TIMOTHY PICKERING

Rhode Island, Maryland and Delaware, argued that the more western territory should become the possession of all the states and be used for their common benefit rather than for the aggrandizement of a few states. In 1783, Timothy Pickering and a group of Revolutionary officers drew up a plan for the organization of a state out of the new territory. This plan envisioned the settlement of veterans and their families in communities beyond the Ohio, the adoption of a constitution before settlement, the exclusion of slavery and rapid admission into the Union on terms of equality. This plan was not actually adopted at the time, but it foreshadowed the ultimate solution to the new nation's territorial problem.

In March 1784, Thomas Jefferson brought another plan before the Continental Congress. Jefferson, in this ordinance, attempted not only to legislate for the northwest but also to set up governments in the areas immediately west of South Carolina and Georgia. He proposed a temporary government with a large measure of home rule, to

RUFUS KING

be followed by rapid admission into the Union once a certain population level had been reached. In this plan, it was declared that throughout the new territories, "After the year 1800 of the Christian era there shall be neither slavery nor involuntary servitude . . . otherwise than in punishment of crimes, whereof the party shall have been duly convicted to have been personally guilty." The southern states, to be sure, could not accept this limitation. Jefferson stood alone in his delegation in his attempt to retain the antislavery clause, and six northern votes were defeated by seven southern votes. This ordinance, without the antislavery clause, was passed on April 23, 1784. It never went into effect but is significant as an early attempt to organize the West and as a precursor of the tragic argument over slavery in the new territories.

As the law stood, slavery was to be admitted into all the western states—a plan unacceptable to many northerners. In a letter to Rufus King of Massachusetts, Timothy Pickering wrote:

> To suffer the continuance of slaves till they can gradually be emancipated, in States already overrun with them, may be pardonable, because unavoidable without hazarding greater evils; but to introduce them into countries where none now exist—countries which have been talked of, which have been boasted of, as asylums to the oppressed of the earth—can never be forgiven.

The issue of the organization of the Northwest and of revision of the 1784 ordinance was permitted to remain in abeyance until 1787. Fear of western political domination and a pessimistic report by James Monroe, then a member of Congress, over the possibilities of settlement in the new areas, served to retard the organizational process. Thus, it was only when Congress was pushed by a group of prominent New Englanders who wished to invest in western lands that the 1784 law was revised.

The ordinance of 1787 provided for a smooth transition from territorial status to statehood. It explicitly limited itself to the territories north of the Ohio River. The ordinance provided that there would be no slavery in the northwest, although provision was made for recapture of fugitives who had escaped into the territory from whom labor was "lawfully claimed in any one of the original states." Thus, the first fugitive-slave law was embodied in this "most liberal" territorial legislation.

The causes for the adoption of this action have been interpreted in many ways. One of the contemporary observations was made by Thomas Grayson to James Monroe: "The clause respecting slavery was agreed to by the southern members for the purpose of preventing tobacco and indigo from being made on the northwest side of the Ohio, as well as for several other political reasons." This act made the Ohio River a boundary between slavery and freedom, confining slavery to the South.

THE CONSTITUTION AND THE NEGRO

The Articles of Confederation governed the colonies from 1781 to 1788. During these years, several proposals were made to amend the Articles because they were inadequate to the maintenance of the union of states. In 1786, a large number of representatives assembled at Annapolis, Maryland, and passed a resolution proposing a national convention to be held in Philadelphia in May 1787 to consider the revision of the Articles. On May 25, the convention assembled. As soon as the task of organization was completed, differences of opinion began to appear among the delegates—between the large states and the small ones, the Tidewater section and the Piedmont section, the states'-rights supporters and the central government supporters and, finally, the slaveholding and the nonslaveholding representatives.

Many of the men who came together at Philadelphia in May 1787 were determined to establish a firm and stable union of the former English colonies. Not the least of their worries was the issue of slavery. In examining their actions with regard to slavery—as they dealt with the legal status of the slave, the problem of the fugitive slave and the slave trade—we find an overall pattern of deference to the claims of the southern ruling class.

The first issue on which the North and South were divided was similar to the requisition issue dealt with by the authors of the Confederation a decade previously. The southern delegates argued that, for purposes of apportionment of representatives in the lower house, the slaves should be considered as people. This meant that the South would have a larger representation. The North argued that slaves should be considered strictly as property and not be counted, therefore, for purposes of representation. The irony of the situation, of course, was that while the North proposed to consider slaves as human beings, they did not want them numbered in the population figures. The South, on the other hand, wanted slaves counted as regular people, but in effect treated them as property.

The seriousness of the situation can be appreciated when we recall that the delegate from North Carolina threatened that his state would never enter the Union on any terms that did not provide for at least three-fifths representation of the slaves. Gouverneur Morris of Pennsylvania, however, said that the people of Pennsylvania would revolt if they were considered on an equal footing with slaves. The final compromise was part of Article I, Section 2, and read as follows:

> Representatives and direct Taxes shall be apportioned among the several States which may be included within this Union, according to their respective Numbers, which shall be determined by adding to the whole number of free Persons, including those bound to Service for a Term of Years, and excluding Indians not taxed, three fifths of all other persons.

John Hope Franklin (*From Slavery to Freedom*) suggested that this compromise "was perhaps satisfactory to no one, but it demonstrates clearly the strength of the proslavery interests at the convention."

But the problem of whether or not the slave was actually a person or was simply property had certainly not been solved. James Madison sought to resolve the question of slave status by arguing that slaves were in some respects persons and in others property. He said that the United States Constitution properly viewed slaves in their mixed character.

The authors of the Constitution were faced also with the necessity of arriving at some decision on the status of the slave trade. The Pennsylvania Abolition Society had drafted a memorandum to be presented by Benjamin Franklin, asking that a discussion of the slave trade be placed on the agenda. However, when it became clear that many delegates wished to discuss the question, the proposition was withdrawn for fear of offending the southern delegates.

The debate was fiery and bitter. New England was divided because of the role which her merchants had played in the trade; the middle states, perhaps because of the influence of the Pennsylvanians, were firmly opposed to the trade. While many of the leaders of the delegations from the upper South desired a limit to the trade, the delegates from South Carolina and Georgia were militant. Charles Pinckney of South Carolina promised that his state would not enter a Union which barred the slave trade, although he added that "if the States be all left at liberty on this subject, South Carolina may perhaps do of herself what is wished, as Virginia and Maryland have already done." His cousin, General C. C. Pinckney, suggested that Virginia had abandoned her sister slave states on

LUTHER MARTIN

this issue so as to ensure a market for her surplus slaves.

Many delegates, including even Luther Martin from North Carolina, found a sanctioning of the slave trade noxious in a nation that had just fought for its own liberty. James Madison rebelled against the idea that the Constitution would even recognize the existence of property rights over human rights. But once again compromise was necessary. Article II, Section 9, reads as follows:

> The Migration or Importation of such Persons as any of the States now existing shall think proper to admit, shall not be prohibited by the Congress prior to the Year one thousand eight hundred and eight, but a Tax or duty may be imposed on such importation, not exceeding ten dollars for each Person.

Finally, toward the end of the session, in August 1787, the problem of fugitive slaves demanded attention. The Northwest Ordinance had already established the right of extradition of slave property, as had various Indian treaties concluded during the 1780's. With these precedents in existence, and with the tired delegates anxious to return home, the insertion of a fugitive-slave clause in Article IV, Section 21, met little opposition. The basic decisions on the legality of slavery, obviously, had been made long before, and the fugitive-slave clause was only a logical extention of the three-fifths compromise and the slave-trade compromise.

While the adoption of the federal Constitution firmly established the independence and republicanism of the new nation, it also marked the beginning of a period of reaction against the Negro. Slavery was recognized and allowed. The writers of the Constitution believed that good government rested on the right to own property—and slaves were as much property as land or currency.

Several explanations have been offered for this reactionary shift. Perhaps it grew out of an upper-class fear that the political revolution of 1775–83 would turn into a social rev-

DANIEL SHAYS AND HIS FOLLOWERS AT THE SPRINGFIELD, MASSACHUSETTS, COURTHOUSE.

The rebellion of Daniel Shays and other poor farmers against the practices of the wealthy merchants and property-owners in Massachusetts convinced the upper classes of the need for a strong federal constitution. Their fears for their property rights caused them to demand that the constitution not only safeguard against further outbreaks but also explicitly guarantee and defend their right to own property. The ratified Constitution thus virtually ensured the continuance of slavery, since slaves were an extremely valuable property.

olution. The rebellion in western Massachusetts led by Daniel Shays and the disorders in Rhode Island clearly tended to recommend to the wealthy the constitutional safeguards on slavery. For these upper classes, agitation over the slavery issue was clearly a part of the incipient social revolution that they so greatly feared. There may have been additional causes for the reaction. The rebellion of the blacks of the French colony of Santo Domingo, led by Toussaint L'Ouverture, struck fear into the hearts of the slaveholding South.

THE EMERGENCE OF A BLACK CONSCIOUSNESS

During the Revolution and the period of reaction that followed shortly thereafter, we find the first real emergence of a self-conscious Negro community in the United States.

Too often, the history of the Negro people in the United States has been written as though it were really the history of legislative and other efforts by "good-hearted whites" to uplift the "degraded masses" of black people.

During the years immediately after the Revolution, however, we find a new dynamism within the black community. There may have been several reasons for the development of the race consciousness and pride that appeared at that time: the growth of the free Negro class during the latter part of the eighteenth century, the experience many had in fighting for the Revolution and the cumulative effect of over one hundred years of insurrectionary activity.

The development of the Negro church was a part of this new self-awareness. It provided black people with the beginnings of a cohesive unit from which they could launch their protests for freedom.

CHAPTER EIGHT

Organization and Achievement

THE closing decades of the eighteenth century saw the emergence of an organized life among Negroes and the appearance of many individuals who showed considerable talent in different areas of activity. Among these individuals and within their organizations were both slaves and free blacks.

THE NEGRO POPULATION

When the thirteen colonies declared their independence, the Negro population was somewhat more than 500,000, but it had climbed to over 697,000 by 1790. Nearly 89 per cent lived in the South. Virginia led the southern states with over 300,000 Negroes, although South Carolina led the Union in terms of density of Negro population. Of the southern states, only Georgia contained fewer than 100,000 blacks. Less than 5 per cent were free.

The mid-Atlantic states contained 50,000 Negroes, of whom 28 per cent were free. Over 50 per cent of these mid-Atlantic blacks lived in New York, with the greatest concentration in and around New York City. New Jersey had 14,000 and Pennsylvania had slightly over 10,000.

By 1790, there were approximately 13,000 Negroes in New England, of whom roughly three-fourths were free men. Vermont and Massachusetts had no slaves at all.

Altogether, the new nation contained more than 697,000 Negroes. The free colored population numbered about 59,500, or 7.9 per cent of the total number. These free blacks were concentrated in the towns and cities. The Negro population as a whole, however, was heavily rural, as was the rest of the American population. The development of the plantation system and the beginnings of the extension of the frontier westward created a greater need for labor than the colonies had ever experienced. The Negro in America, in fact, was largely concentrated in rural areas until well into the twentieth century.

The free Negroes were subjected to restrictions in most of the states that prevented their being as free as the white citizens of their communities. Moreover, the presence of free

Negroes, particularly in the southern states, was regarded as inimical to a "satisfied" slave population. These states, therefore, restricted the increase of free Negroes as well as their activities. By 1790, nonetheless, these free Negroes had attained a firmer economic status. Many who were manumitted remained with their masters and worked for wages; others hired themselves as laborers by the day or week. They were workers in skilled as well as unskilled industries. Thrifty individuals in the free Negro population acquired property, and some also became slave-owners. Before the end of the eighteenth century, it was recorded that nearly one hundred houses in Philadelphia were owned by blacks. The great majority of the free Negroes, however, were still living in conditions of poverty, as were many whites. Leadership was needed to arouse their cooperation and to encourage them to pool their weak individual efforts in order to build efficient institutions for their race.

THE FORMATION OF NEGRO CHURCHES

The first evidences of cooperation among Negroes in group activities were shown in the churches. Organized bands of free Negroes had met for many years in the woods and in out-of-the-way places for the purpose of worship. Groups of people came together to associate themselves in the permanent establishment of a church. The first independently organized church efforts resulted in the formation of the Negro Baptist Church at Silver Bluff on the South Carolina side of the Savannah River, twelve miles from Augusta, Georgia. This church had been started during the Revolutionary War on the plantation of George Gaplain, who acted as patron to the small congregation. It continued its existence until the British occupation of Savannah in 1778. After the Treaty of 1783, the Silver Bluff Church revived under the leadership of Jesse Porter. The Silver Bluff Church eventu-

ally transferred its activity to Augusta, and in 1793, it became the first African Baptist Church in this city.

In this same period, a slave named George Liele began the task of organizing a Negro Baptist Church in Savannah. Liele left with the British at the end of the war, and at Kingston, Jamaica, he organized a church that soon had 500 members. In the meantime, another slave from Savannah, Andrew Bryan, continued Liele's early work. With the assistance of his benevolent white master, Bryan prevailed against the unwillingness of the local whites to permit blacks to organize their own churches. On January 20, 1788, a church was formed, and Bryan was ordained minister of the First Baptist Church of Savannah. The congregation grew steadily, numbering 700 by 1800. Bryan continued his religious activities in Savannah until his death in 1812.

In Virginia, Negroes increasingly began to move into their own Baptist churches during this period. Black Baptist churches were organized in Petersburg in 1776, in Richmond in 1780 and in Williamsburg in 1785. In the North, the same pattern prevailed. In 1809, thirteen Negro Baptists in Philadelphia organized their own church. In this same year, the Negro Baptists of Boston organized themselves under the Rev. Thomas Paul. Paul also assisted in the formation of what was to become the Abyssinian Baptist Church in New York City. Throughout these years in New England, a black Revolutionary War hero, Lemuel Haynes, preached to white congregations. A story of Haynes' relations with his congregations runs as follows: upon Haynes' appointment to the pastorate at the church in Torrington, Connecticut, a distinguished citizen sought to show his displeasure by wearing his hat during the service. "He had not preached far," recalled this pillar of Christianity," when I thought I saw the whitest man I ever knew in the pulpit, and I tossed my hat under the pew."

RICHARD ALLEN

FRANCIS ASBURY

ANDREW BRYAN

DANIEL COKER

The Bethel A.M.E. Church as it appeared early in the nineteenth century.

The Methodist churches also were popular among the blacks, and during this period, Negro Methodists, slave and free, began to develop their own organizations. During the late colonial period, missionaries under Bishops Thomas Coke and Francis Asbury were sent out to make arrangements for the religious training of Negroes. Negro missionaries were soon sent also. Prominent among this group were "Black Harry" Hoozier, a companion of Asbury, and Richard Allen of Philadelphia. Hoozier became a popular preacher with both Negro and white congregations; Dr. Benjamin Rush referred to him as "the greatest orator in America." He traveled extensively with Asbury and Coke and attracted many Negroes to Methodism.

Richard Allen purchased his freedom in 1777 and was converted to Methodism that same year. In 1786, he moved from Delaware to Philadelphia and became an active church worker in the mid-Atlantic states. From the beginning, he began to set up prayer meetings for his own people, but his proposals to establish separate organizations for Negroes met with opposition from both whites and blacks during these early years. On one occasion, Allen and two other black companions, Absalom Jones and William White, were pulled

from their knees in the midst of prayer and ordered to move to the balcony. Allen had brought many Negroes into this church, St. George's in Philadelphia, but as their numbers increased they were subject to many insults, which made separation inevitable.

The split from St. George's led to the formation of the Free African Society of Philadelphia. Under the leadership of Allen and Jones, this group gave rise to two church organizations. The Bethel African Methodist Episcopal (A.M.E.) Church was founded in 1794, with Allen as pastor. Jones led the St. Thomas Protestant Episcopal Church, having been ordained in the Episcopal Church in August 1794. Historically more important, however, was the fact that, in 1799, Bishop Asbury ordained Richard Allen as a deacon. The organization of Allen's church and his ordination really mark the founding of the African Methodist Episcopal church.

In 1791, Allen purchased a lot for his church, and in 1793 a blacksmith shop was hauled to the site and converted to a place of worship. Asbury dedicated the building even though Allen and his colleagues had issued a manifesto in which they said that they "thought it necessary to provide for ourselves a house separate from our white brethren."

Branches of the A.M.E. Church were set up in Baltimore, Wilmington and various towns in Pennsylvania and New Jersey. Among those assisting Allen were Daniel Coker, Nicholson Gilliard and Morris Brown. In 1816, the churches joined together in a national organization. Daniel Coker was chosen bishop, but he resigned and Allen assumed the post. The A.M.E. Church quickly became the leading organization among Negro Methodists: by 1820, there were 4,000 members in Philadelphia and almost 2,000 in Baltimore. The organization spread west to Pittsburgh and south to Charleston, although the Vesey insurrection of 1822 checked the growth of all separate Negro organizations in the South, including the A.M.E. Church.

James Varick, first bishop of the African Methodist Episcopal Zion Church.

The free Negro population, partly in response to white hostility from the John Street Methodist Espiscopal Church in Philadelphia, founded the African Methodist Episcopal Zion Church in 1796. This movement was led by Peter Williams, Francis Jacobs, Charles Anderson, George Collins, Christopher Rush and James Varick, who was elected the church's first bishop in 1822. Although in the beginning they tended to be closer to the white church than Allen's group, they split with the whites totally in 1820.

Other denominations also went about setting up separate organizations. In 1809, thirteen Negroes were dismissed from a white Baptist congregation in Philadelphia. Led by the Rev. Burrows, they decided to form their own church. Under the leadership of Thomas Paul, Negro Baptists in Boston organized their own church in 1809. Paul also helped to set up the Abyssinian Baptist Church in New York City at about the same time.

It is possible to argue that the establishment of separate Negro churches actually represented the full acceptance of white cultural hegemony by the blacks who were involved in these organizations. They fully accepted Christian values, and since in early Protestant America these values often tended to be identical with "white values," this acceptance might be considered as further acknowledgment that they were subservient to the whites. This is not the whole truth, however. For the organization of separate churches was really a very important step forward in the development of a specifically black consciousness. These churches were sometimes formed as a strong answer to exclusion by white churches. And sometimes, as in Savannah, the Negro churches organized despite the determined opposition of many white leaders.

The Black Baptist Church at Williamsburg, Virginia, was driven underground at one point in its early existence. The formation of separate churches gave free and slave Negroes an opportunity to develop their separate identity and their own group of leaders. Certainly, there was no break from the dominant racist ideology, but there was at least an organizational break with the oppressing groups.

THE FIRST AFRICAN MASONIC LODGE

Following closely in the path of the first church organizations, the secret societies came in rapid succession. The first one of significance was the African Masonic Lodge. The organization of this lodge was due to the efforts of Prince Hall at Boston, Massachusetts. He had come to America from Barbados in March 1765, at the age of thirty. He became associated with a group of young men who were interested in the life of the community and who were concerned because they could have little participation in it. Negroes were not welcomed in public places, not even in the churches. They were restricted in their occupations, and no adequate provision was made for their education.

Prince Hall determined to lead Negroes toward a larger place in Boston for themselves. Toward this end, he applied himself to his studies while he continued to work at his trade of soapmaking. Within a short time, he was ordained a minister, which gave him the opportunity for greater public activity. He had to make his way forward under handicaps, and his struggle for recognition was intensely difficult. He was actively interested in the antislavery movement and an advocate of citizenship and education for Negroes. He was a leader in the organization of the Sons of the African Society, which was established in Boston to aid in the amelioration of the condition of the Negro population. Between 1773 and 1778, Hall sent several petitions and protests to the Massachusetts legislature, denouncing slavery and the abuses of discrimination. He served creditably with a Massachusetts regiment during the War for Independence and fought at Bunker Hill.

Prince Hall had been interested in Freemasonry from the period of his travels to England as a sailor. It was a distinction to be a Mason in the eighteenth century, and no man who was a slave could become one. The proposal to establish a Masonic lodge for Negroes was regarded then as an idle dream even among the 9,600 free colored people in Massachusetts. Hall called together fourteen of his contemporaries in Boston, nonetheless, and endeavored to persuade the American Masonic bodies to grant them recognition. These attempts failed. He then turned to the soldiers of the British Army stationed near Bunker Hill. The request was granted by these soldiers, who had constituted themselves into a British Army Lodge. This lodge, according to the customs of that period, petitioned the Mother Grand Lodge in England for a warrant to set up the new lodge requested by the Negroes of Boston.

PRINCE HALL

This warrant was issued in England on September 29, 1784, to African Lodge No. 459. With the sanction of the English body, the African lodge became the African Grand Lodge so that it could issue dispensations to African lodges in other places. These events leading to the establishment of an African Lodge of Free and Accepted Masons were significant in the history of the development of black organizations. Prince Hall was the first Grand Master of a state Grand Lodge of Free and Accepted Masons who were Negroes. He guided the extension of the privileges of the order to other cities and assisted in the order's growth and expansion until his death in 1807. By 1825, chapters of black Masonry existed in Rhode Island, New York, Pennsylvania, Maryland and the District of Columbia. The Masons in turn gave birth to other uplift societies—the Colored Knights of Pythias, the Grand United Order of True Reformers, the Knights of Labor and the International Order of Good Samaritans.

Although these early fraternal organizations worked diligently against slavery, their

To all and every our Right Worshipful & loving Brethren, we, Thomas Howard, Earl of Effingham, Lord Howard, &c., &c., &c., Acting Grand Master under the authority of His Royal Highness, Henry Frederick Duke of Cumberland &c., &c., &c., Grand Master of the Most Ancient and Honorable Society of Free and Accepted Masons, sends greeting:

Know Ye, that we, at the humble petition of our right trusty and well-beloved Brethren, Prince Hall, Boston Smith, Thomas Sanderson and several other Brethren residing in Boston, New England in North America do hereby constitute the said Brethren into a regular Lodge of Free and Accepted Masons, under the title or denomination of the African Lodge, to be opened in Boston aforesaid, and do further at their said petition, hereby appoint the said Prince Hall to be Master Boston Smith, Senior Warden, and Thomas Sanderson, Junior Warden, for opening the said Lodge, and for such further time only as shall be thought proper by the Brethren thereof, it being our will that this our appointment of the above officers shall in no wise affect any future election of officers of the Lodge, but that such election shall be regulated agreeable to such by-laws of said Lodge as shall be consistent with the general laws of the society, contained in the Book of Constitution; and we hereby will and require you, the said Prince Hall, to take special care that all and every the said Brethren are or have been regularly made Masons, and that they do observe, perform, and keep all the rules and orders contained in the Book of Constitutions; and further, that you do, from time to time, cause to be entered in a book kept for that purpose, an account of your proceedings in the Lodge, together with all such rules, orders and regulations, as shall be made for the good government of the same, that in no wise you omit once in every year to send to us, or our successors, Grand Masters, or to Rowland Holt, Esq., our Deputy Grand Master, for the time being an account in writing of your said proceedings, and copies of all such rules, orders, and regulations as shall be made as aforesaid, together with a list of the members of the Lodge, and such a sum of money as may suit the circumstances of the Lodge and reasonably be expected, toward the Grand Charity. Moreover, we hereby will and require you, the said Prince Hall, as soon as conveniently may be, to send an account in writing of what may be done by virtue of these presents.

Given at London, under our hand and seal of Masonry, this 29th day of September, A.L. 5784, A.D. 1784.

"By the Grand Master's Command,
R. Holt, D. G. M."

"Witness
Wm. White, G. S."

A copy of the original charter of the African Lodge.

basic ideology did not actually question existing race relations to any significant degree. The Masons were primarily a self-help organization with strong ties to existing white organizations. Thus, in one sense, because they did not readily break with the established social ideology, they were conservative. In paternalistic fashion, Hall urged his colleagues not to waste their money on vain, transitory pleasures and excesses but rather to labor and save in order that they might help raise up their fellows. "Make you this beginning," he declared, "and who knows but God may rise up some friend or body of friends as he did in Philadelphia, to open a school for the blacks here, as that friendly city has done." In a period of acute class conflict, Hall sided with the upper classes. Speaking of Shays' Rebellion in 1786, Hall wrote to the governor of Massachusetts to offer him the assistance of black Masonry: "We, by the Providence of God, are members of a lodge that not only enjoins upon us to be peaceable subjects to the civil power where we reside, but it also forbids our having concern in any plot or conspiracies against the state where we dwell." These organizations might be considered progressive or radicalizing influences insofar as they fostered a sense of black identity, but Prince Hall did not deceive himself or his followers as to the status of the Negro in post-Revolutionary Boston:

> Patience, I say; for were we not possessed of a great measure of it, we could not bear up under the daily insults we meet within the streets of Boston, much more on public days of recreation. How, at such times are we painfully abused, and that to such a degree that we may be said to carry our lives in our hands, and the arrows of death are flying about our heads.

THE FREE AFRICAN SOCIETIES

The Free African Societies contributed substantially to the development of racial awareness among the urban free Negroes.

The Prince Hall Monument in Boston, Massachusetts.

The concentration of free Negroes in the cities of Philadelphia, New York, Boston and Newport led to the development of social and economic problems related to their presence. Organizations of the self-help and mutual-aid type sprang up in response to these needs. The first of these organizations, the Free African Society, was started in Philadelphia in 1787. It combined the purposes of a beneficial society and an ethical improvement society. Its functions were to assist the sick and the needy, to bury the dead and to maintain the standards of marriage and family life among its members. Its constitution and by-laws were drawn up on April 12, 1787.

The preamble to the constitution directed attention to the two men who were responsible for the organization, Absalom Jones and

Richard Allen, "who for their religious life and conversation have obtained a good report among men." Eight persons assembled at a meeting to draw up the society's constitution, which provided that the qualification for membership was sober and clean living. Instances occurred in which members were expelled for breaking these rules. The payment of dues by the members led to the building up of a treasury. In 1790, the society had deposited in the Bank of North America the sum of forty-two pounds, nine shillings and one penny. The society agreed to cooperate with the Pennsylvania Abolition Society. The Free African Society was the first of the Negro organizations for the advancement of the moral as well as the economic condition of the Negro population.

Similar organizations arose in other cities where there were large numbers of Negroes. The African Society was organized by forty-four Negroes in Boston in 1796. Perhaps

to calm the white populace, it avowed its aims to be solely benevolent. It pledged to admit to membership "no one . . . who shall committ any injustice or outrage against the laws of their country." In 1798, another group of Boston Negroes founded the Sons of the African Society "for the mutual benefit of each other," while "behaving ourselves as true and faithful Citizens of the Commonwealth in which we live." For its members, the organization sought to ensure spiritual growth, the care of widows and decent burial.

Such benevolent organizations were not confined to the North. At Charleston, South Carolina, in 1790, the Brown Fellowship Society was organized for mutual aid in distress and for the promotion of social relationships among its members. The laws, however, of the southern states, which prohibited meetings of free Negroes, tended to drive these groups underground.

THE FIRST AFRICAN SCHOOLS

Closely associated with the program of the abolitionists for the emancipation of the slaves were plans for the education of slaves and free Negroes. By the dawn of the Revolution, Negro education was beginning. In 1770, the Quakers of Philadelphia established a school and provided for its supervision by a committee of the Friends' Monthly Meeting. It was supported by the contributions of Friends. Anthony Benezet, a member of the committee of supervision, became in 1782 the teacher of the school, remaining there until his death in 1784. His will provided for the maintenance of the school, which was continued through the years as a monument to his work. Another school was opened by the same Friends' committee to teach the fundamentals of elementary education to the boys and sewing to the girls. There were also two schools in which white and colored children were taught, supported by funds controlled by the

---

The Free African Society

Preamble

Wheereas, Absalom Jones and Richard Allen, two men of the African race, who, for their religious life and conversation, have obtained a good report among men, these persons, from a love to the people of their complexion whom they beheld with sorrow, because of their irreligious and uncivilized state, often communed together upon this painful and important subject in order to form some kind of religious society, but there being too few to be found under the like concern, and those who were, differed in their religious sentiments; with these circumstances they labored for some time, till it was proposed, after a serious communication of sentiment, that a society should be formed, without regard to religious tenets, provided, the persons lived an orderly and sober life, in order to support one another in sickness, and for the benefit of their widows and fatherless children.

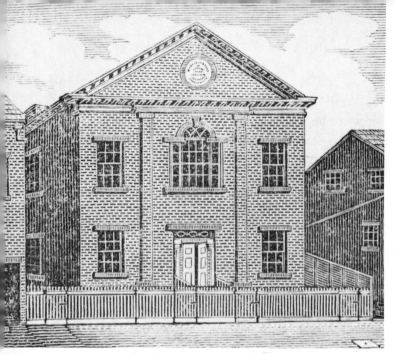

The New York African Free School.

trustees of "the Associates of Dr. Bray in London."

Two schools supported by Negroes also existed at this time. One was held at the St. Thomas Protestant Episcopal Church, where Absalom Jones was the rector; and the other was maintained by Richard Allen's Bethel African Methodist Episcopal Church. In 1789, the Society for the Free Instruction of Orderly Blacks and People of Color conducted an evening school for adults. By 1797, there were seven schools for the education of Negroes in the city of Philadelphia, and the average attendance was reported to be nearly three hundred.

Other cities in the East showed the same developments during this period. The first New York African Free School was established in 1787 through the efforts of the Manumission Society of that city, and forty pupils were admitted in November 1787. Cornelius Davis, the teacher of this school, had given up teaching in a school for white children in order to teach in the newly opened school for Negro children. A female teacher was employed in 1791 to teach sewing to the girls. The school continued for many years, and some of the outstanding Negro leaders of subsequent periods were educated there.

Boston was a center of education for Negroes from the earliest period of their presence. The Negro children at one time could attend school along with the white, although the number who accepted this opportunity was small. An effort, however, was made to establish a separate school for Negroes in 1798, which led to the founding of a school that was later moved to the African Meeting House. The existence of this school did not affect the right of Negroes to attend the other schools in the city. A group of clergymen began the maintenance of a school for Negroes in 1773 at Newport, Rhode Island; it was opened with thirty children, who were to be taught the fundamentals. New Jersey also briefly contained several Negro schools.

Some religious groups in the southern states considered the educational situation facing the Negro population and in their meetings and conferences passed resolutions enjoining their members to aid in the religious instruction of Negroes. The Annual Meetings of the Quakers held in Baltimore, Maryland, in 1770, 1785 and 1793 passed resolutions on this subject. In 1781 and 1782, the Quakers of Virginia appointed committees to plan for the education and religious instruction of Negroes. Robert Pleasants, a Quaker, was instrumental in the organization of a school near Graweely Run, Virginia. The Methodists and the Baptists gathered the children into Sunday Schools, where many learned to read and write as well as to understand religious teachings.

The apprenticeship laws of Virginia, administered first by the Anglican church and later by state officials, made provision for the education of children and for teaching trades. By 1787, Thomas Jefferson asserted that educated Negroes could boast of some accomplishments, for he knew that "many of them have been brought up to the handicraft arts and from that circumstance, have always been associated with the whites." He added that some had been liberally educated.

EARLY MILITANTS

There were several early writers and activists who were less equivocal in their attitudes toward slavery and toward the lot of their own people. Among these was a native African by the name of Gustavus Vassa. Vassa was born in West Africa in 1745 and was brought to a Virginia plantation in 1756. As a young man, he saved money and purchased his own freedom. He eventually made his home in Great Britain, where he labored in the cause of the early abolition movement. In 1789, he published his two-volume autobiography, using both his African and American names: *The Interesting Narrative of the Life of Olaudah Equiano, or Gustavus Vassa, the*

GUSTAVUS VASSA

African. Eight editions of the book were sold within five years.

Equiano-Vassa's militancy was uncompromising. In his writings, he ceaselessly attacked the cultural values of the white Protestant "nominal Christians" who could condone and encourage the evil of slavery. He reminded these people that they had learned from their God the rule of treating others as they themselves would wish to be treated. "Is it not enough," he demanded of them, "that we are torn from our country and friends, to toil for your luxury and lust of gain? . . . Why are parents to lose their children, brothers their sisters, or husbands their wives? Surely this is a new refinement in cruelty."

Another early militant was the New England product of a Negro-Indian marriage, Paul Cuffee. He was a skilled seaman who, in 1780, began to organize his own company to build ships. He was a striking financial success, and attempted to turn his wealth to some social and political purpose. During the war, he and his brother, as taxpayers, unsuccessfully sued the state of Massachusetts for the right to vote. He became a Quaker, and this fostered his interest in Negro improvement. He assisted in the foundation of Negro schools and became interested very early in the colonization of Negroes in Africa.

THE

INTERESTING NARRATIVE

OF

THE LIFE

OF

OLAUDAH EQUIANO,

OR

GUSTAVUS VASSA,

THE AFRICAN.

WRITTEN BY HIMSELF.

VOL. II.

Behold, God is my salvation : I will trust and not be afraid, for the Lord Jehovah is my strength and my song ; he also is become my salvation. And in that day shall ye say, Praise the Lord, call upon his name, declare his doings among the people, Isaiah xii. 2, 4

FIRST AMERICAN EDITION

NEW-YORK:

Printed and Sold by W. DURELL, at his Book Store and Printing-Office, No. 19, Q. Street. M,DCC,XCI.

ACHIEVEMENTS IN THE ARTS

American Negro writing had its beginnings in the eighteenth century, which saw the birth of a distinctive literary form—the slave narrative. These records were sometimes dictated to others and sometimes written by the slave or ex-slave himself. The earliest of the published slave accounts, *A Narrative of the Uncommon Sufferings and Surprizing Deliverance of Briton Hammon, a Negro Man* (Boston, 1760), was a summary, by Hammon, of his capture and imprisonment (while on an errand for his master) by Indians and Spaniards, his eventual escape and his accidental reunion with his master.

Jupiter Hammon, one of the first Negro poets of whom there is record, was a slave belonging to Henry Lloyd of Long Island, New York. His first poem, dated December 25, 1760, was composed of eighty lines of rhyme printed on a double column broadside. Although very little is known of his life, several of his poems have been discovered. Among them are "An Evening Thought"; "An Address to Miss Phillis Wheatley, Ethiopian Poetess"; a dialogue entitled "The Kind Master and the Dutiful Servant"; and "A Poem for Children, with Thoughts on Death." Hammon was no militant; he published an "Address to the Negroes of the State of New York" in 1787 in which he declared that Negroes should bear the burden of slavery lightly. He did believe, however, that slavery was evil and that young blacks should be manumitted.

A former slave dictating the story of his life.

PHILLIS WHEATLEY

Negro poetess Phillis Wheatley was born about 1753 and brought to the United States at the age of eight from her home in Senegal, West Africa. Miss Wheatley lived as a slave with the Wheatley family of Boston, Massachusetts. The members of this family manumitted her and took a genuine interest in her until their deaths. Her poetry was as good as much American poetry of her time and gained for her a prominent place in contemporary Boston literary circles. In spirit and in execution, her poetry is not unlike other poems of the day, which were in style largely imitative of English poetry. Artfully, she produced an accomplished reproduction of the idioms of the school of Alexander Pope, the English group of neoclassical versemakers.

Her first poem was published in 1770. It was "An Elegiac Poem, on the Death of . . . the Late Reverend, and Pious George Whitefield." Within a few months, it passed through six editions in Boston, Philadelphia and New York, bringing her considerable renown. Her work was mentioned by George Washington and was highly praised in Great Britain, where Miss Wheatley lived for a time as the guest of the Countess of Huntingdon.

Phillis Wheatley wrote not as a Negro but as a member of fashionable late eighteenth-century literary society. Having never experienced the hardships of field labor, but only the benevolent treatment of a kind master and mistress, she did not really identify herself with the oppressed slaves. Thus, she wrote:

> Twas mercy brought me from my Pagan land,
> Taught my beknighted soul to understand
> That there's a God, that there's a Saviour too:
> Once I redemption neither sought nor knew.

Limited by current literary fashions, Miss Wheatley could only express rather conventional sentiments. But, on at least one occasion, she abandoned these conventions and seemed to attempt to speak for her people. To the Earl of Dartmouth she wrote:

> Should you, my lord, while you peruse my song,
> Wonder from whence my love of Freedom sprung,
> Whence flow these wishes for the common good,
> By feeling hearts, alone, best understood,
> I, young in life, by seeming cruel fate
> Was snatched from Afric's fancied happy seat:
> What pangs excruciating must molest,
> What sorrows labor in my parent's breast!
> Steeled was that soul, and by no misery moved,
> That from a father seized his best beloved:
> Such, such my case. And can I but pray
> Others may never feel tyrannic sway?

Another important body of early writings by American Negroes is concerned with social problems, particularly with slavery or with discrimination against free Negroes. In the 1790's, Benjamin Banneker, a free Negro who distinguished himself as a mathematician and astronomer, wrote and published an almanac. In one issue, he submitted an advanced and liberal plan for a Peace Office (as opposed to a War Office) for the United States. Richard Allen and Absalom Jones, at about the same time, published their account of the help rendered by Negroes to the citizens of Philadelphia during the yellow fever epidemic of 1793.

It is thought that American Negro art began with the work of the skilled craftsmen, both slave and free, who in parts of the South became the community's wood-carvers, cabinetmakers and metalsmiths. The fine wrought-iron balconies of New Orleans built from 1788 to about 1830 (but not the later, coarser cast-iron work) are believed to be the work of these Negro craftsmen. One craftsman whose name has come down to us was Tom Day, a cabinetmaker who worked in North Carolina in the early nineteenth century and whose fine pieces are now collectors' items.

Patrick Reason was a prominent engraver of New York, who was known as "a gentleman of ability and a fine artist." Some of his engravings were later used as frontispieces for the biographies of fugitive slaves. One of these was an engraving of James Williams, whose experiences in slavery were given wide publicity by the antislavery people. One of Phillis Wheatley's poems was dedicated "To S. M., a Young African Painter, on Seeing His Works." This referred to Scipio Moorhead, who had a number of paintings to his credit.

ACHIEVEMENTS IN SCIENTIFIC INQUIRY

Science was advancing in the United States toward the close of the eighteenth century. Many obstacles were faced by pioneer Americans in this field, and Negroes who were interested in the sciences were uncommon. Individuals with talent had little opportunity to become acquainted with scientific advances. There were a number of Negroes, nevertheless, who did show enthusiasm for scientific fields in spite of the peculiar obstacles in their way. Their beginnings, as elementary as they may now appear, do demonstrate the existence of a potential that might have been realized more fully had there been more opportunity for these thinkers in American intellectual life.

The art of practicing medicine developed very slowly in the period just before, during and after the Revolutionary War. There was a shortage of trained physicians; and even those who were trained were not informed of the causes and cures for most diseases. Harmful methods of healing were practiced. Charlatans peddled their nostrums from village to village. Among whites and Negroes, superstitions about sicknesses and their cures abounded.

The practice of medicine among the nation's blacks began with the transfer here and continuation of the practices of the medicine man in Africa. His conjuration was well known in many slave communities in the South. Some, however, discovered useful remedies. One of these men, known only as Caesar, developed a cure for poisoning in 1792, as well as many remedies using roots and herbs. The Assembly of South Carolina was so impressed with Caesar's value to the community that his freedom was purchased, and he was provided with an annuity of one hundred dollars. A slave in Charleston, South Carolina, in 1797, was known as a "Doctor" and practiced medicine in that city. Other Negroes who were barbers learned how to "bleed" and united these two functions in the practice of phlebotomy. Bleeding was the treatment given for many ailments, generally performed by those who knew the barber's trade. Since Negroes were the most numerous barbers in the southern states, they were also the most active users of this method of treating diseases.

James Derham, referred to as "a practicioner of physics," was born in Philadelphia in 1762. While a boy, he was transferred by his master to Dr. John Kearsley, Jr., who employed him in the mixing of medicines and in the routine duties of his practice. Following the death of Dr. Kearsley, Derham passed through the hands of several owners. Among these were Dr. George West, surgeon in the Sixteenth British Regiment, and Dr. Robert

DR. BENJAMIN RUSH

Benjamin Banneker was born in Maryland in November 1731 and died in October 1806. Since his mother was a free white woman, although his father was a slave, Banneker was born free. He was sent at an early age to a "pay school" conducted for white children, but to which several Negro children were admitted. He was especially interested in mathematics and mechanics and developed a talent for science. In 1790, he was able to construct a clock with a small watch as a model. Three years later, entrepreneur George Ellicott began the erection of flour mills near the Patapsco River, a short distance from Baltimore, near the Banneker home. Banneker visited the mill regularly to observe the machinery. Ellicott showed interest in his progress and supplied him with books on mathematical and astronomical subjects. He was described by one who saw him at Ellicott's Mills as a man "of black complexion, medium stature, of uncommonly soft and gentlemanly manners and of pleasing colloquial powers."

Dove of New Orleans. Derham was employed by these physicians in ministering to their patients. After several years of service, Dr. Dove permitted Derham to purchase his freedom. He then became a practitioner in New Orleans, making use of his knowledge of medicine and becoming exceptionally proficient in treating the diseases prevalent in the city's tropical climate.

At the age of twenty-six, Derham's practice was bringing him the sum of three thousand dollars a year. Dr. Benjamin Rush, who was professor of the Institutes and Practice of Physics at the University of Pennsylvania, stated in an address to the Pennsylvania Society for Promoting the Abolition of Slavery, on January 5, 1789, that he had talked with James Derham concerning most of the diseases of the section of the country in which he was living and had found him acquainted with the modern methods for their treatment. Dr. Rush had expected to make suggestions to him regarding the medicines to be used; instead, Derham suggested others to him.

BENJAMIN BANNEKER

Banneker began to devote much time to his studies, and in 1791 he published an Almanac for 1792. This was the first of the series of annual almanacs that Banneker had published between 1792 and 1802 through Goddard and Angel, Almanac Publishers, in Baltimore. This brought him to the attention of prominent persons, and correspondence was opened with some of them. Among these, Thomas Jefferson stood foremost. Along with a copy of his first almanac, Banneker sent to Jefferson his now famous letter entreating him to use all his powers to put an end to slavery. He appealed to the then Secretary of State on Jefferson's own principles of democracy and libertarianism. Jefferson replied to Banneker with high praise for his work, stating that no one could wish more than he to see such proofs as from this publication "that Nature has given to our black brethren talents equal to those of other men, and that the appearance of a want of them is owing only to the degraded condition of their existence, both in Africa and America." In a letter to the Marquis de Condorcet on August 20, 1791, Jefferson related that he had obtained a position for Banneker "under one of our chief engineers laying out the new Federal city on the Potomac."

In 1789, commissioners were appointed to lay out the lines of the District of Columbia. The work of surveying and laying out this territory was given to Major Pierre L'Enfant, formerly a French engineer and an officer in the American Army during the Revolution. His assistants were Benjamin Ellicott, Andrew Ellicott and Isaac Roberdeau. Shortly after beginning the work, L'Enfant resigned and Andrew Ellicott was appointed chief engineer.

When Ellicott assumed his new post, he recommended that Banneker be attached to the commission. It is probable that Banneker had some previous connection with the work, for the *Georgetown Weekly Ledger,* March 12, 1791, made note of the arrival of Major Pierre L'Enfant "who was accompanied by Benjamin Banneker, an Ethiopian, whose abilities as a surveyor and astronomer have been recognized by Secretary Jefferson." Banneker was one of the distinguished Negroes of his time whose unusual talents set him off from the majority of his contemporaries, both white and black. His achievements were evidence of the potentialities of many other Negro Americans who were prevented from developing their talents by the strictures of a racist society.

CHAPTER NINE

The Period of Reaction

REVOLUTIONARY doctrines concerning the rights of man gradually assumed secondary importance as the problems involved in organizing and unifying the new government became paramount in 1790. While there were those who refused to abandon the liberalism of the Revolution, conservative trends were clearly emergent. The continuation of sectional strife over the question of slavery and the slave trade was one major demonstration of these opposing forces in action.

The divisions that arose during the debates in the Constitutional Convention were carried over into the state ratifying conventions. There were serious divisions between the proslavery states and the nonslaveholding states. There were men in the northern states who described the Constitution as a proslavery document and those in the South who declared that the safeguards for their property were totally inadequate. Curiously, however, only one amendment was offered treating any aspect of slavery. Rhode Island proposed that "as a traffic tending to establish and continue slavery of the human species is disgraceful to the cause of liberty and humanity, Congress shall as soon as may be possible promote and establish such laws as may effectually prevent the importation of slaves of every description." Congress took no action upon this proposal, although there were frequent discussions concerning slavery and the slave trade.

SESSIONS OF THE FIRST CONGRESS

The first Congress met in New York and began its work on April 6, 1789. The question of the slave trade was injected into the debate on the duties of the House of Representatives. An amendment to Representative Porter's slave-trade bill called for a tax of ten dollars on each slave imported. Opposition was immediately presented by the delegates from South Carolina and Georgia. After a short discussion, the amendment was withdrawn, and it was stated that it would be introduced later as a separate measure. The measure was introduced as proposed, but it was delayed until the next session and then was not given final action. The philosophy of the Revolution was evident during these debates only in rare instances, and then it was followed by no positive action. It was clear that the representatives from the South were determined not to tolerate any taxation of the trade.

Slavery was discussed following the presentation of memorials urging action against the continuation of its evils. On February 11, 1790, the Society of Friends sent to Congress the first petition against slavery and the slave trade. The Friends requested Congress to abolish the slave trade. Congressman Thomas Hartley of Pennsylvania made a motion to refer the petition to committee. William L. Smith of South Carolina objected to this procedure, and Burke of the same state also objected to having outsiders meddling in their local problems. Elbridge Gerry of Massachusetts defended the right of petition and expressed the hope that every nation would wipe out this stain. The House committee to which the memorial was referred said that "Congress has no authority to interfere in the emancipation of slaves, or in the treatment of them within any of the states." On the following day, the Pennsylvania Society for Promoting the Abolition of Slavery presented another memorial that directed attention to

BENJAMIN FRANKLIN

slavery and its inconsistency with the Preamble to the Constitution and the avowed aims of the American people. Benjamin Franklin had signed the paper as president of the society.

The Pennsylvania Society's memorial occasioned another debate on slavery. Smith of South Carolina declared that the southern states would never have entered the union "unless their property had been guaranteed to them." He said that "when we entered this confederacy, we did it from political and not from moral motives." Slaves were, he argued, necessary to till the rice and indigo lands. The Representatives from Virginia and Maryland were willing to prohibit the foreign slave trade. Their motivation, however, was clearly economic rather than moral, for such legislation would give those states the opportunity to transport their own surplus slaves to the other southern states.

ELBRIDGE GERRY

AN ADDRESS TO THE PUBLIC

*From the Pennsylvania Society for Promoting the Abolition of Slavery, and
the Relief of Free Negroes unlawfully held in Bondage*

It is with peculiar satisfaction we assure the friends of humanity, that, in prosecuting the design of our association, our endeavors have proved successful, far beyond our most sanguine expectations.

Encouraged by this success, and by the daily progress of that luminous and benign spirit of liberty which is diffusing itself throughout the world, and humbly hoping for the continuance of the divine blessing on our labors, we have ventured to make an important addition to our original plan; and do therefore earnestly solicit the support and assistance of all who can feel the tender emotions of sympathy and compassion, or relish the exalted pleasure of beneficence.

Slavery is such an atrocious debasement of human nature, that its very extirpation, if not performed with solicitous care, may sometimes open a source of serious evils.

The unhappy man, who has long been treated as a brute animal, too frequently sinks beneath the common standard of the human species. The galling chains that bind his body do also fetter his intellectual faculties, and impair the social affections of his heart. Accustomed to move like a mere machine, by the will of a master, reflection is suspended; he has not the power of choice; and reason and conscience have but litttle influence over his conduct, because he is chiefly governed by the passion of fear. He is poor and friendless; perhaps worn out by extreme labor, age, and disease.

Under such circumstances, freedom may often prove a misfortune to himself, and prejudicial to society.

Attention to emancipated black people, it is therefore to be hoped, will become a branch of our national policy; but, as far as we contribute to promote this emancipation, so far that attention is evidently a serious duty incumbent on us, and which we mean to discharge to the best of our judgment and abilities.

To instruct, to advise, to qualify those who have been restored to freedom, for the exercise and enjoyment of civil liberty; to promote in them habits of industry; to furnish them with employments suited to their age, sex, talents, and other circumstances; and to procure their children an education calculated for their future situation in life,—these are the great outlines of the annexed plan, which we have adopted, and which we conceive will essentially promote the public good, and the happiness of these our hitherto too much neglected fellow-creatures.

A plan so extensive cannot be carried into execution without considerable pecuniary resources, beyond the present ordinary funds of the Society. We hope much from the generosity of enlightened and benevolent freemen, and will gratefully receive any donations or subscriptions for this purpose which may be made to our Treasurer, James Starr, or to James Pemberton, Chairman of our Committee of Correspondence.

Signed by order of the Society,

B. Franklin, *President*

Philadelphia, 9th of November, 1789

THE FUGITIVE SLAVE ACT OF 1793

SECTION 1. *Be it enacted by the Senate and House of Representatives of the United States of America in Congress assembled,* That whenever the executive authority of any state in the Union, or of either of the territories northwest or south of the river Ohio, shall demand any person as a fugitive from justice, of the executive authority of any such state or territory to which such person shall have fled, and shall moreover produce the copy of an indictment found, or an affidavit made before a magistrate of any state or territory as aforesaid, charging the person so demanded, with having committed treason, felony or other crime, certified as authentic by the governor or chief magistrate of the state or territory from whence the person so charged fled, it shall be the duty of the executive authority of the state or territory to which such person shall have fled, to cause him or her to be arrested and secured, and notice of the arrest to be given to the executive authority making such demand, or to the agent of such authority appointed to receive the fugitive, and to cause the fugitive to be delivered to such agent when he shall appear: But if no such agent shall appear within six months from the time of the arrest, the prisoner may be discharged. And all costs or expenses incurred to the state or territory making such demand, shall be paid by such state or territory.

SEC. 2. *And be it further enacted,* That any agent, appointed as aforesaid, who shall receive the fugitive into his custody, shall be empowered to transport him or her to the state or territory from which he or she shall have fled. And if any person or persons shall by force set at liberty, or rescue the fugitive from such agent while transporting, as aforesaid, the person or persons so offending shall, on conviction, be fined not exceeding five hundred dollars, and be imprisoned not exceeding one year.

SEC. 3. *And be it also enacted,* That when a person held to labour in any of the United States, or in either of the territories on the northwest or south of the river Ohio, under the laws thereof, shall escape into any other of the said states or territory, the person to whom such labour or service may be due, his agent or attorney, is hereby empowered to seize or arrest such fugitive from labour, and to take him or her before any judge of the circuit or district courts of the United States, residing or being within the state, or before any magistrate of a county, city or town corporate, wherein such seizure or arrest shall be made, and upon proof to the satisfaction of such judge or magistrate, either by oral testimony or affidavit taken before and certified by a magistrate of any such state or territory, that the person so seized or arrested, doth, under the laws of the state or territory from which he or she fled, owe service or labour to the person claiming him or her, it shall be the duty of such judge or magistrate to give a certificate thereof to such claimant, his agent or attorney, which shall be sufficient warrant for removing the said fugitive from labour, to the state or territory from which he or she fled.

SEC. 4. *And be it further enacted,* That any person who shall knowingly and willing obstruct or hinder such claimant, his agent or attorney in so seizing or arresting such fugitive from labour, or shall rescue such fugitive from such claimant, his agent or attorney when so arrested pursuant to the authority herein given or declared; or shall harbor or conceal such person after notice that he or she was a fugitive from labour, as aforesaid, shall, for either of the said offences, forfeit and pay the sum of five hundred dollars. Which penalty may be recovered by and for the benefit of such claimant, by action of debt, in any court proper to try the same; saving moreover to the person claiming such labour or service, his right of action for or on account of the said injuries or either of them.

The memorials were referred to committee, where it was reported that the Constitution had been examined, that the slave trade could not be prohibited until 1808 and that the national government could not interfere with slavery within the states. It was asserted that Congress could tax the slaves imported, regulate the home traffic and forbid the traffic to foreign nations. The debate was a heated one, showing that there was a wide breach between the friends of freedom and the supporters of slave labor. The original report, nonetheless, was finally adopted as written, and it represented the congressional position on slavery for several decades. Memorials from abolition societies in Pennsylvania, New York, Rhode Island, Connecticut and Virginia were presented in 1791. No action was taken. Congress did not vary from this attitude in the subsequent debates that centered about the slave question.

FEDERAL LEGISLATION

The Constitution had provided for the return of fugitive slaves in Article IV, Section 2, and the supporters of slavery sought to secure enforcement of this section. A committee was appointed in the Senate in November 1792 to consider it, and a bill was prepared and passed. On February 4, 1793, the House of Representatives started consideration of the bill, which was passed the following day by a vote of forty-eight to seven. The Fugitive Slave Act of 1793 was the basis for the return of persons escaping from slavery. Under this act, however, free persons also were seized and sold into slavery, and as a result, free Negroes petitioned for revision of the act.

The law provided that the owner of the escaped slave could take the fugitive before any United States judge or any magistrate from the area in which the seizure was made and give proof that the defendant was an escaped slave. Upon receiving this proof, the officer was to issue a certificate enabling the owner or his agent to take the fugitive back to his home state. Any person concealing a fugitive was liable to a penalty of five hundred dollars. Kidnaping became so flagrant in Delaware in 1794 that Congress was petitioned to interfere.

In 1797, four North Carolina blacks petitioned for relief from seizure under the Fugitive Slave Act. They stated that they had been set free by their masters but that there were slave owners who, having secured from the state legislature an act giving them the right to seize and sell free Negroes, had hunted and inconvenienced them. By a vote of fifty to thirty-three, however, their petition was voted down in the House of Representatives.

A petition from the Quakers of the same state said that 134 freed Negroes had been seized and enslaved again. After long debate, the petition was referred to committee. When the House finally voted, it requested that the petitioners take back their petition. Again, the House had declined to act.

In 1794, Congress passed an act prohibiting the participation of any American citizen in the foreign slave trade. Any vessels engaging in this trade were to be confiscated; persons who engaged in the trade were to forfeit two thousand dollars, one half of which was to go to the United States and the other half to those prosecuting the case. This was the government's first move toward suppression of the slave trade. This act was amended and strengthened in 1799.

STATE LEGISLATION

Vermont was admitted into the Union on February 18, 1791. Its constitution contained a bill of rights that declared that no person either born in the country or brought from overseas should be bound "as a servant, slave or apprentice" after the age of twenty-one. Slavery had been abolished in Massachusetts before 1789, but Connecticut lagged behind.

HENRY CLAY

It was not until 1797 that gradual emancipation was legalized in Connecticut. By this act, no Negro could be held in slavery beyond the age of twenty-one years. Among other northern states, only New York and New Jersey were slower in acting against slavery. In 1799, the New York legislature passed an act providing that all male children born of slaves should be freed at the age of twenty-eight and all female slaves, at the age of twenty-five. It was not until 1804 that the first step was taken to end slavery in New Jersey. Efforts in Illinois and Indiana to repeal the prohibition against slavery ended in failure.

Kentucky was admitted to the Union with a constitution denying the legislature the right to emancipate slaves without the consent of the owners and without compensation to them. Owners could not be prevented from bringing their slaves into the state, but their importation for purposes of sale could be prohibited. Slaves could be emancipated by their owners if special laws were granted to this effect. Security would have to be given that those who were emancipated would not become charges upon the state. An effort was made in 1799, under the leadership of Henry Clay, to change these sections of the constitution; this effort, too, ended in failure.

Georgia also forbade the emancipation of slaves without the consent of the owner. The revised constitution of 1798, however, prohibited the future importation of slaves from "Africa or any foreign land." The state legislature of Virginia passed an act in 1796 making more difficult the manumission of slaves, and North Carolina, in the same year, prosecuted a group of Friends because of their efforts on behalf of slaves. They were termed "authors of common mischief." Tennessee was admitted as a slave state in 1796. The extension of slavery into the Mississippi territory was considered in 1797, and it was decided that slaves could not be brought in from outside the United States.

When Georgia ceded its lands in the west, the state provided that slavery should not be restricted there. During the legislation for the Louisiana Territory in the congressional session of 1804–05, it was provided that slaves could be imported into the territory if they had come to the United States prior to 1789. This last date was selected in order to avoid conflict with South Carolina's prohibition of the slave trade in 1787. The system of slavery had become an established institution in the life of the nation.

COTTON AND THE COTTON GIN

American slavery, in the style of life and economic policies that it fostered, was pre-industrial. But it is important to remember that it was the industrial revolution that increased the importance of slavery.

After about 1750, revolutionary developments were taking place in the industrial life of England. Inventions of spinning and weaving machinery in the eighteenth century made cotton textile production possible on a mass scale. The new textile industry lacked only a reliable source of raw cotton.

The situation was ideal for the American southern planter. Immediately after the Revolutionary War, there had been a crisis in the southern economy. Lacking a reliable and subsidized market in England, southerners began to experience a profound depression. The prices of traditional southern staples, tobacco, indigo and naval stores, dropped precipitously. It seemed, indeed, as if slavery would have to be abolished and as if the southern ruling class would need to seek a new basis for its economy.

The development of the textile industry changed all this. The South had produced cotton on a small scale before the Revolution, and the new situation seemed to open possibilities for the development of this small

crop as a staple. The demand seemed absolutely insatiable. Without further technical developments, however, the South could not fill this demand. The bottleneck in cotton production lay in the fact that it took one worker one day to clean one pound of cotton —that is, to separate the seed from the fleecy lint. So serious was this problem that, in 1792, Georgia appointed a commission to explore the possibilities of an invention that would speed up this process.

The "saw tooth" cotton gin was invented in 1793 by a New England schoolteacher named Eli Whitney. His machine was successful; and because Whitney failed to establish a monopoly over the production of gins, they were soon available fairly cheaply throughout the South. Now a worker with a hand-operated gin could clean fifty pounds of cotton per day, while a gin run by horsepower could separate from 300 to 1,000 pounds a day.

An early drawing of a hand-operated cotton gin.

The effects from this invention were immediate. The cotton crop in 1791, before Whitney's invention, was 4,000 bales (with 500 pounds to a bale). By 1800, production had risen to 75,000 bales. From 1791 to 1795, the average annual production of cotton in the United States was 10,000 bales; between 1796 and 1800, the average annual production was 26,000 bales. The importance of the English market for the southern cotton planter becomes clear when we realize that average annual exports rose from 3,500 bales in 1791 to 36,000 bales in 1800.

Certain obvious effects of the ginning process determined the broad outlines of southern history for the next three-quarters of a century. Increasingly, cotton exports to Great Britain provided, in cash returns, the basis for northern industrialization and thus made of the South, in a sense, an economic dependent—a producer of raw goods. As the cotton plantations moved westward, they created and reinforced a patriarchal style of life that set the tone for the southern social system. Small farmers were soon unable to compete with the wealthier planters and were pushed into less fertile areas, where their resentment festered. The South, as a whole, became increasingly unable to produce its own foodstuffs and its own semi-industrial goods. South Carolina exported over 100,000 bushels of corn in 1790, but by 1806, not enough corn was grown there for its own population.

The increased importance of the cotton plantation vastly increased the value of slavery. Slave prices rose and fell with the value

Slaves cutting sugar cane on a plantation in the Deep South.

of cotton exports. Cotton appeared to be an ideal crop for slave labor; and as cotton became more important to the economy, the South became increasingly tenacious in holding onto its "peculiar institution."

For the slave, cotton production meant the increased use of gang labor, which was inevitably a movement toward depersonalization of the master-slave relationship. His increased value meant that, on the one hand, the slave was frequently treated rather well, in a paternalistic sense; but, on the other hand, his chances for gaining his freedom decreased as the value of cotton production increased.

THE CULTIVATION OF SUGAR

The cultivation of sugar developed during the same period as the cultivation of cotton. Along the banks of the Mississippi River, especially in the alluvial delta region in Louisiana, were fertile lands that raised the expectations of planters in the sugar industry. French planters settled around New Orleans, and Negro slaves were soon introduced into the area. The Creole population grew rapidly, and many purchased plantations. Many free Negroes also became landowners. The demand for slaves in the region rose sharply. Prior to the Revolution, fruitless attempts had been made to produce sugar. During the period 1794–95, a Creole, Etienne de Boré, planted a field of sugar cane north of New Orleans and set up an apparatus for grinding the cane and preparing the sugar. His experiment proved successful, and the number of sugar estates increased. Refugees who were familiar with sugar cultivation came over during the Haitian Revolution and settled in the neighborhood of New Orleans. It was not, however, until after the purchase of Louisiana and the prohibition of the slave trade that sugar became the leading industry in the delta lands of the Southwest.

THE GROWTH OF THE NEGRO POPULATION

The invention of the cotton gin and the extension of cotton and sugar cultivation led to an increase in the slave population. There were over 638,000 slaves in 1790, comprising about one-fifth of the total population. In 1800, the number of slaves had increased by over 70 per cent, so that they formed about one-fourth of the population. A similar growth characterized the next ten years, when the slaves increased to one-third of the total population. Georgia experienced an even more rapid growth. The increase in the slave population was not rapid enough to meet the demand, however, resulting in an increase in the price of slaves. Before the invention of the cotton gin, a slave could be purchased for about five hundred dollars, but within the next two decades the price had doubled. The Negro population had grown steadily during the years from 1790 to 1800. The free Negroes had increased from about 59,000 in 1790 to over 107,000 in 1800. The slaves had increased from over 638,000 in 1790 to approximately 893,000 in 1800.

TOUSSAINT L'OUVERTURE AND THE REVOLUTION IN SANTO DOMINGO

One of the immediate results of the French Revolution in 1789 was a successful slave insurrection in the French Colony of Santo Domingo (now Haiti), which occupied the western half of the Island of Hispaniola.

Santo Domingo had been one of the centers for Negro slavery under the French. The cultivation of sugar, coffee, chocolate, indigo, dyes, spices and cotton employed roughly 450,000 slaves, who were under the tenuous control of 38,000 Europeans. An intermediate caste of 28,000 free Negroes and mulattoes was despised by the whites and, in turn, lorded it over their slave relatives.

During the latter part of the eighteenth century, the planters of Santo Domingo had become some of the wealthiest men in the New World. They concentrated increasingly upon sugar—and the island became a vast gold mine for bankrupt noblemen who came there to recoup, in a few years, their family fortunes, at the expense of the slaves. As frequently as not, they returned to France to dissipate their gains. These planters, unlike the American planters, often were not permanent residents of the island and thus had no commitment to Haiti aside from exploiting it as rapidly as possible. They never developed a powerful and autonomous social system that could maintain itself. Thus, the capital city of Le Cap Français, according to one French historian, "resembled nothing so much as a vast hotel."

Slaves were harshly treated and vast plantations worked by several thousand blacks were not unusual. New slaves from Africa were brought in regularly to replace those who had died of overwork. The planters thereby created a revolutionary situation. Unlike many planters in the United States, they did not seek to annihilate the cultural heritage of the blacks or their independent cultural life. As long as the slaves produced, they were more or less left alone to develop their own cultural institutions. This measure of independence, along with the horrendous treatment they received, bolstered the slaves' consciousness of their own numerical superiority and led to a revolution.

War broke out when the local whites appeared to be holding back on the promises of the Revolution of 1789. One night in August 1791, the northern portion of the island seemed to burst spontaneously into flames. Within a week, "200 sugar plantations, 600 coffee plantations" and more were laid to the torch, and their masters were killed. An English writer recalled: "We arrived in the harbor of Le Cap at evening . . . and the first sight which arrested our attention as we approached was a dreadful scene of devastation by fire . . . ruins still smoking and houses and plantations at that moment in flames." And this was only the beginning. In rapid succession, the blacks, with the occasional and undependable collaboration of the mulattoes, attacked the Creoles, the English and the Spanish. In 1793, French commissioners formalized the freedom of the slaves, but for over a decade the blacks were forced to fight to retain their precious liberty.

The man who had given form and direction to all this was a former carriage driver named Toussaint L'Ouverture. It was Toussaint who, joining the movement after the initial outbreak, gave discipline to the enthusiastic but untutored Negroes. He restored both agricultural and commercial life on the island and, in July 1801, declared the island's independence. Thrown suddenly into the world of international diplomacy, this military and political genius put the established powers to shame. According to the abolitionist Wendell Phillips:

> You think me a fanatic, for you read history not with your eyes but with your prejudices. But fifty years hence, when Truth gets a hearing, the Muse of history will put Phocion for the Greeks, Brutus for the Romans, Hampden for the English, LaFayette for the French; choose Washington as the bright, consummate flower of our earliest civilization; and then, dipping her pen in the sunlight, will write in the clear blue, above them all, the name of the soldier, the statesman, the martyr, Toussaint L'Ouverture.

The Peace of Amiens in 1802 gave Napoleon Bonaparte, then master of France, the opportunity to plan the colonial empire in America of which he had long dreamed. One obstacle in his way was the "Black Napoleon" who acted as ruler of an independent state. Control of Santo Domingo was necessary before any attempt could be made to possess the Louisiana territory. The island could be used as a stopping place for ships sailing from France, which would offset the

TOUSSAINT L'OUVERTURE

NAPOLEON BONAPARTE

advantages held by the British Navy. The re-establishment of the slave system would be a boon to the French economy.

Napoleon sent his brother-in-law General Leclerc, in command of 30,000 men, to subdue the blacks and reinstitute slavery. Fierce fighting between the Haitians and the French was the consequence. The resistance offered by Toussaint's forces and their raids on the French forces finally led to discussion of terms of peace. Toussaint went to the meeting and, while under a flag of truce, was treacherously seized and sent to France. He was put in a prison dungeon at Fort Joux in the Jura Mountains and died there in April, 1803.

Toussaint L'Ouverture was one of the greatest Negro leaders in history. He established the first independent Negro government outside of Africa. He led thousands of slaves in one of the very few successful slave insurrections of all times. The effects of the uprising and revolution in Santo Domingo were monumental for the United States. For the news of General Leclerc's death in 1802 and the decimation of his army by the blacks and by tropical fevers—as well as the reopening of the war in Europe—led Napoleon to sell the Louisiana area to the United States for a pittance. Thus, vast areas of the Southwest were opened to the planter class, and the cotton economy received a new impetus. Toussaint had indirectly paved the way for the extension of the slave system into the Mississippi Delta.

There were other effects of L'Ouverture's success. Southern planters were terrified by the Haitian massacres, and they began to watch over their slaves more carefully. They were particularly concerned lest Haitian Negroes find their way into the United States. The high proportion of native African slaves involved in the rebellion made many southerners look with more favorable countenance upon legislation to end the importation of additional slaves. In 1793, South Carolina

GENERAL CHARLES LECLERC

barred the importation of Negroes from Africa and the West Indies for two years. North Carolina soon followed suit, and Virginia and Maryland strengthened existing legislation. In 1794, the Senate and the House of Representatives passed a law to prevent the fitting out of foreign ships for the slave trade in American ports. The Fugitive Slave Act of 1793 was also partially a result of the concern that the Haitian rebellion caused in the United States.

THE ABOLITION OF THE SLAVE TRADE

Economic and political trends favored slavery in the twenty years following the adoption of the Constitution and were responsible for the change in sentiment toward liberty for the slaves. Small groups of people kept up the struggle in the abolitionist societies, and the Quakers joined with this number; but the cause of abolition had declined.

President Jefferson brought the question of the slave trade into prominence with his Annual Message on December 2, 1806. He said that "although no law can take effect until the day of the year one thousand eight hundred and eight, yet the intervening period is not too long to prevent, by timely notice, expeditions which cannot be completed before that day." In the following days, bills were introduced in both the Senate and the House. They were debated and amended during the succeeding days. A bill was passed on March 2, 1807, providing that, after January 1808, those who imported slaves were to be punished by fines and imprisonment. Restrictions were placed also on interstate coastal trade. Masters of vessels in the coastal trade were required to furnish manifests and certificates that the slaves had not been imported into the United States since 1808. Smuggled slaves were to be subject to disposal according to the laws of the state or territory in which they were seized.

Twenty-three days after the Act of 1807 was passed in the United States, the British Parliament, under the leadership of Thomas Clarkson, Granville Sharp and William Wilberforce, prohibited the slave trade to the English colonies. This act was to be effective for vessels leaving England after May 1, 1807, and for vessels arriving in the colonies after March 1, 1808.

The law forbidding the slave trade was so weak that from 1808 on there was virtually no enforcement of it by the United States government. The English, earnestly trying to enforce their law, exhibited distress that the traffic, once forbidden, operated so openly. In the Treaty of Ghent, following the War of 1812, England insisted that the treaty once again affirm the dual intentions of both powers to do what they could to suppress the illegal trade in slaves.

That this treaty obligation was virtually ignored is evident. In 1817, Congress passed an act prohibiting the fitting out of slave vessels and the transportation of slaves to any country. This act, though again unenforced, corroborated the assertion that the trade was continuing.

There were several locations off the coasts of South Carolina, Georgia, Texas, Louisiana and Florida where traders arrived with their contraband cargoes. The slaves were unloaded in these various islands and shipped to areas farther inland to be sold. According to reports made by the Treasury Department, under whose jurisdiction the laws forbidding the traffic fell, no defined policies were ever handed down to enforce the acts prohibiting the trade. Secretary William Crawford, in 1820, in a report to Congress stated: "It appears from an examination of the records of this office, that no particular instructions have ever been given, by the Secretary of the Treasury, under the original or supplementary acts prohibiting the introduction of slaves into the United States."

Historian W. E. B. Du Bois, in his monumental work on the suppression of the slave trade, concluded that the trade did not operate as fully between 1825 and 1850 as it had prior to and following those years. In 1850, the trafficking in slaves from the African Coast to the United States increased to such a point that some historians claim it surpassed the numbers brought to the country before it was outlawed.

While the trade was continuing, further complications arose with Great Britain. In 1830, the *Comet* was apprehended by the British off the coast of the Bahamas when a storm caused her to sail off course. The British refused to release the slaves aboard because of the illegality of the trade. In 1835, a similar incident occurred when the vessel *Enconium* was captured by the British. Again in 1835, the *Enterprise* was forced by a storm to stop at Hamilton, Bermuda, where the British authorities refused to recognize the right of the ship's officers to ownership of the slaves on board.

These three cases remained a thorny diplomatic problem between the United States and Great Britain until they were solved in 1841. The British agreed to pay indemnity for the loss of "cargo" on the *Comet* and *Enconium* because both had been captured prior to 1833, when the British Empire had formally abolished slavery. However, in the case of the *Enterprise,* indemnity was refused because it had occurred after the abolition.

Not all of the slaves who were carried illegally across the ocean were fortunate enough to be apprehended by the British. In many cases, when American vessels carrying slaves were sighted by other ships on the high seas, the unfortunate blacks were brought up on deck still in their chains and thrown overboard to eliminate the possibility of the ship being seized.

From the 1850's to the beginning of the Civil War, the question of the illegal slave trade became one of open argument in the South. In the Southern Commercial Conventions, discussions arose concerning reopening the trade, and there were frequent petitions to the federal government for this purpose. Nothing positive came of these efforts, primarily because the South itself was divided on the issue. On the one hand, those in the lower states, Alabama, Mississippi, Louisiana, Georgia and Florida, were influenced by economic pressures to call for the reopening of the trade. On the other hand, the border states,

whose economy was dependent on raising and shipping slaves south, were in opposition to the foreign trade.

Despite the discussions, laws and constant pleading by the abolitionists for stricter enforcement of the prohibition on the trade, it continued to flourish. The *New York Commercial Advertiser,* in March 1856, claimed that at the very least thirty slave vessels were outfitted annually in New York alone. Fear of legal reprisal by the government was certainly lacking in the case of an advertisement made in the Richmond, Texas, *Reporter* on May 4, 1859. It read: "For sale—four hundred likely African Negroes, lately landed upon the coast of Texas. Said Negroes will be sold upon the most reasonable terms."

One of the most interesting insights into the view of the United States government concerning the traffic was illustrated in the case of the *Wanderer*. This vessel arrived near Brunswick, Georgia, in 1858 with a load of 420 Africans. It was sighted on its arrival by government agents patrolling the area. Its cargo and crew were seized and held for examination and trial. The captain of the ship was arrested, but the crew was not. In a trial that was a mockery of justice, the captain escaped conviction because the judge chose to interpret the laws prohibiting the trade in such a way as to make the owner responsible for breaking the law. The owner was indicted, the vessel forfeited. The owner was never brought to trial, and he later repurchased his ship at a small cost.

The history of the slave trade in the United States, therefore, is steeped in irony. On the one hand, laws were passed to strengthen the authority of the government in its position to outlaw the trade. On the other hand, flagrant disregard for the laws persisted, and the trade flourished even after the start of armed conflict between the states.

CHAPTER TEN

The Negro and the War of 1812

RELATIONS between the United States and Great Britain from 1783 to 1812 were far from satisfactory. In the Mississippi Valley, in the Northwest and on the high seas, the enmity of the two nations increased. British trade policies, especially, occasioned alarm in American shipping circles.

Many deserters from the British Navy had joined the American Navy. In order to reclaim these men, English captains began to stop and search American merchant vessels upon the high seas. Men who were unable to prove their American citizenship were impressed into British service. Negro sailors on American ships were subjected to seizure along with other sailors.

Indian attacks were seen as expressions of British intrigue. General Anthony Wayne's victory at Fallen Timbers and the subsequent Indian treaties gradually opened new territories to American settlement. In one sense, the War of 1812 was a continuation of the struggle of Americans for westward expansion. Americans were anxious for the complete expulsion of England from the North American mainland.

THE WESTWARD MOVEMENT PRIOR TO 1810

The Paris Peace Treaty of 1783, which ended the Revolutionary War, recognized the title of the United States to the territory extending from the Atlantic Ocean to the Mississippi River and from the St. Lawrence River, the Great Lakes, the Lake of the Woods and the forty-fifth parallel southward to the northern Florida line. The signing of the treaty was followed by a continuous westward movement of the population. From this period to 1812, England, Spain and France tried to maintain an interest in this western territory and to win the favor of the settlers so as to separate them from their newly established territorial governments; but their efforts were futile.

Eastern settlers preparing to head west in a wagon train.

The settlers from the East poured through the mountain passes and along the lines where there was least natural resistance. The Northwest Ordinance of 1787 made slave-holding north of the Ohio River illegal, and relatively few travelers from Virginia and the Carolinas attempted to take their slaves into this territory. Nevertheless, there were many slaves in southern Indiana and Illinois for several decades. A convention held in Indiana in 1802 requested of Congress that the Ordinance of 1787 be restricted, but the committee to which their petition was referred reported, on March 2, 1803, that it was inexpedient to restrict or to suspend the ordinance at that time. The same question was raised in the subsequent Congresses of 1805, 1806 and 1807, and Congress continually declined to suspend the antislavery section of the Northwest Ordinance.

The regions to the west of the tidewater region were enticing, for the soil was fertile and the lands were suitable for tobacco production. The exhausted lands of Virginia and North Carolina was abandoned for the virgin western soil. Across the mountains and through tangled woods, packhorses and wagons were driven to new homes. Along the waterways, rafts and boats wended their way to the alluvial lands of the new West. The vanguard was led by Daniel Boone, James Robertson and John Sevier, who pushed into the Cumberland, the Ohio and the Tennessee Valleys. The Virginia planters threaded their way into Kentucky and the Shenandoah Valley. This area proved ideal not only for growing tobacco but for breeding horses and stock as well, especially in the fertile grass lands. The lands in Alabama and Mississippi attracted settlers, and with the dawn of the nineteenth century, immigration there had reached substantial proportions.

With the purchase of the Louisiana area, the tide flowed on into Arkansas and Louisiana. Frenchmen, Spaniards and white and Negro Americans gathered in and about New Orleans. Georgia ceded the territory including present-day Alabama and Mississippi to the United States in 1802, with the condition that the slavery-forbidding article in the Ordinance of 1787 would not apply to that land. Congress agreed, and Alabama and Mississippi became slave states. It was not long before the plantation system was being used in the West. Some settlers, however, declined to adopt the slave plantation system and, instead, sold their lands to the incoming planters and made their way farther west to new land or went into the mountains.

THE LEWIS AND CLARK EXPEDITION

The acquisition of the Louisiana territory led to the desire to learn something of this western section stretching from the Mississippi River into the unexplored West. President Jefferson requested Congress, in 1803, to send "intelligent officers with ten or twelve men to explore" this territory. Jefferson's private secretary, Meriwether Lewis, along with William Clark, brother of General George Rogers Clark, were selected to head the expedition of forty-three men. Setting out in the spring of 1804, the party journeyed along the Columbia River from the mouth of the Missouri River to the Pacific Ocean, reaching it late in 1805. After spending the winter near the Columbia River, the expedition returned to St. Louis in September 1806.

A Negro boy named York was part of this expedition. He was described as a strong, agile fellow able to entertain crowds of Indians with his feats of strength. Clark observed that they were astonished "that so large a man should be so active." Although it is said that York spoke "bad French and worse English," he served at times as interpreter for the expedition. York came from St. Louis, Missouri, and seems to have acquired a knowledge of French through contact with the French traders of the Mississippi Valley. He had also learned several Indian dialects and therefore could serve as the agent in the procurement of food from the Indians, with

MERIWETHER LEWIS

WILLIAM CLARK

JEAN BAPTISTE POINTE DU SABLE

whom he was popular. Clark recorded in his journal: "Those people [the Arikara Indians] are much pleased with my black servant."

An earlier Negro explorer had been Jean Baptiste Pointe Du Sable, the first to settle the area that is now Chicago. In the middle 1700's, Du Sable left Louisiana, where he had emigrated from Haiti, and went north to establish a fur trade with the Indians. While trapping and trading, Du Sable moved farther north and westward. Eventually, he built a fur-trading post on the Chicago River near Lake Michigan, which became the first in a series of buildings that grew into a regular settlement.

THE RISE OF THE DOMESTIC SLAVE TRADE

The basis of the labor supply in the new territories in the Southwest was the domestic slave trade. Even before 1783, the fertility of the best land in Virginia had been exhausted by the unscientific practices of the tobacco planters. At the same time, tobacco production in Kentucky and North Carolina had reached levels competitive with Virginia. Many plantation owners in Virginia went into debt, and plantation slavery began to

lose its economic advantages. Many planters sought ways to get rid of their slaves at a profit; for example, Thomas Jefferson had to order the sale of several of his slaves to help him regain solvency. As Virginians turned away from the production of staple crops, they found themselves burdened with many surplus slaves, for whom they could find no productive work.

With the legal end of the foreign slave trade in 1808, the traffic in slaves between upper and lower South began to be conducted as a business. Beginning in a small way, as migrating farmers and planters obtained excellent prices for the surplus slaves brought with them, the domestic traders gained enormous profits. An advertiser in a Mississippi newspaper in 1810 reported that he had arrived from points north with "upwards of twenty likely Virginia-born slaves now in a flat-bottomed boat lying in the river at Natchez, for sale cheaper than has been sold here in years."

This trade was developed in Maryland and Virginia before the War of 1812. Purchases of slaves were made there for sale farther south and west. Washington, D.C., was one of the centers of the trade. As early as January 1802, the grand jury of Alexandria County described as grievous "the practice of persons coming from distant parts of the United States into this District for the purpose of purchasing slaves." Foreign visitors were often disturbed and astounded to see black flesh being peddled in the streets of the young and hopeful democracy.

Through the efforts of the slave traders, the concentration of slaves began to shift to the west. In 1790, there had been 3,400 slaves in Tennessee; in 1800, 13,500; in 1810, 44,500. In 1790, 89 per cent of the Negro population had lived in the colonies along the coast. By 1810, this figure had slipped to 78 per cent.

There is considerable evidence that the domestic slave trade encouraged the selective breeding of blacks for market, especially in

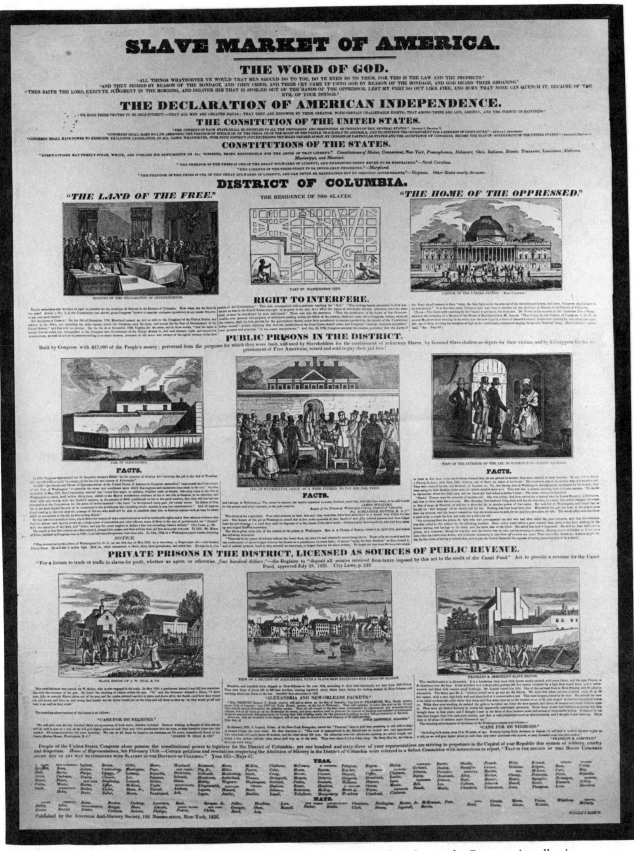

This poster published by the American Anti-Slavery Society bitterly attacks Congress for allowing the slave trade to thrive in the capital of the United States.

the upper South. Even in 1796, a South Carolina slaveholder said that fifty of his slaves had been purchased for breeding purposes. One citizen of Fredericksburg, Virginia, noted that "the chief pecuniary resource of the border states is the breeding of slaves; and I grieve that there is too much ground for the charges that the general licentiousness among the slaves, for the purpose of large increase, is compelled by some masters and encouraged by many."

During the period around the War of 1812, therefore, the slave trade became part of the fabric of southern society. Although the more genteel elements disliked the slave trader, they knew full well how necessary he was to them. Many traders in the upper South amassed vast fortunes by dumping surplus slaves on the growing market in the Deep South as increasing numbers of Mississippi planters called for more Negroes.

NEGROES CARRIED OFF BY THE BRITISH DURING THE REVOLUTION

American diplomacy worked for the return of the Negroes who had accompanied the British armies when they left the colonies. For several decades after 1783, negotiations continued on this question. Dissatisfaction among Americans was most open in the slave-holding territories, of course. It was estimated that about 25,000, or one-fifth of the slaves in South Carolina, had been carried off by the British between 1775 and 1783. Georgia was reported to have lost three-fourths to seven-eights of its blacks. Jefferson estimated that 30,000 Negroes had left Virginia, while North Carolina was said to have lost enough to form two British regiments.

British diplomats admitted that the Negroes had left with their armies but claimed they were free men who had departed voluntarily. Commissioners were finally appointed in 1798 to adjust the losses and damages. Claims for slave losses were pressed upon

them, but negotiations on this matter were generally fruitless. The relations between the two countries were seriously strained after the expiration of the Jay Treaty. The Embargo and the Non-Intercourse Acts were followed finally by war, and once again Negroes were taken off the plantations and put on British ships. The British would eventually pay property holders in the United States $12,000 for slaves who had been carried off by their armies.

NEGRO PARTICIPATION IN THE OPENING CLASHES OF THE WAR

Negroes participated in the clashes between the two nations prior to the actual outbreak of war. The American ship *Chesapeake* was attacked by the British man-of-war *Leopard* as a result of the former's refusal to be searched for deserters. Several of the crew were wounded. The *Chesapeake* was boarded, and Commodore James Barron lowered his flag in surrender. Four sailors were removed, three of whom were Negroes.

When the war actually broke out, a small American army of 6,000 men was pitted against a much larger number of British regulars. Negroes were not included in the standing army at this time, nor did they participate in the opening battles of the war.

New York was the first state to make a formal bid for Negro troops. In October 1814, the legislature authorized the raising of two regiments of Negro soldiers, to be gathered by voluntary enlistment of free Negroes over a period of three years. Each of the regiments was to consist of 1,080 men. The commissioned officers were to be white. The troops were to be transferred out to the service of the United States if the government would assume the cost of maintenance. Two thousand Negroes ultimately enlisted.

Many Negroes served as menials and laborers. They served the American forces by erecting defenses at Bladensburg, Maryland,

COMMODORE JAMES BARRON

The clash of the Chesapeake *with the British man-of-war* Leopard.

The impressment of American seamen by the British.

ABSALOM JONES

when the capital of the nation required protection. Following the occupation of Washington by the British in 1814, the Baltimore Vigilance Committee began to plan its defense. An order of September 3, 1814, stated: "That all free people of color be, and they are hereby ordered to attend daily, commencing with Wednesday, the fifth instant, at the different works erected about the city for the purpose of laboring thereon, and for which they shall receive an allowance of fifty cents a day, together with a soldier's rations." It was obvious, then, that Negroes could be useful but were not to be trusted and armed as soldiers.

The Committee of Defense in Philadelphia was also reluctant to organize and arm the Negroes of that city. The Committee reported on August 30 that the organization of blacks would be improper because of the shortage of supplies for white citizens. The committee recommended, however, that under proper supervision the Negro population could be used as "fatigue parties on the works to act in a manner detached from the white citizens who may be so employed."

At the end of the immediate crisis, 2,500 Negro men were organized by James Forten,

Absalom Jones and Richard Allen to work on the building of defenses. A battalion of Negro troops was later organized and was ready to march to the front when peace was declared. Thus, by and large, Americans were far less willing than they had been in 1775 to organize the Negroes and to give them arms. This is a testimony not only to the unpopularity of the war in the free states, among both races, but also to the fact that racism was increasing in America.

JACKSON AT NEW ORLEANS

In the southern theatre of the war, blacks played their most conspicuous role. In December 1814, General Andrew Jackson found himself sorely in need of a larger force to defend New Orleans against the British. At this time, therefore, he stated that the policy which had deprived the blacks of "participation in the glorious struggle for national rights" was misguided and would no longer obtain. Jackson appealed to the Negroes, calling them America's "adopted children." He stated that all free men would be allowed to enlist and would receive the same compensation as any other soldiers, which meant $124 and 160 acres of land as well as daily rations and clothing. The Negro volunteers were to remain in the Army only for the duration of the war and would be placed in a special regiment, consisting entirely of black enlisted men and non-commissioned officers, commanded by white officers. The segregation was intended, according to Jackson, to forestall "improper comparisons or unjust sarcasm." To the men enlisting he said: "As a distinct independent battalion or regiment, pursuing the path of glory, you will, undivided, receive the applause and gratitude of your countrymen."

The reports of the Battle of New Orleans show that 400 of the 3,600 Americans who defended the city were black. After the fighting, General Jackson said that the two corps

General Jackson at the Battle of New Orleans, where he was assisted by many black Americans.

of Negro volunteers had conducted themselves with great courage and tenacity. So pleased with the Negro performance was Jackson that he declared he would inform the President of their valor. Jackson told his troops of his delight in having discovered in them "a noble enthusiasm which leads to the performance of great things."

There were many other instances of bravery among those Negroes who fought for the United States. When the American troops were being attacked by the British at Mobile, Alabama, a Negro named Jeffreys placed himself at the head of the troops and succeeded in rallying them to a charge that repulsed the enemy. Jordan B. Noble was the drummer who summoned the Americans to arms in the battle of New Orleans. At New Orleans, a Negro named John Julius also gained a reputation as a gallant soldier. He was severely wounded by bayonet gashes but

continued fighting. Congressman Robert Winthrop, speaking in the House of Representatives, stated that "no regiments did better service at New Orleans than did the black regiments." Commodore Stephen Decatur said of the Negro troops: "They are as brave men as ever fired a gun. There are no stronger hearts in the service."

NEGROES IN THE NAVY

Negroes were not proscribed from enlistment in the navy during this period. It was not unusual, therefore, for Negroes to be found among the crews of sailing vessels. Two black men on board the *Governor Tompkins* of New York were slain at their posts during an early battle. Captain Nathaniel Shaler recorded the event. One of the black men, John Johnson, was mortally wounded by a twenty-four-pound shot; yet he lay on deck shouting

Commodore Oliver H. Perry and members of his brave crew during the battles on the Great Lakes.

encouragement to the others. Captain Shaler recorded that John Davis, the other black man similarly shot, fell near him and repeatedly requested to be thrown overboard so as to clear the way for the surviving fighters.

The crews of the ships on the Great Lakes also included Negroes. The guns of Commodore Oliver Perry's vessels were manned by 400 men, of whom 100 were Negroes. When Perry first received his new reinforcements, he complained to Commodore Chauncey that he had been sent "a motley set, blacks, soldiers and boys." Chauncey replied that the men he had sent to Perry were not surpassed by any in the fleet and that he had "yet to learn that the color of the skin, or the cut and trimmings of the coat, can affect a man's qualifications or usefulness." Soon Perry was convinced of his error, for he was later to speak of the bravery and good conduct of his black sailors. He wrote to the Secretary of the Navy that "they seem to be absolutely insensible to danger."

Negroes served in the crews of most of the vessels that saw action in the war. Their loyalty was demonstrated in many heroic deeds. Charles Black, a Pennsylvania Negro, was on board an English ship when the war broke out. He was exchanged as a prisoner of war, joined the navy, and went on to distinguish himself with the American fleet on Lake Champlain.

NEGRO-INDIAN RELATIONSHIPS

During the period of the war, many Negroes continued the tradition of taking advantage of the distracted state of society to seek shelter with the Indians. Since the Indians and the whites regarded each other as mutual enemies, Negroes escaping from their masters often could find a haven with the tribes. Refugee slaves crossed into Florida for shelter with the Cherokees, Choctaws and Chickasaws, Creeks and Seminoles. Negroes and Indians intermarried, and there were Indian

Negroes served on the crews of many American ships during the War of 1812.

Negro seamen demonstrated their courage and loyalty to the American cause during the fierce naval battles of the war.

slaveholders who used blacks for agricultural labor. Near the present site of Muscle Shoals, Alabama, a man named Colbert, half Negro and half Indian, established himself as a prominent farmer using Indian and black labor.

As early as 1783, South Carolina had requested that Georgia aid in the return of fugitive slaves who had formed settlements upon the Apalachicola and Sewanee Rivers and had begun to till the lands. Officials from Georgia were appointed to negotiate a treaty with the Creeks for the return of fugitives. Escaped slaves, throughout the colonial period and well into the nineteenth century, flocked to the Seminoles in Florida. Florida was under, first, the jurisdiction of England and, later, of Spain. The English and Spanish authorities declined to return the fugitives. Finally, however, the United States government felt driven to take Florida for its own, in part to end this avenue of escape.

Georgia sent an armed force into Florida for the purpose of recapturing escaped slaves. The soldiers seized as many runaways as possible from nearby tribes and returned to Georgia. Under General Jackson, a second foray into Seminole territory was made in 1814.

THE NEGRO FORT

During the war, Lieutenant Colonel Edward Nicholas led a small British force into Florida and established an alliance with the Seminoles. Under his direction, a Spanish fort on the Apalachicola River, sixty miles from the American frontier, was rebuilt and named "The British Post on the Apalachicola." Nicholas remained in the fort after the close of the war, uniting the Indians in opposition to the United States and receiving runaway blacks. The Indians were led to believe that the United States would restore the Georgia lands to them. When Nicholas departed, he left a garrison of Negroes and Indians at the

GENERAL EDMUND P. GAINES

fort and supplied them with clothing, military stores and ammunition, including 2,500 muskets, 500 carbines, 500 steel swords, 200 pairs of pistols, 300 quarter casks of rifle powder and 762 barrels of cannon powder. The walls were mounted with four long twenty-four-pound cannon, four long six-pound cannon, one four-pound field piece and a brass howitzer.

In the region stretching for miles up and down the Apalachicola, there were Negroes and Indians with farms and grazing lands. When they saw the post abandoned by Nicholas, they joined the garrison he had left behind, and soon they began to welcome other refugees. Well supplied with arms, they fired on boats in the river and began to harass neighboring whites.

The post became known as the Negro Fort because of the presence in this region of nearly one thousand Negroes. They joined with the hostile Creeks and terrorized American slave-owners for miles around. The military authorities were alarmed, and in May 1815, General Edmund Gaines reported the situation to the Secretary of War. General Jackson was ordered to request the Spanish governor at Pensacola to pacify the area. The governor replied that he could not do so without orders from his superiors and also that he hoped that Spanish territorial rights would not be trampled upon in an attempt to destroy the fort. He was informed that if Spain took no action, Americans would destroy the settlement.

General Gaines had been ordered to take possession of lands along the frontier and to build forts when necessary. He requested authority from General Jackson to build a fort on the Apalachicola, near the boundary between Florida and Georgia, to suppress the troublesome blacks and Indians. In May 1816, Jackson wrote to Gaines that the fort "ought to be blown up regardless of the ground it stands on." He concluded his note by saying that if General Gaines felt the same way, he should "destroy it and restore the stolen Negroes and property to their rightful owners."

Colonel Duncan Clinch, with U.S. troops and Indian allies, was ordered to go down the river and take a position near the fort. Colonel Patterson at New Orleans was to provide a convoy of gunboats to accompany the supplies, which were to be sent up the river. In June, two gunboats were ready to set sail. They arrived at the mouth of the Apalachicola on July 10. Shortly thereafter, a boat crew was fired upon and three of the crew were killed. Upon learning of this, Colonel Clinch prepared to attack the fort. As he approached and demanded its surrender, a red flag with the British Union Jack above it was unfurled above the fort. Colonel Clinch then sent word for the boats to come up and unite in the attack. At this time, the fort sheltered more than three hundred persons including women and children. Nearly all of the inhabitants were Negroes.

On July 27, the attack began. Finding the ramparts much too strong to be battered down by the light guns of the vessels and the defenders courageously opposing their advances, the attackers decided to use red-hot shots. One of these reached the magazine. The 700 barrels of powder exploded and destroyed the fort. Two hundred and seventy people were killed. Those who survived were returned to their masters in Georgia. The Negro Fort had been destroyed, and the Negro-Indian power seemed broken. Other Negro slaves, however, still continued to form alliances with Indians in the hope of winning their freedom. Many Negroes attempted to find freedom by uniting with the British, as their fathers had done during the Revolutionary War. When the British finally admitted defeat and withdrew their forces, a large number of these slaves were returned to vindictive owners. Many slaves who left with the British were betrayed by them and sold into slavery in the West Indies.

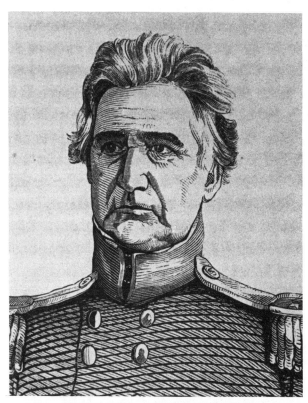

COLONEL DUNCAN CLINCH

CONCLUSIONS

The War of 1812 has very often been called the second Revoluntary War. It was this war, historians believe, that consolidated American independence and freedom and assured the country the respect of the maritime powers. Similarly, the War of 1812 and the events surrounding it consolidated the southern slave system and laid the groundwork for the ante-bellum expansion of that system. For it was during the period immediately after the war and up to 1819 that America experienced its first real cotton boom. Men and money flowed into the new Southwest, as an ambitious young nation began to seek out its natural limits. As settlers poured into Mississippi and Alabama, and the use of slave labor reached a record level, there evolved a new social system that was to characterize the American South.

The end of the War of 1812 marks the birth of a civilization that can truly be called "southern." It is from this date that we trace the development of serious intersectional hostility and bitterness. It is from this date that, with the stabilization of relations with England, we see the beginning of the great trade cycle that made the cotton economy vital to the South and led the planters to buy more and more Negroes in order to plant ever more acreage in cotton.

For the Negro, the period of stabilization and prosperity that followed the war meant that his servitude became more fixed. With the future of the new nation assured, he had less and less possibility of gaining freedom. Increasingly, Negroes were concentrated on large, impersonally run plantations; the Negro became more of a commodity as the southern commercial system expanded. Thus, a study of the history of the blacks during the colonial and early national periods reveals the results of the extension of the plantation system and the development and spread of American racism.

CHAPTER ELEVEN

Colonization and Compromise

THE idea of colonization accompanied Negro slavery almost from its beginnings. Two groups with very different expectations combined in support of it: many antislavery people thought that colonization would lead to the ultimate abolition of slavery; many southerners, concerned with the growing free Negro population, saw colonization as a way of strengthening slavery. Beginning in 1714, various proposals for the removal of the free Negro population to some territory outside of the United States were made.

BACKGROUND

Many Americans who advocated liberal principles in other matters were extremely conservative on the question of abolition. Thomas Jefferson believed "that the blacks, whether originally a distinct race, or made distinct by time and circumstances, are [probably] inferior to the whites in their endowments of both body and mind." Jefferson expressed the view that the abolition of slavery in America would be more difficult than it had been elsewhere because of the racial differences. He cited the Roman case as an example of simple emancipation, comparing it with the American situation, which was more complex: "Among the Romans emancipation required but one effort. . . . The slave, when made free, might mix with, without staining the blood of, his master. But with us a second [step] is necessary. . . . When freed, he is to be removed beyond the reach of mixture." Jefferson favored some kind of emancipation but feared that it would lead to racial war unless the free Negroes were removed. He thought that a growing Negro population ultimately could lead to a revolution that would reverse the roles of slave and master.

In 1773, the Rev. Samuel Hopkins of Newport suggested to Ezra Stiles (later to become president of Yale College), that two students should be trained as missionaries to Africa. Hopkins wanted to spread Calvinism to the unredeemed. Stiles agreed and suggested that a society be set up to promote the project and that thirty or forty "well instructed Negroes . . . inspired with the Spirit of Martyrdom" be sent.

Hopkins instructed some free Negroes in theology and gained financial support from the Society for Promoting Christian Knowledge, at Edinburgh. To ensure that the missionaries would be well trained, he sent two of his most promising students to Princeton for further education. The Revolution interrupted Hopkins' plans, and one of his most important disciples, John Quamine, lost his life in the struggle. After the War for Independence, Hopkins merged his efforts with those of William Thornton.

Thornton was a wealthy Quaker who had recently arrived from England. In 1785, he inherited some West Indian slaves. He proposed that an African commonwealth be established. Hopkins' free Negroes would teach Thornton's slaves morality and religion, while they in turn would train Hopkins' free Negroes to run a plantation. Thornton saw himself as the benefactor of the commonwealth, believing that "by proper laws they [free Negroes] may be made a good and happy people."

WILLIAM THORNTON

He addressed gatherings of free Negroes in New York, Boston, Providence and Newport and claimed to have found them receptive to the idea of colonization. Thornton always argued that a profitable trade in spices, gold dust, ivory, gums and dyes would complement the humanitarian impulse of possible supporters. He obtained the endorsement of Samuel Adams, but his proposal was rejected by the Massachusetts state legislature and he was unable to raise the money elsewhere.

In 1790, Ferdinand Fairfax, who thought it unwise to achieve emancipation through legislation, called for individuals to manumit their slaves. The freed slaves would then be sent to Africa. He wanted Congress to obtain a colony there and to transport the free blacks. Africa, he believed, would be ideal for the Negroes, and they would help to spread Christianity to the Dark Continent. He believed that the colony would also be profitable to American businessmen.

EZRA STILES

St. George Tucker, Professor of Law at William and Mary College, opposed slavery. He warned against the growing population of free Negroes in the United States, who would soon become, he claimed, "the caterpillars of the earth, and the tigers of the human race." Tucker felt that mass federal deportation would be too costly in money and human lives. He proposed as an alternative that free men be encouraged to emigrate in small numbers. The lower portion of the newly acquired Louisiana Territory seemed to him to be the best place, both economically and politically, to establish a colony of free Negroes.

The Virginia House of Delegates, during the session of 1801–02, discussed a proposal to establish a penal colony for rebellious slaves, free Negroes and criminals. The abortive Gabriel insurrection heightened the fear of the potential threat of the growing free

ST. GEORGE TUCKER

Negro population. The Virginia legislature requested Governor James Monroe to ask President Jefferson to establish a territory for free Negroes.

By 1800, the free Negroes in the United States were felt to be a problem. Throughout much of the country, the free Negroes were regarded by the majority of the white population as undesirables. Except among a few ardent friends of the free Negro, the idea of deportation was accepted readily. The Union Humane Society, founded in 1815 by Benjamin Lundy of Tennessee as an antislavery society, had as one of the phases of its program the removal of the Negroes from the United States. Following the close of the War of 1812, the Kentucky Colonization Society petitioned Congress to find suitable territory for use as an asylum for the emancipated Negroes; and the General Assembly of Virginia in 1816 passed a resolution favoring deportation of the Negroes.

Great Britain earlier had established as a settlement for its free Negro population and captured slaves a colony, called Freetown, located at Sierra Leone in West Africa. In

SAMUEL ADAMS

GRANVILLE SHARP

1786, Granville Sharp hired Henry Smeathman to bring the poor blacks of London, most of them former American slaves that Britain had freed during the Revolution, to Sierra Leone. In 1787, about 350 went to Africa. The English philanthropists who supported the venture found the going difficult, however, and surrendered the operation to an English trading company. They attempted a strict regimentation of the colony, but this failed as well.

Freetown was well settled by 1792. Zachary Macaulay, an ardent antislavery leader, was the administrator of the colony from 1793 to 1799. In 1794, the French destroyed the settlement at Sierra Leone. After 1808, Sierra Leone was operated as a Crown colony, with the Sierra Leone Company and the African Institution giving organized assistance to the project. Schools and churches were established, seeds and plants were sent over and native industries encouraged. The African Institution was founded in 1807 as a private charitable organization concerned with the welfare of the Africans and the suppression of the slave trade. The British government allowed the institution to manage Sierra Leone's trade, and American trade with the colony was either forbidden or severely restricted. One attempt to increase American trade was made by free Negro Paul Cuffee, who was an important figure in the colonization movement.

PAUL CUFFEE: NEGRO MERCHANT, NAVIGATOR AND COLONIST

Paul Cuffee was born in January 1758, in New Bedford, Massachusetts. He was the son of a manumitted slave, Cuffee Slocum, and an Indian mother, Ruth Moses. His father was a thrifty landowner in Dukes County. In 1772, the father died, leaving his land to Paul and his older brother, John. The land soon proved to be unproductive and the brothers turned to commercial pursuits. In 1778, all the children dropped the name Slocum, which their father had taken when he was a slave.

At thirteen, Cuffee was barely able to read or write. He kept working at his studies, however, securing the occasional help of a tutor. He studied navigation, remarking on his first lesson that it "was all black as midnight." But he did not despair. At the age of sixteen, Cuffee obtained a position as a seaman on a ship conducting a whaling expedition in the Gulf of Mexico. He went on a second trip to the West Indies. His third voyage took place after the start of the American Revolution. Captured by the British, he was kept a prisoner in New York City for three months. After his release, he went back to farming at Westport.

Having served his apprenticeship on the sea, he conceived the idea of building his own boat and becoming a trader. Cuffee, with the help of his brother, built a ship to trade along the Connecticut coast, but he was unable to make his way against the hazards of the sea and the pirates who freely roamed the coast. At the end of the Revolutionary War and with the adoption of the Constitution, the situation was stabilized and the opportunity for business was more secure.

With the aid of a partner and the profits from smaller ventures, Cuffee constructed the *Mary,* a forty-two-ton schooner. He went on a successful whaling expedition, returning to Westport in 1793. He then proceeded to Philadelphia, where he exchanged his cargo for equipment to build a new vessel. In 1795, the sixty-nine-ton ship *Ranger* was completed with borrowed funds. The *Ranger* was launched from Westport with a cargo worth $2,000 and sailed to Norfolk on the Chesapeake Bay. It then advanced to the Nanticoke River, where Cuffee purchased corn.

In 1808, Cuffee launched the *Hero,* a ship in which he had half interest. On one of its trips, it rounded the Cape of Good Hope. In 1810, Cuffee sailed the *Alpha,* a ship in which he had three-quarters interest, and in the same year he also acquired half interest in a 109-ton brig, the *Traveller.* By this time, stated Peter Williams in his funeral oration, Cuffee had become owner "of one ship, two brigs, and several smaller vessels, besides considerable property in house and lands."

At Westport, Captain Cuffee, as he was now known, and his family of six sons and two daughters made their home. Since there was neither a private tutor nor a school in the community, he proposed to his neighbors that they join with him in the erection of a school. He could not secure their cooperation, however, and so he built the school with his own funds on his own farm and opened it to the public.

At an early period in his life, Paul Cuffee had been militant in his opposition to slavery and his demands for equal rights for all Americans. Finally, however, he became discouraged by the limited opportunities available to free Negroes and began to favor coloni-

PAUL CUFFEE

zation as a possible solution for the nation's growing number of free blacks. James Pemberton, his Philadelphia friend, wrote to Cuffee in 1808 concerning the activities of the African Institution of London in the formation of a colony in Africa. Pemberton had obtained the assurance of Zachary Macaulay, Governor of Sierra Leone, that he would cooperate if Cuffee should decide to go to Africa.

Early in 1810, Cuffee wrote to the Friends of Philadelphia telling them of his plans. Later that year, he announced to the Westport Society of Friends, of which he was a member, that he was planning a voyage to Africa. His purpose was to sail to Africa with a cargo and to make observations concerning the desirability of encouraging free Negroes to settle there. The Friends authorized the voyage and gave Cuffee a letter of recommendation.

Captain Cuffee visited Sierra Leone and England in 1811, obtaining the support of the African Institution for his idea of providing the colony with "good sober steady

PETER WILLIAMS

characters," who would be free Negroes currently residing in the United States. In return for his efforts to encourage immigration to Sierra Leone, he was to receive trading privileges in the colony; and he did acquire a trading license from the British government. Cuffee initiated the Friends' Society at Sierra Leone, which was soon headed by John Kirzell, a Sierra Leone merchant and former American slave.

Cuffee returned to the United States and attempted to win the support of other free Negroes for his plan. Daniel Coker, a teacher at the African School in Baltimore, and James Forten, a prosperous sailmaker in Philadelphia, organized an African Institution in Philadelphia. The Rev. Peter Williams organized one in New York. The primary purpose of these societies was to urge free Negroes to go to Africa.

The War of 1812 interrupted Cuffee's plan for a return voyage, and he petitioned Congress for permission to trade with an enemy colony. On January 10, 1814, Senator Christopher Gore of Massachusetts brought up for consideration a bill supporting Cuffee's requests. The bill passed the Senate but was defeated in the House of Representatives by a vote of seventy-two to sixty-five. Cuffee was forced to delay his plans, therefore, until the conclusion of hostilities between the English and the Americans.

With the assistance of the Westport Society of Friends, the *Traveller* left the United States on December 2, 1815, carrying thirty-eight American Negroes and a cargo of tobacco, soap, candles, naval stores and flour. Cuffee himself had paid the expenses of thirty of the free blacks. When he arrived at Freetown, Cuffee discovered that his trading concessions had all been abrogated. The new immigrants were given land grants, but Cuffee returned empty-handed.

Cuffee arrived back in America on June 1, 1816. During the months that followed, preparation was made for the formation of a national organization for the deportation of Negroes to Africa. On his voyages, Cuffee had gathered information that was needed by the leaders of the movement. He corresponded with the leaders of the proposed

CHRISTOPHER GORE

FRANCIS SCOTT KEY

colonization society, and those letters were published. Unfortunately, before he could make more plans, Cuffee's health began to fail, and on September 9, 1817, he died. His name must be placed on the list of those whose efforts led to the organization of the American Colonization Society. He remains an outstanding example of a free Negro who, by personal industry, thrift and devotion to the larger cause of the amelioration of the condition of his race, made for himself a niche in American Negro history.

THE AMERICAN COLONIZATION SOCIETY

In 1816, a conference was organized in Washington, D. C., which led to the formation of the American Colonization Society. Three people who took the leadership in calling the conference were a New Jersey clergyman, the Rev. Robert Finley; Elias Boudinot Caldwell, a clerk of the Supreme Court; and the author of the "Star Spangled Banner," Francis Scott Key. Finley had corresponded with Cuffee, and in December 1816 he had published a pamphlet favoring colonization.

Caldwell and Key had gained some reputation as friends of the free blacks. When a Philadelphia physician, Jesse Torrey, Jr., attempted to help some free Negroes who had been abducted into slavery, Key volunteered his legal services. Caldwell and others gave publicity and money to the cause.

These two gentlemen succeeded in gaining the support of high-ranking politicians, such as the veteran Supreme Court justice and squire of Mount Vernon, Bushrod Washington. The Speaker of the House, Henry Clay, was persuaded to attend, as was John Randolph of Roanoke. A prayer meeting was held December 16, 1816. Later an advertisement was taken in the *Intelligencer*, inviting to the next meeting all "who are friendly to the promotion of a plan for colonizing the free blacks of the United States."

The meeting took place at the Davis Hotel on December 21, 1816, with Henry Clay presiding. Among the men attending, besides those already mentioned, were Ferdinand Fairfax and the Rev. William Meade, who

BUSHROD WASHINGTON

WILLIAM H. CRAWFORD

later became the Episcopal Bishop of Virginia. Many who were in attendance probably shared Clay's feeling that the scheme, for all its good intentions, was impractical. They all had, however, a desire to find an easy way out of the Negro problem.

Clay's opening address reflected many of the ideas recorded by Finley in his pamphlet "Thoughts on Colonization." He sympathized with the ambiguous position that the free blacks found themselves in. He believed that prejudice would always prevent their amalgamation into white society. Furthermore, he maintained that it was morally right to return them to their native lands. Colonization would also rid the United States of a potentially dangerous population and spread civilization to Africa.

Colonization was only to be for free Negroes. The society must avoid the "delicate question" of emancipation. Finley had argued that colonization would be a way of gradually doing away with slavery, but Clay wanted all to understand the limited objectives that

the group must have in order to be effective. Caldwell stressed Finley's argument that the United States would benefit from eliminating this glaring contradiction to its professions of liberty, but by this he meant only the condition of the free Negro and urged that they avoid the troublesome question of slavery. John Randolph emphasized the southern position that, besides the higher motives mentioned, colonization would "materially tend to secure" slavery. It would eliminate the free Negroes, who were seen as a source of potential danger.

With their limited purposes thus clarified, those present voted to establish a colonization society "for the purpose of collecting information" and assisting the federal government in formulating and launching a colony in Africa, "or such other place as Congress shall deem most expedient." On December 28, 1816, they adopted a constitution and a name: The American Society for Colonizing the Free People of Color of These United States. A few days later, fifty men signed the constitution and elected officers.

Judge Bushrod Washington was elected president. The vice-presidents elected were William H. Crawford of Georgia, Secretary of the Treasury; Henry Clay of Kentucky; William Phillips of Massachusetts; Colonel Henry Rutgers of New York; John E. Howard, Samuel Smith and John C. Herbert of Maryland; John Taylor of Virginia; General Andrew Jackson of Tennessee; Robert Ralston and Richard Rush of Pennsylvania; General John Mason of the District of Columbia; and the Rev. Robert Finley of New Jersey. Elias B. Caldwell was elected secretary, and David English treasurer. The actual responsibilities fell to the board of managers and the executive secretary.

On January 14, 1817, John Randolph of Roanoke presented a memorial from the organization to the House of Representatives. It called attention to the "low and hopeless condition" of the free Negroes and urged

THE AMERICAN COLONIZATION SOCIETY 163

GERRIT SMITH

Congress to establish a colony in Africa, in the interest of "moral justice" and "political foresight." This memorial was sent to the Committee on the Slave Trade, which rejected it.

The society realized that it would need more information about Africa if it was to win support for its proposals. In March 1817, the Rev. Samuel J. Mills, who was traveling for the American Bible Society, offered to go to England and to Africa in order to obtain the necessary information. To help raise the $5,000 he believed necessary for the journey, auxiliaries were set up in Philadelphia, New York and Baltimore during the summer of 1817. Mills was joined by Ebenezer Burgess, a professor of mathematics and natural philosophy at Burlington College in Vermont. They borrowed the necessary funds and sailed for England and Africa. Though Mills died before the report was completed, Burgess finished the work and returned with the completed report.

On March 3, 1819, Congress passed the Slave Trade Act, authorizing the President to return all captured Africans to Africa and to provide for them on the West Coast of that continent. President Monroe was urged by Secretary of the Treasury Crawford to construe the act liberally. This interpretation was opposed by Secretary of State John Quincy Adams. Crawford's position won out, and Monroe cooperated with the Colonization Society in sending out agents to select a spot on the African coast for the return of the captured Africans. The result was the eventual chartering of the ship *Elizabeth,* which left America in 1820 with the Rev. Samuel C. Craner, agent of the Colonization Society; two agents of the government; and about eighty free Negroes. The three white Americans and many of the Negroes became ill and died within a short time.

Although this initial attempt at establishing a settlement in Africa was not successful, the society ultimately established the colony of Liberia, whose capital was named Monrovia after the current President of the United States. By 1832, more than a dozen state legislatures had officially endorsed the Colonization Society. Among these were Maryland, Virginia and Kentucky. North Carolina, Mississippi and other states had local societies. At first, only free Negroes were sent; but after 1827, a few slaves were manumitted on the condition that they be sent to Liberia. The Colonization Society had, by 1830, settled 1,420 Negroes in the colony.

The first ten years of the society's life were its most successful. After 1831, abolitionists, many of whom had previously supported it, began to denounce colonization. William Lloyd Garrison, Arthur Tappan, Gerrit Smith and James G. Birney were prominent abolitionists who turned against colonization. Internal problems resulted in the loss of many of the auxiliaries, which declared their independence. The loss of this support resulted in the organization's becoming insolvent in

1834, although it continued to function until its dissolution in the decade preceding the Civil War.

There were other efforts to rid the country of its free Negro population, including an effort to encourage emigration to Haiti. Altogether, approximately fifteen thousand Negroes, the majority from the slaveholding states, migrated from the United States, the Colonization Society having been responsible for the departure of about twelve thousand. Most of the Negroes were sent to Liberia.

There were numerous reasons for the failure of the deportation project. The large number of Negroes living in the United States made deportation economically unfeasible. The Colonization Society was composed of people with extremely divergent views, which tended to make long-term cooperation doubtful. Some of its members sought an end to slavery and the return of the Negro to his rightful homeland. Others believed that the Negroes could never be integrated into Western civilization and that the country would, therefore, be better off without them. Negroes themselves were mostly in opposition to the colonization scheme. Missionaries saw the returning Negroes as apostles of Christ on a holy mission to Africa. Slaveholders believed that the disappearance of the free Negro would strengthen slavery. It was inevitable that men with such divergent purposes could not long work together.

THE REACTION OF FREE NEGROES TO COLONIZATION

One of the most important reasons for the lack of success of the colonization movement was the opposition of the free Negro population to the project. The free Negroes of Richmond, presided over by William Bowler and Lenty Craw, met shortly after the society was established. They agreed that colonization of the free Negroes was perhaps desirable, but they wanted it to be in the United States.

They decided to request the grant of a small portion of territory "either on the Missouri River, or any place that may seem . . . most conducive to the public good, and our future welfare, subject however, to such rules and regulations as the government of the United States may think proper to adopt."

James Forten, the Rev. Richard Allen, Absalom Jones and Robert Douglas called a meeting in Philadelphia at the Bethel Church, which resolved that colonization was "an unmerited stigma attempted to be cast upon the reputation of the free people of color." The United States was their home and they vowed "never to separate [themselves] voluntarily from the slave population of this country."

Since some of these same men had supported Paul Cuffee, their views surprised the Colonization Society. Finley went to Philadelphia and convinced them that colonization was the best possible thing, but his success was short-lived. During the summer of 1817, James Forten led a meeting of 3,000 blacks opposed to colonization. Forten claimed that colonization would strengthen slavery by raising the value of slaves and thus discourage manumissions. "Let not a purpose be assisted," he declared, "which will stay the cause of the entire abolition of slavery." Meetings opposed to colonization were held in Baltimore, Boston, New York, Hartford, New Haven and Pittsburgh. Every Negro convention in the North was opposed to colonization.

There is generally little evidence of opposition among free Negroes in the South to the idea of colonization, probably the result of the severe limitation placed on their freedom of speech and movement. The colonization project was supported by many prominent white southerners, and the risks to be run in opposing them were extreme. In 1832, a free man spoke in Charleston in favor of colonization. He discussed the hostile legislation against the free people of color in both the North and the South and saw emigration as

LOTT CARY

the only solution. In Africa, the Negro could gain true freedom. Thomas S. Grimké wrote to the Society at this time, demonstrating that other free Negroes in Charleston shared these views.

Several ministers supported colonization as a method of extending Christianity. Alexander Crummell and Daniel A. Payne were among those supporting the project for this reason. Lott Cary and Colin Teague, under the sponsorship of the Richmond African Baptist Missionary Society and the General Baptist Missionary Convention, went to Liberia in 1821. Though Cary disagreed with the American Colonization Society, he labored in Africa till his death in 1828. Most free Negroes would have agreed with Martin R. Delany, who, though he felt the Negro would be better off in Central or South America than in the United States, was extremely hostile toward the Colonization Society. He described it as "anti-Christian in its character and misanthropic in its pretended sympathies."

THE MISSOURI COMPROMISE

Slavery had already been established in Missouri when it applied for admission as a state. The area contained approximately ten thousand slaves out of a total population of sixty thousand. When the bill was introduced enabling Missouri to enter as a state, Representative James Tallmadge, Jr., of New York moved to amend the bill so as to prohibit the further introduction of slaves into Missouri and to provide for the gradual emancipation of those already enslaved there. Though the issue of slavery seemed to have arisen slowly, it had been an important topic of discussion for some time. Whether through accident or through design, the tradition of having an equal number of free and slave states was established. Many people held that allowing Missouri to enter as a slave state would upset the delicate sectional balance.

Most of the opposition to slavery in the North came from well-to-do philanthropists.

JAMES TALLMADGE, JR.

The Manumission Society of New York aided runaway slaves. Quakers sought a strengthening of the law prohibiting the African slave trade and another to protect Negroes from being kidnaped and sold back into slavery. Northern opposition to slavery tended to be a combination of humanitarian sympathy for the plight of the slave and political opposition to the power of the slave states.

When Representative James Tallmadge of New York broached the issue of slavery in the House, a storm of protest rose in the South and a wave of support grew in the North. Jefferson stated that the issue was as terrifying as "a fire bell in the night." Many warned that the slavery question could lead to disunion. Tallmadge did not flinch from this possibility: "If a dissolution of the union must take place, let it be so! If civil war, which gentlemen so much threaten, must come, I can only say, let it come!"

A compromise was worked out, however, under the leadership of Henry Clay. Maine, which had recently broken away from Massachusetts, was admitted as a free state, and Missouri entered as a slave state. The rest of the Louisiana Territory was divided between areas open to slavery and areas closed to it. Using the southern boundary of Missouri as a guide, the territory was so divided at latitude 36°30′ N. When Missouri applied for admission, its constitution had a clause forbidding free Negroes to enter the state. Other states had similar laws. According to the Constitution, however, a citizen of one state had the privileges of citizenship in all states. Since certain states, such as New York, recognized the free Negroes as citizens, these provisions created a Constitutional dilemma. Clay introduced a resolution that stated that the clause in the Missouri constitution should not be interpreted as depriving any citizen of his rights. Though Clay's resolution was meaningless, it served to overcome the opposition; and Missouri was finally admitted into the Union in 1821.

Though the crisis was temporarily averted, the debate served as a warning signal of things to come. While northerners were not yet ready to join together and risk war to gain their way, the reaction in the South was much stronger. All previous differences melted away as southerners united to fight to preserve their "peculiar institution."

CHAPTER TWELVE

The Spirit of Freedom

THE free Negro population continued to increase, though at a slower rate, during the remaining period of slavery. The free Negro's position in society was precarious. The southern slaveholder saw him as a constant threat to the slave system. The northern community, while growing increasingly hostile to slavery, showed little sympathy for the Negro as a person. When a slave gained his freedom, the relationship that had existed between him and his master ended; but his freedom did not entitle him to the political, economic and social rights available to the free white population. Free Negroes were constantly subject to restrictive legislation; but despite these limitations, there were instances of individual accomplishment and social development.

PRE-CIVIL WAR METHODS OF EMANCIPATION

There were several ways in which the free Negro population was increased. Children born to free parents or to a slave father and a free mother were considered free. Besides these natural increases in the free Negro pop-

ulation, slaves frequently were manumitted, providing the primary means of increasing the free Negro population.

In the North, the increasing prohibition of slavery was an important factor in the growth of the free Negro population. A slave in the South attained his freedom through the individual action of his master or, sometimes, as a result of action by his local community. Pierre Charting of Mobile, Alabama, obtained his freedom by public subscription. This was done out of gratitude to him for his outstanding service to the community during the War of 1812 and the yellow fever epidemic of 1819. Sometimes, an individual would free his slaves or leave a will with such instructions. John Randolph, upon his death in 1833, allowed for the emancipation of more than four hundred slaves. Many slaves born of a white master and a slave mother were granted their freedom by their fathers.

Slaves also purchased their freedom on their own initiative. The opportunities for employment outside the slave system were severely limited and closely controlled, however, so that few slaves were able to accomplish this. A slave who did attempt to earn

A slave attempting to gain his freedom through flight.

North Carolina and Tennessee passed similar restrictive legislation. Following the Turner rebellion, Maryland passed a law requiring all Negroes who obtained their freedom thenceforth to leave the state. In special cases, permits could be issued to Negroes allowing them to remain.

This attempt to restrict the growth of the free Negro population, particularly in the South, reflected a growing sense of insecurity over slavery. As attacks on the "peculiar institution" increased in the North, the South became more defensive. The South's entire political, social, ideological and economic existence was predicated on Negro slavery. A free Negro population by its very existence contradicted some of the assumptions in the arguments of the slaveholders. Equally important was the constant threat that they would conspire with the slaves and precipitate a revolt. As slavery became more solidified in the South and as the North became more threatening, restrictions on the growth of the free Negro population increased.

his own income needed the permission of his master and lacked the legal recourse to sue an unscrupulous owner. Many slaves' earnings were confiscated by their masters who argued that since the slaves were their property it naturally followed that all that the slaves possessed belonged to the masters. The most obvious method was widely used: thousands gained their freedom simply by running away.

After 1810, the rate of increase in the number of free Negroes fell rapidly, a result of the greater difficulties masters were facing in manumitting their slaves. In many cases, manumitted slaves were required to leave the state. Virginia, in 1806, legislated that all slaves set free after 1806 were obliged to leave the state. Maryland, Kentucky and Delaware soon responded by prohibiting the emigration of free Negroes. In the next twenty-five years, Ohio, Illinois, Indiana, Missouri,

VIII. *Be it enacted* by the authority aforesaid, That no emancipation of any slave shall be valid or lawful, except it be by deed, and according to the regulations above prescribed, and accompanied by the above mentioned certificate. And furthermore, that every person freeing any slave, shall cause to be delivered to him or her, a copy of the deed of emancipation and certificate aforesaid, (within ten days after such deed shall have been executed) attested by the clerk of the court of the district, who shall record the said deed in the respective offices; and that the said clerk shall be paid therefor by the person emancipating, the sum of four dollars; and that all deeds and certificates of manumission, shall be void and of non-effect, unless such deed and certificate shall be recorded within six months from the time the same shall have been executed.

In South Carolina, even when a slave obtained his freedom through emancipation, it was necessary for him to have this fact recorded. Failure to do so meant his return to slavery.

THE GROWTH AND DISTRIBUTION OF THE FREE NEGRO POPULATION

The first United States census was taken in 1790. It revealed that there were approximately 59,000 free Negroes, 32,000 in the South and 27,000 in the North. From 1790 to 1800, the free Negro population showed an increase of 82 per cent. It increased by 71 per cent the following decade, totaling more than 185,000 by 1810. During these twenty years, the free Negro population increased at three times the rate of increase of the slave population. After 1810, however, the rate fell rapidly. From 1820 to 1830, the free Negro population grew at a rate of 36.8 per cent, about the same rate as the slave population. Much of this increase took place in the North as a result of the decline of slavery in that area. After 1840, the slave population increased at a greater rate than the free Negro population. In 1860, the free Negro population totaled about 488,000.

Percentage Increase of the Free Negro
Population

Years	Increased By
1790–1800	82.2%
1800–1810	71.9%
1810–1820	25.3%
1820–1830	36.8%
1830–1840	20.9%
1840–1850	12.5%
1850–1860	12.3%

The free Negro population increased in the South in those areas where the plantation system was declining. In New England, the free Negro population remained stationary after 1840. A similar situation existed in New York. The free Negro population gradually increased in New Jersey and Pennsylvania. While the states of the Deep South had a steady increase in the number of free Negroes living in them, their position relative to the rest of the country declined from almost 54 per cent in 1790 to about 45 per cent in 1860. Particularly after the passage of the Fugitive Slave Act in 1850, states bordering on Canada and the Great Lakes showed the greatest increase in their free Negro populations. These states included Ohio, Michigan and Illinois.

There was a general tendency for free Negroes to settle in urban areas. Of the 83,942 free Negroes in Maryland in 1860, 25,680 resided in Baltimore. Of Louisiana's 18,641 free Negroes, 10,689 lived in New Orleans. One-third of the free Negro population in Pennsylvania resided in Philadelphia. Other cities with high free Negro concentrations were New York in the North and Charleston in the South. The primary reason for this tendency among the free Negroes to settle in urban areas was the greater economic opportunity open to them in the cities. There some prospered as skilled craftsmen while others worked as laborers.

LEGAL STATUS OF THE FREE NEGRO

The free Negro was most secure legally during the period of the American Revolution. After the initial impetus provided by the struggle for the inalienable rights of man had worn off, the position of the free Negro became exceedingly more precarious. It became harder for him to maintain his status. He was constantly threatened, by fraudulent claims of whites or by kidnaping, with return to slavery. Virginia, Tennessee, Georgia and Mississippi required free Negroes to register. All southern states required that they carry passes, and a Negro without one was considered to be a slave.

A free Negro could be enslaved if he aided a runaway slave. It was necessary for him to prove his status if he was accused of being a slave by a white person. If he was unable to do so, he was presumed a slave. If he was unable to pay a fine, he could be returned to slavery. A free Negro could be enslaved in parts of the South for marrying a slave. In Maryland, a free Negro had his ears cut

SEC. 12. No free negro or mulatto, shall be suffered to keep or carry any firelock of any kind, any military weapon, or any powder or lead, without first obtaining a license from the court of the county or corporation in which he resides, which license may at any time be withdrawn by an order of such court. Any free negro or mulatto who shall so offend, shall on conviction before a justice of the peace, forfeit all such arms and ammunition to the use of the informer.

SEC. 13. It shall be the duty of every constable to give information against, and prosecute, every free negro or mulatto, who shall keep or carry any arms or ammunition, contrary to this act.

SEC. 14. If any free negro or mulatto, who shall have been convicted of keeping or carrying arms or ammunition, shall, a second time offend in like manner, he shall, in addition to the forfeiture aforesaid, be punished with stripes, at the discretion of a justice of the peace, not exceeding thirty-nine.

This Mississippi statute made it illegal for any Negro to carry arms or ammunition without a special license.

off for assaulting a white man. South Carolina denied the free Negro the right to trial by jury. The penal code that was applied to slaves usually was applied to free Negroes as well.

The freedom of movement of the free Negro was severely limited. Many seaboard states forbade the free blacks who worked on ships to leave their ships while docked in port. For violations of these restrictions, severe penalties, including a return to slavery, could be levied. Many states made it illegal for a free Negro to carry arms without a special license. By 1835, he had been denied the right to peaceful assembly by almost all states in the South. The presence of white ministers was required at his religious services. Maryland prohibited free blacks from having "lyceums, lodges, fire companies, or literary, dramatic, social, moral, or charitable

societies." Stringent laws attempted to keep their contacts with slaves at a minimum.

The Negro was also limited in his economic pursuits. An 1805 Maryland statute prohibited free Negroes from selling corn, wheat or tobacco without a license. Georgia, in 1829, made it illegal for Negroes to be typesetters. North Carolina prevented Negroes from trading outside the city or town in which they resided. A statute passed in 1831 called for the licensing of all Negro tradesmen in that state. In South Carolina, it was against the law for a Negro to be a clerk. A free Negro needed a guardian's approval to make purchases on credit in Georgia. In spite of these restrictions on their economic life, however, every state required its free Negroes to work and be able to give visible evidence of means of support. In northern cities, besides legal restrictions on his activities, the free Negro faced the added burden of greater competition from whites. Negroes were constantly subjected to attack by white workers who feared their competition. During hard times in Cincinnati and Philadelphia, there were especially severe anti-Negro riots.

For several years following the Revolution, in many areas the free Negro was guaranteed the right to vote. Maryland and North Carolina in the South and New York and Pennsylvania in the North allowed free Negroes to vote. Every slave state that entered the Union after 1789, with the exception of Tennessee, prohibited voting by the free Negro. In the nineteenth century, the free Negro's hold on the vote was severely weakened. Maryland, in 1810, discontinued the franchise for him. In the heyday of Jacksonian democracy, the Negro saw his suffrage disappear—in Tennessee in 1834, North Carolina in 1835 and Pennsylvania in 1838. Indiana disfranchised its free Negro population in 1851. New York, in 1823, required a $250 property qualification and a three-year residency for free Negro suffrage. After

WHEREAS great inconvenience is felt in this state in consequence of free negroes receiving stolen corn, wheat and tobacco, from slaves, and selling the same as the production of their own labour; therefore,

II. BE IT ENACTED, *by the General Assembly of Maryland,* That from and after the first of May next, no free negro shall sell any corn, wheat or tobacco, unless, at the time of his or her so selling the said article or articles, he or she shall be possessed of a certificate, under the hand and seal of a justice of the peace of said county, that he or she is a peaceable and orderly person, and of good character, which certificate shall be of force for one year and no longer.

III. AND BE IT ENACTED, That if any free negro shall act contrary to the provisions of this act, the person so offending shall incur the penalty of five dollars for every such offence, one half to the informer, the other half to be applied to the use of the county, and to be recovered as other fines and forfeitures, before a justice of the peace in the county where such offence shall be committed.

IV. AND BE IT ENACTED, That any person who shall purchase or receive from any free negro any corn, wheat or tobacco, contrary to the provisions of this act, shall forfeit and pay, for every offence, the sum of ten dollars, one half to the informer, the other half to be applied to the use of the county in which such offence was committed, and to be recovered and applied in the same manner as other fines and forfeitures are by this law directed to be recovered and applied.

V. AND BE IT ENACTED, That it shall be the duty of every justice of the peace, sheriff and constable, to give information of every violation of this act that shall come to his knowledge.

This 1805 Maryland act prohibited free Negroes from selling corn, wheat or tobacco without a license.

1830, very few free Negroes were voting anywhere in the United States.

The free black frequently was required to assume the obligations of citizenship without receiving the benefits. In many places, he was forced to pay school taxes while his children were forbidden to attend the public schools. Generally, he had the right to own property. Most states, with such exceptions as Louisiana and New York, excluded the free Negro from the militia. His testimony was not admissible in court cases involving whites. Legally, in general, he tended to fare better in the higher courts. In *Slave and Citizen*, Frank Tannenbaum stated: "The law, the church, and social policy all conspired to prevent the identification of the liberated Negro with the community. He was to be kept as a separate, a lesser, being. In spite of being manumitted, he was not considered a free moral agent."

EDUCATION AVAILABLE TO NEGROES

Facilities for the education of Negroes varied from state to state. In the South, for example, there was little popular interest in education, nor was there a tax base with which to make widespread public education possible. In a plantation society, education was available only by private tutor or in a private academy; thus, the level of education of free Negro children was dependent upon the financial resources of their parents. Added to this, of course, was the fact that many southerners opposed education for free blacks, since this would only provide them with weapons for their insurrectionary tendencies. Nearly all of the southern states passed legislation of one sort or another to make it difficult, if not impossible, for free Negroes to receive any kind of formal education.

There were several attempts, however, in the border states as well as in Louisiana, to provide for Negro education. The A.M.E. Church, for example, opened a school for free blacks, the Bethel Charity School, in 1816. There were also several excellent schools for Negroes in Washington, D.C. Finally, there were scattered attempts in

EDUCATIONAL LAWS OF VIRGINIA.

THE

PERSONAL NARRATIVE

OF

Mrs. Margaret Douglass,

A SOUTHERN WOMAN,

WHO WAS IMPRISONED FOR ONE MONTH

IN THE

COMMON JAIL OF NORFOLK,

UNDER THE LAWS OF VIRGINIA,

FOR THE CRIME OF

TEACHING FREE COLORED CHILDREN TO READ.

"Search the Scriptures!"
"How can one read unless he be taught?"
HOLY BIBLE.

BOSTON:
PUBLISHED BY JOHN P. JEWETT & CO.
CLEVELAND, OHIO:
JEWETT, PROCTOR & WORTHINGTON.
1854.

Many southerners opposed education of any form for Negroes. As a result of this attitude, Mrs. Margaret Douglass, pictured above, spent one month in jail for the "crime" of trying to educate the Negroes of Virginia.

North Carolina, Virginia and even in some sophisticated areas of South Carolina. The wealthy free Negro community of New Orleans supported several schools. Some Negroes of that area even went to Paris to study. In 1850, there were 1,400 Negroes in school in Baltimore and 1,000 in New Orleans.

Although educational opportunities in the North were available to the free Negro, the facilities increasingly tended to be segregated. Separate schools for black children were established in Boston in 1820, and soon after that other towns in Massachusetts followed Boston's example. In many cases, free Negro parents established their own schools for the education of their children. Boston, partly in response to the growing abolitionist sentiment, went against this trend in 1855, when

it integrated its school system. Rhode Island and Connecticut maintained separate facilities for whites and Negroes. The New York legislature passed an ordinance in 1841 allowing communities to set up segregated facilities if they so desired. Earlier, in 1832, Negroes in New York had gained control of the existing New York Manumission Society school. They had replaced the white teachers and principal with Negroes and had run the school themselves. New Jersey also set up a separate school system for the children of free Negroes.

The situation did not improve as the country expanded westward. Ohio excluded Negroes from its school system in 1829. Twenty years later, it provided for the establishment of separate schools for free "people of color," but it never provided the Negro schools with adequate financial assistance. Indiana and Illinois handled the situation in a similar manner. Although conditions tended to be better in Michigan and Wisconsin, real improvement did not come until after the Civil War.

The following table indicates the surprisingly large number of free blacks who were educated before the Civil War. It demonstrates the fact that in such places in the South as Charleston, South Carolina, the restrictions on education were not fully enforced. Thus, in Charleston, only forty-five adults are listed as illiterate in 1850.

School Attendance and Adult Illiteracy among
the Free Negro Population in 16 Cities: 1850

Cities	Free Colored Population Total	Number of Free Colored Attending School for County in which City is Located	Number of Illiterate Adult Free Colored in County
Boston, Mass.	2,038	1,439	205
Providence, R. I.	1,499	292	55
New Haven, Conn.	989	360	167
Brooklyn, N.Y.	2,424	507	788
New York, N.Y.	13,815	1,418	1,667
Philadelphia, Pa.	10,736	2,176	3,498
Cincinnati, Ohio	3,237	291	620
Louisville, Ky.	1,538	141	567
Baltimore, Md.	25,442	1,453	9,318
Washington, D.C.	8,158	420	2,674
Richmond, Va.	2,369	0	1,594
Petersburg, Va.	2,616	0	1,155
Charleston, S.C.	3,441	68	45
Savannah, Ga.	686	0	185
Mobile, Ala.	715	53	12
New Orleans, La.	9,905	1,008	2,279

The first Negro to complete college in the United States was John Russwurm, who graduated from Bowdoin College in 1826. By 1860, Negroes were in attendance at Oberlin, Franklin-Rutland Colleges, Harvard Medical School and elsewhere. In 1851, Myrtilla Miner established an academy for Negro girls in Washington, D.C. The following year, Charles L. Reason founded the Institute for Colored Youth in Philadelphia. The Rev. Charles Avery gave his name and financial assistance to a college for Negroes

JOHN RUSSWURM

in 1849. Religious organizations helped to establish colleges for Negroes: Lincoln University in Pennsylvania was established by the Presbyterians in 1854, and in 1855 the Methodist Episcopal Church established Wilberforce College in Ohio. After the Civil

CHARLES L. REASON

Because of his lack of training while in slavery, the newly freed Negro usually found it necessary to work as an unskilled laborer.

War, black Methodists assumed the sponsorship of the university. There were many more plans for Negro higher education than were realized. A good example is the college that Frederick Douglass planned in the 1850's. It was his conviction that at that time members of his race sorely needed an industrial college to train people in the mechanical arts. Liberal arts education was fine, he insisted, but there were other needs of the country and of the Negro to be met. "We need mechanics as well as ministers," Douglass asserted. "We need workers in iron, clay, and leather, we need orators, editors and other professional men, but they only reach a certain class and get respect for our race only in certain selected circles." Douglass' outline in many ways anticipated Booker T. Washington's philosophy and dream for the Tuskegee Institute.

Since most Negro slaves received little or no education, with few exceptions the Negro had few skills when he obtained his freedom. While most free Negroes survived as unskilled laborers, some did obtain a higher status. Many were able to obtain property and a few became slave owners themselves. In Charleston, South Carolina, free blacks were listed as working in fifty different occupations. Free Negroes in North Carolina were engaged in over seventy different crafts. Boston and New York saw their free people of color participating in over one thousand different occupations. They were paperhangers, engravers and photographers, while a few had become lawyers, ministers and teachers. In Philadelphia, Negro caterers served the city's best families.

Various organizations were set up in pre-Civil War America to help the Negro make the adjustment to freedom. The Society of Friends, one of the first groups in this country to formally condemn slavery, helped the Negroes who had already obtained their freedom. Particularly active in this cause was the Philadelphia Yearly Meeting. The Pennsylvania Society for the Abolition of Slavery and the North Carolina Manumission Society also helped the newly freed Negro. A few masters who granted freedom to their slaves also gave them property.

The free Negro population did achieve a certain amount of economic success. In Philadelphia, as early as 1800, the free Negroes of the city owned nearly one hundred houses and lots. By 1837, the free Negroes in New York City were listed as owning $1,400,000 in taxable real estate. At the same time, they had $600,000 deposited in the city's banks. In Maryland, by 1860, the free Negro population had accumulated $1,000,000 in taxable property, and twelve free blacks were listed as owning property worth more than $5,000. In the same year, the free Negroes of Virginia owned 60,000 acres of farmland and city real estate valued at $463,000. In Charleston, in 1859, 352 Negroes owned $778,000 worth of property. Tennessee's free Negro population had acquired, by 1860, $750,000 worth of property; while in New Orleans, by the year preceding the outbreak of the Civil War, the free Negro population had accumulated approximately $15,000,000 worth of property.

SOCIAL POSITION

One of the striking characteristics of the free Negro population was the high percentage of those with mixed ancestry. This situation resulted primarily from the mechanism by which emancipation was generally gained before the Civil War. While being of mixed ancestry was no guarantee in itself of economic privilege or social success, those Negroes who had some white ancestors usually were also favored by white society in obtaining the education necessary for the very limited opportunities available to free Negroes. Twelve per cent of the slave population was of mixed ancestry in 1850. In the same year, 37 per cent of the free Negroes were listed as being of mixed ancestry. In Louisiana, about 15,000 of 18,500 free Negroes were mulatto. In all, there were at least 159,000 free mulattoes in the nation in 1850.

The family life of the free Negro tended to be less stable than that of the slave, even though his marriage was recognized by law. This was particularly true of the majority, who were poor and lived in urban slums. Those free Negroes who had obtained a degree of economic stability tended to have more stable marriages. The union of a free Negro and a slave required only the master's permission. This "family," therefore, tended to be informal and without explicit legal sanction.

There was not much available in the way of recreation for free Negroes. Two of the more popular pastimes were gambling, which

Dancing was a form of recreation that Negroes enjoyed in slavery and also as free men and women.

was illegal, and dancing. In New York, an African theater was founded in 1821, but it survived only a few years. Most Negroes had neither the time nor the money to support much leisure activity. Living in an extremely hostile environment, their primary preoccupation tended to be a concern for their survival. In the South, the growing fear of slave insurrections made it extremely difficult for the free Negro population to assemble in large numbers. There were, of course, some free Negroes who had achieved a degree of prosperity and did have more time for recreation and other luxuries.

The upper class of free Negroes tended to be mulatto rather than black. They tended to have a greater degree of literacy, education and training. Some mulattoes were landowners, and a few owned slaves. In the North, this group formed a small aristocracy, which held itself apart from most of the other Negroes, particularly the slave population in the South. They were mostly artisans, tradesmen and the better domestic servants. This group was increased by the addition of well-to-do mulattoes who emigrated from the South.

In southern cities, the class distinctions were even greater. The two most important free Negro communities in the deep South were in Charleston and New Orleans. Many free Negroes in both these communities tended to identfy more with the whites than with the slaves. This attitude is reflected in the actions of the free Negro population of Charleston: in 1790, they formed themselves into an organization known as the Brown Fellowship Society.

ORGANIZATIONS OF FREE NEGROES

The situation that the free Negro faced forced him to organize in order to pool his community's meager resources. Some groups were merely social and attempted to provide a release from the pressures to which the free blacks were constantly subjected. Others, such as the convention movement, were more overtly political and sought the twin objectives of the abolition of slavery and an end to second-class citizenship for free Negroes. They sought to overcome the discrimination that left them without the right to vote or to attend public schools and that restricted their efforts to earn a living.

The first colored Grand Lodge was organized in 1845 in Maryland. Two years later, a second lodge was founded. In 1843, Peter Ogden and other free Negroes organized the Grand United Order of Odd Fellows. Negroes in Baltimore had set up a mutual-help organization in 1821. There were thirty-five such organizations by 1835, some of them existing in secret. Among these were the Friendship Benevolent Society for Social Relief, the Star in the East Association and the Daughters of Jerusalem. Similar organizations existed in other areas. The further south they attempted to go, the more difficult organization proved; many cities in the South outlawed these organizations.

The church was definitely the main organization existent among the free Negroes. It is not surprising, therefore, that one of the first major Negro newspapers should have been a religious organ. The African Methodist Episcopal Church founded a weekly magazine in 1847 called the *Christian Herald;* after 1852, its name was changed to the *Christian Recorder.* The church expanded and developed during this period, spreading with the free Negro as he moved to the new states and territories in the West. The two most important denominations were the Baptist and the Methodist. Though the Baptist Church contained the largest number of free Negroes, the Methodist Church, which was organized on a national basis, tended to have greater influence. The Baptist churches in a particular area, if associated with any church, tended to be aligned with the local white Baptist church.

JOHN RANKIN

PETER OGDEN

MORRIS BROWN

As the nineteenth century progressed, the free Negro in the South found increased resistance by whites to his independent religious life. Part of the reaction of the white community to the Vesey plot was the destruction of the African Methodist Episcopal Church in Charleston in 1822. The Rev. Morris Brown was forced to move the church to the North. John Chavis, a Negro minister in North Carolina, was prevented from preaching there in 1831. The white Episcopalians and Presbyterians allowed free Negroes to attend segregated services, a device that helped to set back the development of free Negro independent church organizations. Gradually, as the Civil War approached, the church in the South declined as an important factor in the life of the free Negro.

The first Negro convention took place in Philadelphia in 1817, and was called primarily to condemn the American Colonization Society. Also in 1817, a meeting was called by free Negro citizens of Richmond to protest colonization. In 1830, a more positive call was issued by Peter Williams, rector of St. Philips Church in New York City.

Bishop Allen was elected president of the convention, which met at the Bethel Church "to devise ways and means for the bettering of our condition." Other leaders in attendance were James Forten, John B. Vashon, John T. Hilton and Samuel Cornish. Two major items on the agenda were a project to encourage Negroes to migrate to Canada and the need to raise money for a Negro college. The members attacked the American Colonization Society and set up local auxiliary societies to raise funds for the establishment of a colony of free Negroes in upper Canada.

The convention met regularly for several years. Whites occasionally attended, among them, Arthur Tappan, John Rankin and William Lloyd Garrison. In 1847, while meeting in Troy, New York, the convention urged Negroes to seek admission to white colleges. Among the delegates urging this action was William C. Nell, who believed that if Negroes demonstrated their capabilities they would win the support of whites.

In the 1850's, an increasing number of conventions was held. Meeting at Rochester, New York, delegates formed the National

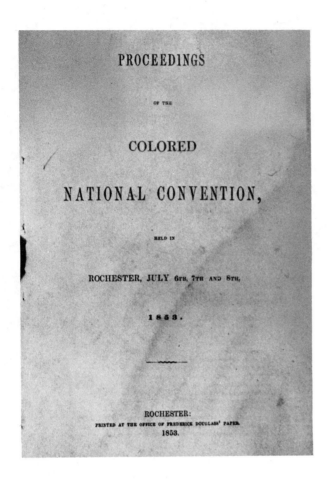

PROCEEDINGS

OF THE

COLORED

NATIONAL CONVENTION,

HELD IN

ROCHESTER, JULY 6TH, 7TH AND 8TH,

1853.

ROCHESTER:
PRINTED AT THE OFFICE OF FREDERICK DOUGLASS' PAPER.
1853.

DAVID WALKER'S *APPEAL* AND *FREEDOM'S JOURNAL*

The Negro convention movement represented an organized attempt by free Negroes to better their position and to deal with the question of slavery. Between the first convention, in 1817, and the second, in 1830, free Negroes had continued to oppose the treatment they received from the rest of society. Two striking examples of printed opposition to their plight are David Walker's *Appeal* and the first Negro newspaper, *Freedom's Journal*.

David Walker was born in North Carolina on September 28, 1785. He moved to Boston, where he sold second-hand clothes. Though he was a free Negro living in the North, his hatred of slavery did not diminish. In September 1829, he published his *Appeal in Four Articles: Together with a Preamble, to the Colored Citizens of the World, but in Particular . . . to Those of the United States Written in Boston, Mass.* This pamphlet was one of the most uncompromising indictments of slavery that was ever printed in the United States. It was widely circulated both in the North and in the South.

The pamphlet was divided into four sections: (1) "Our wretchedness in consequence of slavery"; (2) "Our wretchedness in consequence of ignorance"; (3) "Our wretchedness in consequence of the preachers of the religion of Jesus Christ"; (4) "Our wretchedness in consequence of the colonizing plan." According to Walker, the Negroes had been forced by other Americans into becoming the *"most wretched, degraded* and *abject* set of beings that *ever lived* since the world began." He argued that the Negro should acquire an education and make "tyrants quake and tremble on their sandy foundation."

One of Walker's aims was to dispel the myth of Negro inferiority. "Are we MEN?" was his constant question. He wanted slaves to ponder how it was possible that they were

Council of Colored People. In a declaration signed by Frederick Douglass, among others, the convention declared that, with the exception of the Jews, the Negroes were the most persecuted people in the United States. The New York State Convention of Colored Citizens met in Albany in 1840 for the purpose of considering the political plight of the free Negro. A committee consisting of Alexander Crummell, the Rev. J. Sharp, T. S. Wright, Patrick H. Reason, C. L. Reason and Charles B. Ray was appointed to draft an address to the people of New York. The address was to deal with the lack of political expression available to Negroes.

Another group, the Colored Citizens of Pennsylvania, met in convention at Harrisburg in 1848, with John B. Vashon serving as president. The purpose of this convention was to weld the group into a united front in an effort to confront the evils of discrimination.

subject to men just like themselves, to the very same "dust and ashes" and "dying worms" that can describe the condition of all humanity. Walker declared, further, that America really belonged more to the slaves than to the masters. To him, the slaves had ennobled the land, enriching it with their blood and tears. Religion was part of the problem, according to Walker, for he could see "no greater mockery . . . than the way in which it is conducted by the Americans." But his special wrath was saved for certain Negroes: those who betrayed their racial group in order to further their personal positions.

Basing his attack on portions of the Declaration of Independence, Walker came to the conclusion that slaves were justified in using force to resist the oppression of their masters. He urged Negroes to fight fearlessly to obtain their lawful rights. "The man," he said, "who would not fight under our Lord and Master, Jesus Christ, in the glorious and heavenly cause of Freedom and of God—to be delivered from the most wretched, abject and servile slavery, that ever a people was afflicted with since the foundation of the world, to the present day—ought to be kept with all of his children or family in slavery, or in chains, to be butchered by his cruel enemies."

Some antislavery leaders looked upon the pamphlet as too radical. Benjamin Lundy stated that it was perhaps the boldest and most inflammatory paper published in the United States. He condemned it, claiming that it would injure the cause of freedom. William Garrison did not approve of Walker's radicalism. He said that "a better promoter of insurrection was never sent forth to an oppressed people, [but] as for me, I do not preach rebellion."

The distribution of Walker's *Appeal* caused considerable alarm in the South. Its circulation was prohibited in Virginia, and its suppression was discussed by the North Carolina

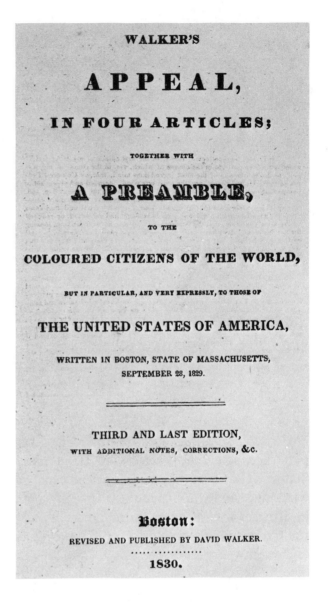

legislature. Georgia passed a law prohibiting the circulation of all incendiary pamphlets. A reward of $1,000 was offered for Walker's "head," and ten times that amount for "the live Walker." The mayor of Savannah wrote Mayor Harrison Grey Otis of Boston and asked him to suppress the work; but Otis replied that he lacked the power to do this. Threats against Walker's life became so numerous that his friends advised him to go to Canada. He declined to do so and remained in Boston, where he died in 1830. Walker's *Appeal* continued to be circulated and was said to have influenced Nat Turner in his insurrection of 1831.

SAMUEL CORNISH

Freedom's Journal was the first periodical published solely by Negroes in the United States. It was a magazine and newspaper combined and was founded in 1827 at a meeting of free Negroes in the home of Boston Cromwell in New York City. Samuel Cornish, a Presbyterian minister, and John Russwurm, the first Negro college graduate in the United States, were selected as the editors. The prospectus stated that the object of the publication was not to be controversial but to champion the defense of oppressed humanity. It declared that "there ought to be some channel of communication between us and the public through which a single voice may be heard in defense of five hundred thousand free people of colour."

Cornish resigned from the paper after the first issue. Russwurm, who was more conservative than Cornish, continued to guide the paper for its remaining two years. In 1829, Russwurm left the United States for Liberia, at which time Cornish resumed the editorship, changing the journal's name to *The Rights of All*. This new paper, however, did not last long either. From 1837 until its demise in 1841, Cornish edited the *Colored American*. *Freedom's Journal* and *The Rights of All* were both precursors of the abolition movement, and during their brief existence they gave voice to the growing dissatisfaction of the free Negro with his own position and with the condition of his enslaved brothers in the South.

CHAPTER THIRTEEN

Revolt and Abolition

DURING the nineteenth century, there were conspiracies and revolts conducted by slaves against the plantation regime, and there is some evidence of day-to-day resistance on the part of individual slaves. It is difficult to estimate the extent and intensity of this resistance to slavery since the South constantly was subject to false rumors of proposed violence, and since many actual disturbances were never recorded because southern newspapers feared that they were "a delicate subject to touch." There were, in the 1800's, three slave insurrections that were of major importance: that led by Gabriel Prosser, the Denmark Vesey conspiracy and Nat Turner's rebellion.

JAMES MONROE

THE GABRIEL INSURRECTION

Gabriel was a slave belonging to Thomas H. Prosser, the proprietor of a plantation in Henrico County, Virginia. In May of 1800, Gabriel began to plan a general insurrection, which was elaborately designed and kept secret for several months. A few weapons were stored away, and approximately a thousand slaves became involved in the conspiracy. The conspirators planned to meet six miles outside of Richmond, where they would begin a three-column attack on the city. One company was to seize the arsenal, another the powder magazine, and a third was to begin the general attack on the population. It was the slaves' intention to kill all whites except the Quakers, Methodists and Frenchmen and then establish their own republic in western Virginia.

During the summer of 1800, there was growing fear in the white community that something was amiss. At the very last moment, two slaves, Tom and Pharaoh, told their master, Mosby Sheppard, of the plot. Governor James Monroe acted quickly to call out 600 troops and alert the local militia. He also obtained the use of the federal armory at Manchester. On August 30, 1800, over a thousand slaves assembled outside Richmond. A violent storm took place that evening, however, and forced cancellation of the rebellion. J. T. Callender, a witness to the events, described the situation in a letter to Thomas Jefferson: "Upon that very evening just about Sunset, there came on the most terrible thunder accompanied with an enormous rain, that I ever witnessed in this State. Between Prosser's and Richmond, there is a place called Brook Swamp which runs across the high road, and over which there was a bridge. By this, the Africans were of necessity to pass, and the rain had made the passage impracticable." Since an attack on the alerted city was now impossible, the slaves dispersed.

Gabriel escaped but was discovered in Norfolk on September 25. Refusing to reveal the names of any of the slaves who had been involved in the attempt, he was convicted and sentenced to be hanged on October 7. After an interview with Gabriel, Governor Monroe declared: "From what he said to me, he seemed to have made up his mind to die, and to have resolved to say but little on the subject of the conspiracy." At least thirty-four of Gabriel's companions were executed along with him.

At his trial, Gabriel delivered one of the most eloquent statements to come out of the black insurrectionary movement. He declared that he had nothing more to offer in his defense "than what General Washington would have had to offer, had he been taken by the British and put to trial by them." Gabriel contended that his only goal had been to obtain the liberty of his countrymen, that he sacrificed his life willingly in their cause and that he desired immediate execution. He knew that his trial was a mere formality and boldly said so in court: "I know that you have predetermined to shed my blood, why then all this mockery of a trial?"

The unsuccessful Gabriel conspiracy left in its wake widespread white hysteria. A correspondent described the situation for a Philadelphia paper: "Let but a single armed Negro be seen or suspected, and, at once on many a lonely plantation, there were trembling hands at work to bar doors and windows, that seldom had ever closed before, and there was a shuddering when a grey squirrel scrambled over the roof, or when a shower of walnuts came clattering down from the overhanging boughs." The courage and daring that the slaves had displayed was extremely upsetting to the whites. "The accused," John Randolph commented, "have exhibited a spirit, which, if it becomes general, must deluge the Southern country in blood. They manifested a sense of their rights, and contempt of danger, and a thirst for revenge which portend the most unhappy consequences." Virginians asked the federal government to establish a colony where they could send recalcitrant slaves, and they established a permanent guard for the state capitol. The request to the national government was not acted upon.

Unrest continued in Virginia during the following year. Plots were reported in Petersburg and Norfolk. Fifteen slaves were executed in North Carolina, allegedly for planning an insurrection. Finally, the situation quieted down, until the next serious outbreak took place in Virginia in 1816. There, George Boxley, a white storekeeper, gained the support of some blacks for an insurrection, but his plot was betrayed by a slave woman. Boxley escaped, but six slaves were hanged, and another six were banished.

JOSEPH CINQUE AND THE *AMISTAD*

Joseph Cinque, one of fifty-three slaves on board the slave ship *Amistad* going from Havana to Puerto Príncipe, led a mutiny of the slaves. The Africans gained control of the ship, killed the captain and the cook and forced their two Spanish purchasers to sail toward Africa. By day the men pretended to sail toward Africa, by night they sought the United States mainland.

After several days, during which the slave-owners (Ruiz and Montez) were held captive on board the *Amistad,* the ship was sighted by the American brig *Washington.* Sensing something awry when they saw a Spanish ship being commanded entirely by Africans, the crew of the *Washington* stopped the *Amistad* and sought an explanation. It was soon discovered that Cinque and the other slaves were in command as a result of mutiny, and the captain of the *Washington* took the *Amistad* and its crew into custody. The capture of the *Amistad* inspired the anti-slavery forces to join together in an effort to help the slaves retain the freedom they had gained on the high seas.

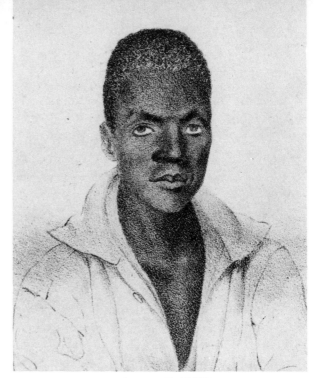

JOSEPH CINQUE

A

HISTORY

OF THE

AMISTAD CAPTIVES:

BEING A

CIRCUMSTANTIAL ACCOUNT

OF THE

CAPTURE OF THE SPANISH SCHOONER AMISTAD,

BY THE AFRICANS ON BOARD;

THEIR VOYAGE, AND CAPTURE

NEAR LONG ISLAND, NEW YORK; WITH

BIOGRAPHICAL SKETCHES

OF EACH OF THE SURVIVING AFRICANS.

ALSO, AN ACCOUNT OF

THE TRIALS

HAD ON THEIR CASE, BEFORE THE DISTRICT AND CIRCUIT COURTS OF THE
UNITED STATES, FOR THE DISTRICT OF CONNECTICUT.

COMPILED FROM AUTHENTIC SOURCES,
BY JOHN W. BARBER,
MEM. OF THE CONNECTICUT HIST. SOC.

NEW HAVEN, CT.:
PUBLISHED BY E. L. & J. W. BARBER.
HITCHCOCK & STAFFORD, PRINTERS.

1840.

In the meantime, the Spanish government pressed its claim for the surrender of the ship. It is probable that President Martin Van Buren would have yielded had not the case already entered the federal courts. In the two lower courts, Cinque and his followers were acquitted of the charge of piracy; then their case was taken on appeal to the Supreme Court. Former President John Quincy Adams argued and won the case for Cinque and his crew. They were released from bondage, and with funds provided by the American and Foreign Anti-slavery Society, they were sent first to England and then back to Africa.

THE VESEY CONSPIRACY

Denmark Vesey was born in 1767 on the Island of Hispaniola. In 1800, he was able to purchase his freedom with money he had won in a lottery. He settled in Charleston, South Carolina, where he had been taken as a slave, and earned his living as a carpenter. He constantly admonished other Negroes to demand better treatment and to assert their dignity. John Lofton (*Insurrection in South Carolina*) quoted a contemporary of Vesey as saying: "Even whilst walking through the streets in company with another, he was not idle; for if his companion bowed to a white person he would rebuke him, and observe that all men are born equal, and that he was surprised that anyone would degrade himself by such conduct; that he would never cringe to the whites, nor ought anyone who had the feelings of a man."

Vesey's outlook reflected both religious and secular influences. He had read the Bible and was particularly impressed by the example of the Israelites escaping from Egyptian bondage. He followed closely the debates in Congress on the Missouri Compromise and read much of the antislavery material being published in England and the North. The successful revolt of the slaves in Haiti and their achievement of independence inspired Vesey and the people who had begun to gather around him, mostly literate slaves working as artisans in the city. Even some functionaries of the African Methodist Episcopal Church joined in the conspiracy, having become angry and frustrated by the harassment they received from the Charleston authorities, although Morris Brown, the minister of the church, was not involved.

The conspirators collected, among other weapons, 250 pike heads and bayonets and 300 daggers. They chose the second Sunday in July 1822 as the day of their revolt. Vesey was careful to select capable and loyal men for his lieutenants. That he chose wisely is indicated by the fact that, when the plot was revealed, only one would divulge the names of his colleagues. The conspirators exercised similar care in enlisting supporters, trusting few domestic servants. Unfortunately, a favorite slave of Colonel Prioleau was told of the plot; he informed his master of the plan. Before the July date, two conspirators, Peter Poyas and Mingo Harth, were arrested.

Vesey attempted to move up the date of the insurrection but was unable to contact all his confederates. Peter and Mingo did not give away the conspiracy and were released the following day. The police kept them un-

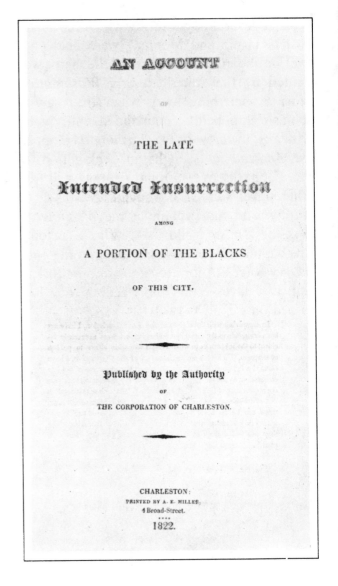

AN ACCOUNT

OF

THE LATE

Intended Insurrection

AMONG

A PORTION OF THE BLACKS

OF THIS CITY.

Published by the Authority

OF

THE CORPORATION OF CHARLESTON.

CHARLESTON:
PRINTED BY A. E. MILLER,
4 Broad-Street.
1822.

der close surveillance, however. A second slave informed, and more arrests were made. One of those arrested agreed to cooperate with the authorities, and the plot was finally broken. Of the 137 arrested, at least 47 were condemned to death. Thirty-seven, including Vesey, were hanged in Charleston, while the rest were removed from the area. Four whites implicated in the plot were fined and imprisoned. The names of the conspirators were kept in code, and Vesey died without revealing their names. Peter Poyas died admonishing his comrades: "Do not open your lips! Die silent, as you shall see me do." It was estimated that as many as nine thousand slaves had been involved in the plan.

NAT TURNER'S REBELLION

The next major attack by blacks upon the slave regime occurred in Southampton County, Virginia, in 1831, under the direction of Nat Turner, a literate slave and an avid reader of the Bible. A Baptist, he often conducted religious services among his fellow slaves. Turner was a mystic who recorded in his confession that he "was ordained for some great purpose in the hands of the Almighty." In 1828, he "heard a loud noise in the heavens, and the Spirit instantly appeared to [him] and said the Serpent was loosened, and Christ had laid down the yoke he had borne for the sins of men, and that [he] should take it on and fight against the Serpent, for the time was fast approaching when the first should be last and the last should be first."

The time was ripe. Virginia was already unsettled by the circulation of Walker's *Appeal*. Turner interpreted a solar eclipse on February 12, 1831, as a sign from God. He interested four other slaves in his plan, and July 4, 1831, was chosen as the date to begin the insurrection. Few preparations were made, however, and Turner spent most of his time in prayer. On the day scheduled for the start of the rebellion, Turner was sick and the insurrection was postponed. On August 13, he saw another "sign." The following day, he addressed a religious meeting of Negroes in Southampton County. Some of the slaves there "signified their willingness to cooperate with him by wearing around their necks red bandanna handkerchiefs."

The revolt started on August 21, 1831. After killing Joseph Travis and his family, Turner and his initial band of slaves roamed the countryside killing whites. Fifty-seven whites were killed within a period of thirty-six hours.

As the largest number of slaves with Turner at one time was seventy, they were easily suppressed by the militia. After six weeks, Turner was caught and executed, along with sixteen others. Twelve slaves were deported, and many Negroes were indiscriminately massacred by the militia after Turner's band was defeated. The *Richmond Whig* alluded to "the slaughter of many blacks without trial and under circumstances of great barbarity."

The discovery of Nat Turner.

The paper estimated that forty Negroes had been killed during the rampage. The rebellion lacked the careful planning and coordination of the two previous conspiracies. Governor John Floyd of Virginia wrote to Governor James Hamilton of South Carolina that, "All died bravely indicating no reluctance to lose their lives in such a cause."

Except for a few small conspiracies, the last thirty years of American slavery were relatively calm. Thus, during a time when sectional tension was heightened over the issue of slavery, the slaves themselves did not offer any organized resistance to their situation or to the planter regime.

OTHER FORMS OF RESISTANCE TO SLAVERY

Over half the Negroes in the South lived on plantations of fifty slaves or fewer, and in some areas the white population was larger than the black. The nonslaveholding whites were loyal to the slave regime and hostile to the Negro, which meant that escape from the plantation was extremely dangerous. Many slaves were dependent on their masters for protection from hostile whites.

Nevertheless, there was a strong current of day-to-day resistance that gives evidence that the surface calm covered an underlying hostility to the regime. The history of slavery abounds with instances of individual violence against the master or overseer. The most independent of the slaves ran away and made the trek to the North and freedom.

U. B. Phillips' study of the criminal offenses of slaves in Virginia demonstrates that many of the crimes committed by slaves took the form of violence against whites. Of 1,418 incidents recorded in Virginia, 1,117 state the nature of the crime. Of these, 346 were convictions for murder. The number of whites murdered by slaves was 194. An additional 60 victims were unidentified. Phillips found an additional 111 convictions for other assaults, such as attempted murder, and only

two of these were recorded as committed against blacks.

Many slaves obtained their freedom by escaping to the North. The Underground Railroad was a systematic effort of whites and Negroes to aid the slave in his escape. Henrietta Buckmaster places its beginning in 1804. At that time, General Thomas Boude refused to return a fugitive slave and was supported in his action by his community, Columbia, Pennsylvania. The term Underground Railroad gained wide usage after 1831. When it first began operating, most of the slaves who attempted to flee were men. Later, as the system became better organized, women and children participated in increasing numbers.

The "railroad" operated in a very simple way. The fugitive slaves would travel at night, stopping for food and rest at "stations" spaced about twenty miles apart. Quakers and other groups raised money to keep the operation going. Harriet Tubman, herself a

HARRIET TUBMAN

fugitive slave, would hire herself out as a domestic when the operation was low on funds.

It is difficult to estimate how many slaves escaped this way. William B. Hesseltine in his *History of the South* estimated that up to two thousand slaves escaped each year on the route through Ohio from 1830 to 1860. Wilber H. Siebert found over three thousand people cooperating in the enterprise in the North, over half of whom worked in Ohio. The journey to freedom was very difficult and dangerous. Harriet Tubman made nineteen trips to the South, emancipating almost three hundred slaves. Rewards for her capture totaled over $40,000. She was always armed with a pistol, which she used to threaten any slave who desired to turn back and thus endanger her party.

ABOLITION BEFORE 1830

The antislavery organizations that had appeared in the closing decades of the eighteenth century grew weaker as the movement for colonization of Negroes gained support and the slave system became more fixed in the South. While the period before 1830 was relatively quiet, there was still some opposition to slavery. These early abolitionists tended to be moderate in their approach, hoping to develop a program of gradual and peaceful emancipation. Many abolitionists cooperated with the efforts of the American Colonization Society, hoping to rid the country of its Negro problem.

Most of the antislavery activity conducted at this time was done through the press. In 1817, Charles Osborn began publishing the *Philanthropist,* an antislavery paper, in Ohio. Two years later, Osborn moved to Tennessee, where he published the *Manumission Intelligencer.* Elihu Embree published the *Emancipator* in Jonesboro, Tennessee. Joshua Leavitt, an intensely religious man, graduated from Yale College of law in 1814, returning

---

THE EMANCIPATOR

(Complete)

Published by ELIHU EMBREE

JONESBOROUGH, TENNESSEE

1820

A REPRINT OF

The Emancipator, to which are added a biographical sketch of Elihu Embree, author and publisher of *The Emancipator,* and two hitherto unpublished anti-slavery memorials bearing the signature of Elihu Embree.

B. H. MURPHY, *Publisher*

NASHVILLE, TENNESSEE

1932

---

later to study for the ministry. During the mid-1820's, he began writing articles attacking slavery for the *Christian Spectator,* and during the 1830's, he edited the *Evangelist* in New York. The latter's mild approach to abolition attracted over ten thousand subscribers before its demise during the depression of 1837. When the *Evangelist* was forced to cease publication, Leavitt began editing the *Emancipator,* the organ of the American Anti-Slavery Society.

The most important figure in the abolitionist movement before William Lloyd Garrison was Benjamin Lundy, a Quaker born in New

BENJAMIN LUNDY

Jersey. He helped Osborn publish the *Philanthropist* in Ohio until it failed, at which time Lundy founded the *Genius of Universal Emancipation*. This antislavery journal published its first issue in January 1821 and continued until Lundy's death in 1839. In 1824, Lundy moved to Baltimore and began publishing the *Genius of Universal Emancipation* on a weekly basis.

Lundy's program of emancipation was extremely mild, coupling the desire for emancipation with support for colonization. In 1825, he helped a number of free Negroes settle in Haiti. Though Lundy was conservative in his approach, he did not escape physical assault. In Baltimore, he was attacked by a group of slave traders and nearly killed. The judge set the assailants free, arguing that Lundy deserved such an attack.

In 1827, there were 130 antislavery societies in the United States, containing approximately 6,600 members. Although 106 of these societies were located in the South, they had little influence since their approach was conciliatory and conservative. The North Carolina Manumission Society had forty-five branches in that state. It favored colonization, gradual emancipation, Negro education and the use of women in the movement. The society published a journal called the *Patriot* for awhile, but after 1828, the group declined as an effective force. Slavery was fast becoming a sectional issue.

WILLIAM LLOYD GARRISON

William Lloyd Garrison was born in Newburyport, Massachusetts, in 1805. At the age of thirteen, he was an apprentice on the Newburyport *Herald*. He and Isaac Knapp published the *Free Press* in 1826, but this journal failed to last out the year. Garrison then moved to Boston, where he became involved with the Reverend William Collier, a temperance supporter. Garrison helped Collier publish the *National Philanthropist*.

WILLIAM LLOYD GARRISON

THE GENIUS OF
UNIVERSAL EMANCIPATION.

"We hold these truths to be self-evident: that all men are created equal and endowed by their Creator with certain inalienable rights, that among these are life, liberty, and the pursuit of happiness."—*Dec. Ind. U. S.*

No. 3. Vol. I. Third Series.]   **JUNE, 1830.**   [Whole Number 255. Vol. XI.

REMOVAL.

The office of the *Genius of Universal Emancipation* is removed to *No.* 49, *Sharp Street*—Second door South of Pratt Street. Subscriptions, Communications, &c. will be received both at the office, and at No. 135, Market Street.

☞The editor of this work has again partially fitted up a Printing Office, in order that the publication may be once more entirely under his own controul. It is expected that the arrangements will be completed in a short time, when it shall be seen whether the abominations of the slave system, and the corruption of its guilty abettors, are not to be properly investigated and exposed. But, in order to effect this desirable object, punctuality in paying up for present subscriptions, as well as more activity in procuring new ones, is absolutely necessary, on the part of the patrons and friends of the work. It would be no difficult matter, one would suppose for those who wish for its success, to procure some further patronage, in almost every part of the country.

I acknowledge, with pleasure, that a few of our friends at a distance have generously used their influence in procuring additional subscribers, and forwarding their payments, since the change from a weekly to a monthly publication: and I sincerely hope that others will speedily follow the example. I cannot now leave home for that purpose myself. The terms of publication, &c. may be seen on the last page of the cover. ☞New subscribers will be supplied from the commencement of the present volume.

THE LIBEL SUIT—AGAIN.

Attempts have been made in various places, and at different times, by some of the high professing "republicans" of this nation, to abridge the freedom of the Press, when it has clashed with what they conceived to be their private interests. This Argus-eyed guardian of the "rights of man" has ever been a thorn in the sides of the corrupt and the tyrannical. We have heard much of the arbitrary proceedings against it, by European despots and oligarchs; but in no country on the globe is such a disposition more completely exemplified than here. With all their vain-boasting, and the egotistical proclamation of their love of liberty, many of the people of this Republic are at heart disposed to be as self-adulatory and oppressive as any that exist. And such are ever desirous to impose curbs, restraints, and gags upon those publishers of periodcals, &c. who stand ready to expose their aristocratic machinations. But in few instances, perhaps, if any, has this spirit manifested itself more fully, than in the numerous attempts to intimidate the editors, and *put down the establishment*, of the "Genius of Universal Emancipation." Not con-

Benjamin Lundy visited Boston, hoping to gain support in New England for his abolitionist crusade. At this time, there were few antislavery societies in New England, and his trip failed to attract much attention. It was Lundy, however, who converted Garrison to the cause. Afterwards, Garrison spent a brief period of time in Bennington, Vermont, editing the *Journal of the Times*. The paper's prime function was to aid the presidential campaign of John Quincy Adams.

Garrison soon left Bennington and moved to Baltimore. There he helped Lundy publish the *Genius*. Garrison, at this time, was moving away from the gradualist approach and adopting a position of immediate abolition. He went so far as to attack a slaver, for which he was fined fifty dollars; and he was jailed when he refused to pay the fine. Finally freed, he moved to Boston, where on January 1, 1831, he began publishing the *Liberator*.

The *Liberator* began with a circulation of about 450 subscribers. It was subsidized by such free Negroes as James Forten and by wealthy, aristocratic whites. Garrison's position on the question of slavery was clear and defiant.

> Oppression! I have seen thee face to face,
> And met thy cruel eye and cloudy brow;
> But thy soul-withering glance I fear not now—
> For dread to prouder feelings doth give place,
> Of deep abhorrence! Scorning the disgrace
> Of slavish knees that at thy footstool bow,
> I also kneel—but with far other vow
> Do hail thee and thy herd of hirelings base:—
> I swear, while life-blood warms my throbbing
>   veins,
> Still to oppose and thwart, with heart and hand,
> Thy brutalizing sway—till Afric's chains
> Are burst, and Freedom rules the rescued land.
> Trampling oppression and his iron rod:
> Such is the vow I take—so help me God!

Nat Turner's insurrection and Walker's *Appeal* became linked in the public mind with Garrison's *Liberator*. But while Garrison became well known, the circulation of the *Liberator* remained small.

THE ANTISLAVERY ARGUMENT

The antislavery crusade was part of a broader movement of reform and religious revival that occurred in the 1830's. There was an increasing concern among the public with the need to improve American life: such movements as temperance, women's rights and world peace gained wide support. In the West, Charles G. Finney's "great revival" became linked with the abolitionist movement. The abolition of slavery was seen as a way of serving God.

James G. Birney in his "Letter to the Ministers" and Theodore Weld in "The Bible against Slavery" attacked slavery as violating the Christian doctrine of the brotherhood of man. Slavery was indicted by others as being contrary to American ideals. The system of human bondage was presented as making a mockery of America's professed concern with

JAMES G. BIRNEY

individual rights. More practical critics attacked slavery as being an inefficient system that kept the South in a state of backwardness. The master-slave relationship was said to have debased the spirit and kept southern culture at a low level. The South was accused of becoming an armed camp, constantly fearful of slave insurrection.

The abolitionists began a direct assault on the doctrine of colonization. They pictured colonization as a planter conspiracy to rid the country of its free Negro population and thereby strengthen slavery. In 1832, Garrison published his *Thoughts on African Colonization.* In part I, he tried to prove by citations from official documents of the American Colonization Society that that organization was really organized to perpetuate slavery and that the free Negroes were being removed from the country in order that slavery might be continued. Part II of the book was devoted to the "Sentiments of the People of Color"

AN

INQUIRY

INTO THE

CHARACTER AND TENDENCY

OF THE

AMERICAN COLONIZATION,

AND

AMERICAN ANTI-SLAVERY

SOCIETIES.

BY WILLIAM JAY.

"Give me the liberty to know, to utter, and to argue freely, according to my conscience, above all liberties."—MILTON.

THIRD EDITION.

STEREOTYPED BY CONNER AND COOKE.

NEW YORK:
PUBLISHED BY LEAVITT, LORD & CO.
180 BROADWAY.
BOSTON: CROCKER & BREWSTER,
47 WASHINGTON-STREET.
....
1835.

and demonstrated that the free Negro population was opposed to the Colonization Society. Another successful exposé of the society was William Jay's *Inquiry,* published by the son of John Jay, the first chief justice of the Supreme Court. The result of this activity was that the Colonization Society lost much of its abolitionist support.

Garrison went to England in 1833, hoping to convince the abolitionists there to oppose colonization. The Colonization Society had sent Elliott Cresson there to win support for its cause. Garrison successfully challenged Cresson and obtained the support of the British abolitionists, who repudiated the principles of the Colonization Society. Garrison's trip to England won him fame both there and

WILLIAM JAY

in the United States. When he returned, he was considered the leading figure in the American abolitionist movement.

THE NEW ENGLAND AND THE AMERICAN ANTI-SLAVERY SOCIETIES

In 1831, Garrison organized the New England Anti-Slavery Society. Of its original seventy-two members, about one-fourth were Negro. Garrison's position urging immediate abolition dominated the organization. Moderates from New York and Philadelphia helped to establish the American Anti-Slavery Society. Arthur Tappan, a wealthy New York merchant, was chosen as the society's first president. Other leaders were Theodore Weld, James G. Birney, William Goodell, Joshua Leavitt, Elizur Wright, Samuel May and Beriah Green.

ARTHUR TAPPAN

THE

ANTI-SLAVERY RECORD.

VOL. I.   SEPTEMBER, 1835.   [FIRST EDITION.]   NO. 9.

THE DESPERATION OF A MOTHER.

"Why do you narrate the extraordinary cases of cruelty? These stories will not convert the cruel, and they wound the feelings of masters who are not so."
REPLY. Cruelty is the fruit of the system.

In Marion Co., Missouri, a Negro-Trader was, not long ago, making up a drove for the Red River country. He purchased two little boys of a planter. They were to be taken away the next day. How did the mother of the children feel! To prevent her interference, she was chained in an out-house. In the night she contrived to get loose, took an axe, proceeded to the place where her [yes, her] boys slept, and severed their heads from their bodies! She then put an end to her own existence.

☞ The negro-trader and planter quarreled, and went to law, about the price!

Garrison was able to influence the American Anti-Slavery Society, and most of his positions on abolition eventually were adopted by the group. Its main program was centered on the need to publicize its views. The group distributed pamphlets on the questions of slavery and colonization throughout the country and published four periodicals: *Human Rights,* the *Anti-Slavery Record,* the *Emancipator* and the *Slave's Friend.*

The full records of membership and organization of the American Anti-Slavery Society cannot be reconstructed. In 1835, the society reported that 328 new branches had formed that year; 254 of these reported a combined membership of 27,182. By 1838, there were approximately 1,350 societies claiming a membership of 250,000. In 1837, there were 145 antislavery societies in Massachusetts, 274 in New York and 213 in Ohio.

Garrison, with the support of John Greenleaf Whittier and Wendell Phillips, tended to

HUMAN RIGHTS.

OUR OBJECT IS LIBERTY FOR ALL; GAINED BY MORAL POWER, AND REGULATED BY IMPARTIAL LAWS.

VOL. II. No. 3.]   NEW-YORK, SEPTEMBER, 1836.   [WHOLE NO. 15.

CAPITOL OF THE UNITED STATES. "HAIL COLUMBIA."

FRANKLIN AND ARMFIELD'S SLAVE PRISON.
Licensed under authority of Congress.

Dr. Torrey, in his account of the "American Slave Trade," states on the authority of a member of the House of Representatives, Mr. Adgate, "That during the last session of Congress, (1815-16,) as several members were standing in the street near the New Capitol, a drove of manacled colored people were passing by, and when just opposite, one of them elevating his manacles as high as he could reach, commenced singing the favorite national song, 'Hail Columbia! happy land.'" &c. Page 64.

"Let it be known to the citizens of America, that at the very time when the procession which contained the president of the United States and his cabinet was marching with triumph to the capitol, to celebrate the victory of the French people over their oppressors, another kind of procession was marching another way, and that consisted of colored human beings, handcuffed in pairs, and driven along by what had the appearance of a man on a horse!"

A similar scene was repeated on Saturday last; drove consisting of males and females chained in couples, starting from Roby's tavern on foot, for Alexandria, where, with others, they are to embark on board a slave ship in waiting to convey them to the south.
(Washington (D. C.) Spectator, A. D. 1830.

"Cash for 500 Negroes,

Including both sexes, from 19 to 25 years of age. Persons having servants to dispose of, will find it to their interest to give us a call, as we will give higher prices in cash than any other purchaser who is now or may hereafter come into the market. FRANKLIN & ARMFIELD, Alexandria."

"Alexandria and New Orleans Packets.

Brig Tribune, Samuel C. Bush, master, will sail as above on the first of January; brig Isaac Franklin, Wm. Smith, master, on the 15th of January; brig Uncas, Nath. Boush, master, on the 1st of February. They will continue to leave this port on the 1st and 15th of each month, throughout the shipping season. They are all vessels of the first class, commanded by experienced and accommodating officers, will at all times go up the Mississippi by steam, and every exertion used to promote the interest of shippers and comfort of passengers. Shippers may prevent disappointment by having their bills of lading ready the day previous to sailing, as they will go promptly at the time. Servants that are intended to be shipped, will at any time be received for *safe keeping*, at 25 cents per day. JOHN ARMFIELD, Alexandria."
(National Intelligencer of Feb. 10, 1833.

[Form of a Petition for the Abolition of Slavery in the District of Columbia.]

TO THE CONGRESS OF THE UNITED STATES.

YOUR PETITIONERS, inhabitants of the town of ____ in the county of ____ and state of ____ beg leave to represent to your honorable body, that the people of the United States have vested in Congress, by the 1st Article of the Federal Constitution, "exclusive legislation, in all cases whatsoever," over the District of Columbia.

Your Petitioners do not ask your honorable body to legislate for the abolition of slavery in the several states where it exists, but they do respectfully represent that duty to their country, to mankind, and to God, forbids Congress to exercise their power of "exclusive legislation," to PERPETUATE SLAVERY AND THE SLAVE TRADE in the Capital of the American Republic. The acts of Congress hitherto passed for the government of said District in fact do this.

If these laws are *ever* to be repealed, and slavery and the slave trade in that District are thereby *ever* to cease, it must be by the action of your honorable body. Your Petitioners believe that no time can be more favorable for such action than the present. They therefore most respectfully but earnestly entreat your honorable body to pass without delay such laws, as to your wisdom may seem right and proper for the entire abolition of slavery and the slave trade in the District of Columbia.

And your Petitioners, &c.

HUMAN RIGHTS.

NEW-YORK, SEPTEMBER, 1836.

SELLING INTO PERPETUAL SLAVERY TO PAY JAIL FEES.

In the District of Columbia, as in the slave states, every colored man is *presumed* to be a *slave*. That is, if any person claims him as a slave, that claim is allowed by the courts *without any proof*, unless the colored person can prove himself to be *free!* By an old law of Maryland which is still in force in that part of the District which was ceded by Maryland, a colored man may be arrested by any body who pleases, and, at the discretion of the nearest magistrate, thrown into jail, and months and ten days, unless he is called for by his owner, which, if he is a *freeman* of course he will not be, he may be sold to the highest bidder to pay his JAIL-FEES, &c.!!! Here is the law. Please to read it.

"Every sheriff that now hath, or hereafter shall have, committed into his custody, any runaway servants or slaves, after one month's notice given to the master or owner thereof, of their being in his custody, if living in this province, or two months' notice if living in any of the neighboring provinces, if such master or owner of such servants or slaves do not appear within the time limited as aforesaid, and pay or secure to be paid all such imprisonment fees due to such sheriff from the time of the commitment of such servants or slaves, and also such other charges as have accrued or become due to any person for taking up such runaway servants or slaves, such sheriff is hereby authorized and required (such time limited as aforesaid, being expired) immediately to give public notice to all persons, by setting up notes at the church and court-house doors of the county where such servant or slave is in custody, of the time and place for sale of such servants or slaves, by him to be appointed, not less than 10 days after such time limited as aforesaid being expired, and at such time and place by him appointed as aforesaid, *to proceed to sell and dispose of such servant or slave to the highest bidder*, and out of the money or tobacco which such servant or slave is sold for, *to pay himself* all such IMPRISONMENT FEES as are his just due, for the time he has kept such servant or slave in his custody, and also pay such other charges, fees or reward as has become due to any person for taking up such runaway servant or slave, and after such payments made, if any residue shall remain of the money or tobacco such servant or slave was sold for, such sheriff shall only be accountable to the master or owner of such servant or slave for such residue or remainder as aforesaid, and not otherwise."— *Laws of Maryland*, act of 1719, *(May session,)* chap. 2.

This is the law *now in force* in the city of Washington! So barbarous did this law appear to Maryland herself, that she abolished it in 1817 within her own jurisdiction. Still it remains in force within the "exclusive legislation" of the Federal Congress. By the law of Maryland, if the suspected runaway is not claimed within a limited time, he must be *released*, and the expense of his confinement *paid by the county*. But by the law of Congress, he is to be sold, no matter whether he have been a slave or not, to pay his JAIL FEES!!! [See Stroud's Sketch of the Slave Laws, pages 85, 87.]

That this abominable law is not a dead letter the following evidence will prove. In a memorial of the inhabitants of the District of Columbia, signed by one thousand of the most respectable citizens of the District, and presented to Congress March 24, 1828, then referred to the Committee on the District, and on the motion of Mr. Hubbard, of New Hampshire, February 9, 1835, ordered to be printed, the following statement is introduced:

"A colored man, who stated that he was entitled to freedom, was taken up as a runaway slave, and lodged in the jail of Washington City. He was advertised, but, no one appearing to claim him, he was, according to law, put up at public auction for the payment of his jail fees, and SOLD as a SLAVE for LIFE. He was purchased by a slave-trader, who was not required to give security for his remaining in the District, and he was soon shipped at Alexandria for one of the southern states.' An attempt was made by some benevolent individual to have the sale postponed until his claim to freedom could be investigated; but their efforts were unavailing; and thus was a human being SOLD into PERPETUAL BONDAGE, at the capital of the freest government on earth, without even a pretence of trial, or an allegation of crime."

In 1822, Mr. Miner, of Pennsylvania, declared in Congress, that in 1826-7, no less than *five persons* were thus sold. The following is a specimen of the notices inserted in the papers of the District in regard to such persons:

NOTICE.

"Was committed to the prison of Washington Co., D. C., on the 19th day of May, 1834, as a runaway, a negro man, who calls himself DAVID PECK. He is 5 feet 8 inches high. Had on, when committed, a check shirt, linen pantaloons, and straw hat. He *says he is free*, and belongs to Baltimore. The *owner or owners* are hereby requested to come forward, prove him and take him away, or he will be sold for his prison and other expenses, as the LAW DIRECTS.

JAMES WILLIAMS,
Keeper of the Prison of Washington County,
District of Columbia.
For ALEXANDER HUNTER, M. D. C."

Mr. Miner stated that within five years previous to 1829, 742 colored persons had been committed to the public prison of the city of Washington. Of these 452 were lodged there by slave-traders for safe keeping previous to exportation, the remaining 290 were imprisoned on suspicion of being fugitives, and if not claimed, were sold under the *authority of Congress* to pay their JAIL FEES!

In 1826, Gilbert Horton, a free citizen of New-York, was imprisoned in the District, and would have been sold into perpetual bondage but for the timely interference of his fellow citizens at the north.

All this is before the nation, yet our enlightened representatives resolve that "Congress ought not to interfere IN ANY WAY with slavery in the District of Columbia, because it would be a violation of the *public faith*, &c." So the old law of

THEODORE DWIGHT WELD

dominate the New England societies. The New York and Ohio groups were more moderate. Theodore Dwight Weld, one of the leaders of the more moderate groups, went to the Lane Theological Seminary in Cincinnati. At his urging, the students discussed the question of the abolition of slavery. After the discussion, the students voted overwhelmingly for a resolution stating that the people in the slaveholding states should abolish slavery immediately. The conservative trustees, much displeased, issued a report on the situation, which concluded that "education must be completed before the young are fitted to engage in the collisions of active life." Forty students resigned, many transferring to Oberlin College. This act of opposition to abolitionist activity in the North was not an isolated one but part of a general reaction.

THE REACTION OF THE COUNTRY TO ABOLITION

There were many instances of antagonism to the abolitionists on the part of the general population. One of the most famous cases of intolerance and repression was the closing of the Crandall School. Prudence Crandall, a Quaker teacher, found her school in Canterbury, Connecticut, boycotted when she attempted to admit a Negro girl. Then Lewis Tappan and Garrison helped her open a school for Negro girls. The school was attacked, and she and her girls were subjected to insults and harassment by the townspeople. Bells and cannons were heard when news came that a bill making her school illegal had been passed into law. She was arrested for violating the law, which forbade the teaching of Negro girls from out of the state. Arthur Tappan went to Canterbury and provided the money for publicity and court action. The trials ended inconclusively, but the school was forced to close because of the constant threat of physical destruction.

There were various instances of mob action against the abolitionists. In 1834, there was a riot at the Chatham Street Chapel in New York City, which was serving as host to the American Anti-Slavery Society. Six hundred delegates met in Utica, New York, to form a statewide antislavery organization in 1835.

PRUDENCE CRANDALL

The meeting was attacked by the townspeople but was finally able to conclude its deliberations when Gerrit Smith invited the delegates to his estate at Peterboro.

In 1833, James G. Birney, a wealthy southerner and former slave-owner, moved from Alabama to Kentucky. He had become a convert to the antislavery cause. In Kentucky, he organized the Society for the Gradual Relief of the State from Slavery. Birney was unsuccessful in gaining southern support for the cause of abolition and moved north to Ohio. He published the *Philanthropist,* a moderate antislavery journal, in Cincinnati. On July 30, 1836, a mob destroyed the press, and Birney barely escaped with his life. The publication of the *Philanthropist* was continued by the conservative Dr. Gamaliel Bailey, but its presses were destroyed on two other occasions in 1847. Dr. Bailey then moved to Washington, D.C., where he edited the antislavery journal *National Era.*

ELIJAH P. LOVEJOY

One of the most notorious instances of mob terror was the murder of Elijah P. Lovejoy in Alton, Illinois. Lovejoy's career as an abolitionist began in St. Louis. In the St.

The Alton, Illinois, riot during which abolitionist Elijah P. Lovejoy was murdered while defending his office and press.

Louis *Observer,* he attacked Judge Luke Lawless for his leniency in a case concerning the burning alive of a Negro by whites. He was run out of the city, and his office and press were destroyed by an angry mob. He moved across the Mississippi River to Alton, Illinois. In November 1837, he was killed while defending his press from the attacks of the townspeople.

Abolitionists found it difficult to find places to meet, to print their views and to gain hearings. The mood of Jacksonian democracy was one of hostility to the antislavery crusade. As an illustration, Dr. Reuben Crandall, a botany teacher and the younger brother of Prudence, was arrested in Washington, D.C., simply for having in his possession abolitionist literature. He was charged with intending to circulate incendiary publications.

LEGAL SUPPRESSION

The American Anti-Slavery Society, in June 1835, developed a program aimed at the free distribution of abolitionist material. When packages prepared by the society arrived in Charleston on July 30, 1835, they touched off a riot. A crowd broke into the city's post office, seized the material and destroyed it. The postmaster of Charleston wrote to Washington seeking instructions. Amos Kendall, the Postmaster General and a leading figure in Jackson's administration, empathized with the South's dilemma. He stated that "we owe an obligation to the laws, but we owe a higher one to the communities in which we live."

Jackson recommended to Congress the passing of a law which would "prohibit, under severe penalties, the circulation in the southern states, through the mail, of incendiary publications intended to instigate the slaves to insurrection." The bill passed the Senate when Vice President Martin Van Buren cast the deciding vote. Though the

SARAH MOORE GRIMKÉ

bill never became law, it gave evidence of the support the southern cause had throughout the nation. In 1836, the gag rule was passed, which meant that no petition dealing with slavery could be discussed. It was vigorously opposed by John Quincy Adams and Joshua R. Giddings but remained the law of the land until 1845.

THE ABOLITIONISTS DIVIDE

The abolitionist movement had been an uneasy alliance from the beginning. The various factions of the American Anti-Slavery Society fought for control of the organization. One of the questions that finally split the organization was the position of women. Sarah Moore Grimké and Angelina Grimké were southern sisters who had converted

ANGELINA GRIMKÉ

of abolition. Garrison quickly responded to these attacks. The Board of Managers of the Massachusetts Anti-Slavery Society voted approval of his policies and reproved the authors of the "Clerical Appeal." A state convention was organized, and it endorsed Garrison's position.

In 1839 and 1840, Garrison and the moderates battled for control of the national organization. In 1840, Garrison emerged victorious with his supporters gaining important positions and women being given positions of responsibility. The New York group, under the leadership of Lewis Tappan, opposed Garrison and formed the American and Foreign Anti-Slavery Society, which sought to

to Quakerism. Once they learned of their brother's children by his slave mistress, they became intensely concerned with the abolitionist movement. First, they gave talks in the homes of abolitionists. There was little opposition to their activity until they started speaking in public places. With Garrison's approval, they toured New England in support of abolition. The moderate abolitionists, however, considered such activity by ladies highly improper and bound to "do more harm than good."

A "Pastoral Letter of the General Association of Massachusetts" contrasted the Grimké sisters' activities with "the appropriate duties and influence of women" and attempted to prevent their speaking in the churches. The "Appeal of Clerical Abolitionists on Anti-Slavery Measures" condemned the *Liberator* for actions harmful to the cause

JOSHUA GIDDINGS

combine moral persuasion and political action. It helped to form the Liberty Party in 1840, which nominated James Birney for president. In 1844, he polled nearly 60,000 votes.

Many abolitionists were moving toward political action, but Garrison and the New England group remained influential. In a country that gave legal sanction to slavery, citing a "higher law" was bound to have appeal. Meanwhile, many abolitionists were beginning to support violence. In 1839, James Hammond of New York stated that only force would end slavery, and he suggested that Negro military schools be set up in Canada and Mexico. When the slaves revolted on the ship *Creole*, Senator Joshua Giddings praised them. Congress promptly censured him; he then resigned but was returned to Congress by his Ohio constituency.

CHAPTER FOURTEEN

Negro Participation in the Abolition Movement and Antebellum Social Progress

THE Negroes of the United States were represented by active participants in the abolition movement. They were allied with numerous antislavery organizations and in many instances initiated independent activities for the freedom and the advancement of the Negro population. The opinion that Negroes accomplished nothing of definite value for their own freedom is not corroborated by the facts. On the contrary, there were Negro men and women who devoted their lives as unselfishly and courageously to the cause of freedom as did the white abolitionists. They were just as active as the whites in the movements for the amelioration of slave conditions and for the emancipation of the slaves. They subscribed to newspapers. They wrote for the papers and acted as agents for their distribution. They organized abolition societies, and in their local communities they joined with the popular movements working for freedom. During the 1830's, antislavery organizations started by Negroes adopted resolutions against slavery and African colonization. The Negroes declined to remain passive in the struggle for freedom, and this was evident particularly in the northern states, where they demonstrated an active interest in abolition.

NEGROES IN THE AMERICAN AND THE NEW ENGLAND ANTI-SLAVERY SOCIETIES

The American Anti-Slavery Society was organized to combat slavery and to advance abolition. In accordance with Article III of its constitution, it was agreed that its aim was "to elevate the character and condition of the people of color by encouraging their intellectual, moral and religious improvement, and by removing public prejudice, that thus they may, according to their intellect and worth, share an equality with the whites, of civil and religious privileges but this society will never, in any way, countenance the oppressed in vindicating their rights by resorting to physical force."

JOHN B. VASHON

These sentiments appealed to the Negro population, and they responded by joining and working for the movement. Among the delegates to its first meeting, December 4, 5 and 6, 1833, were the following Negroes: James G. Barbadoes of Massachusetts; James McCrummell, Robert Purvis, James Forten, John B. Vashon and Abraham D. Shadd of Pennsylvania; and Peter Williams of New York. A *Declaration of Sentiments* was issued by this first meeting. It was drawn up at the home of James McCrummell, and was signed by sixty-two persons, among whom were three Negroes—Barbadoes, Purvis and McCrummell. The Board of Managers of this society included Barbadoes, Williams, Purvis, McCrummell, Vashon and Shadd.

The annual reports of the society showed that there were Negro antislavery societies at Lexington, Ohio; Middletown, Connecticut; and at Nantucket, Massachusetts. At Newark, New Jersey, there were an adult and a juvenile society; at Rochester, New York, there were a society for males and a society

for females; at Albany and Geneva, New York, there were societies; and at New York City, there was the New York United Society and the New York Young Men's Society. There were Negro Literary Societies, in urban centers, that were not directly affiliated with the American Anti-Slavery Society but that gave expression to abolition sentiment and supported abolition activities.

The roll of delegates at the Second Anniversary of the American Anti-Slavery Society in New York, on May 12, 1835, included several Negro delegates. From New York City there came Theodore S. Wright, Christopher Rush and Samuel E. Cornish. Wright and Cornish were elected members of the executive committee of nine members, with Arthur Tappan as chairman. James Forten was named one of the vice-presidents. Wright was also elected one of the delegates to the next meeting of the New England Anti-Slavery Society. The Board of Managers included James McCrummell, James Forten, Robert Purvis, John B. Vashon, and Abraham D. Shadd of Pennsylvania; James G. Barbadoes of Massachusetts; Ray Porter of Rhode Island; and Samuel E. Cornish, Theodore S. Wright and Peter Williams of New York.

The American Anti-Slavery Society met in New York City on May 10, 1836, for its third annual meeting. The Negro members present were Wright, Cornish, Purvis, Forten, McCrummell, Vashon and Shadd. Robert Purvis requested that the meeting regard the results of emancipation in the British West Indies as conclusive proof of the safety of the policy of emancipation. Theodore S. Wright offered a resolution to instruct the Auxiliary Societies to appoint a committee "to introduce our colored brethren to use full [useful] arts," especially those who were desirous of becoming regular apprentices. They were instructed also to use every effort for the improvement of Negroes in literature, morals and religion.

The 1840 Convention of the World Anti-Slavery Society in London, which was attended by Charles Lenox Remond and Dr. James McCune Smith.

The Rev. Charles Gardner, pastor of a Presbyterian church, presented the following resolution at the meeting in 1837: "That sufficient evidence has been given to the world, to convince the enlightened public that the immediate emancipation of the colored people is morally right and politically safe." He supported this resolution by evidence concerning the condition of the colored people in the northern and border states. He stated that there were some low-class whites just as there were some low-class Negroes. He declined to admit that William Lloyd Garrison had induced the colored people to oppose the colonization plan. He explained: "When William Lloyd Garrison was a schoolboy, the people of color in different parts of the country were holding extensive meetings, which

always agreed in declaring that they regarded the scheme as visionary in itself and calculated only to rivet the chains of those who remain in slavery." Henry Highland Garnet, a dynamic personality in a later period, also attended this meeting.

At the annual meeting in 1838, Charles Lenox Remond served as one of the three secretaries of the meeting. He was later elected one of the vice-presidents of the New England Anti-Slavery Society and served also as president of the Essex County Anti-Slavery Society. He was a delegate to the World Anti-Slavery Convention held in London in 1840. Dr. James McCune Smith, who was a graduate of the University of Glasgow, delivered an address on British emancipation and helped audit the treasurer's accounts.

EXECUTIVE COMMITTEE OF THE PENNSYLVANIA ANTI-SLAVERY SOCIETY, 1851.

In the front row from left to right are Oliver Johnson, Mrs. Margaret Jones Burleigh, Benjamin C. Bacon, Robert Purvis, Lucretia Mott and James Mott. In the back row are Mary Grew, E. W. Davis, Haworth Wetherald, Abby Kimber, J. Miller McKim and Sarah Pugh.

LOCAL ANTISLAVERY SOCIETIES

Several states had affiliated abolition societies composed entirely of Negroes. Notable among these was the Massachusetts General Colored Association of Boston, which was affiliated with the New England Anti-Slavery Society. The leaders of this organization were James G. Barbadoes, Coffin Pitts, John E. Scarlett, Hosea Easton, Joshua Easton, William C. Nell, Thomas Cole, Thomas Dalton, Frederick Brimley, Walker Lewis and John T. Hilton. The societies composed entirely of Negroes did not grow rapidly, for there was opposition among Negroes to this type of racial exclusiveness in organizations that were agitating for freedom for all men. Gradually, in the 1840's, the Negro members of these societies joined the white members in the established abolition organizations, and they received recognition by appointments to

committees. Such recognition was received by Charles Gardner, who was appointed to a committee of four at the first Annual Meeting of the Pennsylvania State Anti-Slavery Society. It was the committee's responsibility to prepare the annual address to be given to the public.

The New York Vigilance Committee was one of the most active of these Negro organizations. More than an antislavery society, it was formed originally by five persons who resolved to aid the Negro people by protecting and defending fugitive slaves who were being subjected to arrest and kidnaping under the federal Fugitive Slave Law of 1793. The leading member of this committee was David Ruggles, who was the secretary of the committee for a number of years. He was the proprietor of a grocery store in 1828, the editor of the *Genius of Freedom* from 1845 to 1847, the publisher of pamphlets and tracts, and the founder of a water-cure establishment at Northampton, Massachusetts. He was a "conductor" on the Underground Railroad and is said to have aided more than six hundred slaves escape to freedom in the North and Canada.

The other members of the committee were William P. Johnston, Robert Brown, James W. Higgins and George Barker. In 1837, Theodore S. Wright, Samuel E. Cornish and Thomas Van Rensselaer joined the committee, which devoted itself unselfishly and fearlessly to the task of advancing the cause of freedom by giving aid to fugitives and by encouraging slaves to seek their freedom. Frederick Douglass was aided by this committee when he reached New York as a fugitive slave in 1838.

Negroes were associated with the Pennsylvania Anti-Slavery Society in 1833. Several who were substantial members of the Philadelphia and other Pennsylvania communities served on the board of managers of the society. These persons were James McCrummell, Robert Purvis, Abraham Shadd, John B. Vashon and James Forten. James Forten was one of the influential members of this society and a member of its board of managers. Economically independent as a result of a sail-making business, he was in a position to be of great service to his race. Although possessing only a meager education, he wrote pamphlets and letters to newspapers in defense of his people. The "Letters from a Man of Color," which appeared in several newspapers, both white and colored, were attributed to him. He was an opponent of colonization and strongly expressed his opinions on the subject in his writings.

In 1817, Forten joined Russell Parrott in preparing and publishing an *Address of the Free People of Colour in Philadelphia*. He was a contributor to the *Liberator* and sent twenty-five dollars to aid in bringing out the first edition of this paper. Later, he contributed over a thousand dollars to Garrison's

work. Robert Purvis wrote of Forten and the antislavery movements: "The course pursued by Mr. Garrison he ever thought conformable to the true anti-slavery principles; and those principles, founded upon the immutability of eternal truth had thrown around him, and all others who acted with him, the influences of its divinity."

William Whipper of Pennsylvania was vitally interested in the abolition of slavery, but his attention was divided between other reforms of the period and working for abolition. He was active in the organization of the Moral Reform Society in 1835 and later became the editor of the *National Reformer*. He was a wealthy lumber merchant. He and his partner, Stephen Smith, donated the use of their box cars for hauling fugitive slaves from one place to another. Whipper contributed $13,000 to the antislavery cause. He was frequently called upon to draft resolutions and to deliver addresses before meetings of Negroes in Pennsylvania.

Robert Purvis was a member of the convention that formed the American Anti-Slavery Society and an active member of the Pennsylvania Anti-Slavery Society. He was born in Charleston, South Carolina, the son of William Purvis, and was educated in New England at Amherst College. He generously gave of his time, money and talents for the freedom of the slaves. His home, located on a broad lawn with large shade trees, was one of the stops on the Underground Railroad; and his horses and carriages were used in the service of the escaping slaves. His activity soon earned for him the sobriquet of "President" of the Underground Railroad, and he was active in many slave-rescue cases. In 1838, when it was proposed in the Pennsylvania legislature to disfranchise the Negro population, he wrote a work entitled "Appeal of Forty Thousand Citizens Threatened with Disfranchisement," which was sent to the legislature. He continued to fight slavery throughout his life.

The declaration of an antislavery convention held in Philadelphia in 1833.

Purvis was interested in the Vigilance Committee in Pennsylvania, which was organized for the purpose of aiding the escaping slaves. The same work was carried on in New York by a committee similarly named. Without the help of these committees, the underground system would never have operated so successfully. William Still, who was in the stove and fuel business, was for many years the chairman and corresponding secretary of this committee. At the request of the Pennsylvania Abolition Society, his personal experiences were published in *The Underground Railroad*. This book is a valuable source of narratives, letters, and information concerning the secret activities of these heroic workers.

NEGRO SOCIETIES

The Moral Reform Society was an organization of Negroes in Philadelphia that was started in 1835 through the efforts of William Whipper. It was involved both in abolition and in practical measures for uniting the free people of color. Among the objectives mentioned was one "of encouraging and assisting persons of color who are desirous to adopt agricultural pursuits in the United States or by settling in the Province of Canada." The influence of this society on the moral and intellectual development of the colored people in Philadelphia was widespread, and the results were gratifying to its members.

Negro women were also active in organizing societies. The Female Anti-Slavery Society of Salem, Massachusetts, was formed in February, 1832, for mutual improvement and to promote the welfare of the race. Similar societies were organized by Negro women in the eastern and middle western states. Susan Paul of Boston, wife of Nathaniel Paul, was a life member of the Massachusetts Anti-Slavery Society in 1835 and served as counsellor of the Boston Female Anti-Slavery Society of New York.

WILLIAM WHIPPER

Negroes organized beneficial societies in the large cities of the North, particularly in Philadelphia, New York and Boston, for the purpose of rendering mutual aid and assistance in times of sickness and distress. These societies were influential in limiting pauperism and crime and in fostering the mutual sympathy so needed for the well-being of their group. The funds appropriated for relief were raised by monthly contributions and were disbursed after investigation of need. While these societies were not primarily antislavery organizations, they were interested in the freedom and the advancement of the Negro race. Statistics show that in 1838 there were eighty of these societies listed in Philadelphia and that forty-five of them were organized and directed by Negro women.

Antislavery discussions occupied the attention of the members of these societies at many of their meetings. Such Negro organizations as the Garrison Society, the Boston Mutual Lyceum, the African Freehold Society and a host of similar societies in cities and towns

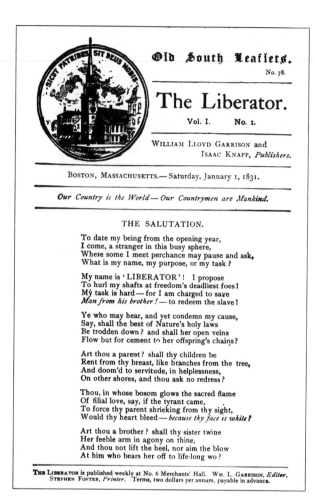

of the northern states showed the desire of free Negroes to participate in the struggle for freedom. It began to dawn upon these champions of liberty, as these societies grew in number, that there was no necessity for independent and "complexional" societies, as they were called; and, beginning with 1833, many of these organizations applied for admission to the New England Anti-Slavery Society and became auxiliaries of it.

NEGROES AND ANTISLAVERY PAPERS

Negroes were contributors and subscribers to the *Liberator* from its first issue, and there were those among them who contributed to the expense of issuing the first number. Garrison placed an appeal in this issue to the "Free Colored Brethren," in which he expressed the opinion that among 300,000 free

Negroes, "some patronage may be given" to the *Liberator*.

Among the outstanding persons who gave aid was James Forten. On December 31, 1830, prior to the publication of the *Liberator*, he sent a letter to Garrison stating that he was happy to learn that the *Liberator* was to be established and that he hoped it would be "the means of exposing more and more the odious system of slavery and of raising up friends to the oppressed and degraded people of colour throughout the union." With this letter, Forten sent fifty-four dollars and the names of twenty-seven subscribers. A significant part of the indebtedness of the *Liberator* was assumed by Forten, who also contributed articles and letters to the paper. In his first published letter, in 1831, he attacked the laws passed by the southern states limiting the freedom of Negroes. Another letter in the same year described his long residence in Philadelphia and stated that he considered himself and his family as thoroughly American and that this country was his home.

James G. Barbadoes of Boston, secretary of the Massachusetts General Association, was another contributor to the *Liberator*. He frequently expressed admiration for Garrison's principles and his opposition to slavery. To protect themselves and their families, Negroes often wrote under such signatures as "A Colored Philadelphian," "A Colored Baltimorean," "A Free Man of Color," "A Gentleman of Color," "A Colored Man of Boston" and under various other pseudonyms. In 1831, James T. Hilton, Robert Wood and J. H. Howe of Boston sent a letter to Garrison thanking him for his efforts in behalf of freedom for the enslaved Negroes and pledging their liberal support of the *Liberator*. With this letter, they sent what Garrison describes as "a very generous and seasonable donation." In the same year, another group of free Negroes from New York City resolved that they would use every effort to procure subscriptions for the *Liberator*.

POEMS BY A SLAVE.

EXPLANATION.

GEORGE, who is the author of the following poetical effusions, is a Slave, the property of Mr. James Horton, of Chatham County, North Carolina. He has been in the habit, some years past, of producing poetical pieces, sometimes on suggested subjects, to such persons as would write them while he dictated. Several compositions of his have already appeared in the Raleigh Register. Some have made their way into the Boston newspapers, and have evoked expressions of approbation and surprise. Many persons have now become much interested in the promotion of his prospects, some of whom are elevated in office and literary attainments. They are solicitous that efforts at length be made to obtain by subscription, a sum sufficient for his emancipation, upon the condition of his going in the vessel which shall first afterwards sail for Liberia. It is his earnest and only wish to become a member of that Colony, to enjoy its privileges, and apply his industry and mental abilities to the promotion of its prospects and his own. It is upon these terms alone, that the efforts of those who befriend his views are intended to have a final effect.

To put to trial the plan here urged in his behalf, the paper now exhibited is published. Several of his productions are contained in the succeeding pages. Many more might have been added, which would have swelled into a larger size. They would doubtless be interesting to many, but it is hoped that the specimens here inserted will be sufficient to accomplish the object of the publication. Expense will thus be avoided, and the money better employed in enlarging the sum applicable for his emancipation.—It is proposed, that in every town or vicinity where contributions are made, they may be put into the hands of some person, who will humanely consent to receive them, and give notice to Mr. Weston R. Gales, in Raleigh, of the amount collected. As soon as it is ascertained that the collections will accomplish the object, it is expected that they will be transmitted without delay, to Mr. Weston R. Gales. But should they ultimately prove insufficient, they will be returned to subscribers.

The introductory page of a collection of poems by George Moses Horton.

Negroes also purchased advertising space in the paper. In one issue, there appeared advertisements of rooming houses for traders and workmen. Pulaski W. Flanders of Boston advertised his school of music in its columns. The advertisement read: "Instruction offered in sacred music on Sunday evenings in the African School House on Belknap Street, Pulaski W. Flanders, teacher."

Support was given to the *Liberator* by Negro agents who aided in its distribution. These agents were especially active in Philadelphia, New York, Boston and Providence. A circular was issued in 1834 by Garrison and Knapp, editor and publisher, respectively, which stated that only one-fourth of the total number of subscribers was white. The circular stated: "The paper then belongs especially to the people of color—it is their organ—and to them its appeal will come with peculiar force."

In May 1833, when the national antislavery paper the *Emancipator* began publication in New York City, with Arthur Tappan as its leading spirit, Negro agents were selected for it. David Ruggles was known as the general agent. Other agents were John D. Classon of Newark, New Jersey; Thomas Van Rensselaer of Princeton, New Jersey; Abraham D. Shadd and John Carlisle of Pennsylvania. Meetings were held by Negroes in New York City and Philadelphia to obtain subscriptions and contributions to the *Liberator* and the *Emancipator*. Without the assistance of Negroes, these papers would have had greatly reduced audiences and income.

NEGRO ABOLITION LITERATURE

There was a large body of literature printed by Negroes about slavery and freedom. There were over two hundred publications by Negroes prior to 1835. The largest number of publications came from the state of Massachusetts, which was the place of publication of forty-two imprints. Pennsylvania and New York each had forty. These writings included narratives, poems, sermons, addresses, almanacs, letters, a large group of petitions, and records of societies.

Several narratives of the life and experiences of Negroes appeared in the decade prior to 1830; but with the rise of abolition, narratives began to appear in larger numbers because of their value to antislavery societies for propaganda purposes. Some of these were written by whites about Negroes, and others were written by Negroes themselves.

George Moses Horton's first volume of poems, *Hope of Liberty,* was published in North Carolina in 1829; the first northern edition was published in 1837 in Philadelphia, under the title *Poems by a Slave.* The *Mirror of Liberty,* a quarterly magazine, advocated the rights of the Negro and opposed the demands of slaveholders. It seems probable that only two numbers of this magazine

PHILIP A. BELL

ever appeared, one in 1838 and the other in 1839. This was the Negro's first attempt at magazine publication. It was made up of antislavery materials and sentiments. Its belief was that Negroes would secure their freedom only by their own efforts.

After the establishment of *Freedom's Journal,* in 1827, a period of ten years passed before another Negro newspaper came into being. In 1837, the *Weekly Advocate,* edited by Samuel E. Cornish, was published. The proprietor, or business manager, was Philip A. Bell. After a two-month period, the name of the paper was changed to the *Colored American.* This paper suspended publication in 1842. Charles B. Ray was at first the general agent and a contributor. In 1839, he became the editor of the paper, when Cornish and Bell withdrew from participation in the publication of the paper. The *Colored American* had difficulties in continuing its publication, and its issues contained repeated appeals for aid and for subscriptions. In addition to

the editorial staff, there were twenty-two agents who assisted in the distribution of the paper. In 1837, there were 1,250 subscribers; a year later, an increase in this number was reported.

The prospectus of the paper called for "producing an organ for Colored Americans devoted to their interests through which they can make known their well-known sentiments. Terms of the paper: The *Colored American* is published weekly by Charles B. Ray at No. 9 Spruce Street, New York, at two dollars per annum in advance, excepting where a local agent will be responsible to collect the balance, when one-half may be received in advance." In the prospectus of Volume III the editor wrote: "This is the only paper in the United States, published and edited by a colored man, and expressly for the colored people. Its objects are, more directly, the moral, social, and political elevation and improvement of the free, colored people; the peaceful emancipation of the enslaved. The Editor, being a colored man, necessarily feels an interest in the welfare of the colored people, wherever found. The paper, therefore, will not be regardless of the welfare of colored people of other countries."

The *National Watchman* appeared in 1842. It was published in Troy, New York, by William G. Allen, in association with Henry Highland Garnet. Allen had graduated from Oneida Institute and later studied law in Boston. After the discontinuance of the *National Watchman* in 1847, he became a teacher at Central College in McGowanville, New York. The *Elevator* made its appearance also in 1842, in Albany, New York. It was published by Stephen Myers and was conducted entirely for the abolition cause. Lack of funds prevented its regular publication, but it served an important purpose in expressing the views of free Negroes in its area. Between 1845 and 1847, two other papers were published by Negroes. The *Ram's Horn,* started with W. A. Hodge as editor and Thomas Van

THE

Anglo-African Magazine.

VOL. I.   JANUARY, 1859.   NO. 1.

Apology.

(INTRODUCTORY.)

The publisher of this Magazine was 'brought up' among Newspapers, Magazines, &c. The training of his boyhood and the employment of his manhood have been in the arts and mysteries which pertain to the neighborhood of Spruce and Nassau streets in the city of New York. Of course the top of the strata, the upper-crust of the laminæ in his geologic region is—the Publisher. . . . To become a Publisher, was the dream of his youth (not altogether a dream, for, while yet a boy he published, for several months, the People's Press, a not unnoticed weekly paper,) and the aim of his manhood. He understands the business thoroughly, and intends, if the requisite editorial matter can be furnished, to make this Magazine 'one of the institutions of the country.'

He would seem to be the right man in the right place; for the class of whom he is the representative in Printing House Square, sorely need an independent voice in the '*fourth estate*.' Frederick Douglass has said

that 'the twelve millions of blacks in the United States and its environs must occupy the notice and the care of the Almighty:' these millions, in order to assert and maintain their rank as men among men, must speak for themselves; no outside tongue, however gifted with eloquence, can tell their story; no outside eye; however penetrating, can see their wants; no outside organization, however benevolently intended, nor however cunningly contrived, can develope the energies and aspirations which make up their mission.

The wealth, the intellect, the Legislation, (State and Federal,) the pulpit, and the science of America, have concentrated on no one point so heartily as in the endeavor to write down the negro as something less than a man: yet at the very moment of the triumph of this effort, there runs through the marrow of those who make it, an unaccountable consciousness, an aching dread, that this *noir faineant*, this great black sluggard, is somehow endowed with forces which are felt rather than seen, and which may in ' some grim revel,'

' Shake the pillars of the commonweal!'

Rensselaer as proprietor, continued for eighteen months. The *Genius of Freedom* was another of the papers edited by David Ruggles. Its period of publication was very brief.

The *Anglo-African Magazine* made its appearance in 1859 under the editorship of Thomas Hamilton in New York City. It was devoted to literature, science, statistics and the advancement of freedom. Its publication was suspended in 1861, but it was later published infrequently for a very short time. Among the contributors to its columns were Bishop Daniel A. Payne, Dr. James McCune Smith, William C. Nell, Frederick Douglass and John M. Langston.

These papers used plain, direct language. The general theme was the reduction of the oppression of the free colored population and the extension to Negroes of the rights of American citizenship. The policy of immediate and unconditional emancipation was openly sponsored by all of these papers. Generalizations about freedom and liberty were indulged in frequently, but specific recommendations were few.

NEGRO CHURCHES

The legislation restricting religious instruction and worship that began in the 1830's continued to be operative in the South until the Civil War. White ministers preached to the slaves, while discreet Negroes, under their direction, were permitted to function in subordinate capacities.

The independent religious organizations among Negroes became channels through which the religious message was spread in the free states. In 1856, there were 210 A.M.E. churches with six bishops, 165 ministers, 19,914 members and church property valued at $425,000. Their churches were first located in 1816 in parts of Pennsylvania, New Jersey, Delaware and Maryland. Within the next two decades, they had spread into New York, Massachusetts and Haiti. By 1856, the churches were also established in Illinois, Indiana, Missouri, Louisiana, Kentucky and lower Canada.

The African Methodist Episcopal Zion Church experienced a similar expansion. In 1855 in New England, it had seventeen ministers, 504 members and six Sunday Schools with 285 students. In its Allegheny conference, by 1854, this church had twelve ministers and 407 members; its general conference in New York state had a total of ten ministers and 217 members.

The general conference of the African Methodist Episcopal Zion Church in 1854 demonstrated its support of the antislavery cause by the adoption of a set of antislavery resolutions. One of these stated that it was "the duty of the ministers of this General Conference to take a Gospel stand against the sin of slavery, as against all other sins, in teaching, preaching, praying and voting." The conference pledged its members to labor ever in the cause of the enslaved, whether white or black, stating that their motto was and ever should be, "Liberty and Freedom forever."

NEGROES IN THE ARTS

Autobiographical accounts by slaves were extremely popular in the nineteenth century. Among the better known of these are narratives by Moses Roper (1837), Lunsford Lane (1842), William Wells Brown (1848), Henry Bibb (1849), James W. C. Pennington (1849), Samuel Ringgold Ward (1855) and, of course, Frederick Douglass, whose *Narrative of the Life of Frederick Douglass, an American Slave* (Boston, 1845) remains a classic. Early nineteenth-century writers who fought the institution of slavery and who concerned themselves with other social problems included—in addition to Douglass—James Forten, David Walker, David Ruggles, James McCune Smith, Henry Highland Garnet, William C. Nell and Martin R. Delany.

The great American Negro actor of this period—and one of the leading Shakespearean actors of his day—Ira Aldridge, spent his adult life in Europe. Aldridge, who was born about 1807 and grew up in the United States, was sent to the University of Glasgow to complete his education. Eventually, his love for the theatre led him to London, where he soon achieved renown as an actor. His Othello, to which Edmund Kean often played Iago, was particularly famous. Aldridge toured Europe many times and received numerous awards and honors. He died in Poland in 1867. Today, a chair is dedicated to him at the Shakespeare Memorial Theatre in Stratford-on-Avon, England.

The early nineteenth century was also a period during which a rich folk music flourished among Negroes. It included spirituals,

Ira Aldridge in his famous role as Othello.

Negro authors did not turn to the writing of fiction until shortly before the Civil War. The first Negro novel was William Wells Brown's *Clotel: Or the President's Daughter* (London, 1853), which recounts the adventures, and ultimate tragedy, of a beautiful slave who is supposedly the illegitimate daughter of Thomas Jefferson. Other early novels were *The Garies and Their Friends* (London, 1857), by Frank Webb; and *Blake: Or the Huts of America* (which appeared in the *Anglo-African Magazine* [New York] in 1859), by Martin R. Delany.

In 1821, a Negro theatrical group, the African Company, was established in a theatre on Bleecker Street in New York. This venture, which lasted until 1832, was devoted to the performance of Shakespeare's works and other classics. After this theatre closed its doors, Negro actors had virtually no opportunities, until late in the century, to appear on a stage in this country.

ELIZABETH TAYLOR GREENFIELD

children's songs, work songs, ballads, sea chanteys (one of which is the still-popular "Shanadore" or "Shenandoah") and street cries. Negro classical musicians began to attract notice during the 1840's—particularly in such cities as New York, Boston, Philadelphia and New Orleans. This last city was the home of Eugene V. MacCarty, a fine baritone, trained in Paris, who also composed light music. In about 1850, Richard Lambert, father of the talented Lambert family of musicians, taught in New Orleans.

Perhaps the most famous of these musicians was the singer Elizabeth Taylor Greenfield, who began her concert career in the early 1850's. After a highly successful year in London, during which time she once sang at Buckingham Palace for Queen Victoria, she settled in Philadelphia, where she taught. One of her pupils there was the talented young Negro tenor Thomas J. Bowers. Bowers' voice earned him the title of the "American Mario," after Mario, the great Italian tenor of this period.

Portraiture was popular in America in the late eighteenth and early nineteenth centuries, and the first paintings by Negroes were portraits. Early artists were Julien Hudson, of New Orleans (in the early nineteenth century), Joshua Johnson, of Baltimore (active between 1789 and 1825) and Patrick Reason, of New York (active in the 1830's).

The first major Negro painter was Robert Duncanson (1817–1872), a painter of Romantic landscapes. Eugene Warbourg (1825–1861), the first of the Negro sculptors, worked in Europe. These were the pioneers. The years following the Civil War would see Negroes taking increasingly important roles in the arts.

CHAPTER FIFTEEN

Early Negro Crusaders

FREDERICK DOUGLASS

THE plans of the American Anti-Slavery Society from the time of the first convention meetings were to employ agents and lecturers who would distribute literature and spread propaganda against slavery. From the ranks of the Negro people there arose outstanding contributors to the antislavery movement. Among the first crusaders were James Forten, William Whipper, Robert Purvis and William Wells Brown.

One of the first Negroes to join the abolitionists after they became organized was Charles L. Remond. Prior to the public appearance of Frederick Douglass, Remond was the most prominent of the Negro representatives. He was born free and was interested not only in the abolition of slavery but also in the termination of color prejudice. A frequent contributor to the liberal newspapers and magazines, he was president of the Essex County Anti-Slavery Society and has been noted as one of the vice-presidents of the New England Anti-Slavery Society. In 1838, he was chosen as a lecturer by the American Anti-Slavery Society, and in 1840 he went to London, England, as a delegate to the World Anti-Slavery Convention.

FREDERICK DOUGLASS

One of the outstanding leaders of the abolitionist movement was the former slave Frederick Douglass. He was born on the Eastern Shore of Maryland around 1817 and was looked after by his grandmother since his mother worked on another plantation. He never knew his father; and his mother died when he was young. His master, Captain Aaron Anthony, sent Douglass to Baltimore when he was ten years old. There he served Hugh Auld as a household servant and as a laborer in Auld's shipyard.

When Douglass saw Mrs. Auld teaching her children to read and write, he asked for and received the same privilege. As soon as Mr. Auld learned of the lessons, however, he forbade them, saying that "learning would spoil any nigger." Douglass once described his reflections on Auld's attitude: " 'Very well,' thought I, 'Knowledge unfits a child to be a slave' . . . and from that moment I understood the direct pathway from slavery to freedom." In spite of the beatings he received, Douglass continued his education, first with Mrs. Auld's help and then on his own.

Douglass was troubled constantly by his status as a slave. "Why," he would ask, "am I a slave? Why are some people slaves, and others masters?" As Mr. Auld had feared, Douglass soon was able to read the abolitionist propaganda. From reading the *Baltimore American* he learned of the petitions being submitted in support of the abolition of the internal slave trade and took heart: "There was hope in those words."

Captain Anthony, who had lent Douglass to Auld, died when Douglass was sixteen years old. Having become his legitimate master, Thomas Auld then sent Douglass to Edward Covey, a professional Negro-breaker. Douglass was overworked, beaten and nearly starved to death. He took this treatment for six months and then attacked and beat the Negro-breaker. After the beating, Covey left Douglass alone. The incident was another turning point in Douglass' life: "I was a changed being after that fight. I was nothing before, I was a man now . . . with a renewed determination to be a free man. . . . I had reached the point at which I was not afraid to die. This spirit made me a freeman in fact, though I still remained a slave in form."

Douglass worked for two years on a plantation in Maryland. An attempted escape was thwarted, and Douglass was shipped back to Baltimore. In that city, he met Anna Murray, a free Negro, and desired to marry her—not as a slave but as a free man. On

NARRATIVE OF THE LIFE

OF

FREDERICK DOUGLASS,

AN

AMERICAN SLAVE.

WRITTEN BY HIMSELF.

What, ho!—our countrymen in chains!
The whip on *woman's* shrinking flesh!
Our soil still reddening with the stains,
Caught from her scourging, warm and fresh!
What! mothers from their children riven!
What! God's own image bought and sold!
Americans to market driven,
And barter'd, as the brute, for gold!—*Whittier*.

SECOND DUBLIN EDITION.

DUBLIN:
WEBB AND CHAPMAN, GT. BRUNSWICK-STREET.
1846.

September 2, 1838, he escaped. Posing as a free Negro, he fled first to Philadelphia and then to New York City, where he met David Ruggles, who took care of him until Anna could join him. They were married on September 15, 1838, and moved to New Bedford, Massachusetts.

In New Bedford, Douglass began to subscribe to the *Liberator* and to attend abolitionist meeting. At one of these meetings, Garrison was much impressed by Douglass' speaking ability. His speech at an antislavery convention meeting in Nantucket was extremely powerful; the crowd listened intently as he related his experiences as a slave. John A. Collins, an agent for the Massachusetts Anti-Slavery Society, induced Douglass to become a lecturer for the group.

In 1843, he participated in the one hundred antislavery conventions that took place from New Hampshire to Indiana. Douglass attended the National Convention of Colored Men, coming into contact with William Wells Brown and Henry Highland Garnet. The reception Douglass received was not always friendly. William A. White described one incident he witnessed in 1843. The leader of a mob overtook Douglass, knocked him down and began to beat him. Convinced that the assailant was intent on murder and clearly besting Douglass, White rushed to his defense. Others also assisted Douglass, who, though severely injured, did manage to lecture the next day.

Douglass was such an excellent speaker that many doubted that he had been a slave. During 1844 and 1845, he wrote his *Narrative of the Life of Frederick Douglass.* Once he had published the book, he left for England to avoid recapture resulting from the information in his autobiography. Douglass stayed in England for two years, after which time some of his English friends purchased his freedom so he could return to the United States.

By the time Douglass returned, he had acquired an international reputation. In addressing the Anti-Slavery Convention in Boston, he explained why he had returned to the United States, stating that he had put aside the life of ease and comfort that his friends in England offered, in order to share the suffering of his American brethren. He declared that slavery and prejudice too much disturbed him to live in peace on the other side of the Atlantic.

Douglass was concerned with the failure of the free Negro population to maintain its own newspaper. Several papers had appeared, but each had had only a brief existence. He believed that a newspaper that appeared regularly would serve to counteract the racists who justified the enslavement of his people. It would be "a powerful evidence that the Negro was too much a man to be held a chattel." Garrison and Phillips opposed Douglass on this issue because they believed that putting out a newspaper would take up too much of Douglass' time, which could be more advantageously spent on the lecture circuit. By September 1847, however, Douglass decided that it was more important to have a weekly paper and began to make definite plans for publishing one.

The *North Star* made its appearance on December 3, 1847. Douglass was the editor of the paper, assisted by Martin R. Delany. Though the paper later changed its name to *Frederick Douglass' Paper* and then to *Douglass' Monthly,* it lasted for sixteen years. During this period, it was one of the outstanding abolitionist papers, always remaining true to the objectives stated in its Prospectus: "To attack slavery in all of its forms and aspects; advance Universal Emancipation; exact the standard of public morality; promote the moral and intellectual improvement of the colored people; and to hasten the day of freedom to our three million enslaved fellow-countrymen."

Douglass found maintaining the paper to be extremely difficult. Since most of the Boston abolitionists refused to support the paper financially, Douglass soon found himself in debt. He continued the paper, however, despite the lack of full support from the friends of abolition. A few supporters in the United States and England lent financial assistance, and Douglass, when funds were low, would go on lecture tours, using the fees paid him to further subsidize the paper. Gerrit Smith contributed to the maintenance of the paper; and Julia W. Griffiths of the Rochester Ladies Anti-Slavery Society sponsored fairs and other money-raising events.

Douglass was also a stationmaster for the Underground Railroad in Rochester. He used some of the money that he raised on his speaking tours to help the fugitive slaves. While he was extremely concerned and helpful, he realized that the real guiding spirit of the operation was Harriet Tubman. "Most that I have done has been in public, and I have received much encouragement. . . . You [Harriet Tubman] on the other hand have labored in a private way. . . . I have had the applause of the crowd . . . while the most that you have done has been witnessed by a few trembling, scared and footsore bondmen. . . . The midnight sky and the silent stars have been the witnesses of your devotion to freedom and of your heroism."

DOUGLASS AND GARRISON DISAGREE

As Douglass became more involved in the movement for emancipation, he began to question some of Garrison's positions. Garrison favored the use of moral suasion and opposed the use of violence or political action to obtain his objectives. He believed that the Constitution was an important bulwark of the slave system and that it would be necessary to write a new one if slavery was to be defeated. Douglass tended to support this approach and was opposed to militant abolitionism. It will be remembered that Douglass had succeeded in defeating Garnet at the Buffalo convention in 1843—the convention that adopted a resolution in favor of moral suasion.

In 1847, Douglass met John Brown and began to move away from his previous position. Brown was not only opposed to slavery but also thought that the "slaveholders had forfeited their right to live, [and] that the slaves had the right to gain their liberty in any way they could." Although impressed with Brown, Douglass still believed at that time that the slaveholders could be persuaded to see the error of their ways. But Douglass

JOHN BROWN

was soon to change. In 1849, he declared: "I should welcome the intelligence tomorrow . . . that the slaves had risen in the South, and that the sable arms which had been engaged in beautifying and adorning the South, were engaged in spreading death and devastation." Three years later, he stated that, "The only way to make the Fugitive Slave Law a dead letter is to make a half-a-dozen or more dead kidnappers."

Meanwhile, however, Douglass also began to adopt Gerrit Smith's position on the efficacy of political action and the usefulness of the Constitution. In May 1851, he opposed a resolution submitted to the American Anti-Slavery Society that would have withdrawn support from any paper that did not view the Constitution as a proslavery document. Garrison attacked Douglass' position, stating that, "There is roguery somewhere." Douglass was upset at Garrison's remarks, and their close friendship ended at that moment.

OTHER NEGRO ABOLITIONISTS

Another of the active Negro abolitionists was Charles B. Ray. He was born on December 25, 1807, at Falmouth, Massachusetts. He studied at Wesleyan University, where he was held in high esteem. In 1832, he went to New York City and operated a shoe store. During the next year, he became associated with the abolition movement, co-operating with Henry Ward Beecher, Gerrit Smith, Lewis Tappan and other antislavery leaders in New York City. He was secretary of the New York Vigilance Committee, and his home was one of the stations on the Underground Railroad.

In April 1837, he became general agent for the *Colored American,* a weekly newspaper, and in this capacity he traveled extensively and spoke on behalf of the paper. He attended the annual meeting of the New York Anti-Slavery Society in September 1838 and secured forty dollars for his paper. In 1838, he became one of the proprietors of the paper, and he became its editor in 1839.

He continued as editor until 1842. Throughout this period, he was an active abolitionist. As he himself said, "It was my good fortune in the providence of God to become early identified with the Abolition Movement and associated as one of them."

Lewis Hayden was another of these abolitionists. He was born a slave in Kentucky in 1815 but escaped and made his way to Boston, where he was soon recognized as a leader by the Negroes of the city. He was an active worker and organizer of endeavors for the liberty of the slaves. His home was not only a haven for them but a place of meeting for the Negro antislavery leaders.

Hosea Easton published, in 1837, a *Treatise on the Intellectual Character and Civil and Political Condition of the Colored People of the United States, and the Prejudice Exercised towards Them.* Although he tended to deny that color was at the root

CHARLES B. RAY

of the anti-Negro programs and the maintenance of the slave system, he admitted that moral and spiritual education could not combat prejudice and discrimination sanctioned by laws, churches, schools and patriotic institutions. He then asked, "What could accord better with the objects of this Nation in reference to the blacks, than to teach their [white] little ones, that a Negro is part monkey?"

The South furnished another outstanding abolitionist in Lunsford Lane. He was born a slave in Raleigh, North Carolina, of African slave parents. He learned to read and write at an early age. He worked in the tobacco industry, and through his knowledge of the product he was able to manufacture a superior kind of smoking tobacco. He saved the money paid to him by his master, and at the end of eight years purchased his freedom for $1,000. To make this purchase legal, the procedure had to be carried on in New York rather than in North Carolina, where

LUNSFORD LANE

manumission was recognized only for meritorious service. Lane purchased his wife and children for $2,500. He was arrested shortly afterwards in Raleigh and charged with "delivering abolition lectures in Massachusetts." He was arraigned before the mayor's council and in his defense made what is regarded as one of the few abolition speeches delivered by a Negro in the South. His case was dismissed. After being attacked by a mob, he left Raleigh and went to Philadelphia and then to New York. He attended the antislavery meetings there and was engaged as a lecturer, traveling through New England. Bassett, in his *Anti-Slavery Leaders of North Carolina,* lists Lunsford Lane as one of the four prominent abolitionists of his state. Other Negro leaders gained greater prominence after 1840.

Negro women also worked for abolition. Sarah Douglass was one of the life members of the New England Anti-Slavery Society and was a member of the Central Committee of the Anti-Slavery Women of the United States. She was a lecturer in the New England states. Sarah Forten was a lecturer and an agent

for the abolition societies, writing as well as speaking for the cause. One of Miss Forten's poems was published in a pamphlet issued by the New England Anti-Slavery Society. The closing lines addressed to American women were:

Our skins may differ but from thee we claim
A sister's privilege and a sister's name.

Miss Forten was a member of the Board of Managers of the Pennsylvania Anti-Slavery Society. Margaretta Forten was the treasurer of the Philadelphia society, and Grace Douglass was a member of the board of managers.

Frances Ellen Watkins Harper was engaged as a lecturer and was a faithful advocate of the abolition cause. Sarah Parker Remond, a physician and a sister of Charles L. Remond, was an active antislavery agent and lecturer. She accompanied her brother on his lecture tours and later became a public lecturer herself. She lectured abroad in Scotland, Ireland and England for the antislavery cause. Susan Paul was an active worker in the New England Anti-Slavery

FRANCES ELLEN WATKINS HARPER

SOJOURNER TRUTH

Society. These women were censured and ridiculed for their public appearances, for it was believed that a woman's place was in the home, but they persisted in their efforts against slavery.

Another outstanding Negro woman was Sojourner Truth, who was born in Ulster County, New York, probably between the years 1797 and 1800. For a number of years, she spoke only Dutch, until she was sold to an English colonist. As the years passed, she was sold several times, experiencing the hardships of whippings and punishments as she passed from master to master. Her interest in religion helped her keep up her courage. She fled from slavery and later married. When one of her sons was abducted and sold as a slave, her spirit was fired against slavery, and she began to preach wherever she could find hearers.

She attended an antislavery convention in Washington County, New York, in 1851 and delivered an address. She was forceful, plain in her expressions, and used the speech of an illiterate person; but she was able to draw audiences to her lectures and to hold them in rapt attention.

A vigorous writer was William C. Nell, who contributed to the *Liberator* and later to *Frederick Douglass' Paper* and the *Anglo-African*. He was one of the first Negro writers to attempt a historical account of the Negro in the United States. In 1851, Nell published a pamphlet entitled *Services of Colored Americans in the Wars of 1776 and 1812.* In 1855, he published *The Colored Patriots of the American Revolution, with Sketches of Several Distinguished Colored Persons: To Which Is Added a Brief Survey of the Condition and Prospects of Colored Americans.* This account covers not only the colored patriots of the Revolution and the War of 1812 but also a survey of aspects of Negro life in the United States during the nation's history prior to 1850.

James McCune Smith was a practicing physician in New York City, who managed to complete, nevertheless, considerable historical writing. Among his works was a study of the leader of the Haitian revolution, *Toussaint L'Ouverture,* published in 1841.

JAMES McCUNE SMITH

MARTIN R. DELANY

Martin R. Delany, who grew to manhood in Pittsburgh and attended the Harvard Medical School, also became a physician and writer and was editor of a weekly newspaper, *The Mystery.* In 1852, he wrote *The Condition, Elevation, Emigration, and Destiny of the Colored People of the United States, Politically Considered.* He was associated with the editorship of the *North Star* in 1847. Later, he migrated to Canada, then went to Africa, where he participated in the Niger Valley exploration. He returned and enlisted in the army during the Civil War, attaining the rank of major. He was assigned to the 104th U.S. Colored Troops and was sub-assistant commissioner on the staff of the Freedmen's Bureau.

Born a slave in Maryland, Henry Highland Garnet was educated at a private academy in New Hampshire and the Oneida Institute in New York. He began the publication of the *Clarion,* a paper in Troy, New York. He was one of the radical Negro leaders, surpassing Douglass in his desire for overt action by Negroes against slavery. His address be-

fore the convention of 1843, during which he clashed with Douglass, was published in 1848. His other address, *The Past and the Present Condition and the Destiny of the Colored Race,* was published in the same year. He was pastor of Shiloh Presbyterian Church in New York and the Fifteenth Street Presbyterian Church in Washington, D.C.

William Wells Brown had a varied life as an author. He was the first Negro to publish a novel, a drama, a history and a travelogue. He was born in Lexington, Kentucky, in 1816, but grew up in Missouri, where he labored on plantations, worked as an office boy and served on a Mississippi steamer. Later, he was an assistant in the newspaper office of Elijah P. Lovejoy in St. Louis. He escaped from slavery in 1834 and worked at various jobs in Cleveland and Buffalo and as a boat steward on Lake Erie. This activity made it possible for him to aid fugitive slaves escape to Canada.

WILLIAM WELLS BROWN

From 1849 to the beginning of the Civil War, Brown made frequent contributions to antislavery journals, with such articles as "A Lecture Delivered Before the Female Anti-Slavery Society of Salem," published in 1847, and "St. Domingo: Its Revolution and Its Patriots," published in 1855.

In 1847, *The Narrative of William W. Brown* appeared in its first edition through the Massachusetts Anti-Slavery Society. Approximately eight thousand copies of this book were sold in less than eight months. Other editions were issued at subsequent periods. The *Anti-Slavery Harp,* edited by Brown, was published in 1848. This was a collection of abolition poems and songs.

Contemporary with Douglass and Brown was Samuel Ringgold Ward, whose literary fame rests mainly upon a single work. Ward entered the field of journalism in 1848 with a paper, the *Impartial Citizen,* which had only a brief existence. His major contribution was *The Autobiography of a Fugitive Negro: His Anti-Slavery Labor in the United States, Canada and England,* written in London and published in 1855. The book contained a sketch of his life and a discussion of slavery. Ward also served as a teacher, a Congregational minister, an active agent of abolition and a lecturer.

NEGRO MILITANCY

The position of the free Negro in the North was never secure. His rights were never firmly established, and there was good reason for him to remain quiet. The free Negroes were a small minority, living in a generally hostile environment. It is in this context that their refusal to remain silent in the face of the continued enslavement of their brothers in the South and the discrimination in the North must be evaluated. Their willingness to expose themselves to great harm is impressive.

During the 1830's, most of those Negroes who were active in the abolitionist movement

NARRATIVE

OF

WILLIAM W. BROWN,

AN AMERICAN SLAVE.

WRITTEN BY HIMSELF.

———— Is there not some chosen curse,
Some hidden thunder in the stores of heaven,
Red with uncommon wrath, to blast the man
Who gains his fortune from the blood of souls?
Cowper.

ELEVENTH THOUSAND.

LONDON:
CHARLES GILPIN, BISHOPGATE-ST. WITHOUT.
1849.

tended to support the abolitionists' pacifist program. It was only after this peaceful approach failed that some of the free Negroes turned to greater militancy. Many free Negroes supported the Liberty Party, hoping that political action would prove to be a more effective weapon than mere moral suasion. As the actions of the federal government grew more hostile to the abolitionists, the hostility of the free Negro to the federal government increased. Many Negroes began to favor a program of direct action in support of their demands for an end to discrimination in the North and slavery in the South. This was related to the growing self-awareness of the Negro community, which had been fostered in part by the convention movement.

David Walker's *Appeal* was distributed throughout the country in 1829. Along with Garrison's *Liberator,* it became directly associated with Turner's unsuccessful insurrection. When Garrison came under attack, James Forten of Philadelphia wrote to him and praised his courage. Forten believed that Turner's rebellion would help the abolitionist movement in the North by "bringing the evils of slavery more prominently before the public." "Indeed," he declared, "we live in stirring times, and every day brings news of some fresh effort for liberty, either at home or abroad—onward, onward, is indeed the watchword."

In 1837, Phillip A. Bell declared that "It matters not what our friends may do; they make OUR CAUSE their perpetual theme . . . Yet all will be of no avail, so far as we, ourselves, are personally interested without our thinking and acting, as a body, for ourselves." Other Negroes expressed similar ideas. In 1840, the free Negro leaders in New York stated their position: "If we act with our white friends . . . the words we utter will be considered theirs, or their echo. That will be the general impression, the voice of the majority only will be heard, theirs only be considered."

In 1837, an essay by William Whipper in the *Colored American* urged the use of nonviolence as the most effective means of achieving emancipation. Editor Cornish, however, made his sentiments clear when he wrote, "But we honestly confess that we have yet to learn what virtue there would be in using moral weapons, in defense against kidnappers or a midnight incendiary with a torch in his hand." David Ruggles once declared, "Know you not who would be free, Themselves must strike the first blow."

The predominant mood of the most active free Negroes tended to be more conservative than these statements would indicate. The meeting of the National Convention of Colored Citizens in Buffalo in August 1843 can serve to illustrate the mood of moderation which prevailed. The first speaker declared that "We love our country, we love our fellow-citizens—but *we love our liberty* more." When Henry Highland Garnet attempted to be more specific on the right to use violence, however, his speech to the convention was suppressed.

Garnet began life as a slave in Maryland, but escaped with his parents to New York, where he attended school and came under the influence of the Rev. Theodore S. Wright. Garnet later studied at the Oneida Institute in Whitesboro, New York. In 1840, he began teaching in Troy and later was appointed the pastor of the Negro Presbyterian Church in that city.

Garnet's speech to the Buffalo audience was one of the most militant abolitionist statements ever delivered: "Brethren, arise, arise! Strike for your lives and liberties! Now is the day and the hour! Let every slave throughout the land do this, and the days of slavery are numbered. You cannot be more

HENRY HIGHLAND GARNET

oppressed than you have been; you cannot suffer greater cruelties than you have already. Rather die freemen than live as slaves." Garnet declared that "there is not much hope of Redemption without the shedding of blood." The convention then voted nineteen to eighteen to suppress his speech. (Frederick Douglass was one of those who called for suppression.) The speech was finally published a few years later.

There were other instances of growing militancy among the ranks of Negro abolitionists. Maine and New Hampshire Negroes, meeting in Portland, Maine, in 1849, debated the question of whether the free Negro was obligated to come to the aid of the slaves if they rebelled. At a state Convention of Colored Citizens of Ohio in 1849, it was decided to publish a pamphlet consisting of Walker's *Appeal* and Garnet's *Address*. With the Compromise of 1850, and its new Fugitive Slave Act, Negro militancy increased.

The same day that the Fugitive Slave Act became effective, a Miss Brown of Baltimore successfully sued to recover James Hamlet of New York City, who she claimed was a runaway slave. Hamlet was sent to Baltimore before news of his arrest could be circulated. When the free Negroes of New York City learned what had happened, 1,500 met and raised the money necessary to ransom Hamlet. Other Negroes began urging less peaceful methods of overcoming the hated Fugitive Slave Act.

In further response to the Fugitive Slave Act, a convention of runaway slaves met at Cazenovia, New York, on August 21, 1850. The convention urged slaves to continue to run away and exhorted them to arm themselves and to use their weapons boldly against their pursuers. The group declared that if revolution had been just in 1776, it was that much more proper for the slaves to rebel. This statement was qualified, however, by the convention's insistence that it did not encourage violence.

SEC. 6. *And be it further enacted,* That when a person held to service or labor in any State or Territory of the United States, has heretofore or shall hereafter escape into another State or Territory of the United States, the person or persons to whom such service or labor may be due, or his, her, or their agent or attorney, duly authorized by power of attorney, in writing, acknowledged and certified under the seal of some legal officer or court of the State or Territory in which the same may be executed, may pursue and reclaim such fugitive persons, . . . In no trial or hearing under this act shall the testimony of such alleged fugitive be admitted in evidence . . ..

SEC. 7. *And be it further enacted,* That any person who shall knowingly and willingly obstruct, hinder, or prevent such claimant, his agent or attorney, or any person or persons lawfully assisting him, her, or them, from arresting such a fugitive from service or labor, either with or without process as aforesaid, or shall rescue, or attempt to rescue, such fugitive from service or labor, from the custody of such claimant, his or her agent or attorney, or other person or persons lawfully assisting as aforesaid, when so arrested, pursuant to the authority herein given and declared; or shall aid, abet, or assist such person so owing service or labor as aforesaid, directly or indirectly, to escape from such claimant, his agent or attorney, or other person or persons legally authorized as aforesaid; or shall harbor or conceal such fugitive, so as to prevent the discovery and arrest of such person, after notice or knowledge of the fact that such person was a fugitive from service or labor as aforesaid, shall, for either of said offences, be subject to a fine not exceeding one thousand dollars, and imprisonment not exceeding six months, . . . and conviction before the District Court of the United States for the district in which such offence may have been committed, . . . and shall moreover forfeit and pay, by way of civil damages to the party injured by such illegal conduct, the sum of one thousand dollars, for each fugitive so lost as aforesaid, to be recovered by action of debt, in any of the District or Territorial Courts [where] the said offense may have been committed.

Sections of the Fugitive Slave Law of 1850.

SAMUEL R. WARD

In Cleveland, Ohio, Negroes stated that "slaves owe no service nor obedience to their masters." They also declared their intention to protect fleeing slaves "from recapture, whether the kidnapper comes to us as an officer of the government, or otherwise." Negroes in Chicago stated their intention to work together and to use violence if necessary. The New York leadership quoted an epigram of Thomas Jefferson: "Resistance to tyranny is obedience to God."

A state convention of Negroes in Ohio declared that if, as a result of the Fugitive Slave Act, they had no protection, then neither did they owe allegiance to the United States Government. A state convention of free Negroes meeting in New York also demonstrated their opposition to this law, claiming it violated the Declaration of Independence as well as the Constitution. The New York Convention of the African Methodist Episcopal Zion Church, in May 1851, passed a resolution condemning the law.

Negroes who had emigrated to Canada joined those in the United States in attacking the law. Henry Bibb and Samuel R. Ward established emigré newspapers in Canada. Bibb's paper, the *Voice of the Fugitive,* urged Negroes to flee to Canada. He also maintained that fugitive slaves had the right to kill in self-defense. His views were adopted by the North American Convention, which met in 1851 in Toronto at his urging. Two years later, in 1853, a convention in Amherstburg declared that Negroes owed no loyalty to the United States and should emigrate to Canada.

Vigilance committees to block arrests and to rescue fugitive slaves were organized throughout the North. In the *Boston Commonwealth* of March 1851, it was reported that in New Bedford, "Between six and seven hundred colored citizens many of whom are fugitives are here and are determined to stand by one another and live or die together."

Countless individual Negroes had been working to abolish slavery and to improve the conditions under which their people lived since the mid-seventeenth century. Now American blacks were organizing and becoming increasingly militant in their demands for better lives for themselves and freedom for their enslaved brothers.

CHAPTER SIXTEEN

Plantation Life and Southern Labor

THE free Negro population in 1850 was approximately 434,000, an increase of over 12 per cent since 1840. This number was distributed so that 45 per cent was in the North, 54 per cent was in the South, and about 0.03 per cent was in the West. The number of free Negroes increased in spite of the Fugitive Slave Act of 1850. The increase between 1850 and 1860 was about 24,000 in the slave states and 30,000 in the free states. Free Negroes were found in all southern states, although they were most numerous in Maryland, Louisiana, North Carolina and Kentucky.

Cotton factories throughout the South used Negro labor during the mid-nineteenth century.

By 1860, there were about four million slaves in the United States and close to half a million free Negroes. Nearly all of the slaves lived in the South and worked in agriculture.

THE NEGRO AND SOUTHERN INDUSTRIALISM

The introduction of Negro slaves to the new industrialism of the South had been proposed prior to 1850. Governor James Henry Hammond of South Carolina, in 1845, stated: "We are beginning to manufacture with slaves." It was also suggested that the United States had become the second greatest commercial power of the world by slave labor, and that it could become the first when a portion of slave labor was turned to manufacturing.

The use of Negroes in industry was undertaken in cotton factories in South Carolina and Tennessee. Iron furnaces in Tennessee and Virginia also used Negro slaves. At the Saluda factory near Columbia, South Carolina, all the operators were Negroes except the overseers and the superintendent. A cotton factory operated by Negro labor was situated at Arcadia, near Pensacola, Florida.

Slaves were employed in "a manufacturing village" at Scottville in Bibb County, Alabama. Other mills and shops with Negro workers were located in South Carolina, Mississippi and Georgia.

Many progressive leaders, especially those connected with the various agricultural improvement societies, were convinced that the only recourse for the South in the face of economic exploitation by the North was for it to develop its own industries. They argued that one source of the labor supply for this industry would be slaves.

GROWTH AND DISTRIBUTION OF THE SLAVE POPULATION

The external slave trade was ended legally in 1808. Thereafter, though there were illegal importations, external sources of slave manpower declined in importance. Illegal trade declined during much of the antebellum period, although it experienced some renewal shortly before the Civil War. Historians have estimated the total number of slaves imported at this time at figures ranging up to 270,000. W. E. B. Du Bois placed the number at 250,000. The principal source of slaves was natural increase. The average rate of natural increase, however, declined in the latter part of the antebellum period, probably due to the relative fall in the adult population as the imports from Africa decreased.

The proportion of slave population relative to total population, which had declined in the last decade of the eighteenth century, increased during the first twenty years of the nineteenth. The relative number of slaves remained steady until about 1840, then began a slight decline that lasted until 1860. The decline in numbers during the antebellum years was small, however, with the slave population remaining at about one-third of the total population throughout the period.

As the plantation system expanded westward, it received its supply of slaves from the established eastern regions. The distribution of the slave population in the South, therefore, tended to gravitate westward. It is difficult to estimate the exact number of slaves involved in the transfer from the selling to the buying states. A close study of the problem indicates that as much as 40 per cent of the total slave population may have been involved, that is, hundreds of thousands of slaves.

Estimates of the Transfer of Slaves from the Selling to the Buying States

Years	Number of Slaves Transferred
1820–1830	124,000
1830–1840	265,000
1840–1850	146,000
1850–1860	207,000

The trade was well organized, with slave traders active in many southern towns. The slaves were either transported on land in coffles or were shipped along the coast. The sale of slaves from east to west was an economic necessity, but was one of the cruelest, most unpopular aspects of southern slavery. Most respectable community members in the South disliked the practice and looked down on the persons involved in the slave trade.

Per Cent of Slave Population to Total Population by States, 1800–60

States	1800	1810	1820	1830	1840	1850	1860
Southern States	32.7	33.4	34.0	34.0	34.0	33.3	32.3
Border States	30.8	30.1	29.6	29.0	26.7	24.7	22.3
Lower South	40.3	44.7	45.6	46.0	46.0	45.4	44.8

A gang of slaves being driven toward auction blocks in the Deep South.

A busy slave auction in the South.

HEWLETT & BRIGHT.

SALE OF

VALUABLE

SLAVES,

(On account of departure)

The Owner of the following named and valuable Slaves, being on the eve of departure for Europe, will cause the same to be offered for sale, at the NEW EXCHANGE, corner of St. Louis and Chartres streets, on *Saturday,* May 16, at Twelve o'Clock, *viz.*

1. **SARAH,** a mulatress, aged 45 years, a good cook and accustomed to house work in general, is an excellent and faithful nurse for sick persons, and in every respect a first rate character.

2. **DENNIS,** her son, a mulatto, aged 24 years, a first rate cook and steward for a vessel, having been in that capacity for many years on board one of the Mobile packets; is strictly honest, temperate, and a first rate subject.

3. **CHOLE,** a mulatress, aged 36 years, she is, without execption, one of the most competent servants in the country, a first rate washer and ironer, does up lace, a good cook, and for a bachelor who wishes a house-keeper she would be invaluable; she is also a good ladies' maid, having travelled to the North in that capacity.

4. **FANNY,** her daughter, a mulatress, aged 16 years, speaks French and English, is a superior hair-dresser, (pupil of Guilliac,) a good seamstress and ladies' maid, is smart, intelligent, and a first rate character.

5. **DANDRIDGE,** a mulatoo, aged 26 years, a first rate dining-room servant, a good painter and rough carpenter, and has but few equals for honesty and sobriety.

6. **NANCY,** his wife, aged about 24 years, a confidential house servant, good seamstress, mantuamaker and tailoress, a good cook, washer and ironer, etc.

7. **MARY ANN,** her child, a creole, aged 7 years, speaks French and English, is smart, active and intelligent.

8. **FANNY or FRANCES,** a mulatress, aged 22 years, is a first rate washer and ironer, good cook and house servant, and has an excellent character.

9. **EMMA,** an orphan, aged 10 or 11 years, speaks French and English, has been in the country 7 years, has been accustomed to waiting on table, sewing etc.; is intelligent and active.

10. **FRANK,** a mulatto, aged about 32 years speaks French and English, is a first rate hostler and coachman, understands perfectly well the management of horses, and is, in every respect, a first rate character, with the exception that he will occasionally drink, though not an habitual drunkard.

☞ All the above named Slaves are acclimated and excellent subjects; they were purchased by their present vendor many years ago, and will, therefore, be severally warranted against all vices and maladies prescribed by law, save and except FRANK, who is fully guaranteed in every other respect but the one above mentioned.

TERMS:—One-half Cash, and the other half in notes at Six months, drawn and endorsed to the satisfaction of the Vendor, with special mortgage on the Slaves until final payment. The Acts of Sale to be passed before WILLIAM BOSWELL, *Notary Public,* at the expense of the Purchaser.

New-Orleans, May 13, 1835.

PRINTED BY BENJAMIN LEVY.

The slave trade was well organized and planned, especially in the South. Traders posted detailed descriptions of their "merchandise" to attract potential customers.

The prices slaves brought generally followed the fluctuations in the cotton market. The prices were high after the War of 1812: slaves then averaged $700 in the older regions and $1,100 in the newer areas. Prices fell during the depression following the panic of 1819. During the prosperity of the 1830's, prices increased until the panic of 1837. By the middle 1840's, prices were increasing again.

PLANTATION OWNERSHIP

The plantation system dominated southern life before the Civil War; yet the vast majority of southerners did not own slaves. In 1860, three-fourths of the white population did not own slaves. There were only 384,884 owners of Negro slaves in the United States at the start of the Civil War, and most of these masters were not owners of large plantations. More than 200,000 of them had fewer than six slaves. Almost 90 per cent of American slaveholders maintained farms with less than twenty slaves.

A relatively few slaveholders held most of the slaves and produced most of the crop. While one-quarter of the slave population lived on farms with less than ten slaves, another quarter resided on plantations with fifty slaves or more. The rest of the slave population was on plantations with between ten and forty-nine slaves. The most efficient and largest plantations, most of which were in the Deep South, had about thirty to sixty slaves. Production statistics demonstrate the economic importance of the larger plantations in the lower South. In 1860, over five million bales of cotton were produced. Four states in the lower South—Mississippi, Alabama, Louisiana and Georgia—produced over three million bales. These same states had the highest proportion of slaveholders owning twenty or more slaves.

It is significant, nevertheless, that there were so many persons who did not own slaves. The planter aristocracy dominated the South because it was able to impose its goals and aspirations on the rest of society. The small middle class, comprised of many merchants, bankers, lawyers and professional men, shared the ideology of the large planters. The small farmers, mechanics and tradesmen were also proslavery. The poor whites, many of whom lived in the mountains, were anti-Negro and supported slavery as a way of maintaining what little self-respect they had.

THE POOR WHITES

The poor whites were one of the unfortunate groups in the South's population. They were known by such names as "crackers," "hillbillies," "tar heels," "red necks" and "bob-tails." They lived in the worst areas, where production was most difficult. Their homes—usually one-room log cabins—were in wretched condition. The furniture was crude, typically consisting of a bench, a bed, a cupboard and a spinning wheel. Very few could read or write. They were constantly subject to hookworm and the usual fevers of the area. Generalizations about this group, however, must be made carefully. Their standards, manners, interests and morals varied with their locality and opportunities. Poverty was their major handicap and whiskey one of their weaknesses. Fannie Kemble, in her journal, described them as "the most degraded race of human beings claiming an Anglo-Saxon origin that can be found on the face of the earth." Many of these persons drifted from the hills to become tenants or squatters on near-barren lands.

Living conditions of the poor whites were similar to those of the Negroes, in many cases. Their food and dress were similar. Hog meat, greens, hominy, rice, corn meal, molasses and coffee of some kind were the essential elements of the daily fare. Homespun dress and bare feet were common sights. Men and women of both groups worked in the

JOURNAL

OF

A RESIDENCE ON A

GEORGIAN PLANTATION

IN

1838—1839.

BY FRANCES ANNE KEMBLE.

SLAVERY THE CHIEF CORNER STONE.

'This stone (Slavery), which was rejected by the first builders, is become the chief stone of the corner in our new edifice.'—*Speech of* ALEXANDER H. STEPHENS, *Vice-President of the Confederate States: delivered March 21, 1861.*

LONDON:
LONGMAN, GREEN, LONGMAN, ROBERTS, & GREEN.
1863.

the term "po' white trash" is said to have originated with Negroes. Daniel R. Hundley (*Social Relations in Our Southern States*) declared that the Negroes looked "with ineffable scorn on the poor white man." This was not always true, of course, but good relations rarely prevailed between the two groups.

THE YEOMEN

As a group, the yeomen related differently to Negroes than did the poor whites. As small farmers, mechanics and lesser tradesmen, they were economically more secure than the poor white group. They held small plots of land and owned few, if any, slaves. Some of them became overseers; others migrated to the frontiers and the border states. While they supported slavery, they were not as hesitant about working at tasks with Negroes. Hundley wrote that a man traveling in the South would surely "come up with some sturdy yeoman and his sons working in company

fields and carried on their housework after the day was done.

Mutual dislike developed between the lowest group of poor whites and the Negroes. Most whites regarded themselves as superior to the Negro. They resisted any semblance of slaves' work. Many would endure the effects of pinching poverty rather than engage in servile labor.

The poor whites wanted Negroes kept in their place. Frederick Law Olmsted recorded the sentiments of one who insisted that the Negro ought not be permitted to get to the place where he would be "feeling just as good as a white man." Negroes looked with disdain upon this element of the white population;

Plantation overseers were often uneducated men who cruelly mistreated the Negroes.

with their Negroes." It was reported that, in certain factories in Georgia, South Carolina and Tennessee, both races and sexes "worked together without apparent repugnance or objections."

There were certain types of work that the yeomen would not do, tasks they considered to be essentially for the Negro. There were those among them who would drive a wagon but not a carriage, because the latter was too closely associated with the traditional concept of the Negro coachman. In Georgia and Virginia, groups protested against the hiring of Negro slaves and their entrance into mechanical trades—an attitude reflecting the competition that Negro workers offered.

PLANTATION ORGANIZATION

The plantation was intended to be a unit that could survive in near isolation. It was to be complete, with its primitive agricultural efforts, its noncooperative attitude and its use of slave labor. While most of the small plantations were managed by their owners, the larger ones had stewards, managers, superintendents, overseers, foremen and drivers. It was customary for an owner of large sections of land to have several plantations, often located in different places in the same area. The management of these plantations was in the charge of one person, who received his orders from the plantation owner; and over each plantation, there was an overseer. The overseer supervised the foreman or "driver," who headed each gang of slaves. There were some absentee owners who sent orders by mail. While this type of ownership may have been profitable, the distance between the owner and his land and workers fostered the development of many abuses.

The owners of southern plantations having large numbers of slaves employed several overseers. These men were drawn from the yeoman and the poor-white classes and often were uneducated and uncultured. They were described to Olmsted as men who were "passionately careless, inhuman generally, intemperate and totally unfit for the duties of the position." Such a generalization does not, of course, fit all overseers. It must be remembered, nonetheless, that there was nothing in this system of delegated authority to encourage the development of a higher type of supervisory personnel. Some were benevolent despots and others were cruel taskmasters.

In the eighteenth century overseers worked with the gangs and received shares from the profits of the masters. Later, the average overseer was paid a salary, usually on a yearly basis, estimated at from $250 to $600 a year. He was expected to show a profit by "making his crops," which meant that he was required to see to it that the slaves did their work. Owners did not always concern themselves with the methods used by their overseers, who were often rigid and severe in their discipline in order to encourage obedience. Their objective was to maintain an effective laboring force, indicated by a large harvest.

Negro foremen and drivers were placed directly in contact with groups of slaves. Some assisted the overseers in the management of the plantations. Their interest in the work was more closely related to the views of the overseer than to those of the workers. In fact, their jobs depended upon seeing things from his point of view. Many of them, accordingly, gained the overseer's favor by spying and tattling, as well as by demanding that the orders of the overseer be obeyed. The drivers were the head men of the gangs. At times, they were given whips or canes for use against the slaves who did not perform the work that was expected of them. At other times, they worked in the fields and set the pace for the other workers, reporting later to the foreman or overseer concerning the work of the day.

There were three types of Negro plantation workers: field hands, artisans and house servants. Distinctions were drawn between the house servants and the field hands. The house servants were generally more intelligent and were more highly regarded by the masters and overseers; they have been called a black aristocracy. Close attachments between the families of the masters and their house servants often developed. Frederick Douglass wrote that "the delicately formed colored maid rustles in the scarcely-worn silk of her young mistress, while the servant men were equally attired from the over-flowing wardrobe of their young masters, so that in dress, as well as in form and features, in manner and speech, in tastes and habits, the distance between these favored few and the sorrow- and hunger-smitten multitudes of the quarter and the field was immense."

Some of these servants slept in the hallways of the big house where the master's family lived, while others slept in the separate slave quarters. Nursemaids, housemaids, cooks, butlers, waiters and coachmen were in this group. The "Mammy" tradition grew out of the relationship between white children and their black nurses. It is well known that some of them were related by blood to the master's family and were more kindly treated than other slaves on the plantation; certainly they showed more "intelligence" as a result of these contacts. There were owners who permitted their house servants to be taught to read. The evidence for this lies in the writings and speeches of fugitive slaves.

SKILLED SLAVE LABOR

The plantation required the development of skilled workers. The ablest and most promising slaves who were not assigned to service in the master's house were trained in the skilled crafts. The plantations were, to a large extent, self-sustaining units that did all their own repairing and made a large proportion of their supplies. The masters found it easier and cheaper to have their slaves trained in carpentry, masonry, blacksmithing and other

The "Mammy" tradition grew out of the use of Negro house servants to care for the master's children. These Negroes were exposed to far better conditions than their less fortunate brothers and, as a result, exhibited greater "intelligence" than the field hands.

mechanical trades than to depend upon outside labor. Much of the work of the slave artisan on the plantation was rough and crude. Some of it, however, was of the highest quality, as the beautiful southern mansions built by Negro labor still testify.

The mechanical needs of the plantation and of the towns were served mainly by Negro artisans. Southern mansions were built, painted, decorated and repaired by Negro workers. Most of the crafts were in the hands of Negroes—the making and repairing of carriages, harnesses, mills and plows and the shoeing of horses. Albert Bushnell Hart, in *Slavery and Abolition,* estimated that about one-twentieth of the able-bodied men were engaged in the skilled trades. Among these workers were the blacksmith, carpenter, wheelwright, mason, bricklayer, plasterer, painter, tanner, miller, weaver, shoemaker, harness-maker and cooper.

FAMILY LIFE

The majority of the plantation workers were field laborers who lived with their families in the slave quarters, small cabins of log or board walls with mud plaster between them. Some of them were whitewashed on the outside. Oystershells and broken crockery or stones were used for the paths to the doors. In *The Southern Plantation*, Francis Pendleton Gaines wrote that the two main physical features of the plantation tradition were the great mansion and the neat, comfortable slave quarters. This latter picture, however, is not corroborated by the fugitive slaves.

Living conditions did, of course, vary considerably. The general picture we get from the slave writings, however, is a grim one. Frederick Douglass described his quarters on the Eastern Shore of Maryland as a hut built of clay, wood and straw. Louis Hughes in his 1897 autobiography, *Thirty Years a Slave, From Bondage to Freedom*, stated that the cabins of the slaves "were built of rough logs and daubed with red clay or mud of the region." He stated that the quarters were not whitewashed and that no attempt was made to give them a neat appearance inside or out. The one-room cabins he knew were about fourteen feet square with dirt floors.

Slave quarters on the plantations were small and poorly constructed. They often had log or board walls with mud plaster between them and little or no protection at the windows.

NARRATIVES

OF THE SUFFERINGS OF

LEWIS AND MILTON CLARKE,

SONS OF A SOLDIER OF THE REVOLUTION,

DURING A

CAPTIVITY OF MORE THAN TWENTY YEARS

AMONG THE

SLAVEHOLDERS OF KENTUCKY,

ONE OF THE

SO CALLED CHRISTIAN STATES OF NORTH AMERICA.

DICTATED BY THEMSELVES.

BOSTON
PUBLISHED BY BELA MARSH,
NO 25 CORNHILL.
1846

All Orders to be sent to the Publisher.
PRICE, 25 CENTS.

Lewis Clarke, in *Narratives of the Sufferings of Lewis and Milton Clarke,* issued in 1846, described the houses on the plantations as small log cabins ten to twenty feet square. Clarke gave an account of the living conditions he saw: "In the corners, or at the sides there are pens filled with straw for sleeping. Very commonly, two or three families are bundled together in one cabin. Large families were usually found in the two or three room tenements." Hughes described the furniture of the cabins with which he was familiar as consisting of "one bed, a plain board table and some benches made by the slaves themselves. Sometimes a cabin was occupied by two or more families, in which case the number of beds was increased proportionately." The presence of any furniture at all, however,

may have been a comparative luxury. Father Josiah Henson stated in his *Truth Stranger Than Fiction: Father Henson's Story of His Own Life,* that the room in which he grew up had no furniture. "Our beds," he said, "were collections of straw and old rags thrown down in the corners and boxed in with boards; a single blanket the only covering. . . . In these wretched hovels were we penned at night, and fed by day; here were the children born and the sick neglected."

There could be little family life where sales of slaves were likely to occur since the existence of slavery made the institution of marriage unstable. There was, of course, evidence of affection and close relationships. Heartrending scenes have been described of the separation of families when members were "sold down the river" or transferred to other plantations.

Marriages were permitted and encouraged by some masters. When slaves on different plantations wished to marry, some masters

JOSIAH HENSON

One of the most serious problems facing Negro slaves was that their families were often separated. This made it almost impossible for enslaved Negroes to build cohesive family units.

gave their approval and others discouraged them, preferring that their slaves marry among the other slaves on their own plantations. Simple marriage ceremonies were performed at times by the plantation ministers. Some masters, acting as lay readers, were also known to take the initiative in pronouncing their slaves husband and wife. The termination of the slave marriage was not difficult, since it was not necessary to have court action. In general, the consent of the master was the only necessity. Children were usually welcomed by the masters because they were future workers and potential wealth. Large families were characteristic of the slave population.

Healthy, robust laborers were essential to plantation profits, so many masters did make an effort to maintain their workers' health so that a minimum of time would be lost as

a result of illness. Other masters, however, were careless and indifferent about such matters. Antislavery writers alleged that the food of the slaves was generally bad and that even convicts fared better. Some of these assertions were true, but there were masters who were concerned about the well-being of their slaves because of the capital investment the slaves represented. The ordinary food allowance for a slave was a quart of corn meal and a half pound of salt pork or bacon per week. Slaves were also allowed sugar and such vegetables as they themselves raised. On one Maryland plantation of the Eastern Shore, the monthly allowance was eight pounds of pork or fish and one bushel of Indian corn. This food was of the poorest kind, said to be fit only for the hogs. One observer on another plantation stated that the weekly allowance was three and a half pounds of bacon and enough corn to make a peck of meal. Where the slaves' food supply was inadequate and there was a plentiful supply in the storehouse, kitchen or field, the habit of pilfering and foraging for food readily developed. As a result of this situation, it was asserted that the habit of stealing was a fixed racial trait of Negro slaves. When such habits developed, they were, of course, the result of the conditions slaves were forced to live under rather than an indication of racial proclivities.

The wealth and status of the slave owner often determined the amount of food given to his slaves. When the planters experienced production shortages the slaves also suffered. Even when there was sufficient food, the slaves stated that it was poor in quality. Some slaves had their own produce from their gardens; with fish from the waters and game from the woods, their food allowance was more abundant.

Slaves were clothed in the coarsest and cheapest type of material, widely known as "slave cloth." In the summer, on some plantations, the men had one shirt and one pair of pants. In the winter, there were two pairs of pants, two coats, a hat and one pair of slave shoes. Douglass described the winter clothing on his plantation: "A pair of trowsers and a jacket of woolen, most lazily put together, one pair of yarn stockings and one pair of shoes of the coarsest description were provided for the men." The women wore heavier wool and cotton cloth, shoes and a turban.

They were not given undergarments or stockings. The household servants wore the castoff clothing of their owners.

A traditional picture has developed of the plantation and its joys. Gaines, in *The Southern Plantation,* described this romantic view: "Everybody was happy, the old planter with a julip, the young cavalier with horses, dogs, and slaves, the plantation beauty in the first ecstasy of romance, the old servants grinning with pleasure from multitudinous favors."

This tradition is not based upon fact. In the letters of overseers and in the narratives of slaves, another world is found. There were occasions when sports, fishing, barbecues, picnics, horse-racing and dancing were major attractions, but these occasions were often reported by observers while the darker spots went unnoticed. In truth, the evidence in slave reminiscences of such good times is very scanty. The Christmas season was generally an occasion for the suspension of work and a holiday celebration. Josiah Henson described these occasions and also the reaction of the slave-owner to them when he wrote: ". . . The fun and freedom of Christmas, at which time the master relaxed his front, was generally followed by a portentious back action, under which he cursed and drove worse than ever." There were many dark shadows in the actual state of living, particularly for those who were denied the basic human rights that were enjoyed by the rest of society.

CHAPTER SEVENTEEN

Facing Political and Social Issues

THE Civil War brought to a close the era of American slavery. The nation was divided into two hostile camps, with the North committed to a system of free labor and the South committed to slavery. Both societies had developed their own institutions and outlooks, and each section was convinced that its way of life was superior. Each believed that its institutions would be best for the future of civilization. More and more northerners came to view slavery as an anachronism that should be limited and ultimately destroyed. The South, seriously committed to slavery, chose to risk going to war rather than to submit peacefully to the will of the North.

Jacksonian democracy represented the triumph of laissez-faire capitalism. The defeat of John Quincy Adams by the Jacksonians ended the mercantilist phase of controlled growth. The productive forces set loose transformed the North into a major industrial area, and by the 1850's, the forces of industrialism were beginning to collide with the slavocracy's power. Western farmers searching for new lands to settle were confronted by planters seeking to extend the slave system. The industrialists' attempts to gain high protective tariffs were thwarted by southern opposition. Free labor feared the possibility of competition with slave labor. All three groups were incensed at southern opposition to internal improvements.

Alongside these material concerns working against slavery, a heightened moral opposition began to emerge in the North. In the 1840's, many church groups divided over the question of slavery. The northern churches, freed from the constraining hand of their southern counterparts, became more outspoken in their criticism of the institution. Abolitionists continued to make headway with their arguments that slavery was a stain on American life that eventually could threaten everyone's freedom. The popular success of Harriet Beecher Stowe's *Uncle Tom's Cabin* also demonstrated the growing northern abhorrence of slavery.

PICTURES AND STORIES
from
UNCLE TOM'S CABIN.

Published by John P. Jewett & Co., Boston.

THE PROSLAVERY ARGUMENT

Southerners responded vigorously to the growing northern opposition to slavery. They insisted that they were not businessmen casually investing in black labor; instead, the issue of slavery was a matter of their own existence, their entire way of life. There was an increasing tendency to stress the aristocratic and non-material values of the South. Southerners distinguished their attitudes towards monetary gain from those in the North by saying that they sought money not for its own sake but in order to live as gentlemen.

John C. Calhoun, a leading southern politician, attacked the North as a society consisting of antagonistic individuals and classes, unlike the South, which was a true community of responsible individuals. In the North, said its detractors, no human relationship could withstand the pressures of the marketplace. Southerners pictured northern family life as seriously deteriorated and professed indignation at the use of women and children in factories. The South, its spokesmen claimed, was the last outpost against rampant anarchy and materialism: the South was civilization's last hope.

George Fitzhugh, author of the first major sociological work in the United States, *Sociology for the South,* developed one of the more sophisticated attacks on the North. It was his viewpoint that northern political economists failed to see that they were creating a moral code. "Laissez-faire, free competition begets a war of the wits, which these economists encourage, quite as destructive to the weak, simple and guileless, as the war of the sword." It placed men in antagonistic positions, he claimed, each out for his own gain, and set capital at war with labor.

Fitzhugh argued that the individual human being is the most helpless of animals. Actions should be determined by social good, not individual greed. "It makes each society a band of brothers, working for the common good, instead of cats biting and worrying each other. The competitive system is a system of antagonism and war; ours [slavery] of peace and fraternity."

SOUTHERN EXPANSIONISM

As the system of slavery spread westward, older areas, where the land had deteriorated from overuse, found it difficult to compete with the more fertile new sections. The land owners of this area maintained their economic viability by selling surplus slaves to settlers in the West. The money from these sales financed the process of land reclamation. The viability of the American slave system was dependent on its ability to expand. Thus, any attempt to limit slavery was a potential economic crisis that could destroy the system. The formation of a northern political party based on opposition to the expansion of slavery was a direct threat to the planters' position and, as a result, was completely unacceptable to southerners.

JOHN C. CALHOUN

The South was dependent on westward expansion for political as well as economic reasons. Since the North had been populated at a much more rapid rate than the South, it soon possessed a clear majority in the House of Representatives. The Senate became the political protector of southern interests. As long as parity in the number of states remained, the South could veto any hostile legislation. The South faced the dilemma of eventual need for the expansion of its borders, but planters could not rely on acquiring new lands until they could be assured of expanding their institution of slavery as well. The battle for control of the western territories was therefore fundamentally a struggle over the existence of slavery.

POLITICAL ABOLITIONISM

In 1838, the New York Anti-Slavery Society resolved to deny its votes to any candidate who did not support abolition. The next year, the American Anti-Slavery Society adopted a similar position. Garrison soon repudiated this attempt to become directly active in the political life of the nation, and his opposition to political action resulted in the formation of new antislavery societies intent on participating in politics.

One of the weaknesses in the political abolitionists' position was that many Negroes in the North were excluded from voting. In a few of the states where Negroes were permitted to vote, they were limited by special

As wagon trains rolled west, the battle between the forces of slavery and abolition for control of the western territories grew more intense.

legislation. In New York, there was a property qualification solely for Negro citizens. The Negro had the right to vote in Maine, New Hampshire, Vermont, Rhode Island and Massachusetts, but in these states social pressure was almost as formidable a barrier to Negro political activity as legal disfranchisement.

The election of 1840 marked the formal emergence of an abolitionist political party. The Democrats, under the leadership of Jackson and Martin Van Buren, had vigorously supported the South's attempts to limit abolitionist activity. The Whigs were led by Henry Clay, a one-time opponent of slavery. Clay, as his national ambitions heightened, drew away from his previous position. "I prefer the liberty of my own country to that of any other people, and the liberty of my own race to that of any other race," he told Congress. It was soon after this attempt to appease southern sentiment, and after losing his race for the presidency for the third time, that he declared he would "rather be right than be President."

The Liberty Party was founded on April 1, 1840, in Albany, New York. It was to become the main thrust in a political effort to peacefully overthrow slavery. The party claimed that both the Declaration of Independence and the Constitution were antislavery documents. In taking this stand, they emphasized their differences with Garrison, who believed the Constitution was a proslavery document. The party nominated James G. Birney for President and Thomas Earle for vice president.

Many Negroes decided to support the Liberty Party. Samuel Ringgold Ward, whose abilities were praised by his fellow Negro abolitionists, declared his support. Ward later stated that, in 1840: "I then became for the first time a member of a political party; with it I cast my first vote; to it I devoted my political activity; with it I lived my political life." Henry Highland Garnet declared that he was "a Liberty Party man." J. W. Loguen, a Negro minister, campaigned in New York State for the Liberty Party ticket. William Wells Brown lectured for the party.

Other abolitionists besides Garrison opposed the Liberty Party because they thought it would weaken the abolition movement. Birney spent most of the campaign period attending the World Anti-Slavery Convention in London. William Henry Harrison, the Whig candidate, ran a banal campaign seeking to offend no one. The Democrats were in serious trouble due to the panic of 1837 and tried to picture Harrison as a potential abolitionist. However, Van Buren was beaten in all sections of the country. Birney received only 7,100 votes nationally and 2,798 in New York State.

Negroes, during the 1840's, were never united on the advisability of creating an abolitionist political party. In 1842, the Colored State Convention meeting at Rochester, New York, urged Negroes to support the Liberty Party. Frederick Douglass remained a supporter of Garrison and an opponent of political action. Douglass' objection to the formation of a third party was the fear that it would dispose men to rely upon political rather than upon moral action, two realms that he saw as disparate. Of the abolitionists, he demanded: "Was it political action that removed your prejudices and raised in your mind a holy zeal for human rights?" For Douglass, then, morality and politics were mutually exclusive, or at least the one was not to be fostered by the other.

The National Convention of Colored Citizens that met in 1843 passed a resolution advocating the principles of the Liberty Party. Douglass and Charles L. Remond, both delegates from Massachusetts, cast the only dissenting votes. Opposition to political action among the Negroes was similar to that of the whites. Some believed that political action would corrupt the moral force of the abolitionist movement. Since many politicians had

LEWIS TAPPAN

betrayed them in the past, they tended to generalize about the kind of individual who entered politics. Some of this hesitancy was overcome when, in 1843, Lewis Tappan finally declared himself in support of the Liberty Party. His position of leadership among the New York abolitionists, particularly among the Negroes, helped to bring many of the latter into the Liberty Party fold.

At its Buffalo Convention in 1844, the Liberty Party sought a better-known figure to lead its ticket. Neither John Quincy Adams nor William Seward was fully committed to the aims of the abolitionists, though both showed some sympathy for their objectives. Tappan wanted William Jay to receive the nomination, but the latter shunned what he believed to be a hopeless cause. In the end, Birney was renominated for president and Thomas Morris of Ohio was chosen for the second place on the ticket.

Henry Highland Garnet introduced a resolution at this convention, partly aimed at some of the critics of political abolition: "Resolved, That the Liberty Party has not been

organized for any temporary purpose by interested politicians, but has arisen from among the people, in consequence of a conviction, hourly gaining ground, that no other party in the country represents the true principles of American Liberty or the true spirit of the Constitution of the United States." This resolution was adopted by the convention. Another resolution was introduced that sought to gain wider support among the free Negro population: "Resolved, That we cordially welcome our colored fellow citizens to fraternity with us in the Liberty Party, in its great contest to secure the rights of mankind and the religion of our common country." This was the first time that a national party had extended such an invitation and had declared that Negro citizens were of a "common country."

Garnet continued to campaign for the Liberty Party ticket. He spoke to the Liberty State Convention in Massachusetts in February 1844. His typically militant address was well received. He stated that bloody revolution would surely follow if the hope that the Liberty Party offered for rapid, peaceful emancipation could not be fulfilled. The Annual Convention of the Colored Citizens of New York met at Schenectady during September 18–20, 1844. The New York City delegation presented a protest against the endorsement of the Liberty Party by the Rochester Convention in 1842. This attempt to halt political activity was defeated.

The delegation from New York City, however, did not accept meekly the defeat of their efforts against political abolitionism. The Negro community was still seriously split on the tactics to be used. They went home and held their own meeting, at which they passed a resolution implicitly attacking the Liberty Party. They declared that the franchise "would not be worth the having from any one party or parties who denied the patriotic colored citizens of New York the right of thinking as they please."

Statehood for Texas and expansionism were the main issues in the 1844 election campaign. Before the campaign had begun, both Martin Van Buren and Henry Clay, the probable contenders for the presidency, agreed to avoid these issues. The expansionist forces in the Democratic Party thwarted Van Buren's nomination, however, and James K. Polk was nominated instead on an expansionist platform. The country was sympathetic to the cries of manifest destiny, which meant it was a preconceived fact that the United States would expand its borders, and Polk was elected.

Though this was a defeat for the antislavery forces, since the annexation of Texas would add another slave state to the nation, the Liberty Party could console itself with the gains it had made. In 1844, it received 62,324 votes, nearly ten times the 1840 total. It also had achieved a position of holding the balance of power, as their votes in New York were responsible for Clay's defeat. The New York *Express* stated that the abolitionist vote had amounted to 15,812—sufficient to have defeated the Whig presidential electoral ticket in the state, the governor and lieutenant governor, six members of Congress, four canal commissioners, four state senators and twenty-six assembly members. The New York *Express* stated: "The result is most disastrous. . . . There has never been a vote of any fragment of a party so extensively disastrous in its consequences, or so pernicious to the ostensible objects of its authors."

Negro dissatisfaction with the Liberty Party continued to be heard. While the party had always supported full equality for its Negro members, it could not guarantee the racial tolerance of its membership. In 1844, the Michigan State Convention denied voting privileges to two Negro delegates because they were not legal voters. The action was not lost on the national press, which used it to embarrass the party's presidential candidate. Some Negroes in the North, staunchly

JAMES K. POLK

advocating black suffrage, believed that the Liberty Party was not strong enough to secure the vote for the free Negro. Many pledged themselves to support any candidate who favored free Negro suffrage. When a group of Boston Negroes expressed these sentiments, the Garrison wing of the abolitionist movement responded favorably. The Massachusetts Anti-Slavery Society resolved that it was satisfied with "the sagacity of our colored friends in this city and their correct appreciation of their own position and the welfare of the slave in refusing to be made tools of the Liberty Party on a late occasion."

Many Liberty Party members attempted to make good the party's program in support of free Negro suffrage. The New York Constitutional Convention met in 1842 to modernize the state's constitution. An unsuccessful attempt was made to delete the special property qualification that applied only to Negro voters; but the old franchise provision was retained. Gerrit Smith bitterly attacked this development, and began in 1847 to give free land grants to Negroes. Garnet assisted in the distribution of these grants, which went to such individuals as Frederick Douglass, William C. Nell and William Wells Brown.

THE FREE-SOIL MOVEMENT

Polk's election helped to facilitate the annexation of Texas, and the United States soon found itself at war with Mexico. There was much opposition to this war, particularly in the North. Many people pictured the attack on Mexico as a slavocracy conspiracy seeking to extend its area in the Southwest. David Wilmot, a Pennsylvania Democrat, in 1846 introduced his now-famous proviso to reserve the area annexed from Mexico for free states. The House adopted this measure by a vote of eighty-three to sixty-four. The vote did not represent abolitionist sentiment, but rather the growing northern desire to expand into the entire West.

In 1848, the growing free-soil movement met in convention in Buffalo, New York. The convention consisted of disaffected Democrats, Whigs and Liberty Party men. It nominated Martin Van Buren for president and Charles Francis Adams for vice-president, although Van Buren's previous loyalty to the southern cause was to embarrass the party during the election. They adopted the slogan "Free Soil, Free Speech, Free Labor and Free Men." Samuel Ward, Henry Garnet, Charles Remond, Henry Bibb, Frederick Douglass and "other colored gentlemen" were in attendance.

The convention tried to induce Douglass to deliver an address. He declined the invitation, pleading a recent throat operation as his reason. At the close of the convention, Samuel Ward sent Douglass "An Address to the Four Thousand Colored Voters of the State of New York." Ward asked: "But can the colored voters of New York State support the nominee [Van Buren] and join in this movement? I answer no!" Ward urged the election of Gerrit Smith as an "everywhere known, unbroken, uncompromising and truly practical philanthropist." The platform on which Smith ran, Ward stated, promised enfranchisement for all Negroes, emancipation and

MARTIN VAN BUREN

identity with "the great interests of the crushed poor, black or white, bond or free." Douglass' reply to Ward was an editorial stating that supporting a specific party, at that time, would be a violation of his antislavery principles.

The Free Soil Party did gain impressive Negro support. A convention of blacks in Cleveland, Ohio, voted support for the Free Soil Party on a resolution proposed by Martin R. Delany. It also adopted resolutions that were more abolitionist and went further than the platform of the Free Soil Party. Even Douglass was impressed with the wealth and talent of the party. The antislavery cause had reached a wider audience than had been possible previously. Though they weren't abolitionists, they talked much of the evils of slavery. Douglass continued to stress the need to use moral suasion.

In 1848, the Liberty Party splintered and rapidly declined in importance. Gerrit Smith and his followers left the party and formed the Liberty League. The National Liberty Party met at Buffalo, New York, June 14

ZACHARY TAYLOR

and 15, 1848. Douglass attended this convention and was impressed with the National Liberty Party's nominee for president, Gerrit Smith. This was the first time that Douglass had attended a political convention, and he remained dubious as to the wisdom of political action.

As a result of these splits and the rise of free soil philosophy, the Liberty Party was relegated to an extremely minor role in American political life. The regular Liberty Party nominee, John P. Hale, withdrew during the campaign and threw his support to Van Buren. Van Buren received 291,678 votes, approximately 10 per cent of the total. Most of these votes were not for abolition, but rather were cast for the free soil movement.

The Negro vote was not concentrated as a single national force. Frederick Douglass stated that the Negro voters in New Bedford, Massachusetts, supported the Free Soil Party. In Rhode Island, the Negroes supported the Whig ticket. The Democrats of that state had taken the lead in trying to eliminate Negro suffrage. The Whigs had defeated their at-

tempts and were guaranteed the Negro vote. Douglass toured the state and attempted to loosen the hold that the Whigs had on the free Negro vote. He was unsuccessful, however, and most of the free Negroes supported Zachary Taylor, the Whig nominee.

THE FUGITIVE SLAVE QUESTION

The Supreme Court, in interpreting the Fugitive Slave Law of 1793, had maintained the right of Congress to legislate concerning the treatment of escaped slaves. Some American statesmen believed that it was each state's responsibility to return fugitive slaves; others were of the opinion that the federal government should enforce its own law.

Cases involving the interpretation of the Fugitive Slave Law by the federal courts brought the question to public attention. The free Negroes of the northern and border states were often without defense against the claims of slave traders. Many white persons sympathized with the Negroes, who had become easy prey for the slave bounty-hunters. Pennsylvania was the scene of one such case in reference to slave kidnaping. In 1826, the legislature of this state passed an act that prohibited taking from the state any Negro with the intention of selling him as a slave.

Margaret Morgan, a slave woman, fled from Maryland to Pennsylvania in 1832, which led to the case of *Prigg* v. *Pennsylvania* (1842 U.S. 825). Edward Prigg, an agent for the Maryland owner, came to Pennsylvania in 1837 and succeeded in having her arrested. She and her children, one of whom had been born in Pennsylvania, were sent back to her owner. Prigg was then arrested and convicted in the Pennsylvania county court under the existing law. This conviction was upheld by the supreme court of Pennsylvania. An appeal was taken to the Supreme Court of the United States, which decided that the Pennsylvania statute was illegal, being superseded by the federal law of 1793.

In 1839, the authorities of the state of Virginia asked the law enforcement authorities of New York to arrest three Negroes who were accused of aiding a slave to escape. The governor of New York replied that no state could demand the return of a fugitive for an act that was made criminal only by its own legislation. The effort by the slaveholders to compel the prosecution of those who aided fugitives to escape and to make mandatory the return of escaped slaves met with opposition from antislavery people and from those who believed that the constitution did not provide for such oppression. Eventually, some northern states passed Personal Liberty Laws to check the growing demand by slaveholders for the return of their "property." The increasing legislation in the North, combined with increasing numbers of runaway slaves, led to passage of the more stringent Fugitive Slave Law of 1850.

NEGROES IN CANADA AND CALIFORNIA

In 1793, Canada passed an act prohibiting the importation of slaves. In the very year in which Congress passed the first Fugitive Slave Law, therefore, it became legally possible for slaves to obtain their freedom by escaping to Canada. Emigration to Canada increased gradually with the spread of information. It reached its peak after the organization of the Underground Railroad and the passage of the Fugitive Slave Law in 1850, but the total number of slaves in Canada was never large.

The largest number of fugitive slaves entered Canada via the western peninsula of Ontario, which was bounded on three sides by the United States. In this area, several settlements were begun for the new arrivals. The two most successful communities were the Dawn settlement, established in 1842, and the settlement at Buxton, begun in 1850.

The Buxton settlement was established by the Elgin Association, a corporation formed for the purpose of purchasing land and settling black refugee families. Begun by the Rev. William King, a college rector from Louisiana who had brought his own slaves to Canada to free them, the association was able to buy nine thousand acres of land around Lake Erie. Each colonist was allowed to buy fifty acres at a price of $2.50 per acre, payable in ten annual installments. He was expected to build a substantial house and to proceed with the work of clearing the land.

A correspondent from the *New York Tribune* who visited the thriving colony in 1857 was clearly impressed by the moral standards that prevailed there. Dr. Samuel R. Howe, who toured Canada on behalf of the Freedmen's Inquiry Committee, termed Buxton "a perfect success." In *Refugees from Slavery in Canada West,* Howe stated: "Here are men who were bred in slavery, who came here and purchased land at the government price, cleared it, bought their own implements, built their own houses after a model and have supported themselves in all material circumstances and now support their schools in part."

Many Negroes either came or were brought to California once gold had been discovered there. Numbers grew steadily until, by 1860, the census showed nearly four thousand blacks in California, or slightly more than 1 per cent of the total population. In the mining counties, blacks mostly labored in the mines. In the cities, they were employed primarily in the service trades, but they gradually began to succeed as businessmen and artisans as well.

Slavery had been made illegal when California's constitution was adopted in 1849. The constitution, however, failed to determine the status of those slaves brought into the area before or after its ratification. Local judicial sentiment, therefore, determined the outcome of each contested slave case. Many were granted freedom; many were kept in slavery. The broad outlook for race relations, however, was probably better there than in the nation generally, because of the kinds of people the West attracted.

It was the uncommonly energetic and adventurous individuals of all races who went west. This was as likely to be true of the slaves who were brought to California as it was of the free Negroes who came on their own initiative, since masters would tend to choose their hardier and more intelligent slaves to face the rigors and uncertainties of the journey westward. According to Rudolph M. Lapp (*Journal of Negro History,* Volume 49), the Negro population "accumulated more wealth in a shorter period of time in California than anywhere else in the nation."

It is not surprising that Negro leadership in California was especially well organized and articulate. The Franchise League formed in 1852 around the issue of lobbying to have courts accept black testimony in cases involving white men. Though their goal was attained only after passage of the Emancipation Proclamation, the league was able to serve as a basis for organizing three Colored Citizens' Conventions—in 1855, 1856 and 1857—which did much to promote the attainment of civil rights for Negroes in California.

THE COMPROMISE OF 1850

In 1850, the nation had nearly split apart over the issue of slavery in the territories. A compromise was worked out, which averted civil war. This compromise, however, contained provisions that were odious both to the North and to the South. With the admission of California as a free state, the South was forced to give up its position of parity in the Senate. Northerners were incensed at the inclusion of a new and more stringent Fugitive Slave Law. This act threatened the liberties of the ex-slave population in the North and of the whites who attempted to help them. While the compromise was not unanimously

A handbill giving an extract from the speech delivered by Daniel Webster (above) on March 7, 1850.

VOTERS, Read This!

EXTRACT FROM A

SPEECH

DELIVERED BY THE

Hon. Daniel Webster,

IN THE SENATE OF THE UNITED STATES,
ON THE 7th OF MARCH, 1850.

"If the infernal Fanatics and Abolitionists ever get the power in their hands, they will override the Constitution, set the Supreme Court at defiance, change and make Laws to suit themselves. They will lay violent hands on those who differ with them politically in opinion, or dare question their infallibility; bankrupt the country and finally deluge it with blood."

approved, most Americans were thankful that a grave crisis had been avoided.

The furor aroused by this act demonstrated that slavery, not free soil, was the basic issue that divided Americans. When Daniel Webster spoke in support of the compromise on March 7, 1850, many of his constituents considered him a traitor to northern interests. The abolitionist poet, John Greenleaf Whittier, expressed northern sentiments toward Webster in his poem "Ichabod":

> Revile him not, the Tempter hath
> A snare for all;
> And pitying tears, not scorn and wrath,
> Befit his fall!

The South was threatened directly when the slave trade was made illegal in the District of Columbia. While the trade was merely moved across the river to Alexandria, Virginia, the legislation itself was taken as an affront to southern society. The fear that a hostile northern majority would abolish slavery was thus intensified.

It was partly in response to the Fugitive Slave Law that Douglass broke with Garrison and endorsed political action. Other Negroes followed Douglass' lead. In 1851, Douglass was appointed to the National Committee of the Liberty Party. On June 5, 1851, under the financial sponsorship of Gerrit Smith, Douglass' newspaper merged with the *Liberty Party Paper*. Though Douglass' endorsement of political action greatly increased black participation in the political movement for abolition, it did not result in a common Negro front. Negroes continued to divide their support between the waning Liberty Party and the rising free soil movement.

On August 11, 1852, the Free Soil Convention met in Pittsburgh, Pennsylvania. Douglass attended the convention and was elected secretary by acclamation. This time he did not decline the invitation to address the convention. He explained to them that he was "not so much a Free Soiler as others," and he added that he was against slavery not

J. W. LOGUEN

merely in California but in New Orleans as well. In the campaign, he supported the Free Soil Party nationally and the Liberty Party in New York State.

The Democratic presidential candidate was Franklin Pierce, who called for strict enforcement of the Fugitive Slave Law. The main emphasis of his campaign, however, was an attempt to distract from the growing sectional crisis by calling for western expansion. Pierce defeated the Whig nominee, Winfield Scott. Though the free soilers did not receive as many votes as they had during the 1848 campaign, it would be erroneous to attribute this to a decline in their influence. Van Buren and his followers had returned to the Democratic fold. Calling themselves the "Free Democrats," the free soilers nominated John P. Hale for the presidency. Despite the loss of significant political support and the relative obscurity of their standard-bearer, they did receive over 156,000 votes. The poor showing of the Liberty Party ended Tappan's hope for a pure antislavery party.

Negroes were becoming impatient with the limited success obtained from political action. Many had fled to Canada in order to escape prosecution under the Fugitive Slave Law, and many who remained demanded more direct action. The Rev. J. W. Loguen stated that his brethren must "strike the blow for themselves, and not wait for the hairsplitting of politicians and speakers." He added that he had "made an abolitionist of [his] master by whipping him." Douglass agreed that the Free Soil Party had its limitations but believed it was making progress. Douglass continued to divide his allegiance, and in 1855 he was nominated by the Liberty Party for secretary of state of New York.

THE EMERGENCE OF THE REPUBLICAN PARTY

As the West became more settled, popular pressure grew for the construction of a transcontinental railroad. Stephen A. Douglas, Senator from Illinois and leader of the Democratic Party in the northwest, was strongly in favor of the project as a help to the economic development of his section. Senator Douglas wanted a northern rather than a southern route for the proposed railroad and, to strengthen his position, introduced a bill to organize the area west of Iowa and northwestern Missouri into a new territory, to be called Nebraska.

This bill was bound to engender strong southern opposition. It dealt with territory north of the Missouri Compromise line and would mean the addition of another free state. To appease southern interests, Senator Douglas amended his bill in such a way that the Missouri Compromise was almost nullified. The territory was divided into two parts, with the southern half to be called Kansas. Each territorial legislature would decide whether slavery would be permitted in its territory. This, in effect, made inoperative the Missouri Compromise, which stated that slavery would be permitted in no territory in that area. The bill passed with the support of almost the entire southern delegation, Democrats and Whigs. The northern Democrats split on the bill, and almost all the northern Whigs opposed it.

The northern reaction outside Congress was extremely hostile, for the dominance of the slaveholders over the national government had been demonstrated again. The Whig Party ceased to exist as southern Whigs joined the Democratic Party while their northern counterparts began to look elsewhere. Democrats and Whigs who opposed Senator Douglas' bill called themselves Anti-Nebraska Democrats and Anti-Nebraska Whigs. In 1854, these elements joined with the Free-Soilers to form the Republican Party. Their campaign in 1854 was an astounding success: they elected a majority to the House of Representatives and captured various state governments.

BLEEDING KANSAS

Many people who settled Kansas came not merely to establish a new life but as men dedicated to a cause. Many people in the North encouraged their fellow countrymen to save Kansas for freedom. The New England Emigrant Aid Company offered assistance to those who wished to settle there. Though the South attempted to induce settlement of Kansas by its supporters, it operated at a disadvantage. It was extremely dangerous for a planter to take his slaves into an area where there was so much antislavery agitation. He could never be certain that the territorial legislature would adopt a constitution supporting slavery. Should it fail to do so, he could lose all he had invested.

Rampant fraud marked the territorial election of 1855. The proslavery forces were able to secure a majority in the legislature, which enacted laws to legalize slavery in the state. The antislavery forces held their own convention and adopted a constitution that excluded slavery from the territory. President Pierce sided with the proslavery forces, declaring those involved in writing the antislavery constitution to be outlaws committing acts that were close to treason.

CHARLES SUMNER

A civil war broke out in Kansas when a proslavery marshal attempted to arrest the leaders of the free-state movement. The town of Lawrence was nearly destroyed during the attack. John Brown was accused of leading a band of his followers and killing five proslavery settlers in retribution. The war spread, and Kansas was ripped apart. Each section blamed the other for the tragedy that soon became known as "Bleeding Kansas." Charles Sumner, militant abolitionist senator from Massachusetts, delivered an address to the Senate, "The Crime against Kansas." This speech included a personal attack on South Carolina's Senator Andrew P. Butler. Butler's nephew avenged the insult to his uncle's good name by beating Sumner with a cane. As a result of the injuries he received, Sumner was unable to take his seat in the Senate for four years, but his state refused to send a successor. The violence in Kansas demonstrated the growing inability of the nation to resolve its difficulties in a peaceful manner.

THE ELECTION OF 1856 AND ITS AFTERMATH

The Democrats nominated James Buchanan for the presidency and adopted a platform supporting popular sovereignty and the Kansas-Nebraska Act. The Whigs, completely disunited, endorsed Millard Fillmore, the Know-Nothing Party nominee. The major interest of the campaign centered on the Republican Party, which ran John C. Frémont as its first candidate for the presidency. Its platform attacked the Kansas-Nebraska Act and called for a halt in the expansion of slavery. The Republicans also adopted a plank that called for an expanded program of internal improvements. The Political Abolition Party, which had been formed the previous year, nominated Gerrit Smith for the presidency and Samuel McFarland for the vice-presidency.

The Republican Party attracted the support of many Negro voters. While it was not an antislavery party, it was, like its predecessor the Free Soil Party, opposed to the extension of slavery. Its slogan was "no slavery outside of the slave states." It made little effort to attract Negro voters or to win political rights for the Negro in the North. The party's growing strength and success could not be ignored, but many Negro leaders were uncertain about its intentions. Frederick Douglass attacked the Republican Party as "a heterogeneous mass of political antagonisms, gathered from defunct Whiggery, disaffected Democracy, and demented, defeated, and disappointed Native Americanism."

The Republican Party was attracting a large following. It called for an end to the extension of slavery, and many abolitionists hoped that this would be only the first step toward complete abolition. Douglass, in September 1856, reversed himself and declared his support for John C. Frémont. He stated that "a man was not justified in refusing to assist his fellowmen to accomplish a good thing simply because his fellows refuse to accomplish some other good thing which they deem impossible." After the campaign, he wrote Smith: "We have turned Whigs and Democrats into Republicans and we can turn Republicans into Abolitionists." He still refused, however, to become a member of the Republican Party.

Buchanan defeated Frémont in the election, but the Republican Party could look on the results with some optimism. Though the party was only two years old, it received 1,341,000 votes, approximately 500,000 less than went to Buchanan. It outdistanced the fragmented Whig Party and was firmly established as a major political force even though it received support only in the North. Despite the sectional nature of the party, however, a slight shift in the votes in Pennsylvania and Illinois would have given the Republicans the presidency.

THE UNDERGROUND RAILROAD

While political events swirled around them, Negroes in the South did not wait for the election of a political party that might bring them freedom. The desire for freedom was buried deep in the hearts of the enslaved Negroes, and they had been, through the years, escaping from bondage by way of the Underground Railroad. They often spent days on end in swamps or hid in out-of-the-way places. They fled toward refuge in Canada and sympathetic northern states, often finding aid along the way among their own people at neighboring plantations. The routes of the Underground Railroad were many and varied, and word was passed from person to person of designated areas where it was safe to pass. Probably one of history's most intricate networks of conspiracy was developed during the height of the Underground Railroad.

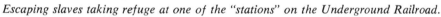

Escaping slaves taking refuge at one of the "stations" on the Underground Railroad.

The passage of the Fugitive Slave Law in 1850 did not deter the freedom-bound slaves. If anything, the act, with its harsh measures, inspired the abolitionists to increase their labors for reform and increased the resolve of those who gave comfort and aid to the escaping slaves. The stories of escapes through the Underground Railroad are legend. There are hundreds of unsung heroes who, like Harriet Tubman, escaped to freedom and then returned to the South to bring others to the North.

Josiah Henson, who had served as an overseer on his master's plantation in the South, escaped and made his way to Canada with his wife and children. He was not satisfied with his own victory over perpetual bondage, however, and returned to the South again and again to bring others to freedom. According to Henson, in his autobiography, he brought out of the South a total of 118 slaves. William Still, another Negro, worked as an agent for the Underground Railroad in the Ohio River area. He was responsible for making contacts between the escaping Negroes and those who aided them.

Perhaps one of the most fascinating accounts of an escape from slavery was that of Henry "Box" Brown. Brown, a slave on a southern plantation, determined to be free even though his was not a harsh and cruel master. Making friends with a white abolitionist in a nearby town, Brown conceived of making his escape by way of the United States mail service. He ordered a box, made by a Negro carpenter, into which he himself could fit. After the proper arrangements had been made with members of the underground in Philadelphia, Brown's abolitionist friend mailed him in the box. He was then placed at the freight station and "mailed" to Philadelphia. Said Brown: "I laid me down in my darkened home of three feet by two, and like one about to be guillotined, resigned myself to my fate." After approximately two days of travel in his cramped quarters, Brown ar-

HENRY "BOX" BROWN

rived at his destination and was picked up, in his box, by the Philadelphia contact. About his release from the confinement of the crate, Brown later exclaimed, "Great God, was I a freeman! . . . My labor was accomplished, my warfare was ended, and I stood erect before my equal fellow men, no longer a crouching slave, forever at the beck and nod of a whimsical and tryannical slave owner."

William and Ellen Craft thought of a unique means of escaping from their Georgia plantation. Ellen was fair enough to disguise herself as a white gentlewoman, ill and traveling with William, her devoted slave. With the assistance of antislavery workers, the Crafts were able to get to England, where they worked hard and prospered. After the Civil War, the Crafts returned to Georgia, purchased a plantation and established an industrial school for Negro youth.

The famous escape of Jane Johnson and her two sons was accomplished under the very gaze of Jane's master. Colonel John Wheeler, Minister to Nicaragua, attempted to take his three slaves from North Carolina to New York by ship. While docked in Philadelphia, Jane indicated to a sympathetic passenger that she desired freedom. The man then notified the antislavery office. Agents William Still and Passmore Williamson boarded the boat, informed Jane of her legal right to freedom in Pennsylvania and urged her to leave with them. As a result of the mobilization of the powerful proslavery forces in the city, Williamson eventually spent eight months in jail. Jane and her sons, however, went free.

Many free Negroes in the North played a considerable role in aiding the escaped slaves. It has been estimated that Robert Purvis and James Forten, of Philadelphia, helped more than three thousand blacks on their road to freedom.

In the 1850's, while the politics of slavery and expansion was being discussed by the

PASSMORE WILLIAMSON

The rescue of Jane Johnson and her children.

public, two incidents occurred in Massachusetts that fanned the flames for freedom. An escaped fugitive, Shadrach, was being held in the Boston Courthouse awaiting trial in accordance with the Fugitive Slave Act, when a Negro minister, Lewis Hayden, and twenty of his congregation spirited Shadrach away to Canada, with the aid of local whites. The preacher and his helpers were then brought to trial for aiding the slave to escape. The jury failed to convict them, however, because one member refused to find them guilty. Later, the member who had refused to vote for conviction related that he himself had driven Shadrach across the Canadian border to freedom.

Another incident occurred in 1854, when Anthony Burns, an escaped Virginia slave, was captured and held for his master. The Boston Vigilance Committee attempted to rescue Burns by force but was deterred by the armed guard surrounding the fugitive.

Burns was returned to his southern master but later was released as a result of legal proceedings in the United States courts.

Other northern states were sympathetic to the escaping fugitives. In Vermont one judge refused to return an escaped slave to the master who claimed him. The judge exclaimed that he would be satisfied with "nothing less than a bill of sale from the Almighty" as proof of ownership. And thus the controversy grew between North and South over the legality versus the morality of the Fugitive Slave Act.

In 1859, John Brown led his famous raid on Harpers Ferry, Virginia. In the North, Brown was heralded as a hero; in the South, he was regarded as a traitor and a menace to the country. The Negro, a pawn in the struggle over economic, political and moral objectives, had but to stand back and watch the opposing sides prepare for their march toward Armageddon.

PICTURE ALBUM

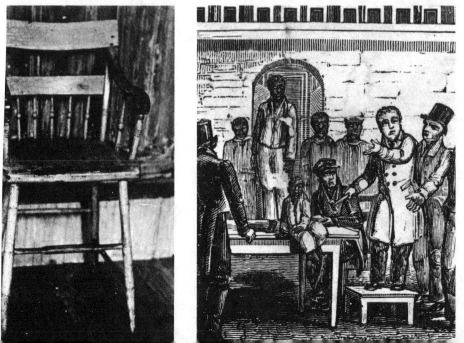

THE SLAVE TRADE

WHILE HUMAN BEINGS were being torn from their homelands, heartless men grew rich. The resulting prosperity blinded nations to the horrors of the slave trade, and an elaborate enterprise developed. The hunting and imprisonment of men, the transporting of human cargoes and, finally, the auctioning of slaves, fostered ruthlessness and inhumanity in those participating in the trade.

Africa was left behind . . . and so was freedom. The terror and grief of leaving homes and families were aggravated by the attendant misery of living in confined and crowded quarters surrounded by filth.

By 1808 men were sufficiently shocked by the evils of the slave trade to pass laws preventing its continuance.

Slave galleys were fitted and launched from major European ports to pick up their human cargo in Afr

Slaves were brought to markets and shore points in coffles.

At various points along the African coast, the captured slaves were forced to await the slave galleys.

Slaves suffering from diseases were left on shore to die.

When battling high seas and rough weather, or when being pursued by hostile vessels, many slave ships met with disaster.

SLAVERY IN THE UNITED STATES

Slave life in the United States began with the fall of the auctioneer's gavel. Once unloaded from the galleys, slaves were dressed up for display like merchandise in a store window, subjected to the ruthless scrutiny of prospective buyers and sold to the highest bidder.

Human beings were bought and sold on the auction block.

The miserable conditions of slavery included poverty, inadequate housing, hunger and illness.

The cooking hearth was often the only source of light and warmth in the barren slave quarters.

Though his clothing is tattered and his cabin windowless, this old man would have been considered fortunate by many slaves whose living conditions were far worse.

To the generations born into slavery, the future held little hope for a better life.

INSTITUTIONAL LIFE

THE EARLIEST EFFORTS by blacks to organize can be seen in the formation of church groups. Tired of being under the guidance of white church leaders, free Negroes began to establish and direct their own religious organizations.

The earliest Negro house of worship, founded by Richard Allen in 1794, was the Bethel African Methodist Episcopal (A.M.E.) Church in Philadelphia. It was from this humble beginning that nearly all organized institutional life among Negroes developed.

MOTHER BETHEL
(FOUNDED BY RICHARD ALLEN)
AFRICAN METHODIST EPISCOPAL CHURCH
has occupied this site continuously since its founding
and in its earliest years enjoyed the active
financial and moral support of Dr Benjamin Rush
Signer of the Declaration of Independence

Its significant relationship
to the historic events commemorated by
INDEPENDENCE NATIONAL HISTORICAL PARK
is hereby recognized by
THE NATIONAL PARK SERVICE
U.S.DEPARTMENT OF THE INTERIOR

The Bethel Hymn

The God of Bethel heard her cries,
He let his power be seen;
He stopp'd the proud oppressor's frown,
And proved himself a King.

Thou sav'd them in the trying hour,
Ministers and councils joined,
And all stood ready to retain
That helpless church of Thine.

Bethel surrounded by her foes,
But not yet in despair,
Christ heard her supplicating cries;
The God of Bethel heard.

Souvenir Historical Chart.

FIRST PLACE OF MEETING.

FIRST BRICK CHURCH.

Pastors of Bethel Church, Phila.,
from 1816 to 1899.

RICHARD ALLEN,
RICHARD WILLIAMS,
JACOB TAPSCIO,
WILLIAM CORNISH,
MORRIS BROWN,
JOSEPH COX,
WILLIAM MOORE,
JOHN CORNISH,
WILLIS NAZERY,
HENRY J. YOUNG,
HENRY DAVIS,
RICHARD ROBINSON,
*JOHN CORNISH,
W. D. W. SCHUREMAN,
JOSHUA WOODLAND,
J. P. CAMPBELL,
*WILLIAM MOORE,

* Served two terms.

Pastors of Bethel Church, Phila.
from 1816 to 1899.

JAMES HOLLEN,
D. DORRELL,
J. M. WILLIAMS,
*HENRY J. YOUNG,
THEODORE GOULD,
R. F. WAYMAN,
G. C. WHITFIELD,
L. J. COPPIN,
J. S. THOMPSON,
C. C. FELTS,
*J. S. THOMPSON,
J. W. BECKETT,
C. T. SHAFFER,
W. H. HEARD,
W. D. COOK,
*T. GOULD,
*L. J. COPPIN,

* Served two terms.

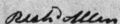

First Bishop,
Born Feb. 14, 1760. Died Mar. 26, 1831.

Successors :

2. MORRIS BROWN,
3. EDWARD WATERS,
4. WM. PAUL QUINN,
5. WILLIS NAZERY,
6. D. A. PAYNE,
7. A. W. WAYMAN,
8. J. P. CAMPBELL,
9. J. A. SHORTER,
10. T. M. D. WARD,
11. J. M. BROWN,
12. H. M. TURNER,
13. W. F. DICKERSON,
14. R. H. CAIN,
15. R. R. DISNEY,
16. W. J. GAINES,
17. B. W. ARNETT,
18. B. T. TANNER,
19. A. GRANT,
20. B. F. LEE,
21. M. B. SALTER,
22. J. A. HANDY,
23. W. B. DERRICK,
24. J. H. ARMSTRONG,
25. J. C. EMBRY.

THE PRESENT CHURCH.

BAND TICKET....BETHEL CHURCH.

If ye then be risen with Christ, seek those things
which are above, where Christ sitteth on the right
hand of God.   Col. iii. 1.

Minister.

FAC SIMILE OF FIRST LOVE FEAST TICKET.

Observe the Landmarks.

The African Methodist Episcopal Church takes great pride in its past,
its first Bethel Church and its first bishop, Richard Allen.

An early view of the Mother Bethel A.M.E. Church.

The original pulpit from which Richard Allen preached.

*The first bishop's chair still sits
in the Mother Bethel Church.*

COLONIZATION AND ABOLITION

RESENTMENT AGAINST SLAVERY grew steadily. Slaves worked tirelessly to buy their freedom. Some emancipated blacks dreamed of returning to Africa and attempted to join with others to set up a colony there. Others favored settling in remote areas of the United States where they could establish black states. Some were determined to make a place for themselves in the mainstream of white society. But both blacks and concerned whites agreed that slavery must be abolished.

Free blacks who were jailed and unable to pay their fines were often sold back into slavery.

264

While the controversy raged over colonization, one black man left his home for the distant shore of Liberia. Daniel Dashiel Warner, born free in Baltimore County, Maryland, in 1815, moved to Monrovia in West Africa in 1823 to start a shipping business and eventually became President of Liberia.

THE

COLONIZATION SCHEME CONSIDERED,

IN

ITS REJECTION BY THE COLORED PEOPLE—IN ITS

TENDENCY TO UPHOLD CASTE—IN ITS

UNFITNESS FOR CHRISTIANIZING AND CIVILIZING

THE ABORIGINES OF AFRICA,

AND FOR PUTTING A STOP TO

THE AFRICAN SLAVE TRADE:

IN A LETTER TO

THE HON. THEODORE FRELINGHUYSEN

AND

THE HON. BENJAMIN F. BUTLER;

BY

SAMUEL E. CORNISH AND THEODORE S. WRIGHT,

PASTORS OF THE COLORED PRESBYTERIAN CHURCHES IN THE CITIES OF

NEWARK AND NEW YORK.

NEWARK:

PRINTED BY AARON GUEST, 191 MARKET-STREET.

1840.

Two free blacks, Samuel E. Cornish and Theodore S. Wright, expressed their opposition to colonization in this pamphlet.

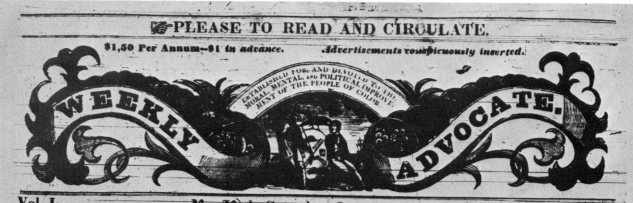

Robert Purvis, the famous Negro Abolitionist.

THE

ANTI-SLAVERY HARP:

A

COLLECTION OF SONGS

FOR

ANTI-SLAVERY MEETINGS.

COMPILED BY

WILLIAM W. BROWN.

SECOND EDITION.

BOSTON
PUBLISHED BY BELA MARSH, NO. 25 CORNHILL.
1849.

THE UNDERGROUND RAILROAD

At a time when abolitionist sentiment was at a peak and when all avenues of escape from bondage were being anxiously explored, hopes and ideas combined to bring about the formation of the Underground Railroad. Through its efforts families were reunited, freedom was purchased and fugitives were given refuge. Efforts were made to educate those it had guided into freedom. Through its innumerable good works, it proved itself one of the greatest benefactors of the Negro.

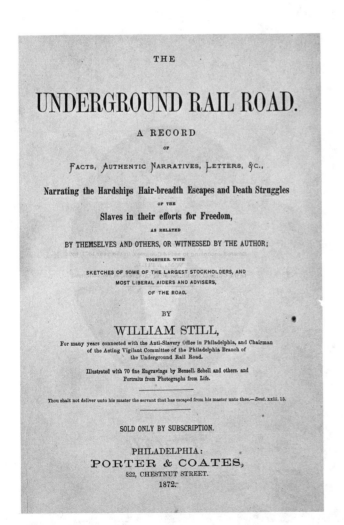

THE

UNDERGROUND RAIL ROAD.

A RECORD

OF

FACTS, AUTHENTIC NARRATIVES, LETTERS, &c.,

Narrating the Hardships Hair-breadth Escapes and Death Struggles

OF THE

Slaves in their efforts for Freedom,

AS RELATED

BY THEMSELVES AND OTHERS, OR WITNESSED BY THE AUTHOR;

TOGETHER WITH

SKETCHES OF SOME OF THE LARGEST STOCKHOLDERS, AND
MOST LIBERAL AIDERS AND ADVISERS,
OF THE ROAD.

BY

WILLIAM STILL,

For many years connected with the Anti-Slavery Office in Philadelphia, and Chairman
of the Acting Vigilant Committee of the Philadelphia Branch of
the Underground Rail Road.

Illustrated with 70 fine Engravings by Bensell, Schell and others, and
Portraits from Photographs from Life.

Thou shalt not deliver unto his master the servant that has escaped from his master unto thee.—*Deut.* xxiii. 15.

SOLD ONLY BY SUBSCRIPTION.

PHILADELPHIA:
PORTER & COATES,
822, CHESTNUT STREET.
1872.

267

Homes such as the Magee House in Canisteo, New York, served as stations for the Underground Railroad.

The overwhelming desire to escape bondage saw the fugitive slaves through many perils.

Traveling at night to avoid pursuers, slaves took to the rivers to erase their tracks.

The Underground Railroad often arranged for fugitives to travel in groups to the safety of the northern states and Canada.

Marie Weems, in a man's suit of clothes and using the alias Jo Wright, fled from a harsh master at the age of fifteen. Only after her safe arrival in New York did she abandon her disguise. From there, through the kindness of many new friends, she traveled to Canada to receive an education.

John Hall was freed from slavery by his courageous Irish sweetheart who was able to make arrangements for his escape. They were eventually reunited in Canada, where they married.

Fugitives utilized ingenious disguises and deceptions to evade slave-catchers and to slip into areas of safety as quietly as possible. Arrest was feared as greatly as death.

Capture was often followed by severe punishment.

Incidents of violence and rebellion continued to increase, until they culminated, eventually, in the Civil War.

Bibliography

BIOGRAPHICAL WORKS

ADAMS, RUSSELL L. *Great Negroes, Past and Present*. Chicago, 1963.

BAKER, HENRY. "Benjamin Banneker, the Negro Mathematician and Astronomer," *Journal of Negro History* III (April 1918).

BALL, CHARLES. *Fifty Years in Chains: Or the Life of an American Slave*. New York, 1859.

BARNES, GILBERT H., and DUMOND, DWIGHT L. *Letters of Theodore Dwight Weld, Angelina Grimké Weld and Sarah Grimké, 1822–1844*. New York, 1934.

BARTLETT, IRVING H. *Wendell Phillips: Brahmin Radical*. Boston, 1961.

BEATTIE, JESSIE L. *Black Moses: The Real Uncle Tom*. Toronto, 1957.

BIBB, HENRY. *Narrative of the Life and Adventures of Henry Bibb, an American Slave*. New York, 1849.

BILLINGTON, RAY ALLEN. "James Forten: Forgotten Abolitionist," *Negro History Bulletin*, XIII (November 1949).

BIRNEY, CATHERINE H. *The Grimké Sisters: Sarah and Angelina Grimké, the First American Women Advocates of Abolition and Women's Rights*. Boston, 1885.

BIRNEY, WILLIAM. *James G. Birney and His Times*. New York, 1890.

BLUETT, THOMAS. *Some Memoirs of the Life of Job . . . Who Was a Slave About Two Years in Maryland*. London, 1734.

BRADFORD, SARAH. *Harriet Tubman: The Moses of Her People*. New York, 1961.

BREWER, W. M. "Henry Highland Garnet," *Journal of Negro History,* XIII (January 1928).

———. "John B. Russworm," *ibid.,* XIII (October 1928).

BROOKES, GEORGE S. *Friend Anthony Benezet*. Philadelphia, 1937.

BROWN, HENRY BOX, *Narrative of the Life of Henry Box Brown*. Manchester, England, 1851.

BROWN, WILLIAM WELLS. *The Black Man: His Antecedents, His Genius and His Achievements*. New York, 1863.

———. *Narrative of William W. Brown, a Fugitive Slave*. Boston, 1847.

———. *The Rising Son: Or the Antecedents and Advancements of the Colored Race*. Boston, 1874.

BRUCE, HENRY. *The New Man: Twenty-nine Years a Slave, Twenty-nine Years a Free Man*. York, Pa., 1895.

BUCKMASTER, HENRIETTA. *Women Who Shaped History*. New York, 1965.

CADE, JOHN B. "Out of the Mouths of Ex-Slaves," *Journal of Negro History,* XX (July 1935).

CHERRY, GWENDOLYN, THOMAS, RUBY, and WILLIS, PAULINE. *Portraits in Color: The Lives of Colorful Negro Women*. Paterson, N.J., 1962.

CHESNUTT, CHARLES WADDELL. *Frederick Douglass*. Boston, 1899.

CLARKE, LEWIS. *Narrative of the Sufferings of Lewis and Milton Clarke . . . during a Captivity of More Than Twenty Years among the Slaveholders of Kentucky*. Boston, 1846.

COAN, JOSEPHUS R. *Daniel Alexander Payne, Christian Educator*. Philadelphia, 1935.

COFFIN, LEVI. *Reminiscences of Levi Coffin*. Cincinnati, 1880.

CONRAD, EARL. *Harriet Tubman*. Washington, 1943.

COOLEY, TIMOTHY MATHER. *Sketches of the Life and Character of the Rev. Lemuel Haynes*. New York, 1837.

CRAFT, WILLIAM, and CRAFT, ELLEN. *Running a Thousand Miles for Freedom*. London, 1860.

DANNETT, SYLVIA G. (ed.). *Profiles of Negro Womanhood: 1619–1900*. Yonkers, N.Y., 1964.

DAVIS, EDWIN A., and HOGAN, WILLIAM R. *The Barber of Natchez*. Baton Rouge, 1954.

DAVIS, NOAH. *The Narrative of the Life of Rev. Noah Davis, a Colored Man*. Baltimore, 1859.

DOUGLASS, FREDERICK. *The Life and Times of Frederick Douglass*. Hartford, Conn. 1881.

———. *My Bondage and My Freedom*. New York, 1855.

———. *Narrative of the Life of Frederick Douglass, an American Slave*. Boston, 1845; Cambridge, Mass., 1960.

DU BOIS, W. E. B. *John Brown*. Philadelphia, 1909.

DUMOND, DWIGHT L. *Letters of James Gillespie Birney, 1831–57*. 2 vols. New York, 1938.

FAUSET, ARTHUR HUFF. *Sojourner Truth: God's Faithful Pilgrim*. Chapel Hill, N.C., 1938.

FELDMAN, EUGENE P. R. (ed.). *Figures in Negro History*. Chicago, 1964.

FISHER, MILES M. *The Master's Slave: Elijah John Fisher*. Philadelphia, 1922.

FLADELAND, BETTY. *James Gillespie Birney: Slaveholder to Abolitionist*. Ithaca, N.Y., 1955.

FONER, PHILIP S. (ed.). *The Life and Writings of Frederick Douglas*. 4 vols. New York, 1950–1955.

FORTEN, CHARLOTTE L. *The Journal of Charlotte L. Forten: A Free Negro in the Slave Era*, ed. RAY ALLEN BILLINGTON. New York, 1961.

FULLER, EDMUND. *A Star Pointed North*. New York, 1946.

GARRISON, WENDELL P., and GARRISON, FRANCIS J. *William Lloyd Garrison, 1805–1879: The Story of His Life Told by His Children*. 4 vols. Boston, 1894.

GRAHAM, SHIRLEY. *The Story of Phillis Wheatley*. New York, 1949.

———. *There Once Was a Slave: The Heroic Story of Frederick Douglass*. New York, 1947.

———. *Your Most Humble Servant: The Story of Benjamin Banneker*. New York, 1949.

GRIGGS, E. L. *Thomas Clarkson: Friend of Slaves*. London, 1936.

GRIMKÉ, ARCHIBALD H. *William Lloyd Garrison, the Abolitionist*. New York, 1891.

HAMMON, BRITON. *A Narrative of the Uncommon Sufferings and Surprizing Deliverance of Briton Hammon, a Negro Man*. Boston, 1760.

HARLOW, RALPH V. *Gerrit Smith: Philanthropist and Reformer*. New York, 1939.

HAWKINS, WILLIAM G. *"Lunsford Lane": Another Helper from North Carolina*. Boston, 1863.

HEARD, WILLIAM H. *From Slavery to the Bishopric of the A.M.E. Church*. Philadelphia, 1924.

HENSON, JOSIAH. *Truth Stranger than Fiction: Father Henson's Story of His Own Life*. With an Introduction by HARRIET BEECHER STOWE. Cleveland, 1858.

HIGGINSON, THOMAS WENTWORTH. *Contemporaries*. Cambridge, Mass., 1900.

HILDRETH, RICHARD. *The Slave: Or Memoirs of Archy Moore*. Boston, 1836.

HOLLAND, FREDERIC M. *Frederick Douglass, the Colored Orator*. New York, 1891.

HUGHES, LANGSTON. *Famous American Negroes*. New York, 1954.

HUGHES, LOUIS. *Thirty Years a Slave: From Bondage to Freedom*. Milwaukee, 1897.

JOHNSTON, JOHANNA. *Runaway to Heaven: The Story of Harriet Beecher Stowe*. New York, 1963.

JULIAN, GEORGE W. *The Life of Joshua R. Giddings*. Indianapolis, 1892.

KORNGOLD, RALPH. *Citizen Toussaint*. Boston, 1944.

———. *Thaddeus Stevens*. New York, 1955.

LANE, LUNSFORD. *The Narrative of Lunsford Lane*. Boston, 1845.

LERNER, GERDA. *The Grimké Sisters from South Carolina: Rebels against Slavery*. Boston, 1967.

LOGAN, RAYFORD W. (ed.). *Memoirs of a Monticello Slave*. Charlottesville, Va. 1951.

LOGUEN, J. W. *The Rev. J. W. Loguen, as a Slave and as a Freeman*. Syracuse, N.Y., 1859.

LUNDY, BENJAMIN. *The Diary of Benjamin Lundy*, ed. FRED LANDON. Toronto, 1921.

———. *The Life, Travels and Opinions of Benjamin Lundy, Including His Journey to Texas and Mexico: With a Sketch of Contemporary Events and a Notice of the Revolution in Hayti*. Philadelphia, 1847.

MAGOUN, F. ALEXANDER. *Amos Fortune's Choice: The Story of a Negro Slave's Struggle for Self-Fulfillment*. Freeport, Me., 1964.

MALVIN, JOHN. *Autobiography*. Cleveland, 1879.

MATHEWS, MARCIA M. *Richard Allen*. Baltimore, 1963.

MERRILL, WALTER M. *Against Wind and Tide: A Biography of William Lloyd Garrison*. Cambridge, Mass., 1963.

MOORE, JOHN H. "Simon Gray, Riverman: A Slave Who Was Almost Free," *Mississippi Valley Historical Review*, XLIX (December 1962).

MORSE, W. H. "Lemuel Haynes," *Journal of Negro History*, IV (January 1919).

MOTT, ABIGAIL. *Biographical Sketches and Interesting Anecdotes of Persons of Color*. New York, 1826.

NORTHUP, SOLOMON. *Twelve Years a Slave*, ed. SUE EAKIN and JOSEPH LOGSDON. Baton Rouge, 1968.

PAULI, HERTHA. *Her Name Was Sojourner Truth*. New York, 1962.

PAYNE, DANIEL ALEXANDER. *Recollections of Seventy Years.* Nashville, Tenn., 1888.

PENNINGTON, JAMES W. C. *The Fugitive Blacksmith: Or Events in the History of James W. C. Pennington.* London, 1850.

PORTER, DOROTHY B. "David Ruggles, an Apostle of Human Rights," *Journal of Negro History,* XXVIII (January 1943).

QUARLES, BENJAMIN. *Frederick Douglass.* Washington, 1948.

REDDING, J. SAUNDERS. *The Lonesome Road.* Garden City, N.Y., 1958.

ROGERS, JOEL AUGUSTUS. *World's Great Men of Color: 3000 B.C.—1946 A.D.* 2 vols. New York, 1946–1947.

ROLLIN, FRANK A. *Life and Public Services of Martin R. Delany.* Boston, 1868.

ROPER, MOSES. *Narrative of the Adventures and Escape of Moses Roper, from American Slavery.* London, 1837.

RUSH, BENJAMIN. *The Autobiography of Benjamin Rush,* ed. GEORGE W. CORNER. Princeton, N.J., 1948.

SEEBER, EDWARD D. "Phillis Wheatley," *Journal of Negro History,* XXIV (July 1939).

SHERWOOD, HENRY N. *Paul Cuffe.* Washington, 1923.

SIMMONS, WILLIAM J. *Men of Mark: Eminent, Progressive and Rising.* Cleveland, 1887.

SMITH, JAMES MCCUNE. *Toussaint L'Ouverture.* New York, 1841.

STEWARD, AUSTIN. *Twenty-two Years a Slave, and Forty Years a Freeman.* Rochester, N.Y., 1857.

TAPPAN, LEWIS. *The Life of Arthur Tappan.* New York, 1870.

THOMAS, BENJAMIN P. *Theodore Weld, Crusader for Freedom.* New Brunswick, N.J., 1950.

THOMAS, JOHN L. *The Liberator: William Lloyd Garrison, a Biography.* Boston, 1963.

THOMPSON, JOHN. *The Life of John Thompson, a Fugitive Slave.* Worcester, Mass., 1856.

TRUTH, SOJOURNER. *Narrative of Sojourner Truth.* Boston, 1875.

VASSA, GUSTAVUS. *The Interesting Narrative of the Life of Olaudah Equiano, or Gustavus Vassa, the African.* London, 1789.

VAUX, ROBERT. *Memoirs of the Life of Anthony Benezet.* New York, 1817.

VILLARD, OSWALD GARRISON. *John Brown, 1800–1859.* Boston, 1910.

WALSER, RICHARD G. *The Black Poet: Being the . . . Story . . . of George Moses Horton, a North Carolina Slave.* New York, 1966.

WARD, SAMUEL RINGGOLD. *Autobiography of a Fugitive Negro.* London, 1855.

WASHINGTON, BOOKER T. *Frederick Douglass.* Philadelphia, 1906.

WESLEY, CHARLES H. *Richard Allen: Apostle of Freedom.* Washington, 1935.

WHITNEY, JANET PAYNE. *John Woolman, American Quaker.* Boston, 1942.

WORK, MONROE N. "The Life of Charles B. Ray," *Journal of Negro History,* IV (October 1919).

YATES, ELIZABETH. *Prudence Crandall: Woman of Courage.* New York, 1955.

GENERAL HISTORY AND LIFE IN THE UNITED STATES

CLARK, GEORGE L. *A History of Connecticut.* New York, 1914.

CRAVEN, WESLEY F. *The Southern Colonies in the Seventeenth Century, 1607–1689.* Baton Rouge, 1949.

DEGLER, CARL. *Out of Our Past: The Forces That Shaped Modern America.* New York, 1959.

GEWEHR, WESLEY M. *The Great Awakening in Virginia, 1740–1790.* Durham, N.C., 1930.

HESSELTINE, WILLIAM B. *History of the South.* New York, 1936.

HUNDLEY, DANIEL R. *Social Relations in Our Southern States.* New York, 1860.

JEFFERSON, THOMAS. *Notes on the State of Virginia.* Paris, 1784–1785.

JOHNSON, GUION G. *Ante-Bellum North Carolina.* Chapel Hill, N.C., 1937.

———. *A Social History of the Sea Islands.* Chapel Hill, N.C., 1930.

MCCRADY, EDWARD. *History of South Carolina under the Proprietary Government, 1670–1719.* New York, 1897.

PAGE, THOMAS NELSON. *The Old South: Essays Social and Political.* New York, 1892.

SCOTT, JOHN A. (ed.). *Living Documents in American History.* New York, 1963.

WEEDEN, W. B. *Economic and Social History of New England, 1620–1789.* Boston, 1890.

THE AFRICAN BACKGROUND

AFRICANUS, JOANNES LEO. *The History and Description of Africa.* London, 1896.

BOAS, FRANZ. *Old African Civilizations.* Atlanta, Ga., 1906.

DAVIDSON, BASIL. *Africa: History of a Continent.* London, 1966.

———. *African Kingdoms.* New York, 1966.

———. *The Lost Cities of Africa.* Boston, 1959.

———. *Old Africa Rediscovered.* London, 1959.

DELAFOSSE, MAURICE. *The Negroes of Africa.* Washington, 1931.

ELLIS, GEORGE W. *Negro Culture in West Africa.* New York, 1914.

FAGE, J. D. *An Introduction to the History of West Africa.* Cambridge, England, 1959.

FROBENIUS, LEO. *The Origin of African Civilizations.* Washington, 1898.

HERSKOVITS, MELVILLE J. *Dahomey: An Ancient West African Kingdom.* 2 vols. New York, 1938.

———. "On the Provenience of the New World Negroes," *Social Forces,* XII (December 1933).

JOHNSON, JAMES WELDON. *Native African Races and Culture.* Charlottesville, Va., 1927.

KIMBLE, GEORGE H. T. *Tropical Africa.* St. Louis, 1966.

MOORE, FRANCIS. *Travels into the Inland Parts of Africa.* London, 1738.

MURDOCK, GEORGE PETER. *Africa, Its Peoples and Their Cultural History.* New York, 1959.

WOODSON, CARTER G. *The African Background Outlined.* Washington, 1936.

THE NEGRO IN AMERICA

GENERAL HISTORY

APTHEKER, HERBERT. *Essays in the History of the American Negro.* New York, 1945.

———. *To Be Free: Studies in American Negro History.* New York, 1948.

———. *Toward Negro Freedom.* New York, 1956.

——— (ed.). *A Documentary History of the Negro People in the United States.* 2 vols. New York, 1951.

BARDOLPH, RICHARD. *The Negro Vanguard.* New York, 1959.

BENNETT, LERONE, JR. *Before the Mayflower: A History of the Negro in America, 1619–1964.* Chicago, 1964.

BONTEMPS, ARNA W. *The Story of the Negro.* New York, 1955.

BRAWLEY, BENJAMIN G. *A Social History of the American Negro.* New York, 1921.

BROWN, INA CORRINNE. *The Story of the American Negro.* New York, 1957.

CALDWELL, ARTHUR B. (ed.). *History of the American Negro.* Atlanta, Ga., 1919.

CHAMBERS, LUCILLE A. *America's Tenth Man.* New York, 1957.

CREGER, RALPH, and CREGER, CARL. *This Is What We Found.* New York, 1960.

CROMWELL, JOHN W. *The Negro in American History.* Washington, 1914.

CUBAN, LARRY. *The Negro in America.* Chicago, 1964.

DAVIS, JOHN P. (ed.). *The American Negro Reference Book.* Englewood Cliffs, N.J., 1966.

DU BOIS, W. E. B. *Black Folk, Then and Now: An Essay in the History and Sociology of the Negro Race.* New York, 1939.

———, and JOHNSON, GUY B. *Encyclopedia of the Negro.* New York, 1946.

EMBREE, EDWIN R. *Brown Americans: The Story of a Tenth of the Nation.* New York, 1943.

EPPSE, MERLE R. *The Negro, Too, in American History.* Chicago, 1939.

———, and FOSTER, A. P. *Elementary History of America: Including the Contributions of the Negro Race.* Nashville, Tenn., 1939.

FOSTER, WILLIAM Z. *The Negro People in American History.* New York, 1954.

FRANKLIN, JOHN HOPE. *From Slavery to Freedom: A History of American Negroes.* New York, 1967.

———. "The New Negro History," *Journal of Negro History,* XLII (April 1957).

FRAZIER, E. FRANKLIN. *The Negro in the United States.* New York, 1957.

GARNET, HENRY HIGHLAND. *The Past and the Present Condition, and the Destiny, of the Colored Race.* Troy, N.Y., 1848.

GINZBERG, ELI, and EICHNER, ALFRED S. *The Troublesome Presence: American Democracy and the Negro.* New York, 1964.

GRANT, JOANNE. *Black Protest.* New York, 1968.

HARLAN, LOUIS R. *The Negro in American History.* Washington, 1965.

HERSKOVITS, MELVILLE J. *The Myth of the Negro Past.* Boston, 1958.

JOHNSON, CHARLES S. *The Negro in American Civilization.* New York, 1930.

JOHNSON, EDMUND A. *A School History of the Negro Race in America, from 1619 to 1890.* Philadelphia, 1892.

KAISER, ERNEST. "Trends in American Negro Historiography," *Journal of Negro Education,* XXXI (Fall 1962).

LAWSON, ELIZABETH. *Study Outline History of the American Negro People, 1619–1918.* New York, 1939.

LITWACK, LEON F. *North of Slavery: The Negro in the Free States, 1790–1860.* Chicago, 1961.

LIVERMORE, GEORGE. *An Historical Research Respecting the Opinions of the Founders of the Republic on Negroes as Slaves, as Citizens and as Soldiers.* Boston, 1862.

LOGAN, RAYFORD W. *The Negro in the United States: A Brief Review.* Princeton, N.J., 1957.

MELTZER, MILTON (ed.). *In Their Own Words: A History of the American Negro, 1619–1865.* Vol. I. New York, 1964.

NORDHOLT-SCHULTE, J. W., SR. *The People That Walk in Darkness.* New York, 1956.

OTTLEY, ROI. *Black Odyssey.* New York, 1948.

PENNINGTON, JAMES W. C. *A Textbook of the Origin and History of the Colored People.* Hartford, Conn., 1841.

QUARLES, BENJAMIN. "Letters from Negro Leaders to Gerrit Smith," *Journal of Negro History,* XXVII (October 1942).

———. *The Negro in the Making of America.* New York, 1964.

REDDING, J. SAUNDERS. *They Came in Chains: Americans from Africa.* Philadelphia, 1950.

SAVAGE, W. SHERMAN. "The Negro in the Westward Movement," *Journal of Negro History,* XXV (October 1940).

SLOAN, IRVING J. *The American Negro: A Chronology and Fact Book.* Dobbs Ferry, N. Y., 1965.

STARKEY, MARION L. *Striving To Make It My Home: The Story of Americans from Africa.* New York, 1964.

TANNENBAUM, FRANK. *Slave and Citizen: The Negro in the Americas.* New York, 1947.

TAYLOR, ALRUTHEUS A. "Movement of the Negroes from the East to the Gulf States from 1830 to 1850," *Journal of Negro History,* VIII (October 1923).

THORPE, EARL E. *The Mind of the Negro: An Intellectual History of Afro-Americans.* Baton Rouge, 1961.

U.S. BUREAU OF THE CENSUS. *Negro Population in the United States: 1790–1915.* Washington, 1918.

VAN DEUSEN, JOHN G. *The Black Man in White America.* Washington, 1938.

WADE, RICHARD C. *The Negro in American Life.* New York, 1966.

WASHINGTON, BOOKER T. *The Story of the Negro: The Rise of the Race from Slavery.* Garden City, N.Y., 1909.

WEATHERFORD, WILLIS D. *The Negro from Africa to America.* New York, 1924.

WESLEY, CHARLES H. *Negro Labor in the United States, 1850–1925: A Study in American Economic History.* New York, 1927.

———. "The Negro's Struggle for Freedom in Its Birthplace," *Journal of Negro History,* XXX (January 1945).

WILLIAMS, GEORGE WASHINGTON. *History of the Negro Race in America, from 1619 to 1880.* New York, 1882.

WOODSON, CARTER G. *The Education of the Negro prior to 1861.* Washington, 1915.

———. *Negro Orators and Their Orations.* Washington, 1925.

———. *The Story of the Negro Retold.* Washington, 1959.

——— (ed.). *The Mind of the Negro: As Reflected in Letters Written during the Crisis, 1800–1860.* Washington, 1926.

WOODSON, CARTER G., and WESLEY, CHARLES H. *The Negro in Our History.* Washington, 1962.

WOODWARD, C. VANN. "Flight from History: The Heritage of the Negro," *Nation,* CCI (September 20, 1965).

WRIGHT, RICHARD. *Twelve Million Black Voices: A Folk History of the Negro in the United States.* New York, 1941.

LOCAL HISTORY

ALLEN, JAMES EGERT. *The Negro in New York: A Historical-Biographical Evaluation from 1626.* New York, 1964.

ALLEN, RICHARD, and JONES, ABSALOM. *A Narrative of the Proceedings of the Black People during the Late Awful Calamity in Philadelphia, in the Year 1793.* Philadelphia, 1794.

ANDREWS, CHARLES C. *The History of the New York African Free Schools.* New York, 1830.

BARTLETT, IRVING H. *From Slave to Citizen: The Story of the Negro in Rhode Island.* Providence, 1954.

BOYKIN, JAMES H. *The Negro in North Carolina prior to 1861.* New York, 1958.

ERNST, ROBERT. "The Economic Status of New York City Negroes, 1850–63," *Negro History Bulletin,* XII (March 1949).

GREEN, CONSTANCE M. *The Secret City: A History of Race Relations in the Nation's Capital.* Princeton, N.J., 1966.

GREENE, LORENZO J. *The Negro in Colonial New England, 1620–1766.* New York, 1942.

———. "The New England Negro As Seen in Advertisements for Runaway Slaves," *Journal of Negro History,* XXIX (April 1944).

HICKOK, CHARLES T. *The Negro in Ohio, 1802–1870.* Cleveland, 1896.

HIRSCH, LEO H., JR. "The Negro and New York: 1783–1865," *Journal of Negro History,* XVI (October 1931).

INGLE, EDWARD. *The Negro in the District of Columbia.* Baltimore, 1893.

JOHNSON, GUY B. *Folk Culture on St. Helena Island, South Carolina.* Chapel Hill, N.C., 1930.

KLINGBERG, FRANK J. *An Appraisal of the Negro in Colonial South Carolina.* Washington, 1941.

PATTERSON, CALEB P. *The Negro in Tennessee, 1790–1865: A Study in Southern Politics.* Austin, Tex., 1922.

ROUSSÈVE, CHARLES B. *The Negro in Louisiana.* New Orleans, 1937.

RUCHAMES, LOUIS. "Race, Marriage and Abolitionism in Massachusetts," *Journal of Negro History,* XL (July 1955).

SHEELER, J. REUBEN. "The Struggle of the Negro in Ohio for Freedom," *Journal of Negro History,* XXXI (April 1946).

SOUTHALL, EUGENE P. "Negroes in Florida prior to the Civil War," *Journal of Negro History,* XIX (January 1934).

TATE, THAD W., JR. *The Negro in Eighteenth-Century Williamsburg.* Williamsburg, Va., 1965.

THORNBROUGH, EMMA LOU. *The Negro in Indiana.* Indianapolis, 1957.

TURNER, EDWARD R. *The Negro in Pennsylvania: Slavery — Servitude — Freedom, 1639–1861.* Washington, 1911.

WASHINGTON INTERCOLLEGIATE CLUB. *The Negro in Chicago, 1729–1929.* Chicago, 1948.

WRITERS' PROGRAM OF THE WORK PROJECTS ADMINISTRATION. *The Negro in Virginia.* New York, 1940.

FREE NEGROES

CLARKE, JAMES FREEMAN. *Present Condition of the Free Colored People of the United States.* Boston, 1859.

ENGLAND, J. MERTON. "The Free Negro in Ante-Bellum Tennessee," *Journal of Southern History,* IX (February 1943).

FITCHETT, E. HORACE. "The Origin and Growth of the Free Negro Population of Charleston, South Carolina," *Journal of Negro History,* XXVI (October 1941).

FLANDERS, RALPH B. "The Free Negro in Ante-Bellum Georgia," *North Carolina Historical Review,* IX (July 1932).

FRANKLIN, JOHN HOPE. *The Free Negro in North Carolina, 1790–1860.* Chapel Hill, N.C., 1943.

FRAZIER, E. FRANKLIN. *The Free Negro Family: A Study of Family Origins before the Civil War.* Nashville, Tenn., 1932.

JACKSON, LUTHER P. *Free Negro Labor and Property Holding in Virginia, 1830–1860.* New York, 1942.

JAY, WILLIAM. *On the Condition of the Free People of Color in the United States.* New York, 1839.

JOHNSON, FRANKLIN. *The Development of State Legislation concerning the Free Negro.* New York, 1919.

MEHLINGER, LOUIS R. "The Attitude of the Free Negro toward African Colonization," *Journal of Negro History,* I (July 1916).

NELSON, ALICE DUNBAR. "People of Color in Louisiana," *Journal of Negro History,* I (October 1916); II (January 1917).

PENNSYLVANIA SOCIETY FOR PROMOTING THE ABOLITION OF SLAVERY. *The Present State and Condition of the Free People of Color of the City of Philadelphia.* Philadelphia, 1838.

ROGERS, W. McDOWELL. "Free Negro Legislation in Georgia," *Georgia Historical Quarterly,* XVI (March 1932).

RUSSELL, JOHN H. "Colored Freemen as Slaveowners in Virginia," *Journal of Negro History,* I (June 1916).

———. *The Free Negro in Virginia, 1619–1865.* Baltimore, 1913.

SCHOEN, HAROLD. "The Free Negro in the Republic of Texas," *Southwestern Historical Quarterly,* XL (April 1926).

SYDNOR, CHARLES S. "The Free Negro in Mississippi before the Civil War," *American Historical Review,* XXXII (July 1927).

TAYLOR, ROSSER H. *The Free Negro in North Carolina.* Chapel Hill, N.C., 1920.

THOMAS, DAVID Y. "The Free Negro in Florida before 1865," *South Atlantic Quarterly,* X (October 1911).

WOODSON, CARTER G. *Free Negro Heads of Families in the United States in 1830.* Washington, 1925.

———. *Free Negro Owners of Slaves in the United States in 1830.* Washington, 1924.

WRIGHT, JAMES M. *The Free Negro in Maryland, 1634–1860.* New York, 1921.

NEGRO SOLDIERS IN EARLY WARS

APTHEKER, HERBERT. *The Negro in the American Revolution.* New York, 1940.

BAIRD, HENRY CAREY (ed.). *Washington and Jackson on Negro Soldiers.* Philadelphia, 1863.

GARRISON, WILLIAM LLOYD. *The Loyalty and Devotion of Colored Americans in the Revolution and the War of 1812.* Boston, 1861.

GREENE, LORENZO J. "Some Observations on the Black Regiment of Rhode Island in the American Revolution," *Journal of Negro History,* XXXVII (April 1952).

HARTGROVE, W. B. "The Negro Soldier in the American Revolution," *Journal of Negro History,* I (April 1916).

JACKSON, LUTHER P. "Virginia Negro Soldiers and Seamen in the American Revolution," *Journal of Negro History,* XXVII (July 1942).

MOORE, GEORGE H. *Historical Notes on the Employment of Negroes in the American Army of the Revolution.* New York, 1862.

NATIONAL ASSOCIATION FOR THE ADVANCEMENT OF COLORED PEOPLE. *Black Heroes of the American Revolution.* New York, 1965.

NELL, WILLIAM C. *The Colored Patriots of the American Revolution.* Boston, 1855.

———. *Services of Colored Americans in the Wars of 1776 and 1812.* Boston, 1855.

QUARLES, BENJAMIN. *The Negro in the American Revolution.* Chapel Hill, N.C., 1961.

RIDER, SIDNEY S. *An Historical Inquiry concerning the Attempt To Raise a Regiment of Slaves by Rhode Island during the War of the Revolution.* Providence, 1880.

WILKES, LAURA E. *Missing Pages in American History: Revealing the Services of Negroes in the Early Wars in the United States of America, 1641–1815.* Washington, 1919.

WILSON, JOSEPH T. *The Black Phalanx.* Hartford, Conn., 1888.

THE NEGRO, THE LAW AND THE FRANCHISE

ADAMS, JAMES T. "Disfranchisement of Negroes in New England," *American Historical Review,* XXX (April 1925).

BEECHER, CHARLES. *The Duty of Disobedience to Wicked Laws: A Sermon on the Fugitive Slave Law.* New York, 1851.

CATTERALL, HELEN T. (ed.). *Judicial Cases concerning American Slavery and the Negro.* 5 vols. Washington, 1926–1937.

CLARK, ERNEST J. "Aspects of the North Carolina Slave Code, 1715–1860," *North Carolina Historical Review,* XXXIX (April 1962).

COBB, THOMAS R. R., *An Inquiry into the Law of Negro Slavery in the United States of America.* Philadelphia, 1858.

EVANS, EMORY G. (ed.). "A Question of Complexion: Documents concerning the Negro and the Franchise in Eighteenth-Century Virginia," *Virginia Magazine of History and Biography,* LXXI (October 1963).

FOSTER, GUSTAVUS L. *The Doctrine of Subjection to "The Powers That Be," in Its Application to the Fugitive Slave Law.* Jackson, Mich., 1850.

FOX, JOHN. *Opinion against Negro Suffrage in Pennsylvania.* Harrisburg, Pa., 1838.

GOODELL, WILLIAM. *The American Slave Code in Theory and Practice: Its Distinctive Features Shown by Its Statutes, Judicial Decisions and Illustrative Facts.* New York, 1853.

GUILD, JUNE P. *Black Laws of Virginia.* Richmond, Va., 1936.

HOLLANDER, BARNETT. *Slavery in America: Its Legal History.* New York, 1964.

HOPKINS, VINCENT C. *Dred Scott's Case.* New York, 1951.

HURD, JOHN C. *The Law of Freedom and Bondage in the United States.* 2 vols. New York, 1858–1862.

McDOUGALL, MARION G. *Fugitive Slaves, 1619–1865.* Boston, 1891.

MARCUS [pseud.]. *An Examination of the Expediency and Constitutionality of Prohibiting Slavery in the State of Missouri.* New York, 1819.

Memorial of Thirty Thousand Disfranchised Citizens of Philadelphia to the Honorable Senate and House of Representatives. Philadelphia, 1855.

MOORE, WILBERT E. "Slave Law and the Social Structure," *Journal of Negro History,* XXVI (April 1941).

NYE, RUSSEL B. *Fettered Freedom: Civil Liberties and the Slavery Controversy, 1830–1860.* East Lansing, Mich., 1949.

OLBRICH, EMIL. *The Development of Sentiment on Negro Suffrage, to 1860.* Madison, Wis., 1912.

SHUGG, ROGER W. "Negro Voting in the Ante-Bellum South," *Journal of Negro History,* XXI (October 1936).

SIRMANS, M. EUGENE. "The Legal Status of the Slave in South Carolina, 1670–1740," *Journal of Southern History,* XXVIII (November 1962).

SMITH, GERRIT. *Abstract of the Argument on the Fugitive Slave Law: Made by Gerrit Smith in Syracuse, June 1852, on the Trial of Henry W. Allen, U.S. Deputy Marshal, for Kidnapping.* Syracuse, N.Y., 1852.

SNETHEN, WORTHINGTON G. *The Black Code of the District of Columbia, in Force September 1st, 1848.* New York, 1848.

SOULSBY, HUGH G. *The Right of Search and the Slave Trade in Anglo-American Relations, 1814–1862.* Baltimore, 1933.

STROUD, GEORGE M. *A Sketch of the Laws Relating to Slavery in the Several States of the United States of America.* Philadelphia, 1827.

WESLEY, CHARLES H. *Negro Citizenship in the United States.* Washington, 1966.

WHEELER, JACOB D. *A Practical Treatise on the Law of Slavery: Being a Compilation of All the Decisions Made on That Subject, in the Several Courts of the United States, and State Courts.* New York, 1837.

WRIGHT, MARION T. "Negro Suffrage in New Jersey, 1776–1875," *Journal of Negro History,* XXXIII (April 1948).

YATES, WILLIAM. *Rights of Colored Men to Suffrage, Citizenship and Trial by Jury.* Philadelphia, 1838.

CHURCHES, ORGANIZATIONS AND INSTITUTIONS

BENNETT, LERONE, JR. "Founders of the Negro Press," *Ebony,* XIX (July 1964).

BRAGG, GEORGE F. *History of the Afro-American Group of the Episcopal Church.* Baltimore, 1922.

CRAWFORD, GEORGE W. *Prince Hall and His Followers.* New York, 1914.

CROMWELL, JOHN W. *The Early Negro Convention Movement.* Washington, 1904.

DAVIS, JOHN W. "George Liele and Andrew Bryan, Pioneer Negro Baptist Preachers," *Journal of Negro History,* III (April 1918).

DE COSTA, B. F. *Three Score and Ten: The Story of St. Philip's Church.* New York, 1889.

DOUGLASS, WILLIAM. *Annals of St. Thomas' Church.* Philadelphia, 1862.

DU BOIS, W. E. B. *The Negro Church.* Atlanta, Ga. 1903.

FRAZIER, E. FRANKLIN. *The Negro Church in America.* New York, 1963.

FULLER, THOMAS O. *History of the Negro Baptists of Tennessee.* Memphis, Tenn., 1935.

GROSS, BELLA. *Clarion Call: The History and Development of the Negro People's Convention Movement in the United States, from 1817 to 1840.* New York, 1947.

———. "The First National Negro Convention," *Journal of Negro History,* XXXI (October 1946).

———. "*Freedom's Journal* and the Rights of All," *ibid.,* XVII (July 1932).

JOHNSTON, RUBY F. *The Development of Negro Religion.* New York, 1954.

KOGER, A. BRISCOE. *History of the Negro Baptists of Maryland, 1836–1936.* Baltimore, 1935.

LOVE, E. K. *History of the First African Baptist Church: From Its Organization, January 20, 1788, to July 1, 1888.* Savannah, Ga., 1888.

PAYNE, DANIEL A. *History of the African Methodist Episcopal Church.* Nashville, Tenn., 1891.

PENN, I. GARLAND. *The Afro-American Press and Its Editors.* Springfield, Mass., 1891.

PORTER, DOROTHY B. "Organized Educational Activities of Negro Literary Societies, 1828–1846," *Journal of Negro Education,* V (October 1936).

SINGLETON, GEORGE A. *The Romance of African Methodism: A Study of the African Methodist Episcopal Church.* New York, 1952.

UPTON, WILLIAM. *Negro Masonry.* Cambridge, Mass., 1902.

VOORHIS, HAROLD VAN BUREN. *Negro Masonry in the United States.* New York, 1940.

WESLEY, CHARLES H. *The History of the Prince Hall Grand Lodge of Free and Accepted Masons of the State of Ohio, 1849–1860: An Epoch in American Fraternalism.* Wilberforce, Ohio, 1961.

WOODSON, CARTER G. *The History of the Negro Church.* Washington, 1945.

ANTI-SLAVERY

ARGUMENTS PRO AND CON

ADAMS, CHARLES FRANCIS. *What Makes Slavery a Question of National Concern? A Lecture, Delivered by Invitation, at New York, January 30, at Syracuse, February 1, 1855.* Boston, 1855.

ARMISTEAD, WILSON. *Five Hundred Thousand Strokes for Freedom: A Series of Anti-Slavery Tracts, of Which Half a Million Are Now First Issued by the Friends of the Negro.* London, 1853.

ATLEE, EDWIN P. *An Address Delivered before the Female Anti-Slavery Society of Philadelphia, in the Session Room of the Second Presbyterian Church (on Cherry Street) in the First Month (January), 1834.* Philadelphia, 1834.

BEECHER, CATHERINE E. *An Essay on Slavery and Abolitionism: With Reference to the Duty of American Females.* Philadelphia, 1837.

BENEZET, ANTHONY. *A Caution and Warning to Great Britain and Her Colonies.* Philadelphia, 1766.

———. *A Serious Address to the Rulers of America on the Inconsistency of Their Conduct Respecting Slavery.* Trenton, N.J., 1783.

BIRNEY, JAMES G., and SCOTT, ORANGE. *Debate on Modern Abolitionism in the General Conference of the Methodist Episcopal Church, Held in Cincinnati, May 1836.* Cincinnati, 1836.

BRANAGAN, THOMAS. *A Preliminary Essay on the Oppression of the Exiled Sons of Africa.* Philadelphia, 1804.

BURRITT, ELIHU. *A Plan of Brotherly Copartnership of the North and South for the Peaceful Extinction of Slavery.* New York, 1856.

CHANNING, WILLIAM ELLERY. *Remarks on the Slavery Question, in a Letter to Jonathan Phillips.* Boston, 1839.

———. *Slavery.* Boston, 1835.

CHASE, SALMON P., and CLEVELAND, CHARLES DEXTER (eds.). *Anti-Slavery Addresses of 1844 and 1845.* Philadelphia, 1867.

CHILD, DAVID LEE. *The Despotism of Freedom, or the Tyranny and Cruelty of American Republican Slave Masters: Shown To Be the Worst in the World.* Boston, 1834.

———. "Texas," *Quarterly Anti-Slavery Magazine,* I (January 1836).

CHILD, LYDIA MARIA. *An Appeal in Favor of That Class of Americans Called Africans.* Boston, 1833.

CLARKSON, THOMAS, et al. *Abstract of the Evidence Delivered before a Select Committee of the House of Commons in the Years 1790 and 1791, on the Part of the Petitioners for the Abolition of the Slave Trade.* London, 1791.

COLEMAN, ELIHU. *A Testimony against That Anti-Christian Practice of Making Slaves of Men.* Nantucket, 1733.

DELANY, MARTIN R. *The Condition, Elevation, Emigration and Destiny of the Colored People of the United States Politically Considered.* Philadelphia, 1852.

DUNCAN, JAMES. *A Treatise on Slavery: In Which Is Shown Forth the Evil of Slaveholding both from the Light of Nature and Divine Revelation.* Vevay, Ind., 1824.

DWIGHT, THEODORE. *An Oration Spoken before the Connecticut Society for the Promotion of Freedom and the Relief of Persons Unlawfully Holden in Bondage: Convened in Hartford on the 8th Day of May, A.D. 1794.* Hartford, Conn., 1794.

EASTON, HOSEA. *A Treatise on the Intellectual Character and Civil and Political Condition of the Colored People of the United States, and the Prejudice Exercised towards Them.* Boston, 1837.

EDWARDS, JONATHAN. *The Injustice and Impolicy of the Slave Trade and of the Slavery of the Africans: Illustrated in a Sermon Preached before the Connecticut Society for the Promotion of Freedom and for the Relief of Persons Unlawfully Holden in Bondage, . . . September 15, 1791.* 3rd ed. New Haven, Conn., 1833.

EMERSON, RALPH WALDO. *An Address in the Courthouse in Concord, Massachusetts, on 1st August, 1844, on the Anniversary of the Emancipation of the Negroes in the British West Indies.* Boston, 1844.

FERGUSON, J. B. *An Address on the History, Authority and Influence of Slavery: Delivered in the First Presbyterian Church, Nashville, Tennessee, 21st of November, 1850.* Nashville, Tenn., 1850.

FILLER, LOUIS (ed.). *Wendell Phillips on Civil Rights and Freedom.* New York, 1965.

FITZHUGH, GEORGE. *Sociology for the South.* Richmond, Va., 1854.

GOODELL, WILLIAM. *The Constitutional Duty of the Federal Government to Abolish American Slavery.* New York, 1855.

GRIMKÉ, ANGELINA. *Appeal to the Christian Women of the South.* New York, 1836.

———. *Letters to Catherine E. Beecher, in Reply to an Essay on Slavery and Abolitionism, Addressed to A. E. Grimké.* Boston, 1838.

GUNN, LEWIS CARSTAIRS. *Address to Abolitionists.* Philadelphia, 1838.

HARPER, WILLIAM, et al. *The Pro-Slavery Argument: As Maintained by the Most Distinguished Writers of the Southern States.* Philadelphia, 1853.

HILDRETH, RICHARD. *Despotism in America: An Inquiry into the Nature, Results and Legal Basis of the Slaveholding System in the United States.* Boston, 1854.

HOPKINS, SAMUEL. *A Dialogue concerning the Slavery of the Africans: Shewing It To Be the Duty and Interest of the American States to Emancipate All Their African Slaves.* New York, 1785.

IRISH, DAVID. *Observations on a Living and Effectual Testimony against Slavery.* New York, 1836.

JAMES, HENRY FRED. *Abolitionism Unveiled: Or Its Origin, Progress and Pernicious Tendency Fully Developed.* Cincinnati, 1856.

LAY, BENJAMIN. *All Slavekeepers That Keep the Innocent in Bondage.* Philadelphia, 1737.

LEWIS, EVAN. *An Address to Christians of the [Several] Denominations on the Inconsistency of Admitting Slaveholders to Communion and Church Membership.* Philadelphia, 1831.

NEWTON, JOHN. *Thoughts upon the African Slave Trade.* London, 1788.

PARRISH, JOHN. *Remarks on the Slavery of the Black People: Addressed to the Citizens of the United States, Particularly to Those Who Are in Legislative or Executive Stations in the General or State Governments, and Also to Such Individuals As Hold Them in Bondage.* Philadelphia, 1806.

PHILLIPS, WENDELL. *No Slave Hunting in the Old Bay State: An Appeal to the People and Legislature of Massachusetts.* New York, 1860.

———. *Speeches, Lectures and Letters.* Boston, 1863.

——— (ed.). *The Constitution a Pro-Slavery Compact: Or Extracts from the Madison Papers.* New York, 1856.

RANKIN, JOHN. *Letters on American Slavery: Addressed to Mr. Thomas Rankin, Merchant at Middlebrook, Augusta Co., Va.* Boston, 1833.

RICE, DAVID. *Slavery Inconsistent with Justice and Good Policy: Proved by a Speech Delivered in the Convention Held at Danville, Kentucky.* Philadelphia, 1792.

RUCHAMES, LOUIS (ed.). *The Abolitionists.* New York, 1963.

RUSH, BENJAMIN. *An Address to the Inhabitants of the British Settlements in America, upon Slavekeeping.* Philadelphia, 1773.

SANDIFORD, RALPH. *The Mystery of Iniquity: In a Brief Examination of the Practice of the Times, by the Foregoing and the Present Dispensation.* Philadelphia, 1730.

SEWALL, SAMUEL. *The Selling of Joseph.* Boston, 1700.

SHARP, GRANVILLE. *The Just Limitations of Slavery in the Laws of God Compared with the Unbounded Claims of the African Traders and British American Slaveholders.* London, 1776.

———. *The Law of Liberty.* London, 1776

———. *A Representation of the Injustice and Dangerous Tendency of Tolerating Slavery.* London, 1769.

SIDNEY, JOSEPH. *An Oration Commemorative of the Abolition of the Slave Trade in the United States: Delivered before the Wilberforce Philanthropic Association, in the City of New York, on the Second of January, 1809.* New York, 1809.

SMITH, GERRIT. *Speech before the New York Anti-Slavery Society at Peterboro, October 22, 1835.* New York, 1835.

STANTON, HENRY B. *Remarks of Henry B. Stanton in the Representatives' Hall, on the 23rd and 24th of February, 1837, before the Committee . . . to Whom Was Referred Sundry Memorials on the Subject of Slavery.* Boston. 1837.

SWAN, JAMES. *A Dissuasion to Great Britain and the Colonies from the Slave Trade to Africa, Shewing the Injustice Thereof.* Boston, 1772.

SWIFT, ZEPHANIAH. *An Oration on Domestic Slavery: Delivered at the North Meeting House in Hartford, on the 12th Day of May, A.D. 1791.* Hartford, Conn., 1791.

TAPPAN, LEWIS. *Address to the Non-Slaveholders of the South on the Social and Political Evils of Slavery.* New York, 1843.

THOMAS, JOHN L. *Slavery Attacked: The Abolitionist Crusade.* Englewood Cliffs, N.J., 1965.

TUCKER, ST. GEORGE. *A Dissertation on Slavery: With a Proposal for the Gradual Abolition of It in the State of Virginia.* Philadelphia, 1796.

WALKER, DAVID. *Walker's Appeal in Four Articles: Together with a Preamble, to the Colored Citizens of the World, but in Particular, and Very Expressly, to Those of the United States of America, Written in Boston, State of Massachusetts, September 28, 1829.* 3rd ed. Boston, 1830.

WELD, THEODORE D. *American Slavery as It Is: Testimony of a Thousand Witnesses.* New York, 1839.

WESLEY, JOHN. *Thoughts upon Slavery.* London, 1774.

WHEATON, JOSEPHUS. *The Equality of Mankind and the Evils of Slavery Illustrated: A Sermon.* Boston, 1820.

WHITEFIELD, GEORGE. *To the Inhabitants of Maryland, Virginia, North and South Carolina, concerning Their Negroes*. Philadelphia, 1740.

WISH, HARVEY (ed.). *Ante-Bellum Writings of George Fitzhugh and Hinton Rowan Helper on Slavery*. New York, 1960.

WOOLMAN, JOHN. *Considerations on Keeping Negroes: Recommended to the Professors of Christianity of Every Denomination, Part II*. Philadelphia, 1762.

———. *Some Considerations on the Keeping of Negroes: Recommended to the Professors of Christianity of Every Denomination. Part I*. Philadelphia, 1754.

GENERAL STUDIES

ADAMS, ALICE D. *The Neglected Period of Anti-Slavery in America, 1808–1831*. Boston, 1908.

AMERICAN ANTI-SLAVERY SOCIETY. *The Constitution of the American Anti-Slavery Society: With the Declaration of the National Anti-Slavery Convention at Philadelphia, December 1833, and the Address to the Public, Issued by the Executive Committee of the Society in September 1835*. New York, 1838.

———. *The Legion of Liberty! and Force of Truth: Containing the Thoughts, Words and Deeds of Some Prominent Apostles, Champions and Martyrs*. New York, 1843.

APTHEKER, HERBERT. "Militant Abolitionism," *Journal of Negro History*, XXVI (October 1941).

———. *The Negro in the Abolitionist Movement*. New York, 1941.

BARNES, GILBERT H. *The Anti-Slavery Impulse, 1830–1844*. New York, 1933.

BASSETT, JOHN S. *Anti-Slavery Leaders of North Carolina*. Baltimore, 1898.

BEECHER, EDWARD. *Narrative of Riots at Alton: In Connection with the Death of Rev. Elijah P. Lovejoy*. Alton, Ill., 1838.

BELL, HOWARD H. "Expressions of Negro Militancy in the North, 1840–60," *Journal of Negro History*, XLV (January 1960).

———. "National Negro Conventions of the Middle 1840's: Moral Suasion *vs*. Political Action," *ibid.*, XLII (October 1957).

CURRY, RICHARD O. (ed.). *The Abolitionists: Reformers or Fanatics?* New York, 1965.

CURTIS, CLARA K. *Fighters for Freedom*. Rochester, N.Y., 1933.

DILLON, MERTON L. *The Anti-Slavery Movement in Illinois, 1809–1844*. Ann Arbor, Mich., 1951.

———. "The Failure of American Abolitionists," *Journal of Southern History*, XXV (May 1959).

DRESSER, AMOS. *Narrative of the Arrest, Lynch Law Trial and Scourging of Amos Dresser at Nashville, Tennessee, August 1835*. Oberlin, Ohio, 1849.

DUBERMAN, MARTIN (ed.). *The Anti-Slavery Vanguard: New Essays on the Abolitionists*. Princeton, N.J., 1965.

DUMOND, DWIGHT L. *Anti-Slavery: The Crusade for Freedom in America*. Ann Arbor, Mich., 1961.

———. *Anti-Slavery Origins of the Civil War in the United States*. Ann Arbor, Mich., 1961.

ESTLIN, JOHN B. *A Brief Notice of American Slavery and the Abolition Movement*. London, 1853.

FILLER, LOUIS. *The Crusade against Slavery, 1830–1860*. New York, 1960.

GOODELL, WILLIAM. *Slavery and Anti-Slavery*. New York, 1852.

HAWKINS, HUGH (ed.). *The Abolitionists: Immediatism and the Question of Means*. Boston, 1964.

HESSELTINE, WILLIAM B. "Some New Aspects of the Pro-Slavery Argument," *Journal of Negro History*, XXI (January 1936).

JACKSON, NORMAN B. "The Free Produce Attack upon Slavery," *Pennsylvania Magazine of History and Biography*, LXVI (July 1942).

JAY, WILLIAM. *An Inquiry into the Character and Tendency of the American Colonization and American Anti-Slavery Societies*. New York, 1835.

JENKINS, WILLIAM S. *Pro-Slavery Thought of the Old South*. Chapel Hill, N.C., 1935.

LOCKE, MARY S. *Anti-Slavery in America: From the Introduction of African Slaves to the Prohibition of the Slave Trade, 1619–1808*. Boston, 1901.

LOVEJOY, JOSEPH C., and LOVEJOY, OWEN. *Memoirs of Elijah P. Lovejoy, Who Was Murdered in Defense of the Liberty of the Press, at Alton, Illinois, November 7, 1837*. New York, 1838.

MCKITRICK, ERIC L. (ed.). *Slavery Defended: The Views of the Old South*. Englewood Cliffs, N.J., 1963.

MACY, JESSE. *The Anti-Slavery Crusade*. New Haven, Conn., 1919.

MANDEL, BERNARD. *Labor, Free and Slave: Workingmen and the Anti-Slavery Movement in the United States*. New York, 1955.

MARTIN, ASA EARL. *The Anti-Slavery Movement in Kentucky prior to 1850*. Louisville, Ky., 1918.

———. "The Anti-Slavery Societies of Tennessee," *Tennessee Historical Magazine,* I (December 1915).

———. "Pioneer Anti-Slavery Press," *Mississippi Valley Historical Review,* II (March 1916).

MATTHEWS, ALBERT. "Protests against Slavery in Massachusetts," *Transactions of the Colonial Society of Massachusetts,* VII (1902–1904).

MAY, SAMUEL J. *Some Recollections of Our Anti-Slavery Conflict.* Boston, 1869.

NEEDLES, EDWARD. *An Historical Memoir of the Pennsylvania Society for Promoting the Abolition of Slavery, the Relief of Free Negroes Unlawfully Held in Bondage, and for Improving the Condition of the African Race.* Philadelphia, 1848.

NYE, RUSSEL B. *William Lloyd Garrison and the Humanitarian Reformers.* Boston, 1955.

PEASE, JANE, and PEASE, WILLIAM. *The Anti-Slavery Argument.* Indianapolis, 1965.

PILLSBURY, PARKER. *Acts of the Anti-Slavery Apostles.* Concord, N.H., 1883.

QUARLES, BENJAMIN. "The Breach between Douglass and Garrison," *Journal of Negro History,* XXIII (April 1938).

SAVAGE, WILLIAM S. *The Controversy over the Distribution of Abolition Literature.* Washington, 1938.

SCARBOROUGH, RUTH. *The Opposition to Slavery in Georgia prior to 1860.* Nashville, Tenn., 1933.

SHANKS, CAROLINA. "The Biblical Anti-Slavery Argument," *Journal of Negro History,* XVI (April 1931).

SILLEN, SAMUEL. *Women against Slavery.* New York, 1955.

SYPHER, WYLIE. *Guinea's Captive Kings: British Anti-Slavery Literature of the XVIIIth Century.* Chapel Hill, N.C., 1942.

TUCKERMAN, BAYARD. *William Jay and the Constitutional Movement for the Abolition of Slavery.* New York, 1893.

TURNER, LORENZO. *Anti-Slavery Sentiment in American Literature prior to 1865.* Washington, 1929.

TYLER, ALICE F. *Freedom's Ferment: Phases of American Social History to 1860.* Minneapolis, 1944.

WEBB, SAMUEL. *History of Pennsylvania Hall, Which Was Destroyed by a Mob on the 17th of May, 1838.* Philadelphia, 1838.

WESLEY, CHARLES H. "The Negro in the Organization of Abolition," *Phylon,* II (Fall 1941).

———. "The Participation of Negroes in Anti-Slavery Political Parties," *Journal of Negro History,* XXIX (January 1944).

WILSON, RUTH D. "Justifications of Slavery, Past and Present," *Phylon,* XIX (Winter 1958).

ZORN, ROMAN J. "The New England Anti-Slavery Society: Pioneer Abolition Organization," *Journal of Negro History,* XLIII (July 1957).

THE COLONIZATION MOVEMENT

BANCROFT, FREDERIC. "The Colonization of American Negroes, 1801–65," in *Frederic Bancroft,* by JACOB E. COOKE. Norman, Okla., 1957.

BIRNEY, JAMES G. *Letter on Colonization, Addressed to the Rev. Thornton S. Mills, Corresponding Secretary of the Kentucky Colonization Society.* New York, 1834.

BOARD OF MANAGERS FOR REMOVING THE FREE PEOPLE OF COLOR. *Colonization of the Free Colored Population of Maryland and of Such Slaves As May Hereafter Become Free: Statement of Facts.* Baltimore, 1832.

———. *News from Africa: A Collection of Facts Relating to the Colony in Liberia, for the Information of the Free People in Maryland.* Baltimore, 1832.

BROWN, GEORGE W. *The Economic History of Liberia.* Washington, 1941.

CLEVEN, N. ANDREW. "Some Plans for Colonizing Liberated Negro Slaves in Hispanic America," *Journal of Negro History,* XI (January 1926).

CORNISH, SAMUEL E., and WRIGHT, THEODORE S. *The Colonization Scheme Considered: In Its Rejection by the Colored People, in Its Tendency To Uphold Caste, in Its Unfitness for Christianizing and Civilizing the Aborigines of Africa and for Putting a Stop to the African Slave Trade.* Newark, N.J., 1840.

DOUGLASS, FREDERICK, WATKINS, WILLIAM J., and WHITFIELD, JAMES M. *Arguments Pro and Con on the Call for a National Emigration Convention, To Be Held in Cleveland, Ohio, August 1854.* Detroit, 1854.

FOX, EARLY LEE. *The American Colonization Society, 1817–40.* Baltimore, 1919.

GARRISON, WILLIAM LLOYD. *The Maryland Scheme of Expatriatism Examined.* Boston, 1834.

———. *Thoughts on African Colonization: Or an Impartial Exhibition of the Doctrines, Principles and Purposes of the American Colonization Society.* Boston, 1832.

SHERWOOD, H. N. "Early Negro Deportation Projects," *Mississippi Valley Historical Review,* II (March 1916).

———. "The Formation of the American Colonization Society," *Journal of Negro History,* II (July 1917).

STAUDENRAUS, P. J. *The African Colonization Movement.* New York, 1961.

SLAVERY

THE AFRICAN AND ATLANTIC SLAVE TRADE

BARBOT, JOHN. *A Description of the Coast of North and South Guinea.* In Vol. V, *A Collection of Voyages and Travels,* ed. AWNSHAM CHURCHILL. London, 1732.

BELSHAM, WILLIAM. *An Essay on the African Slave Trade.* Philadelphia, 1790.

BOSMAN, WILLEM. *A New and Accurate Description of the Coast of Guinea.* London, 1705.

BOVILL, E. W. *The Golden Trade of the Moors.* London, 1958.

CECIL, RICHARD. *The Works of the Rev. John Newton and Memoirs of His Life.* New York, 1851.

COUPLAND, REGINALD. *East Africa and Its Invaders.* Oxford, 1938.

DAVIDSON, BASIL. *Black Mother: The Years of the African Slave Trade.* Boston, 1961.

DONNAN, ELIZABETH. *Documents Illustrative of the History of the Slave Trade to America.* New York, 1965.

DORO, GEORGE F. *Slave Ships and Slavery.* Salem, Mass., 1927.

DOWD, JEROME. "The African Slave Trade," *Journal of Negro History,* II (January 1917).

DU BOIS, W. E. B. *The Suppression of the African Slave Trade to the United States of America, 1638–1870.* New York, 1954.

FALCONBRIDGE, ALEXANDER. *An Account of the Slave Trade on the Coast of Africa.* London, 1788.

FOOTE, ANDREW HULL. *Africa and the American Flag.* New York, 1854.

GREENE, LORENZO J. "Meeting on Slave Ships," *Phylon,* V (Winter 1944).

HIGH, JAMES. "The African Gentleman: A Chapter in the Slave Trade," *Journal of Negro History,* XLIV (October 1959).

JACKSON, LUTHER P. "Elizabethan Seamen and the African Slave Trade," *Journal of Negro History,* IX (January 1924).

JOBSON, RICHARD. *The Golden Trade.* London, 1932.

JOHNSTON, JAMES H. "The Mohammedan Slave Trade," *Journal of Negro History,* XIII (October 1928).

LLOYD, CHRISTOPHER. *The Navy and the Slave Trade: The Suppression of the African Slave Trade in the Nineteenth Century.* London, 1949.

MANNIX, DANIEL P., and COWLEY, MALCOLM. *Black Cargoes: A History of the Atlantic Slave Trade, 1518–1865.* New York, 1962.

PHILLIPS, THOMAS. *A Journal of a Voyage Made in the* Hannibal *of London, Ann. 1693–1694. . . to . . . the Coast of Guinea.* In Vol. VI, *A Collection of Voyages and Travels,* ed. AWNSHAM, CHURCHILL. London, 1732.

RINCHON, PÈRE DIEUDONNÉ. *Le Trafic Négrier.* Brussels, 1938.

———. *La Traité de L'Esclavage des Congolais par les Européens.* Brussels, 1929.

ZOOK, GEORGE F. "The Company of Royal Adventurers Trading into Africa," *Journal of Negro History,* IV (April 1919).

AGRICULTURE, LABOR AND THE ECONOMY

BANCROFT, FREDERIC. *Slave Trading in the Old South.* Baltimore, 1931.

BASSETT, JOHN S. *The Southern Plantation Overseer: As Revealed in His Letters.* Northampton, Mass., 1925.

BLAKE, WILLIAM O. *The History of Slavery and the Slave Trade.* Columbus, Ohio, 1860.

CAIN, ALFRED E. *The Winding Road to Freedom: A Documentary Study.* Yonkers, N.Y., 1965.

CHAMBERS, WILLIAM. *American Slavery and Color.* London, 1857.

COLLINS, WINFIELD H. *The Domestic Slave Trade of the Southern States.* New York, 1904.

CONRAD, ALFRED H., and MEYER, JOHN R. "The Economics of Slavery in the Ante-Bellum South," *Journal of Political Economy,* LXVI (April 1958).

DAVIS, DAVID BRION. *The Problem of Slavery in Western Culture.* Ithaca, N.Y., 1966.

DUNBAR, EDWARD E. *The History of the Rise and Decline of Commercial Slavery in America.* New York, 1863.

ELKINS, STANLEY M. *Slavery: A Problem in American Institutional and Intellectual Life.* New York, 1963.

FRANKLIN, JOHN HOPE. *The Militant South, 1800–1860*. Cambridge, Mass., 1956.

FRAZIER, E. FRANKLIN. "The Negro Slave Family," *Journal of Negro History*, XV (April 1930).

FURNAS, J. C. *The Road to Harpers Ferry*. New York, 1959.

GAINES, FRANCIS P. *The Southern Plantation: A Study in the Development and the Accuracy of a Tradition*. New York, 1925.

GENOVESE, EUGENE. "Legacy of Slavery and Roots of Black Nationalism," *Studies on the Left*, VI (November–December 1966).

———. *The Political Economy of Slavery: Studies in the Economy and Society of the Slave South*. New York, 1965.

GOVAN, THOMAS P. "Was Plantation Slavery Profitable?" *Journal of Southern History*, VIII (November 1942).

GRAY, LEWIS C. *History of Agriculture in the Southern States to 1860*. Washington, 1933.

GREENE, LORENZO J. "Slaveholding New England and Its Awakening," *Journal of Negro History*, XIII (October 1928).

GYSIN, BRION. *To Master—a Long Goodnight: The Story of Uncle Tom*. New York, 1946.

HANDLIN, OSCAR. "The Origins of Negro Slavery," in *Race and Nationality in American Life*. Boston, 1957.

HART, ALBERT BUSHNELL. *Slavery and Abolition, 1831–1841*. New York, 1906.

HELPER, HINTON ROWAN. *The Impending Crisis of the South: How To Meet It*. New York, 1859.

INGLE, EDWARD. *Southern Sidelights: A Picture of Social and Economic Life in the South a Generation before the War*. New York, 1896.

JAY, WILLIAM. *Miscellaneous Writings on Slavery*. Boston, 1853.

JOHNSTON, JAMES H. "A New Interpretation of the Domestic Slave System," *Journal of Negro History*, XVIII (January 1933).

JONES, KATHARINE M. *The Plantation South*. Indianapolis, 1957.

LAUBER, ALMON W. *Indian Slavery in Colonial Times within the Present Limits of the United States*. New York, 1913.

MECKLIN, JOHN M. "The Evolution of the Slave Status in American Democracy," *Journal of Negro History*, II (April–July 1917).

NORDHOFF, CHARLES. *America for the Free Working Man*. New York, 1865.

OLMSTED, FREDERICK LAW. *The Cotton Kingdom*. New York, 1953.

PHILLIPS, ULRICH B. *American Negro Slavery: A Survey of the Supply, Employment and Control of Negro Labor as Determined by the Plantation Regime*. New York, 1918.

———. *Life and Labor in the Old South*. Boston, 1929.

ROZWENC, EUGENE C. *Slavery as a Cause of the Civil War*. Boston, 1963.

———, and FREDERICK, WAYNE A. (eds.). *Slavery and the Breakdown of the American Consensus*. New York, 1964.

RUFFIN, EDMOND. *The Political Economy of Slavery*. Washington, 1857.

SIO, ARNOLD A. "Interpretation of Slavery: The Slave Status in the Americas," *Comparative Studies in Society and History*, VII (April 1965).

SMITH, THEODORE C. *The Liberty and Free Soil Parties in the Northwest*. New York, 1902.

SMITH, WILLIAM HENRY. *A Political History of Slavery*. 2 vols. New York, 1903.

STAMPP, KENNETH M. *The Peculiar Institution: Slavery in the Ante-Bellum South*. New York, 1956.

STEPHENSON, W. H. *Isaac Franklin, Slave Trader and Planter of the Old South*. University, La., 1938.

SYPHER, WYLIE. "Hutcheson and the 'Classical' Theory of Slavery," *Journal of Negro History*, XXIV (July 1939).

WADE, RICHARD C. *Slavery in the Cities: The South, 1820–1860*. New York, 1965.

WEBSTER, NOAH. *Effects of Slavery on Morals and Industry*. Hartford, Conn., 1793.

WESLEY, CHARLES H. "Manifests of Slave Shipments along the Waterways, 1808–1864," *Journal of Negro History*, XXVII (April 1942).

WILLIAMS, ERIC. *Capitalism and Slavery*. Chapel Hill, N.C., 1944.

WISH, HARVEY (ed.). *Slavery in the South*. New York, 1964.

WOODMAN, HAROLD D. "The Profitability of Slavery: A Historical Perennial," *Journal of Southern History*, XXIX (August 1963).

LOCAL HISTORY

BALLAGH, JAMES C. *A History of Slavery in Virginia*. Baltimore, 1902.

BASSETT, JOHN S. *Slavery and Servitude in the Colony of North Carolina*. Baltimore, 1896.

BRACKETT, JEFFREY R. *The Negro in Maryland: A Study of the Institution of Slavery*. Baltimore, 1889.

BRUCE, P. A. *The Economic History of Virginia in the Seventeenth Century.* New York, 1896.

COLEMAN, J. WINSTON, JR. *Slavery Times in Kentucky.* Chapel Hill, N.C., 1940.

COOLEY, HENRY S. *A Study of Slavery in New Jersey.* Baltimore, 1896.

FLANDERS, RALPH B. *Plantation Slavery in Georgia.* Chapel Hill, N.C., 1933.

FREEHLING, WILLIAM W. *Prelude to Civil War: The Nullification Controversy in South Carolina, 1816–1836.* New York, 1965.

GIDDINGS, JOSHUA R. *The Exiles of Florida.* Columbus, Ohio, 1858.

HARRIS, N. D. *The History of Negro Servitude in Illinois and of the Slavery Agitation in That State, 1719–1864.* Chicago, 1904.

HENRY, HOWELL M. *The Police Control of the Slave in South Carolina.* Emory, Va., 1914.

LAPRADE, WILLIAM T. "The Domestic Slave Trade in the District of Columbia," *Journal of Negro History,* XI (January 1926).

MCKEE, SAMUEL. *Labor in Colonial New York, 1664–1776.* New York, 1935.

M'KIM, J. M. *A Sketch of the Slave Trade in the District of Columbia, Contained in Two Letters . . . in the* Emancipator. Pittsburgh, 1938.

MOORE, GEORGE H. *Notes on the History of Slavery in Massachusetts.* New York, 1866.

MORGAN, EDWIN V. *Slavery in New York.* New York, 1898.

MOSS, SIMEON F. "The Persistence of Slavery and Involuntary Servitude in a Free State, 1685–1866," *Journal of Negro History,* XXV (January 1950).

PHIFER, EDWARD W. "Slavery in Microcosm: Burke County, North Carolina," *Journal of Southern History,* XXVIII (May 1962).

RIDDELL, WILLIAM R. "The Slave in Early New York," *Journal of Negro History,* XIII (January 1928).

STEINER, BERNARD C. *History of Slavery in Connecticut.* Baltimore, 1893.

SYDNOR, CHARLES S. *Slavery in Mississippi.* New York, 1933.

TAYLOR, ORVILLE W. *Negro Slavery in Arkansas.* Durham, N.C., 1959.

TREXLER, HARRISON A. *Slavery in Missouri, 1804–1865.* Baltimore, 1914.

WERTENBAKER, THOMAS J. *The Planters of Colonial Virginia.* Princeton, N.J., 1922.

WOODSON, CARTER G. "Freedom and Slavery in Appalachian America," *Journal of Negro History,* I (April 1916).

THE UNDERGROUND RAILROAD

BREYFOGLE, WILLIAM. *Make Free: The Story of the Underground Railroad.* Philadelphia, 1958.

BUCKMASTER, HENRIETTA. *Let My People Go.* New York, 1941.

GARA, LARRY. *The Liberty Line: The Legend of the Underground Railroad.* Lexington, Ky., 1961.

PRESTON, E. DELORUS, JR. "The Genesis of the Underground Railroad," *Journal of Negro History,* XVIII (April 1933).

———. "The Underground Railroad in Northwest Ohio," *ibid.,* XVII (October 1932).

SIEBERT, WILBUR HENRY. *The Mysteries of Ohio's Underground Railroad.* Columbus, Ohio, 1951.

———. *The Underground Railroad from Slavery to Freedom.* New York, 1898.

———. *The Underground Railroad in Massachusetts.* Worcester, Mass., 1935.

———. *Vermont's Anti-Slavery and Underground Railroad Record.* Columbus, Ohio, 1937.

SMEDLEY, ROBERT C. *History of the Underground Railroad in Chester and the Neighboring Counties of Pennsylvania.* Lancaster, Pa., 1883.

STILL, WILLIAM. *The Underground Rail Road.* Philadelphia, 1872.

STROTHER, HORATIO T. *The Underground Railroad in Connecticut.* Middletown, Conn., 1962.

SLAVE REBELLIONS

APTHEKER, HERBERT. *American Negro Slave Revolts.* New York, 1963.

———. "Maroons within the Present Limits of the United States," *Journal of Negro History,* XXIV (April 1939).

———. *Nat Turner's Revolt: The Environment, the Event, the Effects.* New York, 1966.

———. *Negro Slave Revolts in the United States, 1526–1860.* New York, 1939.

BAUER, RAYMOND A., and BAUER, ALICE H. "Day to Day Resistance to Slavery," *Journal of Negro History,* XXVII (October 1942).

BONTEMPS, ARNA W. *Black Thunder.* New York, 1936.

CARROLL, JOSEPH C. *Slave Insurrections in the United States, 1800–1865.* Boston, 1938.

COFFIN, JOSHUA. *An Account of Some of the Principal Slave Insurrections.* New York, 1860.

DREWRY, WILLIAM S. *Slave Insurrections in Virginia, 1830–1865.* Washington, 1900.

GRAY, THOMAS R. (ed.). *The Confessions of Nat Turner.* Baltimore, 1831.

HALASZ, NICHOLAS. *The Rattling Chains: Slave Unrest and Revolt in the Ante-Bellum South.* New York, 1966.

HAMILTON, JAMES. *Negro Plot: An Account of the Late Intended Insurrection among a Portion of the Blacks of the City of Charleston, South Carolina.* Boston, 1822.

KENNEDY, LIONEL H., and PARKER, THOMAS. *An Official Report of the Trials of Sundry Negroes Charged with an Attempt to Raise an Insurrection in the State of South Carolina.* Charleston, S.C., 1822.

LOFTON, JOHN M., JR. "Denmark Vesey's Call to Arms," *Journal of Negro History,* XXXIII (October 1948).

———. *Insurrection in South Carolina: The Turbulent World of Denmark Vesey.* Yellow Springs, Ohio, 1964.

OWENS, WILLIAM A. *Slave Mutiny.* New York, 1953.

PORTER, KENNETH W. "Negroes and the Seminole War, 1817–1818," *Journal of Negro History,* XXXVI (July 1951).

SCOTT, KENNETH. "The Slave Insurrection in New York in 1712," *New York Historical Quarterly,* XLV (January 1961).

WISH, HARVEY. "American Slave Insurrections before 1861," *Journal of Negro History,* XXII (July 1937).

CONCEPTS OF RACE

ALPENFELS, ETHEL. *Sense and Nonsense about Race.* New York, 1957.

BENEDICT, RUTH. *Race: Science and Politics.* New York, 1940.

———, and ELLIS, MILDRED. *Race and Cultural Relations: America's Answer to the Myth of the Master Race.* Washington, 1942.

———, and WELTFISH, GENE. *The Races of Mankind.* New York, 1943.

BOAS, FRANZ. *General Anthropology.* Boston, 1938.

———. *The Mind of Primitive Man.* New York, 1948.

BOYD, WILLIAM C. *Genetics and the Races of Man.* Boston, 1954.

COON, CARLETON S. *The Origin of Races.* New York, 1962.

DOBZHANSKY, THEODOSIUS. "A Debatable Account of the Origin of the Races," *Scientific American,* CCVIII (February 1963).

———. *Heredity and the Nature of Man.* New York, 1964.

———. *Mankind Evolving: The Evolution of the Human Species.* New Haven, Conn., 1962.

GARN, STANLEY. *Human Races.* Springfield, Ill., 1961.

GOSSETT, THOMAS F. *Race: The History of an Idea in America.* Dallas, 1963.

HANKINS, FRANK H. *The Racial Basis of Civilization: A Critique of the Nordic Doctrine.* New York, 1926.

HERSKOVITS, MELVILLE J. *The American Negro: A Study in Racial Crossing.* New York, 1928.

HOYDEN, MARGARET T. "The Negro in the Anthropology of John Wesley," *Journal of Negro History,* XIX (July 1934).

MONTAGU, ASHLEY. *Man's Most Dangerous Myth: The Fallacy of Race.* New York, 1952.

SNYDER, LOUIS L. *The Idea of Racialism: Its Meaning and History.* Princeton, N.J., 1962.

STANTON, WILLIAM. *The Leopard's Spots: Scientific Attitudes toward Race in America, 1815–1859.* Chicago, 1960.

THOMPSON, EDGAR T., and HUGHES, EVERETT C. (eds.). *Race: Individual and Collective Behavior.* Glencoe, Ill., 1958.

WASHBURN, SHERWOOD L. "The Study of Race," *American Anthropologist,* LXV (June 1963).

SOCIOLOGICAL STUDIES

ALLPORT, GORDON W. *The Nature of Prejudice.* Cambridge, Mass., 1954.

CUTLER, JAMES E. *Lynch Law: An Investigation into the History of Lynching in the United States.* New York, 1905.

DAVIE, MAURICE. *Negroes in American Society.* New York, 1949.

DEUTSCH, A. "The First U.S. Census of the Insane (1840), and Its Use as Pro-Slavery Propaganda," *Bulletin of the History of Medicine,* XV (December 1944).

FRANKLIN, JOHN HOPE. "History of Racial Segregation in the United States," *Annals of the American Academy of Political and Social Science,* CCCIV (March 1956).

FRAZIER, E. FRANKLIN. *The Negro Family in the United States.* Chicago, 1939.

HOLMES, SAMUEL J. *The Negro's Struggle for Survival: A Study in Human Ecology.* Berkeley, Calif., 1937.

JOHNSTON, SIR HARRY H. *The Negro in the New World.* London, 1910.

JOHNSTON, JAMES H. *Miscegenation in the Ante-Bellum South.* Chicago, 1939.

MYERS, GUSTAVUS. *History of Bigotry in the United States.* New York, 1960.

MYRDAL, GUNNAR. *An American Dilemma.* New York, 1964.

SCHRIEKE, BERTRAM. *Alien Americans: A Study of Race Relations.* New York, 1936.

RELIGIOUS GROUPS: ATTITUDES TOWARD SLAVERY AND THE NEGRO

APTHEKER, HERBERT. "The Quakers and Negro Slavery," *Journal of Negro History,* XXV (July 1940).

BASSETT, WILLIAM. *Letter to a Member of the Society of Friends in Reply to Objections against Joining Anti-Slavery Societies.* Boston, 1837.

BIRNEY, JAMES G. *The American Churches, the Bulwarks of American Slavery.* Newburyport, Mass., 1842.

CADBURY, HENRY J. "Another Early Quaker Anti-Slavery Document," *Journal of Negro History,* XXVII (April 1942).

———. "An Early Quaker Anti-Slavery Statement," *ibid.,* XXII (October 1937).

———. "Negro Membership in the Society of Friends," *ibid.,* XXI (April 1936).

DRAKE, THOMAS E. *Quakers and Slavery in America.* New Haven, Conn., 1950.

FOLEY, ALBERT S. *God's Men of Color: The Colored Catholic Priests of the United States, 1854–1954.* New York, 1955.

GODWYN, MORGAN. *The Negro's and Indian's Advocate, Suing for Their Admission into the Church: Or a Persuasive to the Instructing and Baptizing of the "Negro's" and Indians in Our Plantations, Shewing, that . . . the Wilful Neglecting and Opposing of It, Is No Less than a Manifest Apostacy from the Christian Faith.* London, 1680.

GOODELL, WILLIAM. *Come-Outerism: The Duty of Secession from a Corrupt Church.* New York, 1845.

HAGOOD, L. M. *The Colored Man in the Methodist Episcopal Church.* New York, 1901.

JAMES, SYDNEY V. *A People among Peoples: Quaker Benevolence in Eighteenth-Century America.* Cambridge, Mass., 1963.

JAY, JOHN. *Caste and Slavery in the American Church.* New York, 1843.

JERNEGAN, MARCUS W. "Slavery and Conversion in the American Colonies," *American Historical Review,* XXI (April 1916).

McLOUGHLIN, WILLIAM G., and JORDAN, WINTHROP D. (eds.). "Baptists Face the Barbarities of Slavery in 1710," *Journal of Southern History,* XXIX (November 1963).

MARTIN, DAVID. *Trial of Rev. Jacob Gruber, Minister in the Methodist Episcopal Church, at the March Term, 1819, in the Frederick County Court, for a Misdemeanor.* Fredericktown [Frederick], Md., 1819.

MATHER, COTTON. *The Negro Christianized: An Essay to Excite and Assist That Good Work, the Instruction of Negro Servants in Christianity.* Boston, 1706.

MATHEWS, DONALD G. *Slavery and Methodism: A Chapter in American Morality, 1780–1845.* Princeton, N.J., 1965.

MATLACK, LUCIUS C. *The History of American Slavery and Methodism, from 1780 to 1849.* New York, 1849.

PAXTON, JOHN D. *Letters on Slavery, Addressed to the Cumberland Congregation, Virginia, by Their Former Pastor.* Lexington, Ky., 1833.

REIMERS, DAVID M. *White Protestantism and the Negro.* New York, 1965.

RHOADS, SAMUEL. *Considerations on the Use of the Productions of Slavery: Especially Addressed to the Religious Society of Friends, within the Limits of Philadelphia Yearly Meeting.* Philadelphia, 1844.

SMYLIE, JAMES. *A Review of a Letter from the Presbytery of Chillicothe to the Presbytery of Mississippi, on the Subject of Slavery.* Woodville, Miss., 1836.

TORBET, ROBERT G. *A History of the Baptists.* Philadelphia, 1950.

VIBERT, FAITH. "The Society for the Propagation of the Gospel in Foreign Parts: Its Work for the Negroes in North America before 1783," *Journal of Negro History,* XVIII (April 1933).

WAX, DAROLD D. "Quaker Merchants and the Slave Trade in Colonial Pennsylvania," *Pennsylvania Magazine of History and Biography,* LXXXVI (April 1962).

WEATHERFORD, WILLIS D. *American Churches and the Negro: An Historical Study from Early Slave Days to the Present.* Boston, 1957.

WEEKS, STEPHEN B. *Southern Quakers and Slavery: A Study in Institutional History.* Baltimore, 1896.

WELD, THEODORE D. *A Statement of the Reasons Which Induced the Students of Lane Seminary to Dissolve Their Connection with That Institution.* Cincinnati, 1834.

SLAVERY AND THE NEGRO ELSEWHERE IN THE AMERICAS

AYKROYD, W. R. *Sweet Malefactor: Sugar, Slavery and Human Society*. London, 1967.

BIRD, MARK B. *The Black Man: Or Haytian Independence*. New York, 1869.

BURNS, ALAN. *History of the British West Indies*. London, 1954.

DALLAS, R. C. *The History of the Maroons*. London, 1803.

DREW, BENJAMIN. *A Northside View of Slavery: The Refugee, or the Narratives of Fugitive Slaves in Canada*. Boston, 1856.

EDWARDS, BRYAN. *The History, Civil and Commercial, of the British West Indies*. 5 vols. London, 1818–1819.

GOVEIA, ELSA V. *Slave Society in the British Leeward Islands at the End of the Eighteenth Century*. New Haven, Conn., 1965.

HERRING, HUBERT C. *A History of Latin America from the Beginning to the Present*. New York, 1961.

HOWE, SAMUEL G. *The Refugees from Slavery in Canada West*. Boston, 1864.

JAMES, C. L. R. *The Black Jacobins: Toussaint L'Ouverture and the San Domingo Revolution*. New York, 1938.

JORDAN, WINTHROP D. "American Chiaroscuro: The Status and Definition of Mulattoes in the British Colonies," *William and Mary Quarterly,* XIX (April 1962).

———. "The Influence of the West Indies on the Origins of New England Slavery," *ibid.,* XVIII (April 1961).

LANDON, FRED. "The Buxton Settlement in Canada," *Journal of Negro History,* III (October 1918).

———. "Fugitive Slaves in London, Ontario, before 1860," *Transactions of the London and Middlesex (Ontario) Historical Society,* X (1919).

———. "History of the Wilberforce Refugee Colony in Middlesex County," *ibid.,* IX (1918).

———. "The Negro Migration to Canada after the Fugitive Slave Act of 1850," *Journal of Negro History,* V (January 1920).

———. *Social Conditions among the Negroes in Upper Canada before 1865*. Toronto, 1925.

LESLIE, CHARLES. *A New and Exact Account of Jamaica*. Edinburgh, 1740.

LONG, EDWARD. *The History of Jamaica*. London, 1774.

LOWERY, WOODBURY. *Spanish Settlements within the Present Limits of the United States, 1513–1561*. New York, 1959.

MATHIESON, WILLIAM L. *British Slavery and Its Abolition, 1823–1838*. London, 1926.

NEWTON, ARTHUR P. *The European Nations in the West Indies, 1493–1688*. London, 1933.

OLIVEIRA MARTINS, JOAQUIM PEDRO. *O Brazil e as Colinias Portuguezas*. 5th ed. Lisbon, 1920.

PITMAN, FRANK W. *The Development of the British West Indies, 1700–1763*. New Haven, Conn., 1917.

———. "Slavery on the British West India Plantations in the Eighteenth Century," *Journal of Negro History,* XI (October 1926).

RAGATZ, LOWELL J. *The Fall of the Planter Class in the British Caribbean, 1763–1833*. New York, 1928.

RIPPY, J. FRED. "The Negro and the Spanish Pioneers in the New World," *Journal of Negro History,* VI (April 1921).

SIMPSON, LESLEY. *The Encomienda in New Spain: The Beginnings of Spanish Mexico*. Berkeley, Calif., 1960.

SLOANE, SIR HANS. *A Voyage to the Islands of Madera, Barbadoes, Nieves, St. Christopher's and Jamaica*. London, 1707.

STEDMAN, JOHN G. *Narrative of a Five Years' Expedition against the Revolted Negroes of Suriname*. London, 1796.

STEWARD, THEOPHILUS G. *How the Black St. Domingo Legion Saved the Patriot Army in the Siege of Savannah, 1779*. Washington, 1899.

WALSH, ROBERT. *Notices of Brazil in 1828 and 1829*. New York, 1831.

WILLIAMS, ERIC. "The British West Indian Slave Trade after Its Abolition in 1807," *Journal of Negro History,* XXVII (April 1942).

———. "The Golden Age of the Slave System in Britain," *ibid.,* XXV (January 1940).

———. *The Negro in the Caribbean*. Washington, 1942.

THE NEGRO IN LITERATURE AND THE ARTS

BOTKIN, B. A. (ed.). *Lay My Burden Down: A Folk History of Slavery*. Chicago, 1945.

BRAWLEY, BENJAMIN (ed.). *Early Negro American Writers*. Chapel Hill, N.C., 1935.

BROWN, STERLING A. "Negro Character As Seen by White Authors," *Journal of Negro Education,* II (April 1933).

———. *Negro Poetry and Drama.* Washington, 1937.

———, DAVIS, ARTHUR P., and LEE, ULYSSES (eds.). *The Negro Caravan: Writings by American Negroes.* New York, 1941.

BROWN, WILLIAM WELLS. *Clotel: Or the President's Daughter.* London, 1853.

BUTCHER, MARGARET J. *The Negro in American Culture.* New York, 1956.

CANTOR, MILTON. "The Image of the Negro in Colonial Literature," *New England Quarterly,* XXXVI (December 1962).

CUNEY HARE, MAUD. *Negro Musicians and Their Music.* Washington, 1936.

DELANEY, MARTIN R. *Blake: Or the Huts of America.* Published in *Anglo-African Magazine,* I (January–July 1859).

DOVER, CEDRIC. *American Negro Art.* Greenwich, Conn., 1960.

FISHER, MILES M. (ed.). *Negro Slave Songs in the United States.* Ithaca, N.Y., 1953.

HARPER, FRANCES ELLEN WATKINS. *Iola Leroy: Or Shadows Uplifted.* Philadelphia, 1892.

———. *Poems on Miscellaneous Subjects.* Boston, 1854.

HORTON, GEORGE MOSES. *The Hope of Liberty.* Raleigh, N.C., 1829.

ISAACS, EDITH J. *The Negro in the American Theatre.* New York, 1947.

MARSHALL, HERBERT, and STOCK, MILDRED. *Ira Aldridge.* New York, 1958.

STOWE, HARRIET BEECHER. *Uncle Tom's Cabin.* Boston, 1853.

WEBB, FRANK. *The Garies and Their Friends.* London, 1857.

WEGELIN, OSCAR. *Jupiter Hammon, American Negro Poet.* New York, 1915.

WHEATLEY, PHILLIS. *Phillis Wheatley: Poems and Letters,* ed. CHARLES F. HEARTMAN. New York, 1915.

WHITEMAN, MAXWELL. *A Century of Fiction by American Negroes, 1853–1952.* Philadelphia, 1955.

BIBLIOGRAPHIC WORKS

BROWN, WARREN. *Check List of Negro Newspapers in the United States, 1827–1946.* Jefferson City, Mo., 1946.

DU BOIS, W. E. B. *A Select Bibliography of the Negro American for General Readers.* Atlanta, Ga., 1905.

DUMOND, DWIGHT L. *A Bibliography of Anti-Slavery in America.* Ann Arbor, Mich., 1961.

DUNLAP, MOLLIE E. "Special Collections of Negro Literature in the United States," *Journal of Negro Education,* IV (October 1935).

FOWLER, JULIAN S. *A Classified Catalogue of the Collection of Anti-Slavery Propaganda in the Oberlin College Library.* Oberlin, Ohio, 1932.

HARPER, FRANCIS P. *Catalogue of Unusual Collections of Books and Pamphlets Relating to the Rebellion and Slavery.* New York, 1894.

HOMER, DOROTHY R. *The Negro in the United States: A List of Significant Books.* New York, 1965.

INTERNATIONAL AFRICAN INSTITUTE. *Select Annotated Bibliography of Tropical Africa.* New York, 1956.

KESSLER, S. H. "American Negro Literature: A Bibliographic Guide," *Bulletin of Bibliography,* XXI (September 1955).

LEWISON, PAUL. *A Guide to Documents in the National Archives, for Negro Studies.* Washington, 1947.

MAY, SAMUEL J. *Catalogue of Anti-Slavery Publications in America.* New York, 1864.

MILLER, ELIZABETH W. *The Negro in America: A Bibliography.* Cambridge, Mass., 1966.

NATIONAL URBAN LEAGUE. *Selected Bibliography on the Negro.* New York, 1951; supplement 1958.

NEW YORK PUBLIC LIBRARY. *The Negro: A Select Bibliography.* New York, 1935.

PORTER, DOROTHY B. *A Catalogue of the African Collection in the Moorland Collection.* Washington, 1958.

———. "Early American Negro Writings: A Bibliographical Study," *Papers of the Bibliographical Society of America,* XXXIX (January 1945).

———. *A Selected List of Books by and about the Negro.* Washington, 1936.

———, HUNTON, MARGARET R., and WILLIAMS, ETHEL. *A Catalogue of Books in the Moorland Collection.* Washington, 1939.

SALK, ERWIN A. *A Layman's Guide to Negro History.* New York, 1967.

SPANGLER, EARL. *Bibliography of Negro History, Selected and Annotated Entries: General and Minnesota.* Minneapolis, 1963.

THOMPSON, EDGAR T., and THOMPSON, ALMA M. *Race and Region: A Descriptive Bibliography Compiled with Special Reference to Relations between Whites and Negroes in the United States.* Chapel Hill, N.C., 1949.

WELSCH, ERWIN K. *The Negro in the United States: A Research Guide.* Bloomington, Ind., 1965.

WORK, MONROE N. *A Bibliography of the Negro in Africa and America.* New York, 1928.

NEWSPAPERS AND MAGAZINES

African Repository and Colonial Journal (Washington). 1825–1892.

American Anti-Slavery Reporter (New York). 1833–1834.

Anglo-African Magazine (New York). 1859.

Colored American (New York). 1837–1842. First published as *Weekly Advocate* (1837).

Douglass' Monthly (Rochester, N.Y.). 1847–1863. First published as *North Star* (1847–1851), then as *Frederick Douglass' Paper* (1851–1859).

Freedom's Journal (New York). 1827–1830.

Friend of Man (Utica, N.Y.). 1836–1842.

Genius of Universal Emancipation (Baltimore). 1821–1838.

Liberator (Boston). 1831–1865.

National Anti-Slavery Standard (New York). 1840–1860.

National Era (Washington). 1847–1860.

MANUSCRIPT COLLECTIONS

ASSOCIATION FOR THE STUDY OF NEGRO LIFE AND HISTORY. Carter G. Woodson Papers.

ATLANTA UNIVERSITY. Henry Slaughter Papers.

BOSTON PUBLIC LIBRARY. William Lloyd Garrison Papers; J. Miller McKim Papers.

DOUGLASS MEMORIAL HOME, WASHINGTON. Frederick Douglass Papers.

FISK UNIVERSITY LIBRARY. Special Negro Collection.

HAMPTON INSTITUTE. George Foster Peabody Collection.

HARVARD UNIVERSITY. Wendell Phillips Garrison Papers; Thomas Wentworth Higginson Papers; Samuel Gridley Howe Family Papers.

HOWARD UNIVERSITY LIBRARY. Negro Collection.

JOHNS HOPKINS UNIVERSITY. William Birney Papers.

NEW YORK PUBLIC LIBRARY. Schomburg Collection of Negro Literature and History.

YALE UNIVERSITY LIBRARY. James Weldon Johnson Memorial Collection of Negro Arts and Letters.

Picture Credits

The author is grateful to the following for their aid in the search for unusual and interesting photographs with which to illustrate the text. Those pictures which have not been listed are in the private collection of United Publishing Corporation, Washington, D.C.

Key: T: Top;   B: Bottom;   L: Left;   R: Right;   C: Center

American Oil Company, Chicago: 94L, 144
Bureau of Engraving and Printing, Washington: 102B, 181, 243–245
Cincinnati Historical Society: 40
Historical Society of Pennsylvania, Philadelphia: iiBL, 37, 82, 90, 101B, 106, 114, 120, 137T, 172, 178, 184, 189, 192B, 252, 265
Historical Society of Pennsylvania–Documents Collection, Philadelphia: 39, 145, 204
Historical Society of Pennsylvania–Edward Carey Gardiner Collection, Philadelphia: 213, 222, 262
Historical Society of Pennsylvania–Rosenthal Engravings, Philadelphia: 98R
Historical Society of Pennsylvania–Simon Gratz Collection, Philadelphia: 29, 31, 98L, 138, 143B, 147TL, 153, 161T, 188T, 197B, 242
Historical Society of Pennsylvania–Society Portrait Collection, Philadelphia: 60, 61, 70, 86–88, 91TL, 92, 101T, 104, 105, 161B, 163, 165B, 173B
Historical Society of Pennsylvania–Society Prints Collection, Philadelphia: 41
Historical Society of Pennsylvania–Stauffer Collection, Philadelphia: 74, 113TR, 157T
Library of Congress: iiCTR, CBL, 21C, 30, 44, 47, 51, 85, 94T, 150, 156, 159, 183T, 185, 227B, 240, 251, 257T, 268T
Merkle Press, Washington: 183B
Mother Bethel A.M.E. Church, Philadelphia: 255CR, BL, 261, 263T
Museum of Fine Arts, Boston: 5T
Museum of Primitive Art, New York: 8, 10, 12
National Library of Medicine, Bethesda, Maryland: 125T
National Portrait Gallery, London: 201
New York Historical Society, New York: 77, 227T, 228, 233, 235, 238, 247B, 255CL, BC, BR, 259, 260B, 264
New York Public Library: iiCBR, 2, 16, 21T, B, 22, 23T, 25–27, 33, 35, 43, 49, 53, 55, 56, 65, 66, 75, 81, 83, 84, 91TR, B, 96, 98C, 100, 102T, 108, 109, 122, 128B, 132–134, 137BL, BR, 143T, 147TR, B, 149, 151, 152, 157B, 158, 160B, 162, 174, 175, 191B, 195B, 230B, 232, 234B, 239, 247T, 253B, 255C, 256, 257BR, 258, 260T, 269BR
New York Public Library–Schomburg Collection: iiCTL, BR, 76, 99, 113TL, 121, 148, 173T, 179, 186, 187, 191T, 193, 206, 207, 209, 211T, 214, 219, 221, 230T, 234T, 266T, BR
Smith College Library, Northampton, Massachusetts: 202
Tuskegee Institute, Tuskegee, Alabama: 6T, 11, 18, 23B, 257C
Worcester Art Museum, Worcester, Massachusetts: 5B

Index

Page numbers in *italic type* refer to illustrations.